The
FIVE MILE WOODS
PRESERVE
A History

Don Formigli

Peter Osborne

ALSO BY PETER OSBORNE

The Trains of Our Memory: A History of the Railroad Museum of Pennsylvania 1965-2015

No Spot In This Far Land Is More Immortalized: A History of Pennsylvania's Washington Crossing Historic Park

Where Washington Once Led: A History of New Jersey's Washington Crossing State Park

So Many Brave Men: The Battle at Minisink Ford
- With Mark Hendrickson and Jon Inners -

Lewis and Clark and Me

For Always, Memories of Janis

Our Town: Historic Port Jervis 1907-2007
-With Dan Dwyer -

Vigilance & Perseverance: The History of the Old Decker Stone House

Hail Matamoras: Matamoras, Pennsylvania 1905-2005
- Compiled and Designed –

Put The Dog On The Phone! The Collected Newspaper Columns of Janis Osborne
- Compiled and Designed –

The Delaware River Heritage Trail Guide

Images of America: Promised Land State Park

Images of America: Hacklebarney & Voorhees State Parks, New Jersey

Images of America: High Point State Park and the Civilian Conservation Corps

We Can Take It! The Roosevelt Tree Army at New Jersey's High Point State Park 1933-1941

The
FIVE MILE WOODS
PRESERVE
A History

PETER OSBORNE

With a Foreword
By
DONALD FORMIGLI

The Five Mile Woods Preserve: A History
By Peter Osborne
Foreword by Donald Formigli

Published by
Heritage Conservancy
Doylestown, Pennsylvania

Copyright © 2017 by Heritage Conservancy

ISBN 978-0-692-84234-8 (soft cover)

Library of Congress Control Number: 2017902217

NATURE / Environmental Conservation & Protection
NATURE / Regional
NATURE / Ecosystems & Habitats / General
NATURE / Natural Resources
HISTORY / United States / State & Local / Middle Atlantic
(DC, DE, MD, NJ, NY, PA)

Cover and book design by Peter Osborne and The Wild Horse Creek Company

First Edition
10 9 8 7 6 5 4 3 2 1
Printed in the United States of America

DEDICATED TO

The visionaries who created the Five Mile Woods Preserve

and

To those who have continued on with its mission

THE FIVE MILE WOODS
by
LYNN SIMS

I walked last evening thru the quiet woods.
I saw the orchids rise above the leaves;
Watched the frogs leap o'er the stream,
and the deer go running through the green
Of the Five Mile Woods.

Oh why can't the orchids bloom forever.
Why can't the forest grow untouched.
But in the distance you can hear
The hammers and the dozers near.

There was a stream meandering upon its way
beside the trees reaching to the sky;
such lovely trees to walk beneath or
sit beneath or dream beneath,
now all concrete!

Oh rise ye sleeping people rise.
Oh speak ye silent people speak.
For then your words someone will hear,
And this woodland shall not disappear.

Then the orchids they shall bloom forever,
and the forest grow a century more,
and always there shall be this place
of solitude and subtle grace.
This Five Mile Woods.
This Five Mile Woods.

COMMON BEECH

CONTENTS

CHAPTER 8
REFLECTIONS AND A PASSION FOR THE PLACE
Page 261

In 2016, the Preserve turned thirty-five years old. In this chapter, several of its important leaders reflect on the accomplishments over the years and what the Preserve means to them along with two other advocates of open space in Bucks County.

APPENDIX
Page 283

ACQUISITION MAPS
TRAILS IN THE FIVE MILE WOODS
SPECIES LISTINGS

Today's Preserve is the result of a number of land acquisitions that were made over several decades, and which oftentimes included complicated negotiations with landowners. A series of maps demonstrate how the Preserve came to be acquired. A listing of the Preserve's trails and their most notable features is included. In addition, there are species lists of plants, mammals, birds, reptiles, and amphibians that have been found at the Preserve over the decades.

NOTES
Page 325

BIBLIOGRAPHIC ESSAY
Page 353

BIBLIOGRAPHY
Page 363

INDEX
Page 381

ACKNOWLEDGEMENTS
Page 395

ABOUT THE AUTHOR
Page 405

COLOPHON
Page 409

COMMON BEECH

COMMON BEECH

FOREWORD

The Five Mile Woods Were Worth Preserving.

I T HAS BEEN FORTY-THREE YEARS SINCE I first explored the Five Mile Woods and started photographing the amazing features that I found there. I had been living in Lower Makefield Township (LMT) for ten years and had become increasingly concerned about the rapid development of the area. It was in a conversation with Dan Rattigan, a friend and local businessman, that I first heard about the Five Mile Woods. Dan later became a Lower Makefield Township Supervisor. Around that same time, I was appointed to the Lower Makefield Township Park and Recreation Board; I also started to attend the LMT Planning Commission meetings to learn about how new housing developments were approved. Through exploring, researching and asking questions, I realized that the Five Mile Woods was worth preserving. As more people became interested in the project, we soon started a movement to save the Woods.

This book tells the story of how we saved the Woods. In eight years — from my first exploration in 1974 until the dedication ceremonies on November 21, 1981 — we accomplished something beyond my wildest dreams. Most preserved open space is saved at the national and state levels or by conservation organizations such as The Nature Conservancy, National Lands Trust, or the Heritage Conservancy. However, the Five Mile Woods occupies a unique category: it was saved by a voter referendum and purchased as well as managed by a local government.

Although I did not remain active in the management of the Five Mile Woods Preserve, I continued to visit it. I had also documented and saved everything pertaining to the preservation campaign, including all correspondence, research, newspaper articles, and photographs. I reflected on how to preserve all of this history and ultimately decided that a book would be the best answer, but I needed to find a writer.

In the meantime, many of the documents needed for the book were not accessible. It was not until January 2015, when my family and I decided to sell our home, that I retrieved much of the documentation and many of the slide photos pertaining to the Five Mile Woods. It was by chance that I mentioned to our attorney, Tom Cadwallader, my idea for the book. He was interested in local

Courtesy Peter Osborne

Donald Formigli
2017

history and immediately told me about Peter Osborne, subsequently arranging an introduction. Carting some of my materials for the book, I met with Peter and found that he was excited about the project. Given his involvement with — and his books about — several local and state parks, Peter turned out to be the perfect choice to author the book.

Peter was intrigued not only with how the Woods had been saved, but he also proposed that the book look into the genesis of the Woods, moving forward from there through the intervening years since the Five Mile Woods Preserve was first established.

Although my archive of materials provided the starting point for this book, many of the people originally involved with the movement to save the Woods have cooperated and participated, in countless ways, to make this project complete. Other contributors to this book include the people who have continued to maintain and promote the Preserve until the present day.

As you read this book, you will meet all of the aforementioned people. I am confident that you, the reader, will find the history contained in these pages both comprehensive and fascinating.

Don Formigli
Levittown, Pennsylvania
April 1, 2017

COMMON BEECH

COMMON BEECH

INTRODUCTION

The Essence of History is Remembering

The people of Lower Makefield have done something so unusual, I haven't seen anything like it. Many years from now people will look back at this (the Five Mile Woods Preserve) and be thankful for it.[1]

LLOYD KLATZKIN
CHAIRMAN
LOWER MAKEFIELD TOWNSHIP BOARD OF SUPERVISORS

ONE OF MY FAVORITE THINGS TO do as a writer and historian is to honor the dreams of the people who create our country's museums, historic sites, state and national parks, state and national forests, and natural preserves. It takes someone special to have a vision, such as preserving a significant cultural or natural resource, and then move a complicated process along until there is a dedication ceremony, signs are unveiled and people begin visiting. These are the people who have given us many of the places that we now prize.

There are special characteristics shown by these visionaries, such as Carolyn Pitts who led the effort to save the historic architecture of Cape May, New Jersey, a late nineteenth century seaside resort. Her efforts, during the 1960s, which were controversial at the outset, resulted in the creation of a National Historic Landmark District and a state treasure. The community remains a beautiful place to visit.

Or, perhaps it was the Mount Vernon Ladies Association who saved George Washington's home along the Potomac River in the 1850s. The house sat in a state of disrepair until Ann Pamela Cunningham viewed the venerated founder's home from the river and determined that it needed to be saved. At the time, there were no mechanisms to save historic sites like the preservation organizations or historical societies that are now so common across the country. We enjoy the benefits of their hard work more than one hundred and fifty years later. The Association continues to manage the site.[2]

At nearby Washington Crossing, Philadelphia surgeon Isidor Strittmatter purchased almost three hundred acres of land on both sides of the Delaware River in the early twentieth century. Most of those acquisitions would ultimately become Washington Crossing State Park (New Jersey) and Washington Crossing Historic Park (Pennsylvania). Strittmatter had saved what was then believed to be the most significant tracts on which the famed 1776 Christmas Crossing of the Delaware had taken place.[3]

Another example is the Bowman's Hill Wildflower Preserve (BHWP). This unique area, about one hundred acres in size, was set aside within Washington

Crossing Historic Park. It was one of the early leaders in the native wildflower preserve movement in the United States. Those lovers of wildflowers and native plants created an institution that would become a model for the creation of other preserves across the country. The BHWP remains a dynamic organization.[4]

Among the original organizers of the BHWP in the early 1930s was Dr. Edgar Wherry, a nationally respected botanist, horticulturist, mineralogist, chemist, and museum curator. He became an important supporter of the efforts to save the Five Mile Woods forty years later. Two other supporters of the project, also associated with Bowman's Hill, were Oliver Stark, the long-time botanist there, and his predecessor, David Benner.[5]

An important leader in environmental issues in the county was the Bucks County Parks Foundation, founded in 1958, reorganized as the Bucks County Conservancy, and now known as the Heritage Conservancy. In the years that followed its creation, the members of this esteemed organization were increasingly alarmed by the urbanization of the county and the effect it was having on the environment, its history and historic sites. The Bucks County Conservancy would come to play a critical role in the creation of the Five Mile Woods Preserve and saving significant portions of the Woods not purchased outright by Lower Makefield Township and Falls Township.

Many of the Conservancy's members and leaders were prominent residents of the county, including Ann Hawkes Hutton. Hutton was involved with many efforts to preserve the region's history including creating Historic Fallsington and leading the Washington Crossing Historic Park Commission during its glory years. She served on the Conservancy's board of directors.

Like all of these previous successful efforts to take on what seemed to be impossible tasks, so it was for the residents of Lower Makefield Township. In the end, it was a small group of dedicated people who saved the Five Mile Woods from being destroyed. It was a race against time as houses were being built and developments proposed on neighboring properties.

All of these examples, including the Five Mile Woods Preserve, demonstrate that these visionaries are often single-minded in their focus. They looked for, and found, creative, proactive strategies to implement their goals that often straddled the political divide. Our national, state, and local treasures have often been saved by such people. For their hard work and devotion, we are grateful, even if we do not always know who they are.[6]

While I do not begin a book with an agenda in mind, there is one theme that is consistent in all my books about parks and institutions: They honor the founders and the visionaries who carried those efforts forward. Often, the founders have passed from the scene long ago, moved from the area, or pursued other interests. Their names are forgotten and the current beneficiaries of their hard work and dedication often just assume that the site, building or institution that they are enjoying was always there. Perhaps there is a dusty old picture hanging somewhere of the founder but his or her contemporaries are usually gone and there is no direct connection to that person or the group of people who worked so hard years ago.

However, sometimes those founders come back to those places long afterwards, or continue to maintain an interest in their pet project. And so it is with one of the founders of the Five Mile Woods Preserve, Donald Formigli. Don was the leading visionary who created this wonderful place, and in fact, as the reader will soon discover, he is the *Patron Saint of the Woods*. He later moved from the Township but always kept up an interest in the affairs of the Preserve. When he called me in the winter of 2015 to ask if I was willing to tell this story, I was very excited about the possibility. He is a great example of a founder who still remembers the complicated effort and hard work that it took to create a special place and see it shared by future generations. It is rare to be able to work with someone like Don because his efforts began more than forty years ago. To walk on the trails and eat lunch on logs and rocks at various places with him was not only a pleasure but an honor.

There were others involved in that founding effort including Pat (Fair) Miiller, Gail Hardesty, Hank Miiller, Lloyd Klatzkin, Ann and Paul Rhoads, Carol Dubois, and Lynn Sims, just to name a few. Collectively, in the late 1970s, they developed a comprehensive strategy for a wide-reaching recreational program for Lower Makefield Township. This included recreation facilities for both passive and active interests, the Five Mile Woods Preserve and later, farmland preservation. They used a bipartisan, grassroots approach that was implemented and still benefits the Township today. This effort did not begin with a government mandate but rather with a citizen's initiative. All of these programs required that local residents agree to pay additional taxes which they did in a referendum in 1978.[7]

Then there are the visionaries at the Preserve who have carried that mission forward by sacrificing their time, donating money, dealing with challenges and urging others to do the same. They might give tours and demonstrations, keep the books, clean the bathrooms, cut the grass, maintain the trails, or serve in public office to protect the public investment. While their vision for the site may be different than the founders, they remain committed to that original mission. To those folks, we also offer our collective thanks.

A PLACE WITH A RICH PAST

When one tells the history of the Preserve it must be told through a broader lens. It is not just an inspiring story about local Township residents saving a beautiful parcel of land as the rush of development moved northward from lower Bucks County. That in itself is a remarkable story. However, in many ways the history of the Preserve and the area that immediately surrounds it is the history of the development of Bucks County, the Commonwealth, and the story of our national experience. There are connections with the region's first native peoples and its early European settlers with their ties to American Quakerism.

The establishment of the region's transportation network had a decided impact on the Preserve's history, and its creation came about because of commercial and residential development. It is also significant that the Preserve's destiny fits into a larger narrative of the many conservation and recreation promotional activities that were accomplished in the 1970s and 1980s. This is a story that is set in a much larger context, and in many ways, represents so many far-reaching themes of the era.

Today much of the focus of the interpretive programs at the Preserve, to the credit of its naturalist John Heilferty and the members of the Friends of the Preserve, are on its special environment, including unique plants, trees, animals, reptiles, amphibians, birds, and its fascinating geological past. Taking a tour with them is an experience that opens one's eyes to things not usually seen. Every time we went for a walk at the Preserve I saw something new, wildflowers I had never noticed before, shrubs that I did not know about and amazing geological features.

One of the things that is not emphasized, however, is its interesting cultural history. This is not a criticism of the staff or volunteers, but is only to be expected because the area was saved to preserve its unique natural resources. Aside from Lower Makefield Township historian Ralph Thompson's 1997 report about the historic sites either in or adjacent to the Preserve, there has been nothing written about the Preserve's history. Hopefully this book fills that gap so that its fascinating story can now be told by staff and volunteers.

In 2016, the Five Mile Woods Preserve celebrated the thirty-fifth anniversary of its opening on an auspicious day in November 1981. In 2018, it will commemorate the fortieth anniversary of the first purchase of land that became the basis for future acquisitions and gave us the treasure we now have. To celebrate these remarkable achievements, take this book, go to the Preserve, hike its trails, see the Fall Line, attend a program or admire its amazing wildflowers on a spring day. Maybe you can even find a few of the species of plants or birds found listed in the Appendix. If you do this, you will make those founders and their successors happy and will know that they are deeply gratified.

Peter Osborne
Red Cloud, Nebraska
April 30, 2017

COMMON BEECH

COMMON BEECH

Chapter 1

THE GROUND BENEATH US

The Five Mile Woods contains the only undeveloped section of the Fall Line Zone remaining in Pennsylvania that is of sufficient size for natural processes to dominate.[1]

The Five Mile Woods is also one of the few sites where Coastal Plain flora and fauna persist in the state. The biological significance of the site is enhanced by the mixture of Coastal Plain and Piedmont elements that reflect its location as the boundary of these two physiographic provinces.[2]

NATIONAL NATURAL LANDMARKS
NOMINATION APPLICATION TO THE NATIONAL PARK SERVICE
PREPARED BY DR. ANN RHOADS

2003

I N THE MIDDLE OF A VAST SWATH of residential and commercial development lies a beautiful oasis of woodland and a nature sanctuary called the Five Mile Woods Preserve. Within its borders are the remnants of significant geological events from the distant past along with rare and endangered plants unique to Bucks County and the Commonwealth of Pennsylvania. It is a popular hiking destination and draws local visitors and those from around the region for its programs.

Located in southwestern Lower Makefield Township, the Preserve is home to three important geological features including two distinct provinces - the Atlantic Coastal Plain Province and the Piedmont Province - along with the Fall Line, the place where these two provinces meet. While the Fall Line appears to be just a modest rise in the elevation of the land with a gradual slope in most places, it is a significant geological feature that runs from Carteret, New Jersey, through southeastern Pennsylvania, and all the way to Alabama. The most striking example of the entire Fall Line can be seen at the Great Falls Park, a National Park Service site in McLean, Virginia.[3]

Courtesy United States Geological Survey
The Fall Line runs from
Carteret, New Jersey to Alabama.

The interesting geology of Bucks County has long fascinated scientists, botanists and geologists. Well-known botanists collected specimens here including John Bartram, Thomas Nuttall, Elias Durand, Andre Micheaux, Dr. Benjamin Barton, and Frederick Pursh among others. One of the earliest references to the county's uniqueness comes from Zaccheus Collins, a well-known botanist from Philadelphia.[4]

The most striking example of the Atlantic Seaboard Fall Line can be seen where it crosses the Potomac River at the Great Falls Park in Virginia.

On August 23, 1813, Collins wrote:

I was lately in Bucks county (sic) almost five miles north-west of Bristol, a spot very interesting to me botanically and geologically. Although my opportunity was transient from bad weather. . .[5]

Based on his description, he was not far from the Five Mile Woods.

Three other important botanists who have studied the Woods were Bayard Long, Walter Benner and Ann Rhoads. Long, an important twentieth century botanist, was born in 1885, and was an Associate Curator, and then Curator of Botany, at the Academy of the Natural Sciences of Philadelphia. He placed the specimens he found in the Woods in the Academy's Local Herbarium where they still reside today. Walter Benner was long associated with the Academy, starting as a Research Associate and later becoming a Scientific Associate. In 1932, he completed the *Flora of Bucks County* as part of his Ph.D. coursework. The dissertation, published later as a book, remains a classic today. Born in 1888, he taught biology

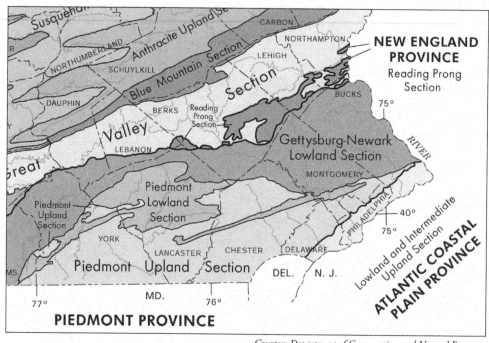

Courtesy Department of Conservation and Natural Resources
The three main geologic provinces of Bucks County are shown here.

at Central High School in Philadelphia for many years. He died in 1970.[6]

Another important botanist who has studied the Five Mile Woods is Dr. Ann Rhoads. She is the co-author of two books, *The Vascular Flora of Pennsylvania: Annotated Checklist and Atlas* and *The Plants of Pennsylvania: An Illustrated Manual.* For many years, she has overseen field surveys in eastern Pennsylvania including directing an effort to gather information for the Pennsylvania Natural Diversity Inventory and a natural areas inventory of Bucks County.[7]

Dr. Rhoads worked as the director of botany at the University of Pennsylvania's Morris Arboretum and also served on the Bucks County Planning Commission. She continues to serve the county with regard to preserving natural areas. In 1987 Rhoads was the recipient of the Science Award given by The Nature Conservancy's Eastern Pennsylvania Chapter. She was an active participant in the efforts to save the Five Mile Woods and prepared the plant species listing that is included in the Appendix of this book.[8]

FROM EONS AGO

The geology of the Five Mile Woods is remarkable because it is the meeting place of two major geological features that have very different characteristics and that developed over millions of years. This process continued until the retreat of the last glaciers more than ten thousand years ago.

To begin a brief journey into the county's geological past, one must first start at its northeastern corner where the Reading Prong Section of the New England Province is located. This lies to the north and south of Riegelsville. The province is a part of the Appalachian Mountains which lie along the eastern seaboard of the United States and run from Maine to Georgia. The rocks found in this region are Pre-Cambrian, the oldest on the geological scale, along with rocks from the early Paleozoic Period which include gneiss and various types of sands and gravels.[9]

Then, moving southward in the county, there is the Piedmont Province which includes ancient rolling hills and plains located along much of the country's eastern seaboard and east of the Appalachians. It includes much of present-day Bucks County. The province's southern boundary includes the communities of Trevose and Langhorne, which are within the county.[10]

The Piedmont Province, also known as the foothills of the Appalachian Mountains, has a complicated geological history but is essentially due to the erosion of mountains over eons of time. This was a result of numerous events, most notably when a massive land mass called Pangea split into two sections, now North America and Africa. As that happened parts of the earth's crust, including parts of the Piedmont Province (Piedmont Plain or Plateau) began to drop and were then covered by eroded material, sands and silt, washed down from the higher elevations.[11]

This section of the Piedmont Province, also described by some geologists as the Triassic Lowlands, dates from the Triassic Period (between 245 million years

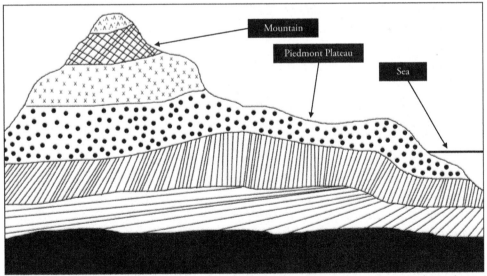

Courtesy Rachel Stenfiennagel

The Piedmont Province was created over eons when materials created by the erosion of mountains took place. That process, along with the shifting of the earth's plates, and further erosion, created the Atlantic Coastal Plain Province.

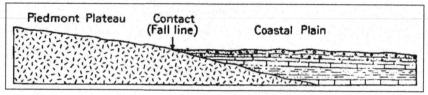

Courtesy United States Geological Survey
The Fall Line is the meeting place of the Coastal Plain and the Piedmont Province.

ago and 206 million years ago). A number of types of rocks can be found here including sedimentary and igneous rocks. They include gray arkose sandstone, dark gray and red shale, red and brown sandstone, gray and black argillite and diabase. Evidence of Pre-Cambrian Baltimore gneiss can be found in the northern parts of the Five Mile Woods Preserve and along Big Oak Road, which fronts the Five Mile Woods Preserve. At least two well-known natural landmarks in this part of the county, Jericho Mountain and Bowman's Hill, were formed during this time.[12]

It was in this period that dinosaurs appeared on the earth's surface for the first time including the Ichthyosaurs, a fish-like lizard, the Pterosaur, a flying reptile, and ancient sharks. There was also the first appearance of crocodiles, turtles, flies and mammals. Fish and dinosaur fossils have been found in Nockamixon State Park along with algae fossils in northern Bucks County. Farther afield plant fossils have been found in Carversville, and dinosaur footprints and lobe-finned fish have been found near Princeton, New Jersey.[13]

The next major feature is the Atlantic Coastal Plain Province which extends out to the Delaware River and across New Jersey to the Atlantic Ocean. It too has a complicated geological history that included the rise and fall of sea levels and the changing of the shoreline as it receded and expanded. Today, Tullytown and Bristol are within this geologic zone. This region includes largely sedimentary rock and sediments and unconsolidated sand, clay, boulders, pebbles and gravel.[14]

The Coastal Plain has been described as:

Characterized by relatively level ground, wider slow-moving streams, extensive marshes and swamps, and a high water table, with frequent flooding after heavy rains . . . the Coastal Plain climate, more influenced by its proximity to larger expanses of water, is somewhat more moderate than the Piedmont.[15]

The contact point between the Piedmont Province and Coastal Plain Province is called the Fall Line, or as it is described by geologists, the Atlantic Seaboard Fall Line, or the Fall Line Zone. The Fall Line runs between Trevose and Morrisville, passing through the Graystone Woods and then crossing the Delaware

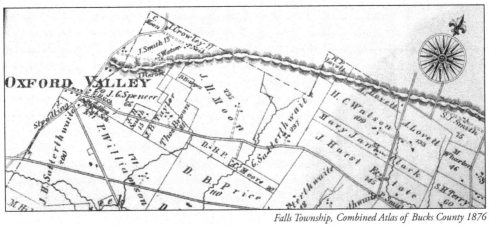

Falls Township, Combined Atlas of Bucks County 1876

The Fall Line is shown as a continuous ridge line on this 1876 Falls Township map. The Preserve is located just north of the J. H. Moon and Giles Satterthwaite tracts.

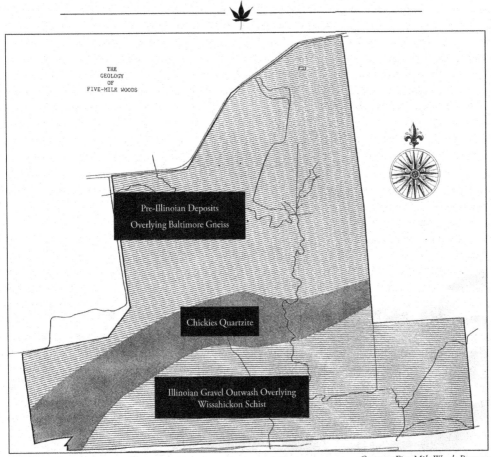

Courtesy Five Mile Woods Preserve
Master Plan for the Five Mile Woods Preserve: Lower Makefield Township Pennsylvania
The Geology of the Five Mile Woods Preserve

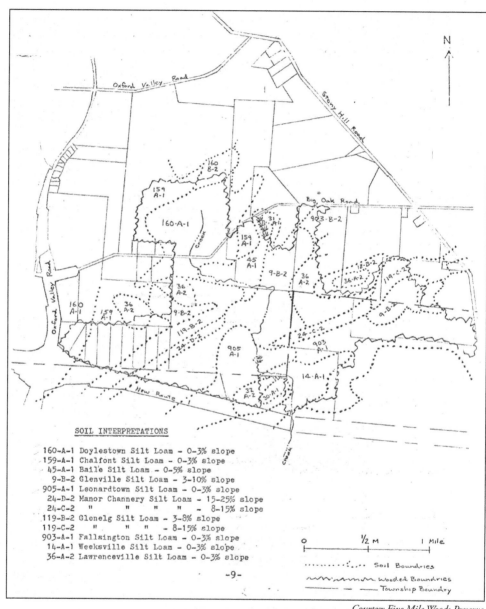

SOIL INTERPRETATIONS

160-A-1 Doylestown Silt Loam - 0-3% slope
159-A-1 Chalfont Silt Loam - 0-3% slope
45-A-1 Baile Silt Loam - 0-5% slope
9-B-2 Glenville Silt Loam - 3-10% slope
905-A-1 Leonardtown Silt Loam - 0-3% slope
24-D-2 Manor Channery Silt Loam - 15-25% slope
24-C-2   "   "   "   - 8-15% slope
119-B-2 Glenelg Silt Loam - 3-8% slope
119-C-2   "   "   "   - 8-15% slope
903-A-1 Fallsington Silt Loam - 0-3% slope
14-A-1 Weeksville Silt Loam - 0-3% slope
36-A-2 Lawrenceville Silt Loam - 0-3% slope

-9-

0   ½ M   1 Mile

.... Soil Boundaries
~~~~~~~~~ Wooded Boundaries
———— Township Boundary

Courtesy Five Mile Woods Preserve
Donald Formigli Collection
Bucks County, Pennsylvania Interim Soil Survey Report

Soil Map of the Five Mile Woods
c. 1975

River. This feature is prominent enough that, on an 1858 farm map of Lower Makefield Township, it is called *Edge Hill*. In Morrisville, there is a housing development built along the Fall Line that is called *Edgehill Gardens*. Falls Township and Fallsington (originally known as *Fallsintown*) both got their names from the rapids in the river created by the Fall Line. [16]

Within the Preserve this ridge can range in height between twenty and thirty feet and between one hundred and sixty and two hundred feet in elevation above sea level. Chickies Quartzite, a greenish quartz rock, can most readily be seen where there are several very small quarries cut into the Fall Line near the southwest corner of the Preserve. The Queen Anne Creek passes over the Fall Line not far from one of the quarries, near the confluence of the Crossing and Creek trails in the eastern part of the Preserve. [17]

The Preserve's geology is described in more technical terms in the Preserve's *Master Plan*, which states that the:

Five Mile Woods straddles a ridge of Lower Cambrian Chickies Quartzite running diagonally across the property from northeast to southwest. Extending north of the ridge for approximately one mile is a formation of Pre-Cambrian Baltimore Gneiss overlain by Pre-Illinoian Deposits, while extending to the south is Wissahickon Schist overlain with Illinoian Gravel Outwash. [18]

Courtesy Peter Osborne

Within the Preserve's boundaries, the Fall Line appears to rise slowly in elevation, but the closer one gets to Route 1, its appearance becomes more distinctive and cliff-like.

Courtesy Peter Osborne

There are only two sections of the Fall Line within the Preserve that have been disturbed. The first is where a small quarry was dug into its edge. This is just a short distance from where the William Dark home was built. The second quarry is located near the southern border and is larger. Its origin is unknown.

This geological formation also impacted construction techniques of the area during the first one hundred-fifty years of its history. Most of the buildings north of the Fall Line are constructed of stone while most of the buildings south of the Fall Line are of wood frame construction. This reflects the rocky nature of the land above the line and the sand and gravel components of the land below it.[19]

It is also here, at the Fall Line, where the two different zones meet, that was described in 1910 by Dr. Witmer Stone as a boundary that:

Marks a great change in plant life.[20]

Five Hundred Million Years Ago

How did this unique place come to be? About five hundred million years ago, the Langhorne Ridge, which crests in Langhorne, was created. It is the base of a former mountain. At the time the ridge served as the bank to the Delaware River, which was much wider than it is today. At that time, all of Bucks County was part of the Piedmont Plain including the bed of the river.[21]

Then, in more recent geological times, the present profile of the county was created. Between ten and fifteen thousand years ago, during the Pleistocene Era, the last glacial ice sheet began melting and receding to the north. While it did not cover Bucks County (the glacier's furthest southward boundary being in the Poconos) the effects of its melting most decidedly impacted the area. The water, sand, and gravel released by the glacial sheet from the higher elevations began to make their way across the county into the Delaware River, and over time, buried sections of the Piedmont Plain. The Coastal Plain region was thus created. The distinctive place where these two features meet became the Fall Line or Fall Zone.[22]

The erosion caused by the melt also created many waterfalls and rapids where numerous rivers cross over the Fall Line. As a result, if one could track the entire route of the Fall Line, one would soon find that it is not a straight line but rather proceeds in an irregular path and varies in height along its length. At some places, it is readily seen, while at others it appears as a simple rise in elevation. During the summer season, it is even more difficult to identify because of the vegetation. To a certain extent, all of these features can be seen in the Five Mile Woods Preserve.[23]

After eons of changes, shifts, and erosion, the Preserve's elevation now varies from one hundred and twenty to two hundred feet above sea level.

Historic Fall Line Cities

The nation's most notable eastern rivers that cut through the Fall Line on their way to the ocean include the Delaware, Schuylkill, Potomac, James, Congaree, and Savannah Rivers. Beginning in the late seventeenth century, and continuing into the early nineteenth century, the towns and cities of the eastern United States were often built along a river's shoreline or near the Atlantic Ocean. Many of them became important commercial centers like Philadelphia and New York.[24]

The rivers provided an important means of transporting goods and moving people. Above the Fall Line, rivers and streams flowed rapidly downstream, and the water was used to operate an assortment of mills. Many of the earliest towns were located at the Fall Line and later became agricultural and industrial centers. Below the Fall Line, the rivers were flat, slower and tidal which also allow for easy navigation up to the Fall Line. Because of the barrier caused by the falls, ships and boats could not easily proceed farther upstream.[25]

Among the more notable towns and cities on the Atlantic Seaboard Fall Line

Courtesy Peter Osborne

The Fall Line crosses the Delaware River at Morrisville. This memorial, at the junction of Crown Street and Highland Avenue, commemorates the starting point of the deed that William Penn negotiated with the area's Native Americans. Across the street, a part of the Fall Line was given the name Graystones. Today the exposed rocks are located within a community preserve called the Graystone Woods.

is Trenton, New Jersey. This was the location of General George Washington's remarkable victories over the British in 1776 and 1777 after the famed Christmas crossing of the Delaware River at McKonkey's Ferry in Upper Makefield Township. Because of the falls at Trenton, the British Navy was unable to sail ships farther up the river and thus cut the colonies off from each other. Today, the rapids created by the Fall Line can be seen from the Calhoun Street Bridge which links Trenton to Morrisville. Below the falls at Morrisville, the Delaware is a tidal river, and at times, there can be a six-foot difference in the height of the river.[26]

After the Revolutionary War, Trenton was considered as a site for the nation's capital. However, another Fall Line community, Washington, D.C., was chosen and became the seat of the federal government. Philadelphia was located where the Fall Line crossed the Schuylkill River, and was the nation's capital for a short time. It was also the state's most important commercial center as well as the center of activities for the nation's founders.[27]

Further to the south and west were other Fall Line communities including Chester, West Chester, Coatesville, and Downington in Pennsylvania; Baltimore and Elkton in Maryland; Wilmington, Stanton and Newark in Delaware; and Richmond, Fredericksburg and Petersburg in Virginia. Farther south there are Raleigh and Greenville, North Carolina; Columbia in South Carolina, and Columbus, Georgia.[28]

Other important communities built on the Fall Lines created by different geological formations include Paterson, New Jersey. Paterson was the birthplace of the American Industrial Revolution. The Society for the Useful Manufacturers, founded by Alexander Hamilton, the first United States Secretary of Treasury, was established there and harnessed the power of the Passaic River for manufacturing purposes. Further to the northeast other Fall Line cities include Albany, New York; Hartford, Connecticut; Lowell, Massachusetts; and Augusta and Bangor, Maine.[29]

Courtesy Library of Congress
Geography and Map Division
Library of Congress Control Number 79695387

This 1771 map of proposed roads in southeastern Pennsylvania reveals how early map makers noted the locations of the waterfalls along the Fall Line.

In the years after the American Revolution the various Fall Lines were recognized as an impediment to the nation's development of its interior and an important consideration in the development of early internal improvement programs such as the building of roads and canals. For example, in 1808, President Thomas Jefferson's Secretary of the Treasury, Albert Gallatin, prepared a report for the United States Senate on the state of roads and canals in the nation. In discussing the state of navigation and the ability to gain access into the interior regions beyond the mountains, Gallatin wrote to the United States Senate:

The most prominent, though not perhaps the most insuperable obstacle in the navigation of the Atlantic rivers consists in the lower falls, which are ascribed to a presumed continuous granite ridge, rising about one hundred and thirty feet above the tide water.[30]

Much of the Fall Line in Pennsylvania, which is forty-four miles in length, was eventually altered as early roads crossed through and over it, railroads and a canal were built, and more recently, when the land was developed for residential and commercial purposes, and when highway systems were constructed. Bit by bit it was covered over, built around, or changed. Some of these changes can be seen just beyond the Preserve's boundaries.[31]

As one walks along the southern property boundary line along Route 1, the Fall Line can be seen proceeding out of the Preserve in a southwesterly direction, and then, as can be seen by the rise in the elevation of the highway, disappearing under the exit for Oxford Valley Road. The Pennsylvania Railroad's line which ran parallel to the southern border of the Preserve, cut through it. To the east of the Preserve, the Fall Line was obscured by development as the topography of the land was changed to accommodate houses.

The Preserve remains the only place in Pennsylvania where the Fall Line, and the land around it, has not been eliminated or changed significantly. Here it runs diagonally from the northeast to the southwest through the Preserve. The best place to see the distinctive features of the Fall Line is near the southwestern corner of the property, and where the Five Mile Trail passes over it, perhaps the remains of an old woods road. Another excellent viewing area includes the channel through it created by the Queen Anne Creek. Here one can see, in miniature form, a rare example of how the Fall Line presented such difficult challenges to the nation's founders.[32]

There is only a small part of the Fall Line within the Preserve that has been disturbed. Sometime in the late seventeenth or in the early eighteenth century it is thought that a very small quarry was opened for stone used in the construction of the foundation of a small house nearby. A second and larger cut in the Fall Line is located at the southeast end of the property. This seems to have been a more extensive effort and the tailing piles are larger, although like the former site, there are no drill marks from the cutting process. This quarry also appears to be newer. Perhaps it was worked as recently as fifty years ago.

THE QUEEN ANNE CREEK

The only significant body of water running through the Preserve is the Queen Anne Creek. Its headwaters begin on the northern side of Big Oak Road, opposite the Preserve in the Yardley Oaks residential development. At this location, the size of the drainage causes surface water to collect and form the creek that meanders through the Preserve with numerous ox bows, or u-shaped turns. Home to sala-manders, frogs, fish and snakes, it is a typical headwater stream and dries up in places during the summer.[33]

From its headwaters, it proceeds southward and over its course in the Pre-serve drops about fifty feet in elevation. It has very little current until it passes through the Fall Line. Overall, from its origins in the Five Mile Woods to its con-fluence with Mill Creek, the Queen Anne Creek's main stem is almost three miles long. It includes a drainage basin of almost seven square miles.[34]

After the creek leaves the Preserve, it passes beneath Route 1 and the railroad tracks, drains into Lake Caroline, and then passes through Queen Anne Park and Oxford Valley Park. It merges with Mill Creek to the east of Frosty Hollow Park. The combined streams unite with Black Ditch Creek and form Otter Creek which flows into the Delaware River at Bristol.[35]

Because of its undeveloped state and its extensive wooded wetlands, John Heilferty, the Preserve's manager, describes the Preserve as one big sponge, ab-sorbing rainfall and preventing flooding. Elsewhere these areas are prone to flood-ing because they do not have good infiltration rates and have high runoff that, as will be seen with the residential and commercial development, has created flooding problems in southern Bucks County. Further south of the Preserve, a one-hundred-year floodplain has been delineated along the creek by the Federal Emergency Management Agency. Queen Anne Creek is classified as a Warm Wa-ter Fishery by the Pennsylvania Fish and Boat Commission.[36]

The larger Otter Creek watershed has also been prone to catastrophic flood-ing largely because residential development has altered the ecological balance. For example, in 1996 more than ten million dollars of damage was done to residen-tial and commercial properties south of the Preserve. Additional major flooding occurred in 1999 during Hurricane Floyd. In 2004, it was calculated that there were at least one hundred and forty residences and more than fifty non-residential structures within the one-hundred-year floodplain of the Otter Creek watershed and thus susceptible to flooding.[37]

In 2014, the Bucks County Planning Commission undertook a feasibility study to consider the development of a Mill-Queen Anne-Black Ditch Creeks

Trail as part of a larger effort to create a trail system along the county's various stream corridors. A trail network like this had been proposed for many years. The idea of connecting the corridors was particularly attractive because most of the land was owned by local or county government agencies and the Philadelphia Electric Company.[38]

The proposed network of short trails began near the headwaters of Bristol Mill, Queen Anne and Black Ditch Creeks respectively, and continued southward as the creeks combined to form Otter Creek. The proposed hiking trail passed through the borough of Bristol and ended at the Delaware. The proposed section of trail that paralleled Queen Anne Creek began in Falls Township, on the southern side of Route 1 at Oxford Valley Park.[39]

Area residents conduct cleanups of the creeks farther downstream as was done in the late fall of 2016. Undertaken by Greenbelt Overhaul Alliance of Levittown, volunteers cleaned debris from streams, removed invasive species and provided educational programs. This not-for-profit organization has worked on a variety of projects in the Levittown area.

A QUEEN, A CROSS-DRESSER AND A MANOR

The origin of Queen Anne Creek's name is not known but there are two streams shown on the circa 1705 version of the *Map of the Improved Part of the Province of Pennsylvania in America: begun by Wil. Penn, Proprietary & Governour thereof anno 1681* that are in the vicinity of its present location. However, neither are named. The 1955 *Place Names of Bucks County* by George MacReynolds describes the reason for the name as *obscure* but does not speculate on how it came to be. Howry Epenshade does not list it in his *Pennsylvania Place Names* written in 1925. The United States Geological Survey (USGS) Geographic Names Information System offers no clues either. The stream appears on various county maps in the early nineteenth century but is not identified. It is believed that there are no Lower Makefield Township deeds that specifically name the creek in their citations.[40]

The creek was identified by name for the first time on the 1858 *Farm Map of Falls Township: Bucks County, Pennsylvania* produced by Thomas Hughes. There it is shown as *Queen Ann's Creek*. It also appears on the Falls Township map in the 1876 *Combination Atlas of Bucks County* by J. D. Scott with the same name. The stream appears on a United States Geological Survey (USGS) topographic map in 1907 (*Trenton West NJ, PA*). The data were compiled from surveys undertaken in 1885-88. It was identified on subsequent USGS maps as *Queen Anne Creek*. In both cases, the headwaters and the section running through the Preserve are not shown or identified. Farther to the south, the name of the stream is indicated.[41]

In trying to determine the origins of the name, but without definitive evidence, one enters the realm of speculation. There is some historical data that al-

Courtesy Peter Osborne

The Queen Anne Creek, the only body of water that runs through the Preserve, meanders from its head-waters on the northern side of Big Oak Road continuing southward until it merges with the Mill Creek and the Black Ditch Creek and flows into the Delaware River at Bristol.

lows for this. Hence, the name of the Queen Anne Creek may date from the eighteenth century. This line of thinking begins with the circa 1705 map previously mentioned. A stream can be clearly seen originating in the William Darte (or Dark as it is also spelled) tract, the location of today's Five Mile Woods Preserve, and proceeding in an easterly direction. During its course, it passes through the northeastern corner of the Mannor of Penns-berry (today's Pennsbury Manor) where it empties into the Delaware River, near the northern end of Biles Island. Some have suggested that this stream's route is the present-day Rock Run, but a review of the USGS topographic maps of the area from various eras show it traveling southward. John Heilferty, the Preserve's Manager and Naturalist, believes that because of the simple facts of the area's geology, the stream could not have substantially changed its course over such a wide area. Therefore, the stream shown leaving the Dark tract on the 1705 map is not the Queen Anne Creek.[42]

A second possibility is the stream shown that begins near the northwestern corner of the Mannor of Penns-berry and empties into the Delaware farther downstream, passing through the property of John Otter. This approximates the combined Queen Anne, Bristol Mill, and Otter Creeks and today's larger watershed. While the Holmes map dates from 1705, and many of its features are remarkably accurate for the time, some of the stream data was probably filled in by a map maker without any actual site knowledge. Mapping data after 1830 confirms the present route of the Queen Anne Creek.

Another factor to consider is that on most maps, even the oldest ones with the creek's name shown, it is not identified until it is in Falls Township. This is probably the mapmaker's recognition of the seasonal nature of the creek's water level as it rises and falls with the season and sometimes runs dry.

There is at least one possible explanation for the creek's name that could tie these various pieces of information together and show a royal connection between the creek's name and the first English owners of the land that now makes up the Preserve. It is possible that the small, and relatively insignificant creek which runs through the Preserve, may have the impressive pedigree which its name implies.

While W.W.H. Davis's 1876 important *History of Bucks County* offers no insight into the origin of the creek's name, Davis does offer a plausible reason for how the name might have come to be. The story begins when England's King William III died on March 8, 1702. One of the potential successors to the throne was Anne Stuart (1665-1714). She was the king's sister-in-law. Davis relays how the news of Anne Stuart's ascension to the throne, on April 23, 1702, was communicated to the residents of Bucks County.[43]

The announcement of the coronation is believed to have been made by Edward Hyde, Viscount Cornbury, a cousin to the queen, and the governor of New York and New Jersey. One of the most powerful men in the American colonies, he came to Burlington, New Jersey with a large entourage, and then visited the Mannor of Penns-berry twice that year, in June and then again in September. To have a ship carry the news so quickly across the Atlantic was possible as trips could be completed in under fifty days.[44]

It is also known that on July 5, 1702, the Provincial Council in Pennsylvania proclaimed Anne as the Queen without an order to do so. Perhaps the official proclamation was done in the aftermath of Cornbury's June visit or in September.[45]

Queen Anne would ultimately recall Lord Cornbury to England. Her reign continued until her death in 1714 when she was succeeded by George I. For more than two centuries Lord Cornbury was described as a colorful figure from the distant past and was said to have been a cross dresser, wearing women's clothing, stating that he did so because he represented a woman. A portrait hanging in the New-York Historical in New York City has been long been assumed to be that of Cornbury. In it, he is attired as a woman. [46]

This curious piece of history is disputed by the most recent historian to investigate this era, Patricia Bonomi, who, in her ground-breaking book, *The Lord Cornbury Scandal: The Politics of Reputation in British America,* demonstrates that the stories that have been passed down may have in fact been fabricated by Hyde's political enemies, and the painting may have actually been of his father.[47]

This series of events suggest a possible scenario for the naming of the creek although it still leaves us without a definitive conclusion. The author believes that one of two events happened. The first is that when Edward Hyde visited the Mannor of Penns-berry one of the colony's officials on hand, someone familiar with the area's geography, might have suggested naming the stream as a token of the colony's esteem for Queen Anne. An even more likely scenario was that William Penn, who was then in England, may have offered the Queen this token of his esteem for her and her realm as a gesture from his proprietorship. When one reads Penn's correspondence of the era it can be readily seen how he would have wanted to make such a gesture in the royal court. However, there is no mention of the creek in the published collection of William Penn's letters.[48]

The issue of a name of a creek passing down from so long ago is not without precedent in Bucks County. Consider the Delaware River that has had its name since the early 1600s. The Neshaminy Creek, in the southern end of the county, was previously named Neshameneth Creek, as it was labeled on the 1705 Penn map. Its historic name is probably derived from a Native American word. The origin of the Core Creek's name dates to at least 1696 and probably predates that, as it is shown on a document laying out a new road near the creek that still bears that name and which feeds Lake Luxembourg. Core Creek Park is about five miles west of the Preserve.[49]

One last possibility, and perhaps less speculative, is that some mapmaker or area resident gave the Queen Anne Creek its name in a moment of whimsy knowing of royal and early colonial history in some distant time. No matter, the name has continued to be used on maps since at least 1858, and probably earlier, and was placed on later USGS maps.

The probability that the name originates from the coronation announcement and celebrations that took place at the Mannor of Penns-berry, or sometime thereafter, is speculative but unless new facts come to light, it remains a possibility. Whether the formal naming came at that moment or in the Queen's court at a time thereafter, it seems likely that the small stream with the royal name was so honored in some way because of her coronation more than three centuries ago.

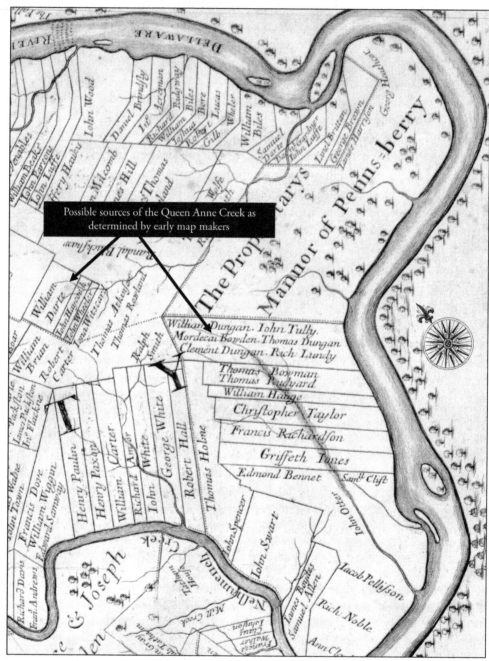

Possible sources of the Queen Anne Creek as determined by early map makers

Courtesy Library of Congress
Geography and Map Division
Library of Congress Control Number 2006625100

This circa 1705 map of Bucks County shows the location of two possible sources of the Queen Anne Creek as determined by early map makers. The Preserve is located on the tract of land that was designated as being owned by William Darte.

Bogs, Wetlands, and Springs

There are numerous other smaller bodies of water within the Preserve's boundaries. These include vernal pools, wetland seeps, emergent wetlands, palustrian (wooded) wetlands, wetlands, and even a small cranberry bog, probably created accidentally. There is a sphagnum moss wetland in the Piedmont Plain area. There are also springs and small streams that last only as long as the season of wetness occurs. Together, this place is home to a variety of unique plants and animals.[50]

At the time of creation of the Five Mile Woods Preserve, it was thought that the endangered bog turtle was a nearby resident. In fact, a student of George Carmichael, an area teacher with a broad knowledge of Bucks County's geological and natural history, brought one into school. The student relayed that it had been found at the headwaters of the Queen Anne Creek on the north side of Big Oak Road. In 1966, according to another source, a bog turtle was found by Harry Smith less than a mile from the bog in the Preserve. Whether these two events are one in the same is not clear but it is known that bog turtles could be found in the Levittown area at the time.[51]

The Preserve's present naturalist, John Heilferty has disputed the bog turtle occurrence in the area. Heilferty is a trained herpetologist and works full-time for New Jersey's Endangered and Nongame Species Program. He has suggested that the turtle sightings were actually of a spotted turtle, a species that can still be found in the Woods. The two turtles are closely related and very similar looking, hence this was most likely a misidentification. There are no formally recognized sightings, present or historic, of a bog turtle in the Pennsylvania Fish and Boat Commissions main database from this time.[52]

Where The Ecozones Meet

Because of the different composition of the soils in the Coastal Plain and the Piedmont Provinces, there are different types of plants and trees that are generally, although not exclusively, found in each of them. Most of the acreage in the Preserve is located within the Piedmont Province. Among the types of trees that can be found generally in this province are the yellow poplar, white and red oak, beech, chestnut, pignut and shagbark hickory, red and silver maple, black gum, white ash, wild black cherry, American hornbeam, dogwood, red elm, black walnut, butternut and bitternut. The chestnut trees that were once so common in the American forests were destroyed by the blight almost a century ago although shoots continue to come up from ancient trees only to die a number of years later.[53]

The Coastal Plain makes up a smaller percentage of the acreage, perhaps one third, and borders the Falls Township line. The Coastal Plain ecology is very rare in Pennsylvania. Species that are endangered in the Commonwealth can be very common in New Jersey, which includes more of the Coastal Plain. There are almost five hundred plant species generally found in the Coastal Plain but not in the Piedmont Province.[54]

However, because these two provinces meet at the Preserve the difference between the types of plants found here is not so clear. Dr. Ann Rhoads in describing the meeting of the Piedmont and Coastal Plain wrote:

A site like 5-Mile Woods, that straddles the geological boundary between two physiographic provinces, shows a blending of the floristic elements of both. Trying to point to areas in the Woods that represent either Piedmont or Coastal Plain plant communities is problematic. Natural boundaries are rarely that sharp and the distribution of species typical of either zone has been further affected by land use history including timbering, clearing for agriculture and subsequent secondary succession. Its more accurate to describe the site as containing species typical of Coastal Plain, such as sweetgum (Liquidambar styraciflua), willow oak (Quercus phellos), sweet pepperbush (Clethra alnifolia), sweetbay magnolia (Magnolia virginiana), American holly (Ilex opaca), swamp dog-hobble (Leucothoe racemosa), soapwort gentian (Gentiana saponaria), cranefly orchid (Tipularia discolor), and netted chain fern (Woodwardia areolata); but plants such as American beech, red oak, white oak, pin oak, mayapple and Christmas fern that are more typical of the Piedmont and areas further north.[55]

In the Commonwealth, the Coastal Plain forests have largely disappeared because of residential development. Only two of any significant size remain, Five Mile Woods and Delhaas Woods.

However, the largest area of undeveloped Coastal Plain forest remaining in Bucks County is Delhaas Woods, a 181-acre tract that is located in Bristol Township. The public access is on Bath Road. Delhaas Woods is part of the Silver Lake Nature Center complex, owned and managed by Bucks County. This parcel was acquired by The Nature Conservancy in 1988. There was a proposal to build a new interchange linking the Pennsylvania Turnpike and Interstate Route 95 which would have devastated this valuable resource, but it was stopped. There are also several smaller Coastal Plain forests remaining in lower Bucks County in Falls, Bristol and Bensalem Townships.[56]

Another example of this is the ability of animals, birds and reptiles to move freely between the two provinces. In reflecting on the wildlife at the Preserve, John Heilferty believes that:

Where wildlife is concerned, the ability of birds and terrestrial wildlife to move freely between the Coastal Plain and Piedmont regions makes the Fall Line a much less significant determinant in species range. However, there are exceptions. And as might be expected, these are more commonly noted among taxa exhibiting low inherent mobil-

ity, which as can be expected, amplifies the effect of any ecotone or geological transition. George Carmichael found in 1975 that the Fowler's toad (Anaxyus fowleri) was not to be found in the Piedmont Plateau but was found in the Coastal Plain. While this is rare for Pennsylvania, it is much more common in the Coastal Plain region. This is thought to be in part due to the Fowler's toad's tendency to self-excavate burrows for refugia, leading to its favoring the sandy or gravelly soils characteristic of the Coastal Plain that are much more conducive to that life history trait. Where Fowler's toads do range into the Piedmont Province, it is typically only along short reaches of stream corridors immediately above the Coastal Plain, where the alluvial deposits of sand and gravel largely mimics Coastal Plain soil conditions. Another example is the occurrence of northern slimy salamanders (Plethodon glutinosus) within the Preserve – a species of salamander not known to occur within the adjacent coastal plain in Pennsylvania, New Jersey or Delaware. [57]

A PLACE OF CONSTANT BUT GRADUAL CHANGE

With the ever-changing nature of the landscape and the various uses of the land over the centuries, particularly those that make up the Preserve and the greater Five Mile Woods, the division between the two ecozones is not always so clear and delineated. The Preserve's landscape has constantly changed, particularly during the last three hundred years, because of the activities of man. Over that time, the land has been put to agricultural use, logged, and since the 1970s, essentially left undisturbed, allowing for a successional forest to develop, mature and to spread into the former agricultural areas and oldfields.[58]

It is thought that the oldest trees in the Preserve range between one hundred-fifty and two hundred years old according to Rick Mellon, the Preserve's first Resident Naturalist, and John Heilferty, the Preserve's current Manager. The Preserve has been timbered on several occasions. The oldest stand of trees includes oaks and beeches and is located not far from the Preserve Headquarters, along Big Oak Road. Several of the oldest beech trees are located along the boundary line between the Preserve and the Guzikowski farm in the lower southeast corner of the Preserve. Those trees may have survived because over the centuries, neighbors did not want to cut down the trees that formed the boundary line. Also, farmers often kept acres of woods and old trees preserved for everyday uses including firewood and lumber.[59]

The Five Mile Woods region has been regularly documented using aerial photography since the late 1930s. These photographs show a gradual evolution of the landscape. In 1938, more than half of the northern section of the Woods was cleared land and was put to agricultural use. Fence rows divided those various lots and there were very few trees. There was for example, an orchard behind the Brelsford House (more recently called the Cutler House), now the Preserve's headquarters. In addition, there was a large nursery of evergreen trees on the west-

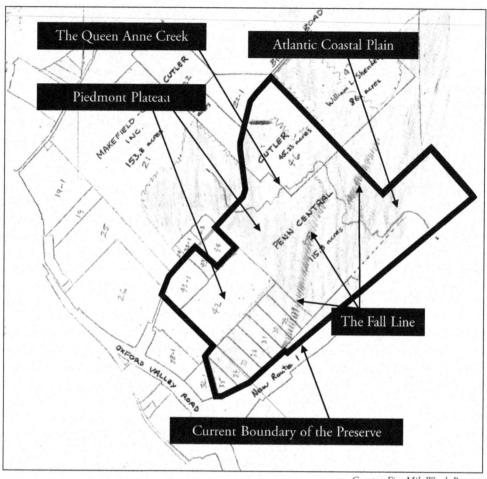

The Queen Anne Creek

Atlantic Coastal Plain

Piedmont Plateau

The Fall Line

Current Boundary of the Preserve

Courtesy Five Mile Woods Preserve
Donald Formigli Collection
Map by Peter Osborne

The Fall Line, as shown on this 1974 tax map, runs through the Five Mile Woods Preserve on a line from the southwest to the east and is most distinctive near the boundary with Route 1. Today the Fall Line and Ridge Trails parallel the route of the geologic feature. Also shown are the Piedmont Plateau, Atlantic Coastal Plain and the Queen Anne Creek.

ern end of the property. This is where today's Evergreen Trail is located. By the late 1950s, some of those open fields were being left undisturbed and were going through natural succession.[60]

The aerial photographs taken in 1971 and again in 1974 reveal not only sections of mature forests, but also younger forests, fewer acres of farmland in active use along with several lots of cleared land being overtaken by forest. In reviewing the photographs, one can also see that the forest itself included sections that varied in age as witnessed by the size of the canopy of individual trees.[61]

With aerial photography, the distinctive shape of the entire Five Mile Woods can be plainly seen, especially as one comes forward in time. As the agricultural uses ended, the land was left undisturbed. The Five Mile Woods of 1981, the time of the dedication of the Preserve, is a very different place than it is today. Today there are several forest types within the Preserve that range from new, to successional growth, to a mature forest.

A PLACE OF ENDLESS GEOLOGICAL FASCINATION

The fascinating geology and ecosystems that lie within the Preserve's boundaries also played a major role in saving it. The meeting place of the Piedmont Plateau and the Atlantic Coastal Plain at the Fall Line helped in the efforts to create and promote the Preserve during the development boom that was taking place in the mid-1970s. Today, those various features remain an important interpretive tool used by staff and volunteers and are of interest to visitors. For lovers of the Preserve, it also remains the largest tract of woodland in lower Bucks County.[62]

But, before its preservation, it was home to Native Americans and Quaker farmers. Their impact on the land and the county's history was an important one. The unique geological events that created the Piedmont Plateau left behind layers of sedimentary rocks that were soft, and hence, shapeable. They became the construction materials of the many stone buildings spread across the county and gave rise to the canal, railroads and highways. The Coastal Plain allowed for the creation of entire industries such as the sand and gravel mining operations across the lower part of the county.[63]

COMMON BEECH

COMMON BEECH

Chapter 2

THE PEOPLE AND THE LAND

A country life and estate I like best for my children.[1]
WILLIAM PENN
REFLECTING ON THE MANNOR OF PENNS-BERRY

(William) Darke arrived in the Delaware River in October 1680 in the company of his younger brother, Samuel Darke, aboard the Content of London. Apparently he lived with his brother at Burlington, West New Jersey, until April 1683, when he warranted 235 acres in Bucks County, Pennsylvania.[2]
LAWMAKING AND LEGISLATORS IN PENNSYLVANIA
A BIOGRAPHICAL DICTIONARY 1682-1709

William Satterthwaite, 1ˢᵗ of Michael and Ester Tyson . . . came to America with a Certificate from Swarthmoor Monthly Meeting held at Rook-How, bearing the Date 12ᵗʰ Month 5ᵗʰ, 1733, he being in the 24th year of his age. He settled in Lower Makefield Township, Bucks County, Pa., on a farm owned by a descendent until 1852.[3]
GENEALOGY OF THE SATTERTHWAITE FAMILY
AMOS SATTERTHWAITE

WHILE THE STORY OF THE FIVE MILES WOODS reflects a long history of geological changes in the landscape, it also reflects the actions of people who inhabited the land. These people included the Native Americans who had been there for at least ten thousand years. After the arrival of European settlers in the mid-1600s, the native peoples slowly made their way westward after having either sold their lands or having been deceived by Europeans as evidenced by the *Walking Purchase of 1737*.

With the arrival in 1682 of William Penn (1644-1718), a prominent English Quaker, lands were fairly purchased from the Native Americans and then parceled out, sold and developed into a vast series of farms and plantations including Penn's own country home, the *Mannor of Penns-berry* (Pennsbury Manor) on the shores of the Delaware River, halfway between present-day Morrisville and Bristol. Those early settlers and subsequent residents changed the landscape with each successive generation. The landscape, which was once mostly covered with trees, was opened up for farming, and, in fact, by 1932, 91% of the county was in agricultural use.[4]

Those early settlers were sometimes anonymous, and their names have been lost to history. The names of others have been preserved like William Penn, William Dark (1622?-1716?) and William Satterthwaite (1709-87). All three, at various times, owned the land that now comprises the Five Mile Woods Preserve. These families also impacted the colony's culture because many of those early settlers were members of the Society of Friends, more commonly known as Quakers. The Quakers arrived after having been persecuted in England for their radical religious beliefs.[5]

Some of the families who came to Bucks County were of the *upper sort* as they were described then, and from the eastern part of England. Most, however, were of the *middling sort*, or the middle class as they might be called today. It is believed that as many as half came from the western part of England.[6]

BUCKS COUNTY

The Five Mile Woods is located in Bucks County, one of the original three counties in the Colony of Pennsylvania. It was created in 1682 by the Provincial Council, the governing legislature, and was named by William Penn to honor the County of Buckinghamshire from where he had lived in England. Prior to the American Revolution, the county was much larger than it is today as Northampton County was removed in 1752, with Lehigh County taken from Northampton in 1812. Today, the county is bounded by Lehigh, Northampton, Philadelphia and Montgomery Counties and then to its east and south, the Delaware River. To the east of the river lie Warren, Hunterdon and Mercer Counties in New Jersey. The county's original townships were Bensalem, Bristol, Falls, Makefield, and Middletown. Bristol served as the first county seat from 1705-24. It was relocated to Newtown until 1813 when it was moved again, this time to Doylestown, where it has been ever since. It is 590 square miles, approximately forty-two miles in length and twenty miles in width at its broadest point.[7]

Bucks County figured prominently in the Revolutionary War on three occasions. The first was the famed Christmas Crossing of 1776, the second was in 1777 when Washington's army passed through on their way to engage the British at the Battle of Brandywine, and lastly in 1778 when Washington and his troops passed through on their way to fight the British at the Battle at Monmouth. There were also skirmishes at Newtown on February 18, 1778, and Bristol on March 17, 1778.[8]

Bucks County also has a rich historical and cultural legacy that extends far beyond the American Revolution. There is a remarkable architectural heritage that includes hundreds of beautiful eighteenth and nineteenth century houses, often located in agricultural and rural settings. Pearl Buck and James Michener, both Pulitzer Prize winners, were residents of the county, as were Oscar Hammerstein, Margaret Mead, and Moss Hart.[9]

The county's rich cultural legacy includes centers at New Hope, the Bucks County Playhouse, the James Michener Art Museum in the cultural district of Doylestown, and the Arts and Cultural Council of Bucks County. The Pennsylvania Impressionist school, which is centered at New Hope, has been active since the 1930s. Bucks is one of the few counties in America that is recognizable by its name.[10]

LOWER MAKEFIELD AND FALLS TOWNSHIPS

The Five Mile Woods is located in the southwestern corner of Lower Makefield Township and includes a smaller parcel that lies within Falls Township. Both townships were among the original five created in the county. Lower Makefield was once part of a larger Makefield Township. It was the second township created in the county in 1692. The name is said to have come from Richard

Hough, a Provincial councilor and landowner, who may have been honoring his hometown of Macclesfield in Cheshire, England. It is thought that the name was corrupted to Makefield.[11]

The northern half of the Township was removed to create Upper Makefield in 1737. This was done because of challenges in administering such a large jurisdiction and the result of land being added to the colony that Penn's sons had acquired as a result of the notorious *Walking Purchase* undertaken in the same year. At the same time the lower half of Makefield was extended further south incorporating a part of Falls Township into what was called Lower Makefield. The southern boundary, which had been subject to some dispute, was drawn to approximate the Fall Line. The borough of Yardley, formerly known as Yardleyville, separated from the township in 1895.[12]

Falls Township, also created in 1692, was an early center of American Quakerism. The Falls Meeting was the first established in the county. As will be seen, the early owners of the land that makes up the majority of the Preserve today were Quakers, and important members of the Meeting. Falls Township's name originates from its location at the falls on the Delaware River at Trenton.[13]

Morrisville, the borough on Lower Makefield Township's southeastern side, was separated from Falls Township and incorporated as a borough in 1804. It is the location of the starting point of the survey of the first purchase of land by William Penn from the Lenni Lenape Indians and is memorialized at the Graystones monument at the junction of Crown Street and Highland Avenue. Summerseat, the headquarters of George Washington during the weeks leading up to the Christmas Crossing of 1776 and the subsequent battles of Trenton and Princeton, is located here.[14]

However, the story of people living on the land that now includes the Preserve began thousands of years ago with arrival of the Native Americans.

The First Peoples

Prior to the settlement of the Delaware River Valley, and then the inland by Europeans, native peoples had lived in the region for thousands of years. They are grouped by category into four general eras: the Paleo-Indian Period, the Archaic Period, the Woodland Period, and the Historic (or Contact) Period. Evidence of all four eras can be found in the region.

The earliest indigenous people in America, the Paleo-Indians (14,000 BC – 8,000 BC), were a hunting culture, and their main quarry was the mastodon. Some have suggested that they may have hunted this large elephant-like animal into extinction. They also hunted woolly mammoths and bison. Fish and birds were also included in their diet. The most notable artifact associated with the Paleo-Indians are the Clovis spear points that were an effective hunting tool along with knives, drills and choppers. Newer research seems to indicate that an even

Courtesy Pennsylvania Geological Survey

Mortars, pestles, adzes and pecking stones were commonly used by the Woodland era peoples.

earlier date can be assigned to the arrival of an indigenous people, now described as the pre-Clovis, perhaps dating as far back as 18,000 to 25,000 years ago.[15]

Between 8,000 BC and 1,000 BC, an era described as the Archaic Period, there was the development of a more diversified culture. They were hunters and gatherers, eating meat and fish and collecting plants to eat. Typically, the kinds of artifacts found representing this era include spear points, knives, axes, drills, scrapers, and choppers. There have been many Archaic sites found and excavated around the region.[16]

The next era, the Woodland Period began about 1,000 BC and lasted until approximately 1600 AD. They were hunters and gatherers who lived in small communities or camps and were the first Native Americans to use bows and arrows. More commonly known as the Lenni Lenapes, these are the native people with whom most people are familiar. The Lenape people used clay pottery, amulets, pecking stones, pestles, axes, knives, scrapers, projectile points which are often still found in farm fields, along with sinkers that were used for fishing.[17]

The Lenape lived in the region until the Historic (or Contact) Period when they encountered Europeans who either simply settled on the land that they had lived on for thousands of years or made small purchases of land from them. Then, beginning in the 1680s, with the arrival of William Penn (1644-1718) and his fellow Quakers, larger purchases of land were made. While they had peaceful relations with William Penn, the native peoples began to move westward as their former lands were developed into plantations and farms. In the eighteenth century, Native Americans were also subjected to diseases and wars. As a result, their numbers were greatly reduced.

The region has been the subject of many archaeological excavations, which are a valuable resource for documenting the lives of these indigenous peoples. One of the most noteworthy Native American archaeological sites on the Eastern seaboard is located at the Abbott Farm. It is located due east of the Preserve less than ten miles away in Hamilton, New Jersey. This is believed to be the largest collection of middle Woodland era sites ever found and there is evidence of Paleo-Indians nearby too. The Abbot Farm was continuously inhabited for ten thousand years and is one of the most important pre-historic sites in the country. Because of its significance, it is a registered National Historic Landmark.[18]

Another important source of research information on the region's Native Americans is the archaeological work recently completed at the planned I-95 bridge site along the Delaware River that will replace the current bridge just north of Yardley. Many artifacts were found from the late Archaic and late Woodland Periods here. Additional research has been conducted in the Point Pleasant and Core Creek areas over the years. There are at least six documented Native American sites north of the Preserve in Lower Makefield Township.[19]

The archaeological sites closest to the Preserve are two locations near the southwestern corner of the Township where it meets Falls and Middletown Townships. Another is located near the junction of Oxford Valley Road and Stony Hill Road. This site investigation was led by Henry Mercer in 1910. There have been no reported sites identified within the Preserve and it is believed that no archaeological testing has ever been undertaken on the property. There are surely many other Native American sites that have not been investigated or reported in Lower Makefield Township or Falls Township.[20]

The shorelines and plateaus on both sides of the Delaware River were ideal locations for native peoples who passed by regularly and occupied seasonally. The area was an important source of stone for Native Americans to make their various utensils, and there were several quarries in the area known to have been used by the native peoples. The region is rich in argillite, a material commonly used by Native Americans to make stone tools, and outcrops of it can be seen along the banks of Delaware and nearby streams.[21]

Other evidence that remains of these ancient peoples are the trails that they used to access the river and the Atlantic Ocean that became the basis for much of the region's road network. It is believed, for example, that Dolington Road was one such road, along with the roads that fan out from it.[22]

The names given to various sites by native peoples sometimes survive such as Sanckhickan, an area west of Trenton in the southeastern corner of Lower Makefield. A street still bears that name in New Jersey's state capital. Other names in Bucks County that survive include Nockamixon, Neshaminy and Aquetong. There is at least one deed in the collection of the Bucks County Historical Society transferring an island in the Delaware River from the local native peoples to William Biles in 1737. The island was called *Manaughanoning*, and today is known as Biles Island.[23]

For Native Americans who had been living in the Delaware River valley region for thousands of years, their world was transformed after the arrival of the first English explorer, John Cabot, who claimed the Delaware River for the crown in 1597. Henry Hudson explored the Delaware River in 1609. By the 1620s the Dutch were making their own claim to the region. At the same time Holland formed an alliance with Sweden, and soon Finns created New Sweden in the 1630s. By the mid-1600s, settlers from across the Atlantic were coming into the valley in increasingly larger numbers.[24]

Sometime in either late 1682 or early 1683, William Penn is said to have negotiated the Treaty of Shackamaxon with Tamanend and other Delaware chiefs, although the historical record is not entirely clear with regard to this much-discussed gathering. Whether it was an actual treaty written on paper or an oral agreement, or in fact, if it even happened, is still not settled history.[25]

THE HOLY EXPERIMENT

On October 27, 1682, the ship *Welcome* arrived in the colony of Pennsylvania carrying with it a prominent Englishman and leader in the Quaker religious movement, William Penn. He came from an important family and his father, Sir William Penn (1621-70), had been an admiral in the British Navy. The elder Penn had personally helped to re-establish the country's navy after a period of civil turmoil in Great Britain. King Charles II, in recognition of that debt and service, wanted to settle it with the elder Penn's son.[26]

In a request to the King, the junior Penn proposed a grant of land in America where Penn could expand upon his ideas for government and religious freedom. A charter was signed on March 4, 1681, giving Penn the land west of the Delaware River, above Maryland and as far north as was plantable. The King suggested the name, *Pennsilvania*, or *Forests of Penn* or *Penn's Woods*.[27]

When Penn stepped off his ship, he was not the first important official to arrive in what became Pennsylvania. William Markham, Penn's cousin and Deputy Governor, and Thomas Holme, the Surveyor General, had arrived earlier to purchase lands from the Indians, deal with settlers who were already there, and study the country. Those settlers included Quakers who had arrived in the 1670s among others. In fact, a small town, called Crewkerne (or Crewcorn), was already established in present-day Falls Township near Morrisville. While the colony of New York did not have any official role in this vast expanse of territory to its west and south, it maintained, by default, some administrative power. Penn incorporated most of those who were already living within the boundaries of his land grant into his proprietorship.[28]

Penn, a lawyer, had already been involved in the New World because of

Courtesy Donald Formigli

A statue of William Penn greets visitors to Pennsbury Manor, the site of the former country home of the proprietor of Penn's Woods.

his association with arbitrating an important legal settlement among several important Quakers over the colony of New Jersey. His efforts culminated in the division of the colonies of East and West Jersey and then for their governance in 1676. Soon ships were arriving at Salem, and then Burlington in the western half of West Jersey. Many of the passengers were Quakers, thereby creating the first Quaker dominated colony. His administrative work with the colonies of East and West Jersey proved to be good experience for his experiment in Pennsylvania, and some of those Jersey settlers soon migrated to Bucks County.[29]

William Penn planned for Pennsylvania's capital, visited the neighboring colony's various leaders, purchased land from the native peoples, organized the colony's government and began planning for the construction of a country estate along the Delaware. Penn's capital would be called Philadelphia, or the *City of Brotherly Love*. It was to be located almost twenty-five miles downstream from where his country home was built.

Penn's plantation site was chosen by Markham, but Penn oversaw the building of the main house and the development of the estate. It was called the *Mannor of Penns-berry* on seventeenth century maps or the *Governor's Plantation*. Known today as Pennsbury Manor, it was situated on the western shore of the Delaware River and located at the sharp turn in the river below the falls at Trenton. The site also included a large swamp that was a valuable source of food for cows and a habitat used by birds which were a good source of food for the settlers.[30]

The construction of the main manor structure began in 1683. The details

William Dark may have traveled to William Penn's home at the Mannor of Penns-berry (Pennsbury Manor), or to Philadelphia, to get his warrant and patent for the land that now includes most of the Preserve. The original mansion fell into disrepair and was lost to history. This reconstruction was built by the Pennsylvania Historical and Museum Commission from 1938-39.

of its construction and other outbuildings are not entirely clear at this late date, and are the source of some controversy. It is believed that a settler who arrived earlier, Thomas King, had already built a house on the proposed location for the manor. After being purchased by Penn, the proprietor may have used the house as his country home even as the new structure was being built. Some have suggested that it may have been incorporated into the new structure. A 1684 session of the Bucks County court was held there along with other official government business. Most recently, historians have suggested that the shell of the building was completed between 1683-86, and was finished between 1700-03 when Penn returned to the colony.[31]

Important visitors and officials came up the river in a small barge using the rising tide from the capital in Philadelphia. Then they disembarked in front of the beautiful home and walked up an allée of poplars to the front door. Located in a picturesque setting, it was maintained by a number of servants and slaves. Native peoples were often guests at Penn's home; he could communicate with them using sign language and he had some understanding of their culture.[32]

THE PROPRIETORSHIP

William Penn's legacy is a remarkable one as he encouraged religious tolerance in Pennsylvania and representative government that became the inspiration for the nation's founding fathers less than one hundred years later. The provincial government was set up with the King as the ultimate authority, William Penn was the proprietor who owned the colony and was the governor who administered the colony along with two legislative bodies. The government evolved over time in scope and size after changes were made to the original charter. The Provincial Council included eighteen members who were elected by the people and wrote the laws. The General Assembly, made up of thirty-six men elected by the people, accepted or rejected the laws.[33]

Penn's belief in religious tolerance and his efforts to undertake a new kind of society came to be called the *Holy Experiment*. He held that people with various beliefs and traditions could live side by side, showing tolerance towards one another. It is one of his most important and enduring contributions to the development of America. By promoting tolerance, he was hoping to avoid the religious persecution he and his fellow Quakers had felt in his homeland. Penn also knew that the Quakers would ultimately be a minority in the colony's population, and wanted them to be treated fairly along with being represented in the economic system.

Once Penn received his grant of land from the King, he began acquiring the land through a number of transactions with the Lenape and paying them what was believed to be a fair price for it. Originally the native peoples had no understanding of the concept of land being sold, instead, they thought Penn generous and would return annually for more gifts. With those initial purchases complete, settlers acquired rights to land with a warrant. The next step, usually occurring several months later, included a survey of the property done by the Surveyor General's office. After this step, the new owner received a patent from William Penn. In return, the new landowner was required to make an annual payment of quit rent, often in pounds' sterling or agricultural goods, normally a peppercorn.[34]

Within two decades most of the land in the southeastern portion of the colony that was included in the original grant was sold. In about 1705, a map of Chester, Philadelphia and Bucks counties was published that listed all of the land owners at that time including one William Dark or Darte as it was spelled on other early maps.

THE QUAKERS ARRIVE

The story of William Penn has a direct connection to the Five Mile Woods Preserve. Since 1683 many people have owned various sections of the greater Five Mile Woods area. To list them all would create a complicated list of transactions that would be difficult to follow. However, there were only two families whose members, over nine generations, and for more than two hundred and fifty years, almost continuously owned the land that now makes up most of the Preserve.

The earliest European family believed to have lived on what is now the Preserve was that of William Dark (c.1629?-1716?). Dark's surname is also spelled with an *e* on several contemporary documents and that has created confusion among historians. It is also shown on the 1687 *Mapp of Improved Part of Pennsyl-*

vania in America, Divided into Countyes, Townships and Lotts and the circa 1705 *Map of the Improved Part of the Province of Pennsylvania in America* as *Dart* or *Darte* respectively.[35]

Dark arrived in America in 1680 along with his younger brother Samuel (?-1723?). They were typical of the *middling sort* of Quaker immigrants of their time and included farmers, merchants, craftsmen, and skilled laborers. William was believed to be at least fifty at the time he came the area. He was originally from Chipping Campden, in Gloucestershire, England. J. H. Battle, in his *History of Bucks County,* speculated that the brothers came to scout out the area. Initially they lived in Burlington, in what was the colony of West Jersey. Then it is thought they acquired land holdings in Burlington County. Nothing has been found about William's time in England.[36]

William Dark was among the first English Quakers to purchase land from William Penn. Penn provided him with a warrant to the property on February 13, 1683, and several months later, on April 20, it was surveyed by the Surveyor General's office. Dark received a patent for the land on May 29, 1684. This transaction was confirmed when a new patent was drawn up by Penn on February 5, 1690, which may have replaced a lost document.[37]

It is possible that Dark traveled down to the Mannor of Penns-berry to obtain both the warrant and patent. The main manor building was under construction at the time although Penn may have been using the former Thomas King house as his headquarters. Or, if not, Dark may have traveled to Philadelphia which was the seat of the provincial government. The receipt of the patent in 1690 would have again required a visit to Philadelphia or Penns-berry as Penn was in England at the time. Dark also had to travel to the Penns-berry or Philadelphia to pay his taxes or quit rent annually on March 1.[38]

The original patent for 235 acres of land was then located in the northwestern corner of Falls Township and included most of today's Five Mile Woods Preserve. The rectangular shape of the parcel can be clearly seen on the 1687 and 1705 maps of Bucks County. The tract was also located in an east-west configuration that was typical as the roads were often built on the same line. The Dark land grant came to be divided into two sections: an eastern tract and western tract, as shown on a 1997 map created by Lower Makefield Township historian, Ralph Thompson.[39]

The land grant north of the Dark tract, bordering Big Oak Road, and partly within today's Preserve's boundaries, was owned by William and Charles Biles, two other important Quakers and associates of William Penn. William Biles was a fell monger, or a dealer in animal hides. To the east was a large tract owned by Richard Hough, the man who is said to have given the Township its name.[40]

The size of the Dark tract is smaller compared to other tracts that Penn sold which were generally five hundred acres and thus indicated a family's social and

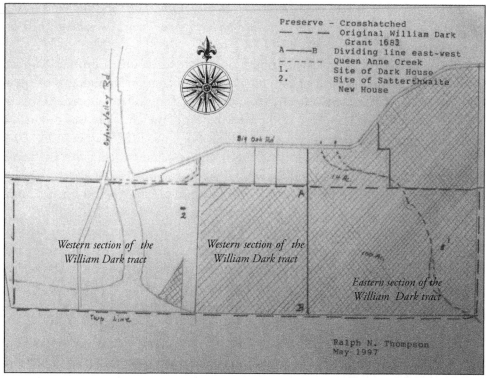

Preserve - Crosshatched
— — — Original William Dark
Grant 1683
A———B Dividing line east-west
----- Queen Anne Creek
1.   Site of Dark House
2.   Site of Satterthwaite
New House

Western section of the William Dark tract

Western section of the William Dark tract

Eastern section of the William Dark tract

Ralph N. Thompson
May 1997

Courtesy Lower Makefield Historical Society
Map by Ralph Thompson

The William Dark tract included most of the Five Mile Woods Preserve as shown on this 1997 map. To the north lay the William and Charles Biles tract which was more than double the size of the Dark property.

economic status. The value of his real and personal property was £62 pounds in the 1690s. As a comparison, the wealthiest resident of the area was worth £146 pounds and the poorest £0.[41]

THE DARK FAMILY LEGACY

William Dark was married twice, first to Honor _____ (?-1670). By this marriage there were said to be six children: Thomas, Mary, Sarah, John (1667-1730), William, and Samuel. Their first son died as an infant. Twin sons William and Samuel survived their mother's death at childbirth. After Honor's death, William married again, in 1671, this time to Allis (also spelled Alice) Butcher (1617-87), who was at least five years older, and raised his children. Allis followed his arrival in America four years later, bringing only John with her.[42]

William Dark was a glover in England and apparently continued in the same line of work in America. In 1684, he took on a five-year-old boy who became his apprentice and was taught the:

. . . art, mistery (sic) and faculty of skinner and glover.[43]

He was involved in the management of the county's administrative affairs and its main religious institution. Dark was a member of the Colonial Assembly in 1685 and served for a single term in which eleven laws were enacted. He also served as grand juror and trial juror from 1685-98 with several interruptions in service, and as a local tax collector in 1690. In 1696, he served as a witness, along with other appointed men, who laid out a road from Newtown to a ferry at Gilbert Wheeler's on the King's Road, present-day Route 413. The original road survey is owned by the Bucks County Historical Society. He served on two additional road committees, the last in 1703.[44]

His son John was married to Jane Rush (1673-1732) and like their parents, both were Quakers. There were a number of children by this marriage, although some of the genealogical data conflicts, as it does with his father. Their children were: John (?-?), Joseph (1702-?), William (1736-?), Thomas (?-?), Mary (?-?) and Susannah (?-?).[45]

John served as a constable, and both he and his father were involved in a 1698 controversy with the Falls Meeting over a trial that had stalled with a deadlocked jury. A coin was tossed into a hat to assist with the final decision. The Meeting believed that the flipping of a coin to determine the outcome had the effect:

To the dishonor of Truth.[46]

The Darks were among the founders of the first Quaker Meeting in Bucks County in the home of William Biles, on March 2, 1683. From that organizational meeting came the Falls Meeting, also known as the *Mother Meeting of Bucks County*. Among the attendees was William Penn, who spoke there when he was staying nearby at the Mannor of Penns-berry. As has been seen, the Darks had an interesting and difficult relationship with the Falls Meeting. After the organizational meeting, Samuel Dark married against the consent of the Meeting. While William tried to reconcile, he did not ever attend Meeting with regularity after that. Son John was also disowned at some point because he married a woman who had joined another faction of Quakers. He was thought to be somewhat of a free spirit.[47]

William Dark's brother Samuel (?-1723?) and his first wife, Ann (?-1683), owned a small tract of land on the Delaware River, not far from the Mannor of

Penns-berry and later a two hundred and thirty-acre tract not far from his brother's farm. He also owned land in Buckingham Township and Burlington, New Jersey, and by the end of his life possessed a considerable amount of property. He was married a second time to Martha Worrall (?-c.1732) in 1686.[48]

Samuel Dark was also involved with the management of the affairs of the colony and had been a cloth finisher in England before coming to America. He served in the Assembly for a number of terms and was considered to be an anti-proprietorship member. Dark was a witness to at least one deed with Native Americans and signed the certificate of removal from the Falls Meeting for William Penn when he returned to England in 1701.[49]

A CABIN ON THE CREEK

William Dark is believed to have built a small house where the Queen Anne Creek passes over the Fall Line and that was near a spring. Ralph Thompson, the late president of the Lower Makefield Historical Society, conducted a groundbreaking study of the historic sites in the Preserve in 1997. In that report, he determined that the original building was a wood-framed structure measuring approximately twenty feet wide by thirty feet long with two fireplaces, one at each end. The existing foundation was constructed of stone taken from a small quarry cut into the Fall Line just a short distance away. Thompson speculated that because the builder had not used mortar that it was an early home, perhaps the oldest in the Township.[50]

The building may have been a one-and a half-story structure with an overhead loft using logs for framing. Its size is representative of the many log houses built during the period and well into the eighteenth century. Another possibility is that it was a two-story log cabin, something that was more common than often thought. The Dark house may have been renovated later and upgraded in the decades that followed to include clapboard siding placed over the logs.[51]

The structure sat directly on the Fall Line, overlooking an open, wide, and flat area and facing to the south. Today, there are no known remnants of any other structures that may have stood close by. A spring is located just beyond the foundation but it is not known if it existed at the time the building was used. If one eliminates the sound of the traffic on Route 1 and stands at the location of the house, it is

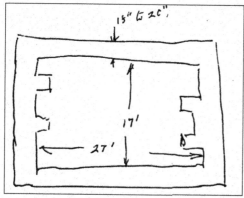

Courtesy Lower Makefield Historical Society
Drawing by Ralph Thompson
All that remains of the Dark home is the foundation. Ralph Thompson documented its dimensions in 1997.

Courtesy Library of Congress
Historic American Buildings Survey
Library of Congress Control Number PA 1687

No images of the Dark home are known to have survived. It was probably a log cabin that may have been subsequently renovated. The Moon-Williamson log cabin in Historic Fallsington, pictured here, may be similar to what the original Dark log cabin looked like. Before its restoration it was two stories in height.

readily apparent that it was an isolated location. This is especially the case because none of his neighbors were very close by, at least not in the first decade of his family's occupancy of the site.[52]

An example of what the Dark home might have looked like is the Moon-Williamson log house still standing in nearby Fallsington. This log house is believed to have been built in 1685 by Edmund Lovett. Before its restoration by Edwin Brumbaugh, one of America's most important historic preservation architects, it was two stories in height. Coincidentally this house is located next to a tract of land that William's brother Samuel owned in Fallsington. On the other side of the Samuel Dark tract was the original Falls Meeting house.[53]

William Dark deeded half of the interest of his property to his son John in late 1696 and left the remaining interest to him when he died in 1716(?).[54] There is one significant piece of information revealed in this deed that includes a description of the property. It states:

> *The tract of land which moiety (half) shall and doth enclude (sic) one half of the houseing (sic) barns stables orchards clear lands or other improvements.*[55]

This description reveals that the land had been developed since its original granting in 1683 to include buildings such as barns, and orchards with fruit trees. Parts of the property had been cleared and, as evidenced by 1684 tax records, he also owned cattle.[56] The appearance of the landscape in the late 1600s and early 1700s was very different than it is today. Aside from some woodlots, which were used for fuel, construction materials, and maple syrup, the level landscape lent itself to farming and pastures for raising livestock. This document also reveals that there were other buildings, including perhaps at least one other house and associated outbuildings. Their locations are unknown and not described.

It is thought that John and Jane Dark and their seven children lived on the property. However, genealogical records show that most of their children were registered at the Byberry Meeting, southwest of today's Preserve. This may indicate that they were leasing the land to a local farmer. It is known that John mortgaged the land and house to the General Land Office in Philadelphia in 1725 for £125. He died five years later in June 1730. John Dark's will, dated April 27, 1730, left all of his real estate and personal property to his wife, Jane. To each of his children, he left five shillings. Jane Dark died just two years later.[57]

It is not known where the Darks are buried although the first generation were probably interred in the first graveyard that was established at the Falls Meeting in Fallsington. The second generation may have been buried at Byberry. Because early Quakers did not formally mark their graves during this time, this information was lost to history.[58]

At least three of John and Jane's children moved to Virginia, far from Bucks County as did the children of a number of the area's early families. One died as a child, and several others are unaccounted for. This is probably the reason for the disposal of the homestead out of the family's ownership.[59]

Since the mortgage had lapsed it reverted to the General Loan Office. The Loan Office sold the two tracts to Bristol Township resident Samson Cary in 1734, ending the Dark family's legal connection to the property. Cary died in 1739, and once again, because the mortgage was not paid off, the property was sold. This time it was acquired by his nephew, Samuel Cary, who owned the eastern tract until 1748 and the western tract until 1764. Neither Cary resided on the property because they lived in Bristol but probably leased the property to local farmers. It was during this period, in 1737, that the Dark tract, which had previously been in the jurisdiction of Falls Township, was incorporated into a newly created Lower Makefield Township. This realignment was the result of the change in the boundary between Makefield and Falls Townships at the time of the *Walking Purchase* and the division of Makefield into Upper and Lower Makefield Townships.[60]

FROM THE SETTLEMENT NEAR THE WOODLAND

The next family to own the Dark tract, after the short interval the Carys owned the property, did so for more than one hundred and fifty years. This was the family of William Satterthwaite Sr. (1709-87). The family's roots can be traced to a community called Hawkshead, near Cumbria, in Lancashire, England. The origins of the family name were the combination of two words: *Setrthwaite – setr*, meaning settlement and *thwaite* or woodland clearing, according to a comprehensive family genealogy written in 1910 by Elizabeth and Amos Satterthwaite.[61]

The family's history also reflects some of the larger themes of American history and was characterized in the genealogy as having:

. . . principally been husbandmen and have nothing in the way of worldly goods of which to boast. We have endeavored to be a law-abiding, honest and industrious people . . .[62]

A late nineteenth century history of Bucks County edited by J. H. Battle says that they were:

Noted for their thrift and enterprise, and are highly respected.[63]

He also wrote that they were:

Whigs and Republicans.[64]

The genealogy is complicated to follow because each succeeding generation used the same first names. For example, there are multiple generations that used the name of William or Giles, which sometimes makes it difficult to untangle not only the various lines of the family but also the land transactions with which they were involved. In addition, there were members of the Satterthwaite family who lived across the Delaware River in southern New Jersey.

One member of the large extended family, William Satterthwaite (? - ?), a teacher in Philadelphia, Durham, Solebury and Buckingham Townships for a number of years, achieved notable fame in the Commonwealth's history as one of its earliest poets. He is thought to have arrived in Bucks County in the 1730s.[65]

One of his most well-known poems includes this verse that has passed down in time, written after he was bitten by a rattlesnake. It states:

Thou pois'nous serpent with a noisy tail,
Whose teeth are tinctured with the plagues of hell.[66]

Another is an untitled poem about a young woman who was not a particularly good singer:

Though singing is a pleasing thing,
Approved and done in Heaven,
It only should employ the souls
Who know their sins forgiven.[67]

The Satterthwaite family was important in the affairs of both Falls, Lower Makefield, and Middletown Townships and were active in Quaker affairs. However, unlike the Darks, the family was not involved in the colony's administration. William Satterthwaite Sr. (1709-87) was among the next generation of settlers in Bucks County, having arrived in 1734. Initially he lived in Middletown. Satterthwaite came to own most of the land that now makes up the Preserve.[68]

Satterthwaite Sr. married Pleasant Mead (1717-87) on February 15, 1736. By their union there were eleven children: Michael (1737-1737), Esther (1739-?), William (1740-1826), Ann (1742-?), Pleasant (1745-?), Rebecca (1748-?), Susannah (1749-?), Sarah (1752-1835), Mary (1755-?), John (1758-?), and Clement (1760-?).[69]

THE NEW HOUSE

William Satterthwaite Sr. purchased the eastern parcel of the Dark tract from Samson Cary on December 6, 1748. Sixteen years later, in 1764, he purchased the remainder of the Dark tract. During this time, it is believed that he and his family lived in the former Dark house. It is known that Satterthwaite built a house in the western tract, along Big Oak Road, in the last years of the eighteenth century. Ralph Thompson speculated that it must have been completed before 1786.[70]

There is a photograph of it in the 1910 *The Genealogy of the Satterthwaite Family* which is labeled:

A part of the . . . residence was the home of Wm. and Pleasant Mead Satterthwaite, and was in the family until 1852.[71]

According to the Genealogy of the Satterthwaite Family, published in 1910, a portion of this building is the New House built by William Satterthwaite, Sr. sometime before 1786. Ralph Thompson believed it was located on the tract of land adjacent to the Preserve where the Shoppe Oxford Oaks Shopping Center is now located. The house has long disappeared although it survived at least until the 1960s.

The building was a typical vernacular stone house common in Bucks County in the late eighteenth and early nineteenth centuries. It appears to be L-shaped and was stuccoed. The windows have both louvered and paneled shutters, and in the background, a short distance away, is another building, a closed forebay barn. Two large trees obscure the view of the building so that more details cannot be ascertained including the window and door configuration. It was described as the *New House* in documents created after its construction.[72]

There are county tax records that indicate in 1775, William Sr. owned four horses, six cattle; twenty-three sheep; and 277 acres in Lower Makefield. He rented part of his land, and perhaps even a house. He had one servant and while some of his Quaker neighbors owned slaves, he did not. Son William Jr. had two horses, five cattle and ten sheep, also in Lower Makefield. In another document the son referred to his holdings as his plantation, a common term in the era, just as his father had. By 1779, William Sr. had three horses and fourteen head of cattle while his son had two horses and four head of cattle.[73]

Names of Owners or Occupants	Names of Owners	Situate Bucks Co Lower Makefield	Number of Houses	Value of each dwelling House £ ℗	Rate of the [assessment]	Assessment $ ℗
55 John Nield	John Nield	Makefield	1	150	.2	30
56 Benjamin Palmer	Benj Palmer	do	1	500	.2	1
57 Henry Pough	Henry Pough	do	1	150	.2	30
58 David Palmer	David Palmer	do	1	400	.2	010
59 Mahlon Paxson	Mahlon Paxson	do	1	110	.2	22
60 Mark Palmer	Mark Palmer	do	1	400	.2	010
61 Amos Palmer	Cornelius Vansant	do	1	600	.3	1 010
62 Jesse Palmer	Jesse Palmer	do	1	600	.3	1 010
63 Henry Praister	Isaac Warner	do	1	150	.2	30
64 Peter Roberts	Peter Roberts	do	1	200	.2	40
65 Rebecca Richey	Rebecca Richey	do	1	110	.2	22
66 Daniel Richardson	Daniel Richardson	do	1	250	.2	50
67 Charles Stackhouse	Charles Stackhouse	do	1	110	.2	22
68 John Stockton	John Stockton	do	1	150	.2	30
69 Giles Satterthwaite	Giles Satterthwaite	do	1	300	.2	60
70 Abra Stackn Jr	Abra Stackn Jr	do	1	600	.2	1 010
71 Thomas Stradling	Thomas Stradling	do	1	150	.2	30
72 Cornelius Stackn	Cornelius Stackn	do	1	150	.2	30
73 James Stackn	James Stackn	do	1	450	.2	90
74 Abra Stackn	Abra Stackn	do	1	700	.2	2 10
75 William Stackhouse	Wm Stackhouse	do	1	250	.2	50
76 John Stackn	John Stackn	do	1	300	.2	60
77 John Stapler	Jno Stapler	do	1	300	.2	60
		do	1	010	.2	010

Courtesy U.S. Direct Tax Lists:
1798 Tax Lists for the State of Pennsylvania

In 1798 the United States government imposed a direct property tax. The listing shown is for a part of Lower Makefield Township. Giles Satterthwaite's house is listed and was valued at $300.

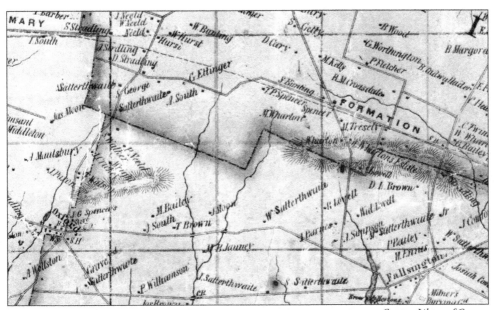

Courtesy Library of Congress
Geography and Map Division
Library of Congress Control Number 2012590185

Members of various Satterthwaite families owned a number of properties in Lower Makefield and Falls townships as shown on this 1850 map.

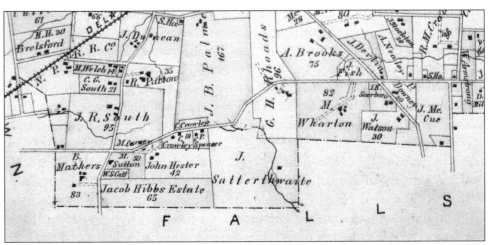

Lower Makefield Township, Combined Atlas of Bucks County 1876

This 1876 map of the southwestern corner of Lower Makefield Township shows how the area was changing with the construction of railroads, increasing residential development and the transferring of ownership of properties that included the Five Mile Woods. J. Satterthwaite's property (actually owned by Giles Satterthwaite) is shown in the center with a house along the Queen Anne Creek.

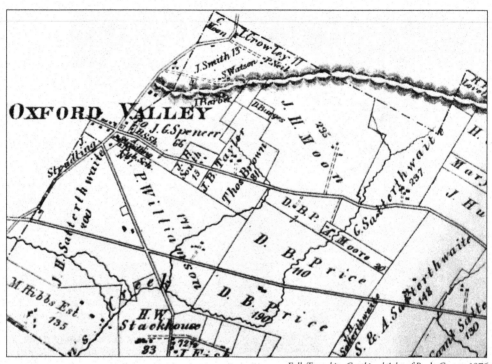

Falls Township, Combined Atlas of Bucks County 1876
This 1876 map shows the Satterthwaite holdings in Falls Township. Giles Satterthwaite's farm is just south of the township's boundary and the Fall Line. It adjoined his property to the north in Lower Makefield.

The *1784 Return of Land for Bucks County* also provides several interesting details about the family. At the time of this tabulation William Satterthwaite, Sr. was living on twenty acres, owned one dwelling house with five white occupants and no black occupants. By this time his son, William, Jr. owned 335 acres and two dwelling houses, (presumably the former Dark house and the other in Falls Township that still stands on Route 1) and two other outbuildings, perhaps a barn and stable. His dwellings were home to a combined eighteen white occupants.[74]

The senior Satterthwaite died in 1787 and left his wife, Pleasant, the *New House* in his will. She is also believed to have died in the same year. He left his land holdings and the remaining existing buildings to his son, the oldest child, William Jr. (1740-1826). In addition, his holdings in Falls and Middletown Townships were passed onto the son. One of the executors of his estate was Samson Cary who was a nephew to the elder Samson who had sold Satterthwaite Sr. his land originally and was a fellow Quaker.[75]

In his will there is a reference that must have included a part of the Five Mile Woods that he owned as well. He wrote:

With all my buildings wood and water their parts . . .[76]

Another section of the will ordered his son William to inherit the ownership of a property that he owned in London. This property contained a dwelling, shops, and other structures on the lot. While it is not known if the father continued to travel back and forth to London, it is clear that he maintained commercial ties to his native homeland. He was typical of the *midling sort* who had both agricultural and merchant interests.[77]

THE NEXT GENERATION
William Satterthwaite Jr. (1740-1826) was married in 1768 to Mary Knight (1750-1822). Her father, Giles Knight, provided muskets to the American cause during the American Revolution, was a member of the Pennsylvania State Legislature and later served as a Bucks County Commissioner. By this marriage, there were ten children including: Michael (1769-1811), Giles (1771-1834), Elizabeth (1773-1854), William III (1775-1859), Joseph (1776-1854), Abel (1779-1867), Susannah (1781-1821), John (1786-1837), James (1788-1793), and Samuel (1791-1858). Satterthwaite, Jr. died on December 30, 1826, and in his 1823 will, he separated the two Dark tracts from each other. He left the original eastern tract that included about one hundred acres, to his son William III (1775-1859).[78]

William Satterthwaite III also inherited an adjoining, rectangular-shaped parcel of 14 acres north of the section of the Dark tract that his grandfather had previously purchased in 1756 from John Palmer. The Palmer family were important land holders who owned a large tract that was part of the even larger tract formerly owned by William and Charles Biles. This smaller tract included part of the Queen Anne Creek and was bounded on the north by Big Oak Road (at the spot where it makes the sharp bend to the northeast). In addition, there was another small, triangular-shaped property that extended north of the former Palmer parcel and followed the route of Big Oak Road for a short distance that was about four acres in size.[79]

The western tract, the larger of the two tracts, was left to another of William Jr.'s sons, Giles (1771-1834). It extended to the west of present-day Oxford Valley Road. Giles (1771-1834) was married to Mary Woolston (1775-1837), and by this marriage there was only one child, Jonathan (1797-1852). During the first twenty-five years of the nineteenth century, Giles generally owned three or four horses and between three and six head of cattle. In 1824, he was worth $7,568, and the value of his farm in 1831 was $36 per acre.[80]

Giles and Mary continued to live in the *New House* until Giles' death in

According to the Genealogy of the Satterthwaite Family this house was owned by William Satterthwaite, Jr. It still stands and is located in Falls Township along Business Route 1 south of the Preserve. It was located in the center of the family's holdings.

1834 and her death in 1837. Giles willed the property to his son, Jonathan (1797-1852). Jonathan continued to prosper and by 1843, he had four horses and nine head of cattle. When he died without heirs (he had never married), the property was disposed of by the estate of his father in a series of land transactions. As a result, the western Dark tract and buildings were sold and passed out of the Satterthwaite family's ownership, and within a few years it was divided into a number of smaller parcels.[81]

As to the eastern tract, it passed down to another family member, William Satterthwaite III (1775-1859), along with eighty-five acres in Falls Township. He married Elizabeth Watson (1779-1869) in 1799, and they had ten children. They were: Amos (1801-1832), William (1804-1882), Mary (1806-1886), Elizabeth (1809-1896), Michael (1811-1811), Joseph (1813-1890), Susannah (1815-1863), Giles (1818-1897), Michael (1820-1898), and Sarah Ann (1824-1828).[82]

With the death of William III, son Giles (1818-1897) inherited the farm and plantation which now included 337 acres in both Townships. Giles was married to Susan Busby (1815-1867), and they were the parents of four children: Joseph (1852-1852), Henry (1853-1937), Margaretta (1855-1910), and Susan (1858-

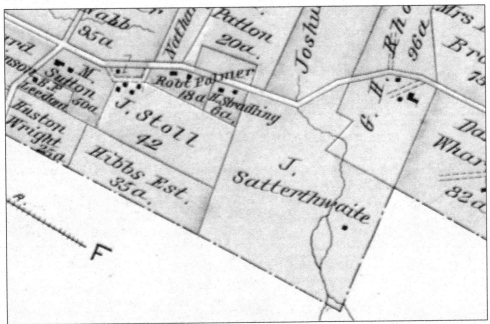

This 1891 map of the southwestern corner of Lower Makefield Township reflects the continuing changes to the former Satterthwaite tract.

1886). As part of her father's will, Margaretta was given a life tenancy. When she died in 1910, Henry owned the property free and clear of any encumbrances. Eight years later the eastern tract of the original Dark land grant passed out of the Satterthwaite's family when Henry sold it. With its sale, the Satterthwaite's ties to the tract of land ended forever.[83]

Curiously, the name of *J. Satterthwaite* appears on a map of Lower Makefield Township included in the 1891 *Atlas of Bucks County, Pennsylvania.* Perhaps Joseph (1813-1890), Giles' brother, was living there just before his death. Or perhaps the mapmaker misspelled Giles' name using a *J* instead of a *G*.[84]

DESCENDANTS RETURN

In the late spring of 1978, brothers William (1911-1982) and Morris Satterthwaite (1915-1990), the great-great-great-great grandsons of William Satterthwaite Sr. (1709-1787), returned to the ruins of their family's ancestral home along the Queen Anne Creek. Morris was a farmer and William worked at the Farmer's Cooperative. Their grandparents were Lucy (1854-1934) and Henry Satterthwaite (1853-1937). The meeting was arranged by Donald Formigli who was then leading the effort to save the Five Mile Woods. All that remained by that

Courtesy Five Mile Woods Preserve
Donald Formigli Collection
William and Morris Satterthwaite stand in front of the ruins of their family's ancestral home in 1978. They could remember their grandfather, Henry W. Satterthwaite, logging on the family's property (today's Five Mile Woods Preserve)and his neighbor's lots as well.

time was the foundation and a portion of the arch of one of the chimney supports. They could still remember when their grandfather Henry (1853-1937) had logged the property along with the neighbor's lots.[85]

THE SATTERTHWAITE FAMILY LEGACY

Some additional details of the family's history have come down through time. Members of the family were generally farmers while some were involved in other occupations. A review of the various maps of Lower Makefield and Falls Townships reveals that various members of the family owned adjoining properties. Their holdings included tracts that crossed over into Falls Township and right up to the boundary line of Fallsington. J. H. Battle wrote that :

At one time they could walk from Fallsington to Oxford on their own land.[86]

Their names regularly appear in the minutes of the Falls Meeting in which births, weddings, and deaths were announced and recorded. Their tombstones can be found in Fallsington, Lower Makefield, and in Middletown. Photographs of various family members also appear on *www.findagrave.com*.

The Bucks County Historical Society owns several items related to the Satterthwaites, including an 1821 school exercise book of William Satterthwaite, perhaps from the fourth generation. Written in a beautiful hand, the book includes written mathematical formulas and surveying problems to solve. There is also a transcription of a 1737 deed between William Biles and the native peoples for an island in the Delaware River to which William Satterthwaite Sr. was a witness.[87]

Because the Satterthwaites were Quakers, they were part of a unique religious organization that became the first to call for the abolition of slavery in the mid-eighteenth century. Quakers believed that the government was divinely inspired and that they should be a part of its success. They were also pacifists, and even as the cannon fire could be heard at Trenton and Princeton in 1776 and 1777, the stalwarts did not participate in the military operations of the American Revolution. The ones who did were driven out of Meeting and often rejoined after the war.[88]

Another theme that runs through the family history is its support of education. Typical of the times, William Satterthwaite, Jr., supported the efforts to build a new school on the northwestern corner of the crossroads of Oxford Valley Road and Big Oak Road. In the fall of 1773, he agreed to support a subscription along with all of his neighbors by pledging money towards its construction. It is believed to have been constructed by either Moses Moon or James Moon, both graduates of Haverford College, a Quaker institution. The building had a datestone from 1775.[89]

The new structure replaced an existing structure. The previous schoolhouse had been located on Thomas Paxson's land, and one can presume that the senior Satterthwaite had been involved with the construction of that building.

The new building was an octagonal stone structure. The shape of the building was unique for a school house, and, in fact, became the accepted design for many schoolhouses in the Delaware River Valley at the time. It is thought to be the first of its architectural design in the country. More than one hundred were built that copied this design and about twenty students are said to have attended school for three months during the winter season for many years.[90]

Called the Nield Schoolhouse, it served Lower Makefield, Falls, and Middletown Townships where they met. A copy of the subscription, along with the design drawings of the building survive in the Lower Makefield Historical Society's collections.[91]

There is some historical dispute as to the building's history. Henry Mercer, one of Bucks County leading historians, believed that the current structure was not built in 1775 but rather in the 1830s to replace the earlier structure. A 1987 newspaper article by Florence White stated that it was closed in 1833. With the passage of a state education law in the 1830s, new schoolhouses were built and used a more standard rectangular design. White wrote that it was later occupied by a series of families and then finally used for storage. It continued to be designated as a school until at least1858, as it is shown on the Falls Township section of the *Hughes Farm Map* but it also appears on an 1860 Township map. By 1876, it was no longer designated as a school.[92]

The building survived in poor condition until recent decades, and was extensively photographed in 1930. Portions of its walls were still intact until the 1970s, and as late as 1987, a proposal was made to restore it. Today, little remains of it. There is, however, another structure with a similar design that can still be seen standing on the corner of Swamp Road and Second Street Pike in Wrightstown Township.[93]

THE ARCHITECTURAL LEGACY

The houses known to be associated with the Darks and Satterthwaites at, or near, the Preserve have long disappeared from the landscape. Consulting mapping data to follow the history of the houses is oftentimes inconclusive and usually offers more questions than answers. For example, the Dark house does not appear on the 1850, 1857, or 1860 maps of Lower Makefield Township. Yet there appears to be a house designated on the 1858 *Hughes Farm Map*. By this time, the center of William Satterthwaite, Jr.'s operations were in Falls Township and in the area surrounding Fallsington where he lived.[94]

Courtesy Five Mile Woods Preserve
Donald Formigli Collection

This chimney foundation is from the home of William Dark. It was built with stone taken from the small quarry cut into the Fall Line, a short distance away. It was also home to the Satterthwaite family. By 1978, aside from the foundation, all that remained of the homestead was one of the arch supports for the two fireplaces.

However, a structure along the Queen Anne Creek does appear on the 1876 and 1891 Township maps in the Bucks County atlases but not on the 1907 USGS map. The 1947 USGS Trenton map confirms that it had disappeared by this time. Aerial photographs are inconclusive because of the dense canopy of the forest. Was the original Dark house destroyed by fire or some other disaster prior to 1850? Did it collapse of its own weight after a roof failure? Was it razed or did mapmakers miss it? Did the Satterthwaites subsequently build a new house on the remaining foundation of the Dark

Courtesy Peter Osborne

All that remains of the Dark-Satterthwaite homestead are the ruins of its foundation.

house? Or was the Dark house somewhere else on the eastern tract? The history of the building remains a mystery and the historical record is not clear. Unfortunately, the earliest maps only designate road systems and major landmarks like churches, but not houses or outbuildings.

This is also true of the Satterthwaite's *New House*. It cannot be determined by the author what happened to the house. Ralph Thompson speculated that any evidence of it was destroyed when the water storage tank was erected by the Pennsylvania American Water Company. He located the site of the house, based on a number of maps, in the vicinity of the northeastern side of the present-day shopping center property.

Additional information has been found since Thompson's 1997 report was published that confirms this. Aerial photography and mapping data show that a house was located along Big Oak Road, sitting on a farm lane, where there had once been a number of other buildings. Steve Willard, whose family owned the adjacent property, stated he could remember the *New House*, when they lived there in the 1950s and 1960s. He did not remember what happened to it although he recalled that the Robinson family lived in it. The building appears to have survived until at least 1971.[95]

It may be that like the Dark house the *New House* fell to the ravages of time but this time the evidence may have been buried when the remainder of the structure was pushed back into the cellar hole and covered. It was probably a victim of the construction of development pressures going on at the time. Once the shopping center was built, whatever evidence remained of any of the buildings at the location was lost forever.

The mapping data can also be confusing with regard to ownership issues. The maps do not always confirm the order of the land transfers laid out here, yet the records that Ralph Thompson used are official land records and his paper appears definitive. For example, the *Lower Makefield Bucks County Historical Map 1798* shows Giles Satterthwaite (1771-1834) as owning the entire Dark tract of 235 acres which apparently was never the case. While he owned the western half from 1827-34, he did not own the eastern tract, perhaps he leased it.

A TRANSPORTATION NETWORK DEVELOPS

With the land settled and a growing farm economy there was the need for a more advanced transportation network to get goods to market. The old cartways and ferries, which had been so important in the first decades, gave way to roadways that would be succeeded by the Delaware Canal, the Reading and Pennsylvania railroads, and the major super highways of today. The families who owned and lived on the land that is now the Preserve, were about to be exposed to new markets and a much wider world in the decades to come. The Quakers, who had established themselves in the region's founding and governing, and in farming and business, quickly became a minority.[96]

COMMON BEECH

COMMON BEECH

Chapter 3

AT THE CROSSROADS

Long before there were (steam) engines to run along them, there existed thousands of miles of American roads . . . The King's Highway, initiated by the colonial governors in 1660 on orders from Charles II following his return from exile, was a road designed to run for 1,300 miles from Boston to Charleston and connect ten of the original thirteen colonies . . . The Fall Line Road linked all of the Eastern river towns that had been built where waterfalls interrupted upstream water travel.[1]

THE MEN WHO UNITED THE STATES:
AMERICA'S EXPLORERS, INVENTORS, ECCENTRICS, AND MAVERICKS,
AND THE CREATION OF ONE NATION, INDIVISIBLE
SIMON WINCHESTER

The country hereabouts is elevated and healthful; is famed alike for its picturesque beauty and its fertility, and the observer with artistic eye will catch glimpses of many a pretty bit of scenery.[2]

ADVERTISEMENT FOR LIZETTE, PENNSYLVANIA
BOUND BROOK RAILROAD DIRECTORY
1880

History tells us that land use and transportation patterns are linked in a continuing cycle, whereby transportation opportunities create an atmosphere for development which in turn generates additional transportation needs.[3]

BUCKS COUNTY COMPREHENSIVE PLAN
2011

THE FIVE MILE WOODS HAS BEEN AFFECTED by geological changes, the actions of people on the landscape, and the transportation corridors that have developed around it. Between the eighteenth century and the mid-twentieth century, Bucks County developed into an important agricultural center. In addition, the county became increasingly connected to the region's major economic centers including Philadelphia, Trenton and New York City because of an expanding transportation network. This network included the Delaware River and its ferries, and a growing and improved road network built on former Native American paths, cartways, and primitive roads. Next came the building of the Delaware Canal and the construction of the Reading Company's railroad system and the Pennsylvania Railroad's Trenton Cutoff.

In the twentieth century, a new road system was developed to service the growing number of automobiles in use. This included enhanced local roadways, the designation of the transcontinental Lincoln Highway, Route 1, Route 13, and Interstate Route 95. All were within a few miles of the Five Mile Woods and had an important impact on the region, incorporating it into the developing national transportation network.

To Meeting and To Market

Initially the plantations and farms of the original Penn grantees were connected by a few unimproved roads, if they can be called that, which were impassible during parts of the year. William Penn was said to have left a thirty-three-foot-wide right-of-way in between selected properties for future roadways, although that policy was not always carried out and the county has been left with many crooked roads. W. H. H. Davis reported that for every one hundred acres purchased from Penn he included an additional six acres to be set aside for future roads. These roads were to be constructed in north-south and east-west configurations and were to be as straight as possible. Up until the 1730s, the roads were laid out in a northwest-southeast direction, paralleling the county's western boundary. They were important because they connected the Meetings and the county seat which was originally located in Bristol in the southern end of the county. As time went by the roads were laid out in a generally southwest to northeast direction and became more numerous and important because they connected the inland settlements to the river crossings and the major routes of the time.[4]

During the eighteenth century, roads were laid out between a growing number of communities. They were built and expanded to service the increasing number of farms in the various townships and county. In addition, by the 1730s stage coach routes were being introduced. Soon small villages and hamlets were sprouting up like those at Oxford, Fallsington and Bile's Corner.[5]

By the mid-nineteenth century the Township's population had grown from 100 individuals (who were taxable) in 1696 to 1,089 in 1810, to 1,340 in 1830 to 1,741 in 1850. The Quakers became less influential as Irish and German immigrants arrived along with those from the Netherlands.[6]

As the county's economy developed, it was almost entirely agriculture-based. Farms averaged about one hundred and fifty acres in size, considerably smaller than the plantations of Penn's original landholders. William Penn's heirs continued to manage the colony until the American Revolution. Many of the descendants of the early landholders retained ownership until the nineteenth century and some even into the twentieth century. The Satterthwaites, and many of their Quaker brethren, were excellent examples of that.

The farms generally were self-sufficient with families growing their own wheat, corn, rye, oats, and hay along with developing orchards. Their livestock included small numbers of cattle, oxen, horses, sheep, goats, pigs, and chickens. The surpluses generated were sold at market. Up until the American Revolution, the county's farmers continued to improve the land and their economic lot. The log cabins that had been erected during the early settlement were discarded in favor of more substantial stone houses or framed buildings: the kinds that are prized by their owners today.[7]

By the middle of the nineteenth century, a new agrarian sector rose to prominence: dairy farming. This new industry served the needs of the growing metropolitan regions of Philadelphia and Trenton along with horse, pigeon and poultry farms. Other agricultural sectors grew in importance including the development of huge industrial greenhouses. As time passed, farmers began growing more specialized crops to serve the growing markets of the metro-Philadelphia area. Locally, several small industries developed facilities in Lower Makefield Township, including fabric fulling and dyeworks businesses, a bleachery, a spice mill, and a light bulb and magnet manufacturer.[8]

The road network that passed both near and through the Five Mile Woods created access for the families that lived there and was important for their ability to bring and sell their products to market. In addition, they could travel easily to Bristol, Newtown, Morrisville, Burlington, Trenton, and Philadelphia. Some of the region's most important roads fanned out from Philadelphia, and one major road, known as the *Great Road,* led to New York City, and passed through Bristol and Trenton. This brought many important figures in early American history through the area, including botanists who came to the area for research.

THE DELAWARE RIVER

A short distance to the east of the Five Mile Woods is the Delaware River, one of the last free-flowing rivers in the eastern half of the United States. From the beginning of its main stem in Hancock, New York, it travels three hundred and thirty miles southward to the Atlantic Ocean. The falls at Trenton are one hundred and thirty miles upstream from the Delaware Capes. The river creates two of the boundaries of Bucks County, on the east and south. The river flow, and its resources, are managed by the Delaware River Basin Commission, a four-state compact. According to the work of previous historians, the original shoreline was believed to have been higher and the shape of islands in the river have regularly changed over time.[9]

Prior to the settlement of the valley by Europeans, native peoples had lived in the region for thousands of years and regularly used the river as a transportation corridor as well as a location for settlements. Early European settlers did the same. While colonists could use it for travel, it was also a barrier that had to be crossed. This necessitated the operation of ferries at numerous locations, and later, the construction of bridges.

In more recent decades the river channel was deepened to allow passage of large iron ore ships to the Fairless Works, just a short distance from Tullytown.[10]

FERRIES

Prior to the construction of covered bridges, river ferries dotted the shoreline of the Delaware from its beginning to its end. They were sited at regular intervals, where roads met the river's edge. Charters were granted by each colony or state for the operation of a ferry and so there were often two ferries at the various locations. In some cases, ferry operations included outright ownership, partnerships, or lease agreements with members of one's extended family. As the ownership of the ferry changed hands so did its name.

The three river crossings closest to the Five Mile Woods were at Yardley and Trenton. The ferry on the Pennsylvania side at Yardley was begun by Thomas Yardley, a nephew of the founder of the small hamlet. Downriver, in Trenton, there were two ferries: one above the falls and one below. The northern ferry was called Kirkbride's, Flower's or Janney's and later, Beatty's Ferry. It was operating at the time of the American Revolution. The lower ferry, below the falls, and chartered in 1718, was in operation in 1675, predating William Penn's arrival. Another important ferry included McKonkey's Ferry farther upriver at what is now known as Washington's Crossing, where the famed crossing by the Continental Army took place. It was in operation as early as 1684, certainly by 1699, and known as Baker's, Slack's and Johnson's Ferry. Another ferry crossed between Bristol and Burlington called Dunk's Ferry after its owner, Duncan Williamson.[11]

The ferries were of great importance for the marketing and shipping of goods and transporting people including the Quakers, who often owned property in both colonies and had family on both sides of the river. They also allowed for communication between the growing cities of the time including Boston, New York, and Philadelphia and dictated where the road networks would finally be constructed.[12]

The river was also the scene of much activity after the valley was settled as Durham boats were used to ship goods downstream. Log rafts came down the river from areas farther north and west beginning in the mid-1700s, continuing until the early twentieth century. Some stopped in the small communities along the river on their way to Trenton and Philadelphia.[13]

Covered bridges, built by private companies, were opened including the first across the Delaware River in Trenton in 1806, and then in Yardley in 1835. With those structures operating as privately owned toll bridges, the crossing of the Delaware became much easier and safer. The Trenton bridge was located at the site of the current Calhoun Street Bridge. In the decades that followed, new bridges were constructed to replace those destroyed in floods or ice jams. They were also built to accommodate increasing amounts of traffic and new highways including U.S. Route 1 and Interstate Route 95.[14]

To follow the early history of the various roads that crisscrossed Lower Makefield Township is a complicated study requiring maps, original deeds, and histories from yesteryear. Often the various sources are not in agreement. Most of the roads had their origins as Indian paths or trails that became cartways or narrow wagon trails with increased use and then finally became dedicated roads that were surveyed and upgraded. Dolington Road is typical of this kind of evolution from Indian trail to an important byway in the eastern part of the county.[15]

Over time, the maps became more accurate and revealed the growing network of roads throughout the region that were critical to, and played an important role in, the area's development. There are several early eighteenth century maps that have survived but they do not have the detail that is required to gain a clear understanding of what roads actually existed at the time.

For example, there is C. Moll's 1729 map entitled *New England, New York, New Jersey and Pennsylvania* that shows the approximate, although distorted, route of the Great Road. There is also T. Kitchen's 1749 *Map of the Province of Pennsylvania* that only shows the most important roads of the era. One of the most detailed contemporary maps of the area's road network dates from the American Revolution. It is entitled *Plan of Operations of General Washington against the King's troops in New Jersey from December 1776 to January 3, 1777* and was drawn by William

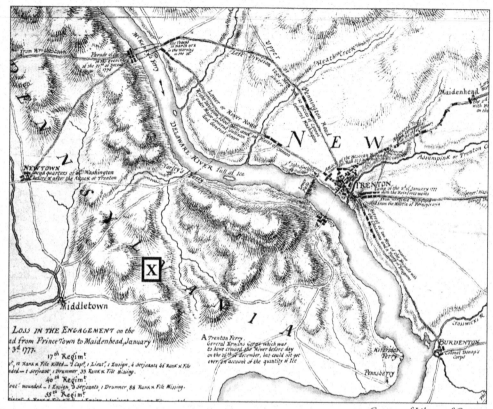

Courtesy of Library of Congress
Geography and Map Division
Library of Congress Control No. GM 71000654

Entitled, Plan of the operations of General George Washington against the King's troops in New Jersey, from December 26, 1776 to January 3, 1777, this map shows the known road configurations in lower Bucks County at the time of the Crossing. The "X" denotes the approximate location of the Preserve.

Faden, a British mapmaker, in the aftermath of the losses Great Britain suffered at Trenton and Princeton. Faden showed three major roads connecting the western part of Lower Makefield Township with the east and the Delaware River. These three important thoroughfares ran generally on an east-west line. However, like so many maps of the time, it contains inaccuracies.

The first road shown on the map (perhaps Route 452) originated in Attleboro (now Langhorne), and then merged with another road just west of Yardley's Ferry. That second road (perhaps Route 332) began at Newtown, and the combined roads ended at Yardley. A third road began at Middletown, proceeded east until it turned sharply to the north, and ended at the ferry at Trenton below the falls. This last road (following the approximate course of Business Route 1) is not shown on the 1776 *Hessian Map of Central New Jersey*, nor is Fallsington. This is

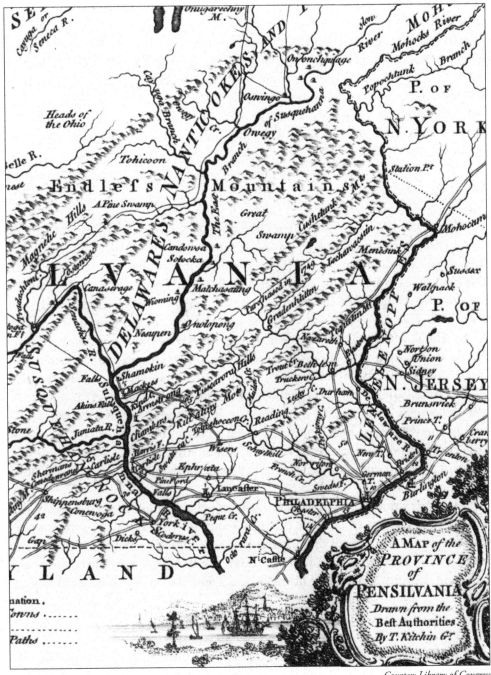

This 1756 map of Pennsylvania shows the Great Road, or the King's Road, between Philadelphia, Bristol and Trenton and also the road that went between Newtown to Yardley.

perhaps the result of inadequate intelligence as other Quaker Meetings, but not all, are shown.[16]

In the decades after the Revolution, the population increased dramatically, which necessitated the construction of a better road network for the area's residents. Many of those byways became turnpikes, operated by private companies, and are today's county, state and federal roads. The first turnpike in Bucks County was the Frankford and Bristol Turnpike, chartered in 1803. It ran from Philadelphia to Morrisville. In the years that followed, other turnpikes were chartered throughout the county.[17]

The following roads were the closest to, or impacted upon, the Five Mile Woods:

THE GREAT ROAD

In the late seventeenth and early eighteenth century, and for many years after that, the most important road in the region was the turnpike that ran from Philadelphia, through Bristol, Falls Township, Tullytown, Tyburn, and then across the Delaware to Trenton. From there it traversed the neck of New Jersey and went onto New York City. This was the most important road that passed near Lower Makefield Township during this era. It was known as the *Great Road* or *King's Path* and is thought to be the oldest road in the county created by the legislature.[18]

Its route was authorized in 1675, but by 1685, it still had not been laid out. At that time, William Biles, Lionel Brittain, and Samuel Dark were assigned the task of laying it out in a more formal way as it had been a vaguely created wagon trail in the wilderness. The first stage coach to travel from Philadelphia to New York completed its inaugural trip in 1756. It took three days to make this journey. To assist riders in determining where they were, mile markers were placed along the route in 1764.[19]

The area through which it passed is much changed but the old Bristol Pike, which includes parts of old U.S. Route 13 and old U.S. Route 1, approximates to some degree the path of the original roadway. Different maps from other eras show it in a variety of configurations. Today, the Bristol Pike parallels Van Sciver Lake and the former main line of the Pennsylvania Railroad and its Trenton Cutoff.

STONY HILL ROAD

While Stony Hill Road does not pass by or through the Five Mile Woods, it is known from deeds of the period that it was in use before the American Revolution. It is also shown on deeds and surveys from the 1760s and on Ralph Thompson's conjectural *Historical Map of 1798* that was based on deeds that he researched. It is also shown on *A Map of the County of Bucks,* prepared from a road survey by Thomas Kennedy in 1817. It was one of two important roads to pass

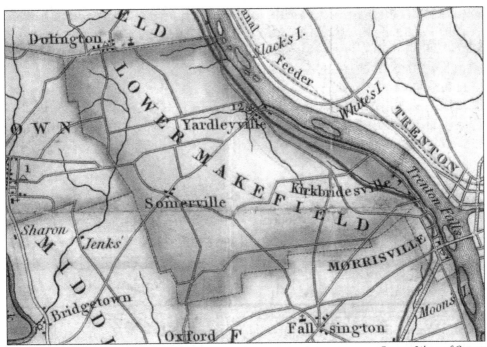

Courtesy Library of Congress
Geography and Map Division
Library of Congress Control Number 200765210

By the 1830s, the road network in Lower Makefield Township had developed further and now included Oxford Valley Road and Big Oak Road. The Delaware Canal had been built on the Pennsylvania side of the Delaware River allowing access to markets and making traveling easier, as shown on this 1831 map.

near what is today's Preserve in the early nineteenth century followed the route of an old Indian path. It was a major north-south route between today's Edgewood (also known as Stradlington (c. 1760), Biles's Corner (c. 1798), Summerville (1830s), Edgewood (1860s) Woodside (1880s), and Fallsington, an important place in the world of Quakers like the Satterthwaites and their neighbors.[20]

Initially Stony Hill Road was designated the *Road to Fallsington*, the *Road from Newtown to Falls Meeting* or the *Fallsington-Newtown Road* as it connected the two Meetings and allowed Quakers from Lower Makefield to get to Fallsington. It became the *Roelof's-Fallsington Road* in the 1920s, and was paved in the 1930s with Depression-era New Deal WPA monies. It was renamed Stony Hill Road at the same time.[21]

THE OXFORD OR MIDDLE ROAD

At Fallsington, Stony Hill Road met the main east-west transportation corridor of the time: the Oxford, or Middle, Road that went from Bustleton (Southampton Township) to Attleboro (Langhorne), through Oxford to Morrisville, and then merged with the main road that went from Philadelphia to New York City. At Fallsington, it converged with several roads at Meeting House Square, including one that began in Andalusia, crossed the Neshaminy Creek, proceeded to Hulmeville (previously called Milford Mills) and then went on to Trenton.[22]

This road, like Stony Hill Road, predates the Revolution as it is indicated on 1760s surveys. It is also shown on the Kennedy survey of 1817. Later, after being converted into a turnpike, it became Route 1 (today's Business Route 1), from Oxford Valley to Morrisville.[23]

BIG OAK ROAD

The Big Oak Road appears on a late eighteenth century survey of properties that were adjacent on the northern side of the Dark tracts and Thompson's *Historical Map of 1798*. It is not shown on Kennedy's 1817 survey. However, it appears on the A. W. Kennedy *Map of Bucks County in Pennsylvania* in 1831 indicating that it was an important east-west route, and probably began as a wagon road. It intersected Oxford Valley Road, as it does today, and continued a short distance beyond that westward. Its route proceeded eastward where it converged with other roads leading to Kirkbride's Ferry, and to Morrisville. As it turns northward beyond Acorn Drive and Oakview Drive, it borders along the north side of the fourteen-acre tract that William Satterthwaite, Jr. purchased from John Palmer to enhance his family's holdings.

One of the mysteries about the history of Big Oak Road is how its route came to be determined. Instead of being on a relatively straight east-west axis as many roads were, it makes two sharp turns toward the north. As a result, a part of John Palmer's land was cut off to the south. This may answer why he sold one parcel of it to William Satterthwaite, and the rest to several others. As roads were being built the county often used property lines for the route so they did not have to compensate farmers for the taking of their land.[24]

The route of Big Oak Road may have been chosen to accommodate the Satterthwaites who may not have wanted a farm road that ran through the center of their property (the former Dark tracts) to be used as a public thoroughfare anymore. The building and maintenance of a bridge across the Queen Anne Creek, or the road's proximity to the family's home on the creek may have also been factors. Perhaps the Satterthwaites did not want the road to cut off the smaller fourteen-acre Palmer parcel from their main holdings. Once Big Oak Road was built, the farm road probably remained a private thoroughfare used just by the Satterthwaites.

Originally this road was known as the Swamp Road, possibly because of the characteristics a section of it took on when it rained and the season was wet. There may also have been a large swamp located on the more direct east-west route which the road commissioners wanted to avoid at the time it was constructed. This might account for the sharp turns that the road makes and that creates the northern boundary of the Preserve.[25]

Its name was later changed to Big Oak Road to honor a large oak tree that was near the general store located not far from the Preserve. In fact, the tree may have been standing when George Washington was in the area during the American Revolution. It was cut down after it was struck by lightning in the mid-twentieth century.[26]

Oxford Valley Road

Oxford Valley Road appears on surveys from the 1760s along with Ralph Thompson's *Historical Map of 1798*. However, it is not shown on the survey by Thomas Kennedy in 1817. It does appear on the 1831 *Map of Bucks County* by A. W. Kennedy. The name of the community for which it was named is located in both Middletown and Falls Townships. Its name is said to be derived from the ford at the Oxford Creek where the Ox Inn was located, and where the community was established. The road connected the communities of Oxford Valley and Woodbourne. Today it ends on the western side of Yardley, at the former Reading Railroad's line.[27]

Roads in the Preserve

Although the Darks may have used one or two of the major roads listed here, depending upon when they were laid out, these roads were certainly used by the Satterthwaites. Within the Preserve today there is some remaining evidence of old farm lanes. There are at least two roads that are known historically to have existed within the Preserve: the first has been designated here as the Dark Farm Road and the second, the Satterthwaite Farm Road.

Dark Farm Road

Just beyond the Dark house foundation there was a farm lane that heads to the south. Perhaps this road connected to another that concluded at or near Fallsington. While the road does not show up on any maps, deeds, or surveys, it is clear that the Darks would have needed a road to travel to areas beyond their farm to the south, east, and north. While no records show that the Darks created or used it, if they did not, then perhaps the Satterthwaites established it. It is shown on Rick Mellon's 1981 *Master Plan for the Five Mile Woods Preserve*.

Satterthwaite Farm Road

A road appears on an 1828 survey of the Satterthwaite tract that includes the Preserve. It cuts diagonally, from northeast to southwest, staying on the upper side of the Fall Line. It does not appear on any of the other maps published before

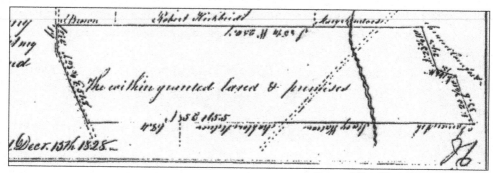

Courtesy Office of Bucks County Land Records

This 1828 survey map shows the Satterthwaite's farm which retains the original boundaries of the William Dark patent of 1684. One curious feature is the road shown that crosses the Queen Anne Creek, not far from where the Dark home was located. Its route, if extended to the northeast, would meet Big Oak Road where it makes a sharp turn to the northeast. It may predate the present route of Big Oak Road's route to Oxford Valley Road, which runs parallel to the western end of the Satterthwaite tract.

or after that. Because it extends beyond the Satterthwaite property it probably connected to Township roads at either end and was a public thoroughfare.[28]

It is not known when the road was built, but it seems likely that its origins are early. If one projects the road out from the boundaries of the Satterthwaite survey it would have allowed the Satterthwaites access to Stony Hill Road, Oxford Valley Road, Big Oak Road, and the small settlement at Oxford. It is not known if it predates the Satterthwaite's ownership or if the road shown on the survey is accurate or an approximation, which seems more likely. At some time after 1828 it must have been vacated and abandoned as a public road.[29]

When one overlays the 1828 survey map over a current Preserve trail map, depending on how it is placed and adjusted, it either follows part of the Fall Line Trail or it approximates the routes of the Ridge, Five Mile and Sweetgum trails.

TRACES OF ROADS

At the time of the creation of the Five Mile Woods Preserve, a master plan was created by Resident Naturalist, Rick Mellon, which showed that several woods roads still remained. He suggested how the Township might create access roads for emergency plans and programming. It is not known when any of these roads were created but the road shown on the master plan map near the Dark/Satterthwaite home site may date to the earliest settlement in the 1680s.[30]

There are additional traces of roads in the Preserve, perhaps left over from various farm and woodlot uses during the many years of occupancy. What appears to be another road follows the route of the Ridge and Coastal Plain trails as they turn eastward near the southern end of the Preserve. There were also old hunting trails remaining at the time of the Preserve's creation.[31]

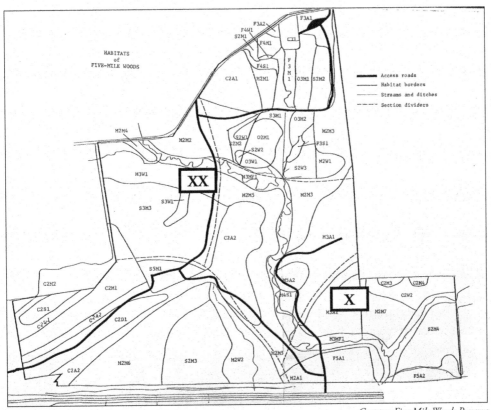

Master Plan for the Five Mile Woods Preserve: Lower Makefield Township Pennsylvania

When biologist Rick Mellon created the first master plan for the Preserve in 1981 he showed the farm roads still remaining and how new roads could be created for a variety of purposes including emergency access and programming. The road designated with an "XX" roughly parallels the road shown on the Satterthwaite survey from 1828. The road designated with an "X" is the approximate route of the Dark Farm Road. The date of the construction of the roads is unknown.

THE DELAWARE CANAL

After the development of the road network, the next new major thoroughfare constructed in the county was the Delaware Division of the Pennsylvania Canal, more commonly known as the Delaware Canal. The waterway, was part of a larger transportation network that included twelve hundred miles of canals running across the Commonwealth of Pennsylvania.[32]

The canal, which ran from Easton to Bristol, followed the stage coach routes of the time, which in turn, followed more ancient Native American trails. Its route along the Delaware River, while convenient and necessary for water supply, was subject to periodic flooding that regularly caused significant damage, even as it continues to do today. The Delaware Canal was constructed and opened in sections, the first from New Hope to Bristol in 1831, and and the second from Easton to New Hope in 1832. It was sixty miles long.[33]

The canal was forty feet wide and five feet deep and crossed a number of streams, necessitating the building of nine aqueducts, twenty culverts, eight turnpike bridges, forty-seven road bridges, and forty-nine farm bridges. There were two wing dams, including one across the Lehigh River at Easton, and another across the Delaware at New Hope. There were twenty-three lift locks, a guard lock, an outlet lock at Easton, sixteen lock houses, and a basin, pier and tide lock at Bristol. In all, it cost almost one and a half million dollars to construct.[34]

Users of the canal shipped anthracite coal, lumber, building stone, lime, cement, iron, and farm produce down its route, and on their return trips boatmen brought finished goods upstream. Canal boats were eighty-seven feet long, ten feet wide and carried ninety tons of freight. At its peak, three thousand boats passed along the waterway transporting more than one million tons annually. Thousands of boatmen and mules were required to operate the boats along with lock tenders, blacksmiths, carpenters and engineering staff.[35]

Most importantly for the region, and for those who lived in the Five Mile Woods area, it created new access for farmers and businesses to market their

Courtesy Library of Congress
Historic American Engineering Record
Library of Congress Control Number PA2215

The Delaware Canal parallels the Delaware River and passes through numerous towns and hamlets including New Hope, Washington Crossing, Yardley, Morrisville, and Bristol. Pictured here is Bridge No. 313, which crossed Letchworth Avenue in Yardley.

goods. Farms, which had been self-sufficient operations, now began to produce excess commodities for the wider market. For the Satterthwaites and their neighbors, this had the potential to improve their economic fortunes. As an aside, it also served as a part of the Underground Railroad, the secret effort to move slaves from the South into the northern states and Canada, a movement that many Quakers would have supported.[36]

The canal also proved to be an important economic stimulus in the areas where it passed because it required the services of farmers, blacksmiths, carpenters, and lock tenders to operate, maintain and repair it. In addition, anthracite coal became available for use in heating and cooking, an important development as the woodlands were increasingly harvested and diminishing in size. Quarries along the canal provided stone for construction purposes not only along the route of the canal but also building materials for homes in Philadelphia.[37]

The Delaware Canal was connected to the Lehigh Canal which linked the anthracite coal regions in Mauch Chunk to Easton. The Lehigh, opened in 1829, terminated at the juncture of the Lehigh and Delaware Rivers. The Lehigh's boats crossed the Delaware and proceeded eastward on the Morris Canal to New York City or further southward on the Delaware Canal to Philadelphia via Bristol. They could also cross over to the Delaware and Raritan Canal on the New Jersey side of the Delaware, at New Hope. Upon entering the Delaware and Raritan at Lambertville, the Lehigh's boats made their way to Trenton or New York City.[38]

After the Civil War, the Delaware Canal's fortunes began a long decline, which paralleled the fortunes of most American canals as a result of increased competition with the railroads. It was purchased in 1858 by a private corporation and then sold to the Lehigh Coal and Navigation Company, the owner of the Lehigh Canal. Traffic declined and finally the last canal boat passed through in 1931.[39] For one hundred years, canal boats drawn by mules were a regular sight as they passed through New Hope, Washington Crossing, Yardley, and Bristol. The canal later provided recreational opportunities along its length as people could take barge rides, canoe, kayak or row along the old waterway and enjoy its natural beauty.[40]

The Main Line of Public Works

During the late 1820s and early 1830s, another transportation revolution took place in the Commonwealth as new routes and methods of moving people and goods were planned and constructed. This network, authorized in 1826, was called the Main Line of Public Works.[41]

Built by the state, it integrated several canal, railroad and inclined plane corridors to connect Philadelphia to Pittsburgh and places farther west. The components included the Philadelphia and Columbia Rail Road, an eighty-mile-long railroad that began in Philadelphia and met the Eastern Division Canal at Columbia on the Susquehanna River.[42]

From Columbia, it proceeded one hundred and seventy-two miles on the Juniata Division Canal to Hollidaysburg. From there, the system traveled thirty-six miles on the Allegheny Portage Railroad via inclined planes over the Allegheny Mountains to Johnstown and then one hundred miles on the Western Division Canal where it ended in Pittsburgh. It took almost five days to go from end to end. From there, goods and passengers could proceed on to the Midwest.[43]

The Philadelphia and Columbia Rail Road, an important component of the Main Line, was chartered in 1826 to build a railroad from Philadelphia to Columbia. The railroad, built during the early 1830s, officially opened on October 7, 1834. At the same time, all the remaining sections of the Main Line were opened to service. Twenty-three years later, in 1857, the entire line was sold by the Commonwealth to the Pennsylvania Railroad (PRR), which had been incorporated in 1846.[44]

The first railroad to pass near the Five Mile Woods was the Philadelphia and Trenton line. Chartered in 1832 and opened in 1834. It was the first railroad built in Bucks County. The line ran northward from Philadelphia, passed through Bristol, crossed the Delaware south of Morrisville and then proceeded on to Trenton. Eventually it was taken over by the Pennsylvania Railroad in 1871.[45]

This series of events catapulted Pennsylvania, and the nation, into a remarkable period of economic growth. With most of its population concentrated in the eastern states, the United States became a world power in less than one hundred years. America's industrial might was born with the railroads, most notably with the PRR. A variety of industries developed as a result including coal, lumber, oil, steel, and manufacturing. It also promoted a tremendous growth in the travel industry. These industries were critical factors in the economic progress of the nineteenth and early twentieth century.

The railroads were remarkable developers of new technologies and wove themselves into the nation's cultural fabric. Ultimately the railroads made Pennsylvania one of the country's richest states. The dominance of the railroads peaked in 1916 when they owned and operated thousands of miles of track and shipped virtually all of the interstate traffic in the country.[46]

One of the results of the remarkable rise of the railroads was the impact they had on the regions they serviced. Cities were connected, farmers began to find new markets available to them and the landscape was physically changed by these developments. This was also true of the residents of the Five Mile Woods as freight trains carrying a variety of goods and raw materials passed nearby every day bound for places all across the nation.

THE TRENTON CUTOFF

In the closing decades of the nineteenth century the PRR embarked on a remarkable long term effort to implement a strategic vision to improve the efficiency of its operations and ultimately make it the *Standard Railroad of the World*. One of the projects undertaken to make the vision a reality was the construction of the Morrisville Line, or the Trenton Cutoff as it was known.[47]

The Trenton Cutoff, or the Trenton Branch of the Philadelphia Division, was built between 1889-1892 and created so the PRR could send its freight trains around Philadelphia creating fewer delays and congestion in the city. Those freight trains were also able to travel more efficiently and quickly because of its level grade and fewer crossings. Built by a subsidiary of the PRR, the Trenton Cutoff Railroad was incorporated in 1889. The shortcut left the main line, which ran from

Courtesy Peter Osborne

The Trenton Cutoff continues to be used. This photograph depicts the line as it appears today looking east towards Morrisville. The catenary poles from the 1930s electrification of the line remain in place.

Harrisburg to Philadelphia, at Glen Lock (located to the west of Frazer in Chester County) and crossed Bucks County to meet with the PRR's Philadelphia to New York main line just south of Morrisville. This bypass was forty-five miles in length and such a success that it would serve as a model for other bypass projects in metropolitan areas by the PRR.[48]

The Trenton Cutoff was built in three sections, the first from Morrisville to the Earnest (located to the southeast of Norristown at the Bucks County line on the Schuylkill River). This section was opened on June 27, 1891. The next section, completed in early 1892, extended the Cutoff further westward to Glen Lock. A second track was added and completed a year later. As part of improving the efficiency of the Cutoff, a new classification yard was built to the south of the Five Mile Woods that extended eastward towards Morrisville. This work was undertaken between 1904-05.[49]

The Cutoff was an immediate operational success. Several decades after its opening it was handling five freight trains per hour with one hundred cars or more. With the immediate financial and operational success of the Cutoff, the

PRR acquired additional land along its right-of-way, and by 1916, expanded its operations considerably as it constructed a new freight terminal with a large receiving yard and improved classification yard. The large facility began near the southeastern corner of the Five Mile Woods Preserve, not far from Fallsington, and continued to the east where it merged with the PRR's main line. The railroad used these yards to distribute freight for all its southern and western customers.[50]

The Trenton Branch was electrified in 1937-38, and today those towers remain, although they have not been used since the 1980s. The Morrisville Yard was upgraded to serve as a new train storage facility for New Jersey Transit in 2004 and is still used. It is also a yard for the Norfolk Southern Railway.[51]

Both the PRR and the nearby Reading Railroad purchased numerous tracts of land along their routes for a number of reasons. First, they were often an investment for future expansion projects. In the case of the PRR, the railroad would continue to expand its Morrisville yards well into the future. These purchases also prevented competitors from moving into their territory. Finally, whenever possible, railroads purchased properties along their routes to lessen the chances of litigation.[52]

THE CUTOFF AND THE SATTERTHWAITES

The Satterthwaite family's holdings were directly impacted by the Trenton Cutoff. First, the Trenton Cutoff passed directly across Giles Satterthwaite's (1818-1897) property and several of his buildings were situated near the tracks. It also passed near several other family-owned tracts south of the Falls and Lower

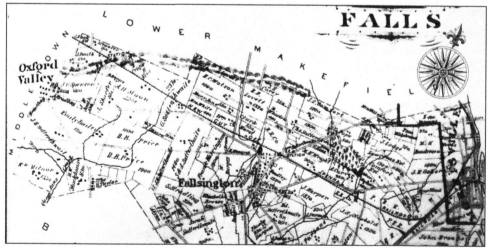

Courtesy Library of Congress
Geography and Map Division
Library of Congress Control Number 2012587544

The Pennsylvania Railroad's newly opened Trenton Cutoff is shown here as the "New Cut Off." The line ran directly through Giles Satterthwaite's property just to the south of the Preserve's southern boundary, as shown on this 1891 map.

Makefield Township's boundary line. There were two new railroad stations constructed a short distance from Giles' farm including one to the northwest and another northeast of Fallsington. This rail connection created new access to markets and to the wider world right in the Satterthwaite's backyard.

This significant chapter in the region's transportation history ultimately came to have a direct role in the creation of the Five Mile Woods Preserve. In 1918, one hundred and seventy years after the eastern section of the original Dark tract was purchased by William Satterthwaite, Sr. (1709-87) in 1748, Lucy S. (1854-1934) and Henry W. Satterthwaite (1853-1937), sold the tract, along with the adjoining farm located to the south in Falls Township to the Pennsylvania Railroad. There were other tracts included in the sale as well, seven in all. The sales price was $30,400.[53]

The Reading Railroad

A second railroad line, built by the North Pennsylvania Railroad between 1874-76, ran from Jenkintown, southwest of the Five Mile Woods, through Lower Makefield, and then passed south of Yardley where it crossed the Delaware River. From there it proceeded through Trenton Junction and Pennington and onto New York City. The line was leased by the Philadelphia and Reading (P&R) and the absorbed into the company three years later.[54]

The P&R, originally chartered in 1833, was one of the earliest railroads in the United States. Its purpose was to carry anthracite coal from north-central Pennsylvania to Philadelphia, and later, to markets far beyond including New York City. This seemingly minor railroad would one day expand into a system that operated more than fourteen hundred miles of track. At one point, its holding company, the Reading Company, was the largest corporation in the world.[55]

The main line of the P&R went north from Philadelphia with various branch lines that extended out from it, including one that passed through Yardley. While this railroad did not have as much significance to the Five Mile Woods as the PRR did, both railroads did intersect a short distance from the Woods at Woodbourne. Beyond the intersection was Roelof's Station or the Bound Brook Station. At that location stood Roelof's Hotel that was owned by Mark Palmer and managed by his daughter, Lizette. The small hamlet came be known as Lizette Station, where vacationers disembarked to spend time in the country in various boarding houses.[56]

The Reading Line shipped locally produced agricultural goods, including eggs, milk, dairy products, ducks, and even manure, along with specialty vegetables, roses and lilacs for mail catalogs, and items manufactured locally. The opening of the line also allowed for the beginning of an exodus of people from the metropolitan areas who wanted to live in the newly developing suburbs. This trend began a real estate development pattern that would culminate in the cre-

The Reading Railroad crossed the Delaware River south of Yardley, first on a bridge put into service in 1876, and then on a much larger concrete bridge built in 1913. The piers from the earlier structure are pictured in the foreground.

ation of Five Miles Woods Preserve one hundred years later.[57]

Today the CSX freight railroad and the Southeast Pennsylvania Transit Authority use this trackage, which is called the West Trenton Branch or Line, to move freight and passengers.[58]

HIGHWAYS AND BYWAYS
U.S. ROUTE 1, U.S. ROUTE 1 BYPASS, AND THE LINCOLN HIGHWAY

The most significant road that affected the Five Mile Woods generally, and the Preserve specifically, was, and is, U.S. Route 1. Today, this major highway borders the southern boundary of the Preserve and its traffic can be distinctly heard as one gets deeper into the Woods. A boundary fence separates the highway right-of-way from the Preserve.

The roadway's history also reflects a chapter of the country's early history that was revealed earlier in the book and that is the development of the various Fall Line communities, in the eighteenth century. In one of those interesting connections of history, Route 1 links many of these communities, along old roads running from Maine to Florida. U.S. Route 1 crossed the Delaware River at Trenton and continued towards Philadelphia. The construction of the original roadbed was completed in 1926.[59]

In the decades to come, there were various projects undertaken to increase the vehicular load Route 1 could handle and to modernize the roadway. For example, in 1928, Route 1 was upgraded to handle the ever-increasing amounts of traffic, and a new toll bridge was constructed across the Delaware. Called the

Courtesy Library of Congress
Historic American Engineering Record
Library of Congress Control Number PA71-30

Three bridges cross the Delaware River just south of the capital building in Trenton, New Jersey. The Trenton Makes bridge is in the background.

Lower Trenton Bridge, it is well known for its illuminated sign that proudly states: *Trenton Makes The World Takes*. It was installed in 1935 and is known locally as the *Trenton Makes* bridge.[60]

The next chapter in that decades long effort to continually improve the highway began with the construction of the Trenton-Morrisville Toll Bridge in 1952. In addition, miles of the highway were modernized in the greater Philadelphia area south of the Five Mile Woods. Route 1 continued westward along the route of present-day Business Route 1.

As the years went by, a more direct route eastward to Trenton from Oakford was built and the highway was designated as Route 281. It was described as a *limited access road* or *superhighway*. In 1972, a new segment of Route 281 between Interstate Route 95 and Oxford Valley Road was opened. This next section, planned from Oxford Valley Road to Trenton Avenue and continuing across the Trenton-Morrisville Toll Bridge, passed directly to the south of the Preserve. Because of funding limitations, the roadway was not completed until 1984. During those years, the roadway simply ended in a farm field beyond the Oxford Valley Road interchange. High school teens from Neshaminy and Pennsbury would regularly gather in this field on Friday nights.[61]

Three years later, the former Route 1 was renamed Business Route 1, and

Courtesy Peter Osborne

An original Lincoln Highway marker still stands on the Pennsylvania side of the Calhoun Street Bridge in Morrisville.

Courtesy Five Mile Woods Preserve
Donald Formigli Collection

It took a decade to build the last section of the Route 1 Bypass from Oxford Valley to Morrisville. In 1975 the roadway ended just east of the Oxford Valley Road exit and entrance ramps. After its completion, it was officially designated as Route 1, and former Route 1 became Business Route 1.

Route 281 was officially designated as Route 1. Today, the business route designation is reserved for the section of old Route 1 that passes through Falls and Middletown Townships to Morrisville.[62]

Aside from its association with the Fall Line, Business Route 1 is a component of the nationally designated Lincoln Highway, so named to honor the memory of President Abraham Lincoln. The historic highway, which runs from the East Coast to the West Coast, was established in 1913.[63]

The Lincoln Highway was originally designated to cross the Delaware River on the Calhoun Street Bridge and a historic marker that designates its route still stands on the Pennsylvania side. However, with various highway rerouting projects over the years the designation was changed as it was originally intended to follow U.S. Route 30. As a result, Route 1 was designated as the Lincoln Highway in the region until it merged with U.S. Route 30 in West Philadelphia. From there it follows the former route of the Philadelphia and Lancaster Turnpike, traveling across the country and holding a prestigious place in American transportation history as the first transcontinental roadway. Today Business Route 1 is designated as the Lincoln Highway where the route is nearest to the Preserve as well as in the rest of the county.[64]

Since the 1950s most of the county's industrial base has been, and continues to be, located along the Route 1, Business Route 1, Route 13 and Interstate 95 corridors.[65]

U.S. ROUTE 13

Another highway that does not border on the Preserve, but played a critical role in the development of Bucks County is U.S. Route 13. Designated in 1926 as a major north-south highway, it runs from North Carolina to its starting point at the Route 1 interchange east of the Preserve and west of Morrisville. Like U.S. Route 1, the highway was regularly improved and its route altered. This was particularly true in the 1950s when a new expressway was built to the north and west of its original route. The former route was the original route of the old Bristol Turnpike.[66]

Its importance to Bucks County lies in the fact that Route 13 served as a major gateway to United States Steel's Fairless Works, which was located to the southeast of the highway, along with two major residential developments, Fairless Hills and Levittown, to its north and west. They were created to house the thousands of steel workers and administrative staff who worked at the steel mill. Those events played an important role in the creation of the Five Mile Woods Preserve several decades later. Today, as it gets closer to Bristol, it runs parallel to present day Interstate 95.

The Route 95 entrance and exit ramp near Washington Crossing, Pennsylvania

U.S. INTERSTATE 95

Interstate 95 is only one mile from the Preserve where it crosses over Route 1. Its impact on the development of Bucks County and the Preserve was, and remains, significant. Several routes were considered including one that went right through Edgewood. However, the final route chosen was to the west of the historic village.[67]

Construction began in 1959, and the last section was completed in 1985. The Scudder Falls Bridge was completed in 1961, but the northern section of Interstate 95 in Bucks County did not open until 1970. Until 1984, commuters had to use Business Route 1 to get to Trenton. However, by tying New Jersey and Pennsylvania more closely together with the Interstate highway system, this highway continued the migration of residents out of Philadelphia, New York City, and New Jersey into the greater Bucks and southwestern New Jersey regions. Today, it carries 59,500 vehicles per day. The Scudder Falls bridge is scheduled to be replaced by a new structure in 2018.[68]

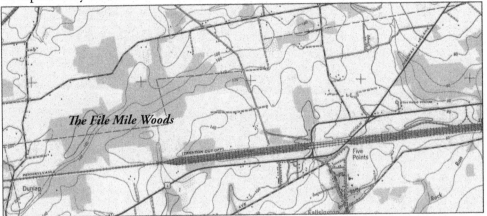

Courtesy United States Geological Survey

This 1947 USGS topographic map (Trenton West, NJ, PA) shows the Five Mile Woods with shading indicating tree cover. The Woods had not yet been impacted by the residential development that would begin in the coming decades. The Fall Line can also be seen at the 160' and 180' contour line, as well as the Trenton Cutoff and U.S. Route 1.

INTEGRATION INTO THE GREATER METROPOLITAN REGION

With the development of each new transportation corridor, the Five Mile Woods area became more and more integrated into the economic development of the county, the greater metro Philadelphia region, and the Commonwealth. With that integration came prosperity for the farmers and area businesses. It also created an interest by real estate developers who wanted to build housing units on the county's prime farmland, and potential buyers who wanted to enjoy the benefits of living in such a beautiful region. These developments played a critical role in the next chapter of the county's history, as well the creation of the Five Mile Woods Preserve.

COMMON BEECH

COMMON BEECH

Chapter 4

.

THROUGH FERTILE BUCKS, WHERE LOFTY BARNS ABOUND

Through fertile Bucks, where lofty barns abound,
For wheat, fair Quakers, eggs, and fruit renowned,
Full fields, snug tenements, and fences neat,
Wide-spreading walnuts drooping o'er each gate
The spring-house peeping from enclustering trees,
Gay gardens filled with herbs, and roots and bees,
Where quinces, pears, and clustering grapes were seen,
With ponderous calabashes hung between;
While orchards, loaded, bending o'er the grass,
Invite to taste, and cheer us as we pass.[1]

THE FORESTERS
WRITTEN AT THE TURN OF THE NINETEENTH CENTURY

The final result of all this new and expanded industrial might can only be guessed. But the immediate results will mix a number of civic headaches with sudden prosperity. Existing school systems already strained will be even more crowded. Housing, even with the new developments, will remain tight. Such utilities as water, electricity, telephone service and sewage disposal will of necessity be expanded at an unnatural rate.[2]

OUR INDUSTRIAL BOOM
HUGH SCOTT
PHILADELPHIA ENQUIRER MAGAZINE
NOVEMBER 11, 1951

WHILE IT WAS NOT UNTIL THE 1950s when the most significant real estate development boom in the history of Bucks County began, the county's population had been steadily increasing since the time of William Penn. Beginning in the 1860s, commuters were traveling back and forth to the suburbs outside of Philadelphia on the Pennsylvania Railroad's Main Line. These included exclusive neighborhoods with names like Villanova, Radnor, and Haverford.[3]

Just before the opening of the 1876 U.S. Centennial Exposition in Philadelphia, the North Penn, Delaware and Bound Brook railroads and the Central Railroad of New Jersey joined forces to create a new Philadelphia to New York route, ending the Pennsylvania Railroad's monopoly of that corridor. Three years later, the Philadelphia and Reading Railroad leased the route. Not only did the line serve the needs of the Centennial's attendees, it also allowed commuters to travel from Yardley to Philadelphia. These railroad suburbs offered new possibilities to upper middle class and wealthy individuals. Yardley's architecture, for example, reflects the tastes of those early commuters with its Second Empire, Carpenter Gothic, Gothic Revival, and Queen Anne styled buildings along South Main Street.[4]

Then, with the introduction of automobiles, a major new societal shift began. While only 458,000 cars were sold in 1910, there were 4.5 million being sold annually by 1929 as Americans began a love affair with the road. In 1930, there were 27 million cars on the road. To accommodate those millions of cars various levels of government began to construct road networks including the opening of the Pennsylvania Turnpike in 1940 and the signing of the National Interstate and Defense Highways Act in 1956 which created the Interstate Highway System to handle the volume of traffic.[5]

With the rise in use of automobiles, Lower Makefield, along with other communities along the Delaware River, became the new home destination for wealthy industrialists and businessmen from Trenton in the 1920s. Here they built large homes, often using the Colonial Revival or Neoclassical styles popular at the time. Others were built using Spanish Eclectic and Tudor themes. Edgehill Gardens, built in 1921-22 on Yardley-Morrisville Road, was the first planned residential development with restrictive covenants in Bucks County as defined by today's standards. Another development built not long after was Morningside Estates to the south.[6]

Washington Crossing Historic Park (Pennsylvania) and Washington Crossing State Park (New Jersey) were both developed during the 1920s, and while there was some camping, tens of thousands of people came to picnic and swim in the Delaware River. The open fields in both parks were often covered with visitors on the weekends during the summer and fall, and hundreds of cars lined the roads.

In addition, during World War II, and in the years after, new industries began moving to the greater Delaware Valley region. Residents of the southern part of the county found themselves unprepared for what happened when U.S. Steel announced in 1951 that it was going to build a new state of the art steel plant called Fairless Works.[7]

At the same time, plans to build thousands of homes south of Lower Makefield Township, at a development called Fairless Hills, were revealed as U.S. Steel needed housing for its employees. Next, William J. Levitt announced his plan to build thousands of homes in lower Bucks County. Parts of these two major residential construction projects were undertaken in Falls Township. At the time, Falls was a rural township whose economy was agricultural-based with a population of three thousand people.[8]

Courtesy Peter Osborne

Edgehill Gardens was one of the first planned communities in Bucks County. Its buildings reflect a number of architectural styles including Colonial Revival, Spanish Mission and Tudor.

All of this was occurring against the national backdrop of returning World War II veterans using their GI Bill benefits to buy homes and returning to school. A major housing shortage began during those years, fueling support for the development of Fairless Hills and Levittown, one of five Levitt developments built on the East Coast.

With all of those developments happening at the same time, the stars aligned for a remarkable housing boom to occur. As dramatic as all those announcements were in 1951, these projects began a decades-long construction spree in which tens of thousands of homes would be built, forever changing the nature and landscape of the county. The population of Bucks County would increase from 107,000 people in 1940 to 479,180 in 1980 forty years later.[9]

There was a tremendous impact on the bucolic and rural Bucks County as some of the best farmland in the United States was lost and the market garden county of Pennsylvania became a place that grew houses instead of produce. Developers from Philadelphia began buying farmland with the hopes of creating new residential housing. Local township officials some became overwhelmed by the flood of projects that were coming across their desks.[10]

THE FAIRLESS WORKS

In 1945, with the conclusion of World War II, a plane owned by Aero Survey of Yardley was sent to Venezuela in search of iron ore deposits to supply U.S. Steel with raw materials for its operations. At the same time, Bethlehem Steel was already shipping ore from Cerro Bolivar Mountain, located along a tributary of the Orinoco River. New deposits were discovered, and so began a development that would forever change Bucks County, thousands of miles away.[11]

In addition, a complicated series of charges were brought by the Federal Trade Commission against the steel company, and other corporations, over their transportation charges. After the company lost its case there was a powerful incentive to build a new steel plant with easier access to raw materials. The Venezuelan ore deposits allowed for cheaper rates to be charged for transporting finished goods.[12]

Starting late in 1948 and completed in early 1950, sixty properties were purchased in lower Falls Township along the Delaware River that totaled approximately thirty-eight hundred acres. Most of it was prime farmland including the Starkey truck farm, which managed 1,884 acres. The entire transaction was coordinated by the Pennsylvania Railroad, long a promoter of various industries that it would be able to assist with their transportation needs and coal supplies.[13]

The company that had direct charge of the project was a PRR subsidiary, Manor Real Estate and Trust Company. Representing Manor Real Estate was Thomas Stockham, the former mayor of Morrisville. His son, Thomas, headed the effort after his father died in the early stages of the project.[14]

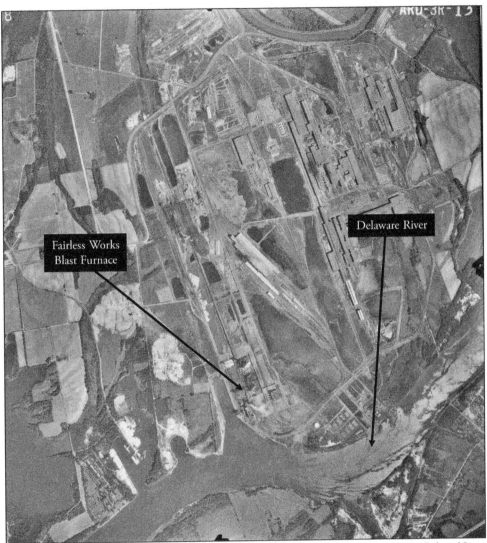

Courtesy Penn Pilot and the Pennsylvania Geological Survey
The Fairless Works is shown in this aerial view taken in 1958.

Initially, land was purchased for $800 an acre, even then a good sum. By the end of the process, Manor Real Estate paid $2,000 an acre, reflecting the growing interest in who was buying the property. In the meantime, as the real estate was acquired, U.S. Steel planned and prepared for the building of the immense structures needed. A ground breaking ceremony was held on March 1, 1951. It was a gala event attended by many of the region's most prominent residents, along with its important political figures. When guests arrived for the ribbon-cutting, there were still abandoned farmhouses dotting the landscape.[15]

On December 11, 1952, seven years after the discovery of ore in Venezuela, the steel works began operation. When Fairless Works was completed, at a price of $450 million, it included:

. . . 75 miles of railroad tracks, 20 miles of roads, 25 miles of sewers, 700,000 cubic yards of concrete and 4,000 feet of concrete bulkhead.[16]

It was the:

Largest integrated steel mill built at one time in the country . . .

and had seen the participation of:

. . . 100,000 companies, 13,000 men working at the site along with three million men working in 27 states to complete it.[17]

The building of Fairless Works and its subsequent worldwide operations was a remarkable accomplishment. Its operation created almost two million tons of pig iron output annually and employed almost five thousand workers. With direct access to the Delaware River and raw materials coming in from South America, U.S. Steel made its products more economically than its competitors. It was the most modern steel manufacturing facility in America and it was located on land that had once been a part of the Mannor of Penns-berry.[18]

It is worth noting that the building of the Fairless plant did not happen in a vacuum. In fact, other manufacturers and affiliates were also building facilities in the region at the same time. Some were steel-based, like the National Tube Company, American Steel and Wire, and General Refractories, while others included chemical plants and oil refining facilities. At the time, it was thought that they would employ almost seventy thousand workers. In addition, other companies built or expanded their facilities. A map that appeared in a 1951 Philadelphia magazine article shows the greater Philadelphia region, including southwestern New Jersey, in the middle of a heyday of industrial expansion.[19]

Located to the west of the Fairless Works, another important industry had operated since the 1930s. Extensive quarrying and dredging operations for sand and gravel had excavated in the area that became present-day Van Sciver Lake. In the decades that followed, the area to the south of the lake became the site for two major landfills.[20]

Both Fairless Hills and Levittown created their own identities. Even today those identities remain, as with the Fairless Hills Fire Department.

FAIRLESS HILLS

Even as the land for the Fairless Works was being purchased, another major development project in Falls Township was unfolding that would also forever change Bucks County. Six weeks after the groundbreaking for the steel plant, work began on a residential development called Fairless Hills. The project's developer was the Danherst Corporation, the builder was Gunnison Magichomes, and the realtor was the John Galbreath Company. Gunnison was owned by U.S. Steel. The company financed the development and the steel plant, which were both named for Benjamin Fairless. Fairless was the President, Chairman, and Chief Executive Officer of U.S. Steel from 1938-55.[21]

This development did not just create new residential housing, but also created a new community. Schools were built along with churches, community golf course, bowling alleys, and a community center. Fire houses were organized and constructed, and a local newspaper was founded. In all, about three thousand families moved into the development, including those who worked for the steel plant and other nearby industries.[22]

Soon, both Routes 1 and 13 were clogged with traffic from residents from the new community and the plant. One observer said in late 1951:

Fallsington is watching in awe as the Danherst Corporation builds a 14,000 population community in its back yard. Each day 16 new homes are completed; each week more houses than Fallsington holds are finished.[23]

The historic community of Fallsington, the birthplace of Quakerism in Bucks County, was less than half a mile to the east of this new development. The Five Mile Woods was also witness to these major undertakings as parts of Fairless Hills were located within one mile of it.

A New Adventure of Suburban Living

With the Fairless Works under construction and the Fairless Hills development well underway by the fall of 1951, a Long Island developer was also planning a residential and commercial development situated between the two major projects. It would be considerably larger and more complex than Fairless Hills. William Levitt, who developed the suburban community of Levittown on Long Island, New York, created another remarkable, planned community situated in Falls, Middletown and Bristol Townships and the borough of Tullytown. As with the Fairless Works project, Levitt acquired thousands of acres of farmland, some bordering Fairless Hills.[24]

More than five thousand acres were purchased with the goal of creating:

A new adventure of suburban living.[25]

When the first sample homes were ready to be shown in Levittown, thirty thousand people came to see them. One could purchase a small home for as little as $9,000 or a larger home for $17,990. Some of the homes required a down payment of just $100. Soon Levitt's company was building houses at the rate of almost twenty per day, all prefabricated and using one of six designs. The first homeowners arrived on June 23, 1952 and with that influx, a huge new community was created where there had been none before. Many of its residents were World War II veterans and employees of the new Fairless Works or other nearby industries. Other skilled workers came from Trenton and the coal regions of northeastern Pennsylvania. Initially, schools could only manage half-day sessions until more were built.[26]

Like Fairless Works and Fairless Hills, Levittown is one of remarkable numbers. The complex covered twenty-two square miles and included ninety-seven miles of roads and 114,000 miles of water and sewer lines. Schools and churches were built, sixty stores were constructed in a mile-long shopping center, year-round recreational facilities with five Olympic swimming pools were created. Even the Pennsylvania Railroad changed the name of their nearby station to Levittown. When it was completely built out in 1958, Levittown included 17,311 new houses and more than seventy thousand inhabitants. Almost four thousand of those houses were in Falls Township increasing its population to thirty thousand.[27]

The completion of Fairless Hills and Levittown did not end the development pressures in the county, but rather began the first chapter of what became a much bigger story. They were the biggest projects undertaken in the county until that time. Levittown remains the largest project ever undertaken in the county, and it is unlikely that something on that scale could ever be built again. In the decades that followed smaller developments of townhouses and single family homes be-

Courtesy Five Mile Woods Preserve
Donald Formigli Collection

Buyers of homes in Levittown had six models from which to choose, as those shown in this advertising flyer.

came more common, as farms were sold and developed across central and lower Bucks County. Among the developments built in Lower Makefield in the 1970s were Kings Hill Cross, Carriage Hill, and Manor Lane. In 1977-78, Toll Brothers built six hundred units at Yardley Hunt.[28]

A Population Explosion

Because of the construction of the Fairless Works, Fairless Hills, Levittown, and then the smaller but numerous developments after that, the population of Bucks County skyrocketed. The population growth between 1950-60 was 113% and it was 34% for the decade of 1960-70. With the construction of Levittown and Fairless Hills, twenty thousand families, many working for Fairless Works or the other important industries nearby, now lived on land that had once been farms. Slowly but surely Falls Township was built out and development made its way north towards, through and beyond Lower Makefield.[29]

The last section of Interstate Route 95 opened in 1985 and with a growing population in the greater Princeton region the need for housing spread westward across the river and into central Bucks County and Lower Makefield.[30]

By 1973, about 25% of Lower Makefield's land mass of 11,187 acres was developed. At the time, it was thought by the Board of Supervisors that the Township's housing stock could increase to eight thousand units from the four thousand it already had. The Bucks County Planning Commission, however, thought it might increase to more than nine thousand units. The commission believed that almost half of the Township could be classified as *resource protection land* which it defined as being farm land, flood plain, or having steep slopes, bodies of water, and wetlands.[31]

Lower Makefield's population almost doubled after World War II, and then from 1950-60, the population of the Township more than doubled again. The next decade also saw tremendous growth as the population increased to almost fifteen thousand residents, a 72% increase. By 1980, the population of Lower Makefield Township had increased almost six-fold since 1950.

The following charts reveal Lower Makefield Township and Bucks County's population and housing growth.

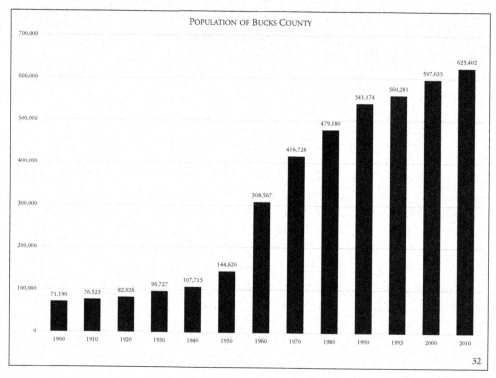

32

Courtesy Peter Osborne

Population of Bucks County

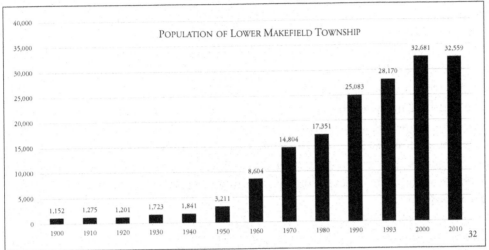

POPULATION OF LOWER MAKEFIELD TOWNSHIP

Courtesy Peter Osborne

Population of Lower Makefield Township

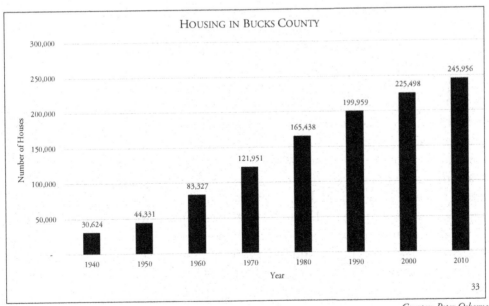

Courtesy Peter Osborne

Housing in Bucks County

The explosive growth created numerous problems in the lower part of the county, which for the previous three hundred years had been primarily rural, with agriculture its main industry. The smaller hamlets and former centers of commerce like Woodbourne, Oxford Valley and Fallsington, were subsumed. Curiously, Yardley did not face the same challenges and retained its distinctive character, probably because the Yardley-Wilburtha bridge was destroyed in the flood of 1955 and not replaced.[34]

Traffic congestion became a major problem, overcrowding in area schools a major challenge, and flooding regularly occurred in areas where new housing had been built, along with a number of other issues. The effect of the suburban sprawl spread across the county, particularly in the lower part was best analyzed by the authors of the 2011 Bucks County Planning Commission's *Comprehensive Plan*. They wrote:

Sprawl has been costly to our county and quality of life. It has been the primary cause of a range of connected regional problems that have been, for the most part, beyond the control of local planning and development review. Among sprawl's most costly effects:

A significant loss of farmland and natural resources
Urban disinvestment
Costly infrastructure development
Physically and socially disconnected neighborhoods
A reliance on fossil fuels
An increased vulnerability to climate change [35]

FULL FIELDS, SNUG TENEMENTS, AND FENCES NEAT

Despite the challenges that the three previous decades of development brought to the region, there were many factors that made Bucks County an attractive place to live in and move to. The county was an accessible location as commuters could easily get to Philadelphia, Trenton, and New York via the railroads that were offering shuttle services and interstate highway connections were open. It was centrally located on the Washington D.C.-New York corridor. The rural landscape of the central and northern part of the county remained relatively undeveloped, and visitors and potential homeowners wanted to enjoy it. Once Interstate 95 was completed and incorporated into the larger interstate highway system, advertisements promoting Bucks County and encouraging people to move there could be found regularly in New York City venues.[36]

Sesame Place, opened in 1980, and was less than three miles from the Five Mile Woods Preserve. It has drawn millions of visitors since it began operations and is the most popular attraction in lower Bucks County.[37]

New Hope became an important regional, and ultimately, a national arts

Courtesy United States Geological Survey

*This 1981 USGS topographic map (Trenton West, NJ, PA) reveals the impact of residential develop-
ment in Fairless Hills and Levittown south of the Five Mile Woods, and the newer development underway in the east and to the north.*

The James A. Michener Art Museum
Doylestown, Pennsylvania

center, known for its *Pennsylvania Impressionism* movement. Washington Crossing Historic Park, a short distance north of Lower Makefield was also a popular destination. In 1952, the famed Emanuel Leutze painting of George Washington crossing the Delaware River on Christmas night in 1776 came to the location it depicted. On loan from the Metropolitan Museum of Art in New York City, millions of visitors from around the country came to see it.[38]

Doylestown, with its historic and cultural sites, brought people to Bucks County from around the nation, the Commonwealth, and the region. Among the important sites was the James A. Michener Art Center, which opened in 1988, and now called the James A. Michener Art Museum. The Bucks County Historical Society, an important force in the preservation of the county's heritage since 1880, occupied a prominent building that had been built by Henry Mercer from 1908-12.

While it is presumed that many were against the massive developments brought to fruition by the Fairless Works, Fairless Hills, Levittown and the subsequent widespread development, there were significant numbers of people who favored the important economic forces at work. In Morrisville, for example, there was support for the new business coming its way. Developers saw the potential of building more houses, and home prices, in some cases, doubled. Families who were able to purchase houses in Levittown and Fairless Hills with small down payments now owned a piece of the American dream in suburbia. Local businesses also saw the potential of new revenue sources.

Many historic structures were demolished as the development swept over Lower Bucks County in the 1950s, although two significant structures were saved by developers. These included the historic Bolton Mansion in Bristol Township and Three Arches in Falls Township. Each had their own important heritage and connections to William Penn and the early Quakers.

Bolton Mansion, along with several acres, was donated by William Levitt who had bought the property in 1952. Construction of the structure was started in 1687 and continued until it completion in 1790. Deeded to Bristol Township, it was first used for the Township's offices. The impressive stone structure was the home of a colleague of William Penn, Phineas Pemberton, who was an important figure in establishing the government for the newly created colony in the 1680s. After the Township decided to move its offices, it was given to the Bucks County Conservancy (now the Heritage Conservancy).[41]

Three Arches was purchased by the Danherst Corporation in 1951 and deeded to Bucks County in 1967. It was subsequently given to Falls Township in 1971. A volunteer group restored the building to its former historic appearance in 1980-82.[42]

Not long after the announcement of the construction of the Fairless Works, and the Fairless Hills and Levittown developments there was a recognition that something needed to be done to better cope with the development forces gathering momentum not only in lower Bucks County but also in the central part of the county. From those announcements in 1951 and 1952 came the creation of several organizations dedicated to slowing the pace of development and preserving the county's agricultural, cultural and historic resources.

Courtesy Peter Osborne

Three Arches
Falls Township, Pennsylvania

131

One of the first groups to be formed was Historic Fallsington, Inc., a non-profit organization dedicated to preserving the history of the historic Quaker village. It was not far from ground zero of the development going on. The historic community, which played such a central part in the lives of the Darks and Satterthwaites and served as a regional economic center, was now completely boxed in by Routes 1, 13, and the Trenton Cutoff. Curiously, those three arteries had, in fact, protected the original crossroads community, even as increasing traffic rumbled by.

In 1953, a historic property, the Burges-Lippincott House, was listed for sale, and it was rumored that it would be demolished for a new gas station. The beautiful historic structure was located at the juncture of Meetinghouse Square, the place where the various Meeting Houses were located. Concerned residents banded together to create a non-profit organization that restored the building. They went on to save a number of other buildings and have the community listed on the National Register of Historic Places.[43]

Several other county-wide groups came into being and would play an important role in the county's future, including the Bucks County Planning Commission, created in 1951 and the Bucks County Department of Parks and Recreation, established in 1953. The Bucks County Parks Foundation, a not-for-profit organization, was incorporated in 1958. (It later became the Bucks County Conservancy and then the Heritage Conservancy.) Collectively, these groups began a series of efforts to preserve the rural landscape where possible, provide a more organized way of allowing for development, to create new parks and recreation areas, and to preserve the county's most important historic structures that were being threatened with demolition.[44]

Two of those entities came to be involved with a remarkable piece of as yet, undeveloped property, called the Five Mile Woods, that lay mostly in Lower Makefield Township along with a smaller area in Falls Township. It was the largest tract of woodland remaining in lower Bucks County.

COMMON BEECH

COMMON BEECH

Chapter 5

THE RACE TO SAVE THE WOODS

People have to have places like this (the Five Mile Woods) to keep their sanity.
They've got to be able to take a walk in the woods.[1]
STEVE WHARTON, PARK AND RECREATION PLANNER
LOWER MAKEFIELD TOWNSHIP

Once you've seen these woods, there's no question you'll vote for it.[2]
DONALD FORMIGLI, CHAIRMAN
LOWER MAKEFIELD PARK AND RECREATION BOARD
ON THE REFERENDUM OF 1978 TO PURCHASE THE FIVE MILE WOODS

The concepts that you and the Park and Recreation Board have developed in the past two to three
years have certainly become the model for many other townships experiencing the growth patterns that
exist in Lower Makefield.[3]
RONALD CHASE, DIRECTOR
COUNTY OF BUCKS DEPARTMENT OF PARKS AND RECREATION
TO
DONALD FORMIGLI
NOVEMBER 6, 1978

B Y THE EARLY 1970S DEVELOPMENT PRESSURES reached Lower Makefield
with full force. For the next twenty years, the Township was swept up
into a vortex of activity and change. Because of its relatively flat topography, access to the area's major transportation corridors and job markets, it was a prime candidate for the construction of new residential housing and
commercial growth. From the south and the east, residential development made
its way to the edge of the Five Mile Woods and came to surround it.

While residents of southern Bucks County were totally unprepared for the
development of Fairless Hills and Levittown, it was now more than a decade after
those projects were completed and the desire to better plan for the future had
been established. Many had the feeling that the rural and agricultural landscape
along with its natural, cultural historic resources should not be allowed to simply
disappear. They also supported the acquisition of park lands, open space, and the
setting aside of recreational areas.

Residents across the county were opposed to massive developments and the
clashing between developers, farmers and residents now became a local affair,
fought at various public meetings. In some cases, extensions of sewer lines were
not granted or storm water control created havoc in the newly built residential
developments. Those who wished to save the central and northern part of Bucks
County from a total build-out were developing new techniques and strategies and
using tools that had been created elsewhere for their cause.[4]

In addition to creating a planning commission in 1951, Bucks County also
created a Department of Parks and Recreation in 1953. The county acquired two
parcels that became county parks: Silver Lake County Park (Bristol Township)
in 1957; and the John J. Stover Tinicum County Park (Tinicum Township) in
1955. There were four state parks previously established in the county including Washington Crossing State Park (now Washington Crossing Historic Park in
Upper Makefield and Solebury Townships), Ralph Stover State Park (Plumstead
Township), the Theodore Roosevelt State Park (the entire length of the Delaware
Canal from Easton to Bristol), and Logan State Park (Bensalem Township) located where the Neshaminy Creek meets the Delaware River.

In 1958, a report revealed the results of a detailed survey of the county's recreation assets by the Department of Parks and Recreation. The report concluded that county residents needed to begin planning and setting aside more areas for parks and recreation. It foresaw that open space and farmland would be lost to residential and commercial developments, all in the not so distant future. The county took up its own challenge and by 1978, just twenty years later, it owned 5,500 acres of parkland along with twenty-two facilities. A 1973 inventory found that the county's townships and boroughs managed one hundred and twenty-five parks. These statistics reflected a trend that was also occurring across the Commonwealth and the country, as the movement to acquire open space was quickly spreading.[5]

A VISION FOR OPEN SPACE AND RECREATION

Lower Makefield Township had been at the forefront of local planning efforts beginning with the creation of a zoning ordinance in 1939, and then a comprehensive plan in 1954. It was one of the first municipalities to adopt a zoning code. All of this was undertaken just as Levittown was being built. So, unlike Falls Township, which had been unprepared for the massive development, Lower Makefield was better able to consider addressing the development pressures coming its way. These planning and zoning efforts allowed for the Township to better anticipate the wave of new residential construction coming northward and how it might address the impact of it on the Township and its quality of life. While some residents would have preferred no residential or commercial development, the simple reality was that the Township could not legally prevent it.[6]

Another area where the Township was a leader was in its creation of the Lower Makefield Historical Commission in 1977. Soon the agency became an important force in preserving the Township's history by saving historic buildings, erecting historic markers and plaques, and establishing an historic district for the architecturally significant Edgewood Village. This was subsequently approved by the Pennsylvania Historical and Museum Commission in 1979. Another important project undertaken by the Commission in 1990, and updated since, was the documentation of over two hundred and fifty historic sites that predated 1900. The Commission also produced the *Tri-Centennial Commemorative History of Lower Makefield Township 1692-1992*, booklets including *A Guide to Lower Makefield's Historic Landmarks* and assisted with the *Historical Map – 1798* and *Map of Original Grantees*.[7]

In addition to these governmental efforts, the Lower Makefield Historical Society was created in 1978. It focused on preserving the Township's history through a variety of methods including the restoration of the Schoolmaster's House, maintaining an archive, conducting monthly meetings and providing public programs and lectures, a role it continues to play today.[8]

Another area where the Township concentrated its efforts was creating a recreation program. This was a theme common to many townships across the county at the time. Included in the 1958 inventory of the county's parks and recreation areas, a map showed that, aside from its schools which provided various forms of recreational programs and open space, and the Yardley Golf Course in the borough, there were no public parks or recreation areas in Lower Makefield. The idea of a community park was not even discussed for the first time until 1965. In the 1974 Township budget, there was no money allocated for parks and recreation.[9]

But there were growing calls for open space preservation and the development of new recreational resources. The leader in the creation and implementation of these programs came to be the Lower Makefield Park and Recreation Board (PRB). Early on this board, with members appointed by the Township's Board of Supervisors, became the most important advocate for recreation in the Township and the preservation of the Five Mile Woods.

In late 1975, the PRB was given the authorization to plan the development of twenty-two acres of land adjacent to the Township's offices on Edgewood Road. With that beginning, the PRB created a strategic plan, entitled *Proposed Park and Recreation for Lower Makefield,* which laid out a strategy for developing recreational facilities in the Township and overseeing the operation of those various sites. The plan included building bike-pedestrian paths linking the Township, streambed preservation, new open space and recreation land set aside, including the Five Mile Woods, farmland preservation, and the development of a recreational complex, called the Community Park, on the property next to the Township's municipal buildings. By 1976, with this new emphasis on recreation, the annual budget request was increased to $27,500.[10]

The organizers of this complex and multi-faceted effort were creative, proactive, bipartisan, and collaborative, which allowed them to reach their goals. And, it is worth remembering that creating this legacy for the future of the Township's residents was also happening at the same time residential and commercial development was reaching its peak.[11]

Meeting monthly, members of the PRB had to deal with a myriad of issues, making complicated decisions that would forever change the Township, while implementing their vision of what the town could look like. The minutes that survive reflect a level of constant activity. In looking at what the Township has today in terms of its recreational resources, much of that legacy can be traced back to this remarkable time in the late 1970s and early 1980s.

Several members of the PRB were critical advocates for saving the Five Mile Woods including Donald Formigli, its chair; Pat (Fair)Miiller, its secretary and later vice chairman, and chairman; and Gail Hardesty. Carol Dubois, a member of the local school board, Ann Rhoads, a botanist, and Township Supervisors Hank Miiller and Lloyd Klatzkin who were also leading advocates. Both supervisors were important local political figures, served as the liaison with the PRB, and used their political clout to get supporting legislation passed.[12]

In addition, the board created partnerships with various groups including Yardley-Morrisville Soccer and Pennsbury Athletic Association, the Society for the Performing Arts, the Friends of the Five Mile Woods, and the Pool Committee. The board also sponsored special events.[13]

There were other critical supporters of saving the Five Mile Woods including the Lower Makefield Open Space Committee (LMOS). The LMOS began as an ad hoc committee in 1974 and was created by Donald Formigli. It lobbied for, and made public appeals to, preserve open space. The committee conducted public programs, including slide shows, distributed maps and handouts, encouraged participants to fill out questionnaires soliciting community input, and compiled a list of properties that were significant and needed to be saved.[14]

Early on, the Five Mile Woods became one of the committee's main areas of focus, along with saving a section of the Brock Creek. Additional concerns included the need to preserve other undeveloped areas in the Township and to keep the public informed. These parcels included the Reading Railroad's land behind the Township Building, the Sandy Run flood plain near the Starkey Farm, several properties along the Delaware Canal, and the Kissing Rock Woods along Big Oak Road. While many presumed that the Five Mile Woods would be lost to development, Formigli and the other dedicated members of this committee did not think that such an outcome was inevitable.[15]

Finally, the Save Our Woods Committee (SOW), another ad hoc group, was created after the supervisors voted to place the purchase of the Woods on the ballot for voters to reject or approve in 1978. The SOW prepared convincing arguments why the Woods should be saved, and why it was also in the Township's best financial interest to do so, putting aside its environmental significance. They conducted a successful public relations campaign that led to the purchase of most of the Woods and its preservation.

THE FIVE MILE WOODS

The first priority of the efforts to preserve open space for the Township's residents was focused on the Five Mile Woods. It was the largest remaining forested area in lower Bucks County and designated in the Township's *Development Plan* created in 1972 as:

> . . . *being worthy of preservation.*[16]

Aerial photographs taken in 1971 show it was located amidst numerous tracts of farmland and new housing developments not too distant to the east and the south. While there were other isolated patches of forests elsewhere in the

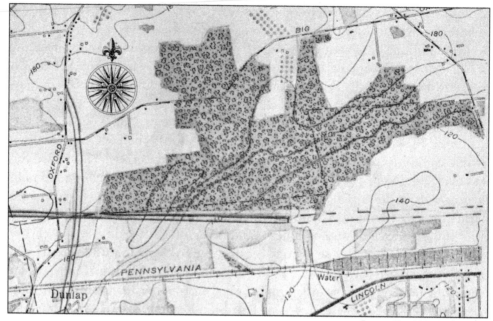

Courtesy Five Mile Woods Preserve
Donald Formigli Collection
Created in 1974-75 and overlaid on the 1955 USGS topographic map (West Trenton, NJ, PA), this map shows the area described as the Five Mile Woods, located within Lower Makefield and Falls townships.

Township, no other tract of forest land was as large or as sprawling.[17]

The Five Mile Woods was not an easily defined area but rather an oddly-shaped tract of land. Its dimensions were not dictated by any natural features, such as a body of water or major change in elevation, but instead was an artificially designated area that had been shaped by its previous and current uses. What was distinctive were its unique natural features which included rare and endangered wildflowers; different stages of forest types, and the Fall Line, that divided the Coastal Plain from the Piedmont Plain. At its center was the Dark tract that had been transferred from William Penn to William Dark in 1683, subsequently owned by the Satterthwaite families, and now owned by the Penn Central Corporation and Manor Real Estate and Trust Company.

While it had been actively farmed, and logged for more than two centuries, by 1938, as shown with aerial photographs, much of what was described as the Five Mile Woods had reverted back to woodland, a process that had been going on for several decades.[18]

At the time that the Preserve was created, there were some interesting and notable features that were not geologic in nature, and can still be seen. There was an evergreen nursery located along the northwestern sector (now a small evergreen forest that one passes when walking on the Evergreen Trail). An orchard was located in the northern sector (behind the Preserve's current headquarters) and forests that varied in age and type were spread across the entire Woods. There were also some open areas bordering the Woods, that were still active farmland, pastures, or reverting to forest. There was even a small cranberry bog, created accidentally, in the western sector, not far from the current shopping center boundary. Most of these areas came to be included within the Preserve. Route 281 (current Route 1), which was completed to its intersection with the Oxford Valley Road, extended several hundred yards east of the exit ramp where it simply ended, a concrete highway to nowhere. It would be almost ten years until it was finished, and opened for use.[19]

One enduring mystery that remains about the Woods is the origin of its name. It is not known exactly when it first came to be called the *Five Mile Woods* as it does not appear on any historical mapping data prior to the mid-1970s. The name is not found, for example, in the 1955 *Place Names of Bucks County* by George MacReynolds, nor is it mentioned in W. W. H. Davis' 1876 *History of Bucks County*.[20]

The name is believed to have been in use in the early twentieth century. The venerated historian of Falls Township, Sam Snipes, remembered camping there with his Scout troop in the 1930s and that his leaders called it by that name. Given that his leaders were probably fifteen or twenty years older, it is possible that the name was in use as early as the 1910s. Steve Willard, a member of the

Courtesy Five Mile Woods Preserve
Donald Formigli Collection

This 1974 aerial view shows the Woods looking from west to east. The Willard evergreen nursery is in the center. There were still open spaces remaining within what is now the Five Mile Woods Preserve.

family who owned a portion of the Woods, and operated a nursery in the 1950s and 1960s also remembered the name being used when he lived there. The name continued in common usage into the 1970s, because support letters written to save the Woods, reference it by that name.[21]

Generally, it is believed that the name *Five Mile Woods* represents some kind of a linear description. One explanation suggests that the name described a forest that began in Langhorne and ended in Morrisville, a distance of five miles. Others have speculated that it was five miles north of Bristol and five miles west of Trenton. The Bristol connection is an interesting one as it has also been suggested that the Woods were logged and the timber used to build piers in Philadelphia. Another hypothesis is that it was five miles from the Meeting House at Fallsington.[22]

Jeff Marshall, the President of the Heritage Conservancy, suggested that farmers would have left wood uncut, especially along the Fall Line because it was unusable land. He pointed out on a map how the Five Mile Woods could have been a long narrow band of woodland using a three-mile section of the Fall Line in Falls Township and Lower Makefield Township as an example. This coincides with what the prevailing thought is about the name.[23]

A different line of thinking relates to the size of the Woods. A 1975 report, prepared by Donald Formigli and entitled the *Five-Mile Woods*, reported that the total acreage of the Woods was 375 acres and that it measured 3.3 miles on an east-west line and 1.8 miles on a north-south Line. The total of the two lines would be 5.1 miles. The Woods in 1975 were about the same size as it had been during the time that Sam Snipes was camping there.[24]

Another contemporary document, the narrative for a slide program prepared by Formigli about saving open space in Lower Makefield Township, reported that the name had come about because the Woods contained five square miles of forest. Another source for the name is said to come from the fact that there are five miles of trails at the Preserve. This theory can be dismissed at the outset.[25]

An alternative that follows this linear line of thinking comes from John Heilferty who took a map of the Five Mile Woods and drew a line around the greatest extent of the Woods and comes up with a five-mile long boundary. However, it is hard to imagine a reason for someone taking the time to measure that line and to what end.[26]

There are several other possibilities that, while not as scientific in their approach, may actually point to an answer that has not been considered because of their seeming obscurity. John Heilferty wondered if perhaps people used a part of the Woods for regular recreational activities and that it was five miles from where they lived. Another possibility worth mentioning comes from Rick Mellon who suggested, with his good sense of humor, that the origin of the name may have a simpler one. Perhaps he thought, it was named for *Joe Five Mile and his Woods*.[27]

Are any of these possible explanations the source of the name? Even today no one can be certain. However, the linear approach seems to point to the most likely of answers.

WHERE ARE THE WOODS

The following chart, compiled in 1974-75, lists the parcels located in all or part of the Five Mile Woods. The total acreage of each parcel is shown along with the Township in which they were located:

Owner Name or Project Name	Tax Parcel Lot No.	Total Acreage of Parcel
Falls Township		*115 acres*
Manor Real Estate and Trust Penn Central Railroad	13-3-8	9.69 acres
Manor Real Estate and Trust Penn Central Railroad	13-3-9-5	37.6 acres
Joseph and Catherine Guzikowski	13-3-10	140.6 acres
Michael Sadowski	13-10-1	37.5 acres
Lower Makefield Township		*260 acres*
Russell Broadnix	20-32-28	5 acres
Independence Development	20-32-29, 32, 33, 35	20 acres
John Deas	20-32-30	5 acres
Marion and Alfred Conrad	20-32-31	5 acres
Jacqueline and Eugene Hieber	20-32-34	4.84 acres
Oxford Valley Assn.	20-32-36.1	5.73 acres
Margaret and James Foulds	20-32-44	6.38 acres
Manor Real Estate & Trust Penn Central Railroad	20-32-45	115.33 acres
Victor and Milton Cutler	20-32-46	45.23 acres
William Shender, Inc.	20-32-47w	39.99 acres

OWNER NAME or PROJECT NAME	TAX PARCEL LOT NO.	TOTAL ACREAGE OF PARCEL
Charles Guzikowski	20-32-47e	46.11 acres
J.H. and A.B. Milnor	20-32-19-2	34.58 acres
Makefield Oak, Inc	20-32-21	147.5 acres [28]

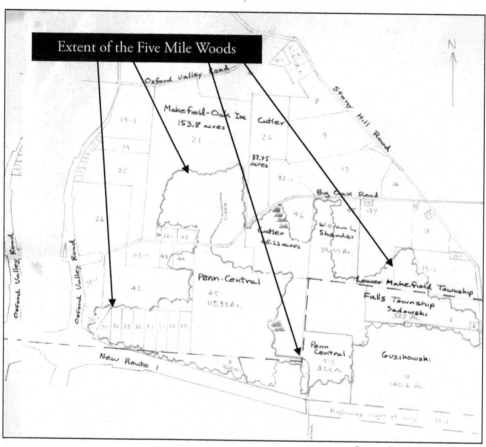

Courtesy Five Mile Woods Preserve
Donald Formigli Collection

In the early 1970s, the greater Five Mile Woods, shown here overlaid on a township tax map, remained intact. But, by the end of the decade, a number of the tracts were built over including one of the two Cutler tracts (No. 22), and now known as Big Oak Bend. The eastern half of the Shender tract (No. 47), now called Big Oak Woods, was developed. A portion of the western half of the property. which included a part of the Woods, was preserved by conservation easement.

THE PENNSYLVANIA RAILROAD AND THE WOODS

The largest tract of land, and the most significant, within the Five Mile Woods, was owned by the Penn Central Corporation (PC). The PC was the corporation that resulted from the merger of its predecessors, the Pennsylvania Railroad and the New York Central Railroad in 1968.

The story of the Penn Central began in the early years of the twentieth century when railroads across the Northeast began to falter after World War I. First, passenger service decreased, then freight traffic declined after a resurgence during World War II. There were a variety of reasons for this including nationalization during World War I, lack of capital improvement and maintenance and then the Great Depression.[29]

In addition, the amount of railroad trackage began to fall dramatically. The decline of trackage in the Commonwealth corresponded with the national decline. Pennsylvania trackage achieved its greatest number in 1915 when there were 11,693 miles of rail. By 1930, railroads operated 11,141 miles of lines in the Commonwealth and by 1960, that number had declined to 9,092.[30]

From 1923-29, the Pennsylvania Railroad hauled almost fifty billion ton miles of freight revenue and generated almost five billion miles of passenger revenue. It carried more passengers than any other railroad in the country and was one of the most important corporations of its day.[31]

However, trouble loomed on the horizon for American railroads as the nation began to depend increasingly on automobiles to travel both locally and nationally. By 1930, there were about thirty million automobiles in the United States. That number increased dramatically after World War II and with the creation of the Interstate Highway System. As such, the nation became more dependent on automobiles for their transportation to work and for recreational purposes. In addition, beginning with the first commercial flights in 1957, jet airplanes allowed for quicker trips back and forth across the nation.[32]

Another important development was the movement of America's population from urban areas to suburban and exurban areas. This migration impacted areas that had been largely served by the railroads, particularly in the Northeast.[33]

By the 1940s and 1950s, passenger service was losing money for the railroads, and freight revenue was declining precipitously. For example, in 1957, there were 112,000 miles in the passenger rail network; by 1971, it had slid downward to 49,000 miles.[34]

The most ominous trend for the railroads was the increasing amount of America's freight being shipped by truck on the newly built interstate system.[35]

Also, the United States Postal Service ended the practice of shipping the mail by train in 1977, an important revenue source for railroad companies.[36]

Furthermore, the anthracite coal market, previously a major source of income for the northeastern railroads and a significant percent of the tonnage shipped on railroads like the PRR, had collapsed as Americans shifted to other sources of energy including oil and natural gas. The first diesel locomotives were introduced in 1925, and by 1952, the number of diesel powered engines exceeded the number of steam locomotives which ran on coal. This added another significant blow to the declining coal market.[37]

Beginning in the late 1940s, a series of events unfolded that were warning signs of more difficult times ahead for the railroad corporations, as some of the most important lines began to cease operations, or abandoned parts of their business. Then, in 1956, the Baldwin Locomotive Works, the famed manufacturer of locomotives, dropped their production from its product lines.[38]

There were also the corporate combinations of financially weakened railroads such as the Pennsylvania Railroad and New York Central Railroad merger in February 1968.[39]

It was just two years later that the Penn Central collapsed after losing more than $328 million, the largest corporate financial failure in American history up to that time. The fate that beset the Penn Central would soon engulf most of the Northeastern railroads, including other Pennsylvania railroads. It was an astonishing turn of events.[40]

The list of the *fallen flags* as they were known, included the Erie Lackawanna, the Lehigh Valley, and the Reading Company. In 1973, the U.S. Congress passed the Regional Rail Reorganization Act that cobbled together the failing railroads to create the Consolidated Rail Corporation, or more well-known by its shortened name, Conrail. Conrail began its operations on April 1, 1976.[41]

On the passenger side of service, Amtrak, (National Railroad Passenger Corporation) a quasi-government corporation, was created on May 1, 1971 by federal legislation. It assumed control over a collection of passenger lines to relieve the railroads of their unprofitable passenger service. It would take years for passenger service to recover. It was the nadir of the long and glorious history of American railroads which in 1916 had 254,037 miles of track, but by 1963 had declined to 214,387 miles. It was a remarkable collapse of what had been the lifeblood, critical to the development of the nation in the nineteenth and early twentieth centuries. [42]

The bankruptcy proceedings of the Penn Central required a complicated legal effort to dispose of unprofitable railroad assets, and to save the profitable entities. At the time, in 1970, the company's assets and operations were divided between two entities. The railroad operations were owned by the Penn Central Transportation Corporation (PCTC), and subsequently absorbed into the newly created Conrail on April 1, 1976. The bankruptcy court required that the PCTC sell off all its non-operating railroad assets, such as land, as the bankruptcy and reorganization process moved forward.[43]

The profitable and marketable assets, including some railroad properties, were retained by the Penn Central Corporation (PCC). This was the original holding company of the PCTC that continued to survive after the merger of the PCTC's railroad assets into Conrail. (It is also called the Penn Central Company in various documents.) The PCC emerged from the financial disaster as a solvent corporation that owned a number of smaller subsidiaries, some of these were purchased by the Pennsylvania Railroad before the merger, including a stake in Madison Square Garden in New York City and the New York Knicks and New York Rangers.[44]

This complicated story and the resulting chaos from the bankruptcy had a direct impact on the creation of the Five Mile Woods Preserve as the Trustees of Penn Central Transportation Company and the Manor Real Estate and Trust Company, the subsidiary real estate company, owned the most environmentally significant tract within the Woods. It had come into the possession of the Pennsylvania Railroad in 1918 when the railroad purchased it from Henry Satterthwaite.[45]

Initially, the property may have been leased out to local farmers for planting, but by the 1930s it is clear from aerial photographs that the forest had overtaken much of the former farmland. The land may have also been timbered, and it was a place that area hunters used. Locals camped on the property, some damaged the distinctive beech trees with graffiti or buckshot, and others dumped their garbage and tires there. In spite of those problems, this parcel, with its fascinating natural and cultural history, became the central focus of all the stakeholders active in the efforts to save the greater Five Mile Woods.[46]

DEVELOPMENT ARRIVES AT THE FIVE MILE WOODS

The Woods, as an ecosystem, was still remarkably well preserved as the 1970s began. All the parcels that made it unique, remained undeveloped. However, by 1975, the pressures of residential and commercial development that had taken place in lower Bucks County for the previous two decades, were arriving at Lower Makefield's border with full force. Land was purchased in anticipation of it being developed, particularly open farmland. The plans and projects that had been prepared by various developers and property owners were making their way through the approval process. Or, in some cases, were preparing for construction. In fact, in 1977, almost fifteen hundred units of housing were in various stages of design, approval or under construction in the Township. By 1979 there were forty-four development projects in various stages of review or construction that represented almost four thousand five hundred individual units. Most of the land included within the Woods was in some stage of design or review.[47]

In 1973, the Five Mile Woods area was zoned R-3, or Residential, Single Family High Density which could include single family homes or townhouses. There could be as many as four units per acre, a situation particularly attractive

Courtesy Five Mile Woods Preserve
Donald Formigli Collection
Before Yardley Oaks was developed it was open fields, as shown in this 1974 photograph.

to developers. The far western end of the Woods was zoned C-2 or Commercial – Highway Services. A small section of the Woods to the south and the east, and which was in Falls Township, was zoned for low density single family homes.[48]

The proposed developments on the properties that either included the Woods or were adjacent to it included two residential projects called Oxford Glen and Yardley Oaks, being constructed by Herbert Burstein and Makefield Oak, Inc. a developer from Philadelphia. Their development, located on Big Oak Road, was directly across the road from the present-day Preserve; it called for the building of 590 units on 147 acres.[49]

William Shender, owner of William Shender, Inc., another developer from Philadelphia, proposed building a development called Cambridge Estates (previously called Stacey Meadows). It included 147 single family homes, although that number was later increased to 176 units. This was located directly to the east of the present-day Preserve and included forty acres. Diagonally across from Cambridge Estates, on the other side of Big Oak Road, was a planned development called Bexley Orchards (previously called Cherry Hill Orchards) where twenty-nine lots were proposed on fourteen acres.[50]

On the western end of the Woods, Independence Development, Inc., from Newtown, proposed a residential complex named Independence Square. This was to be located at the corner of Oxford Valley Road and Big Oak Road and called for sixty-eight individual houses and 155 duplexes on sixty acres. Its preliminary plan was approved in the fall of 1977, and a final plan was dated September 2, 1978. Beyond that, the developer proposed building a shopping center. Along the Route 1 right-of-way were eight parcels, several of which were owned by Independence Development. The smaller parcels, five acres each, were not slated for development at the time.[51]

At the center of the Five Mile Woods were located two prime, relatively level, developable tracts. The first, and the larger of the two, was the Penn Central parcel. The proposed development was to be called Penn Treaty Woods, an interesting irony given the ties of the Dark family to William Penn. The project was

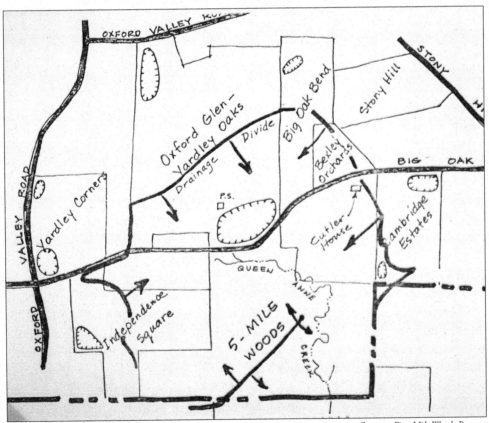

Courtesy Five Mile Woods Preserve
Report on the Hydrology of the Five Mile Woods

This 1981 drawing shows the water runoff patterns from the developments that were either being built around the Preserve or in the final planning stages.

Construction of the Cambridge Estates.
1978

designed to include 430 units of housing.

The adjoining property was owned by Victor and Milton Cutler, developers from Jenkintown, Pennsylvania. This parcel, also level and ideal for development, was divided by Big Oak Road. Plans called for 176 units of housing to be constructed on it. The tract on the south side of the road was the second most significant of the tracts that made up the Woods.[52]

As approvals were given, construction soon began and several of these developments were built. The Cambridge Estates, later renamed Big Oak Woods, bordered the eastern side of the Preserve, and was built between 1977-79. The northern Cutler parcel of thirty-eight acres was ultimately developed and called Big Oak Bend. Oxford Glen and Yardley Oaks were developed and built out as was Bexley Orchards.[53]

Work on the proposed Independence Square residential development, located at the corner of Oxford Valley Road and Big Oak Road was to begin in 1978, but did not, and in fact, the residential community was never built. Years would pass until it was finally developed as a shopping center with a Kohl's department store serving as an anchor along with other retail stores.[54]

The parcels that made up the Five Mile Woods not acquired or preserved with easements by Lower Makefield Township were ultimately developed. Several parcels were acquired from Independence Development, Inc. as part of an agreement to build its shopping center. Later, the Township acquired a five-acre parcel on which the present-day water storage tank was built. The water company leased the land from the Township for ninety-nine years. Only four parcels that included parts of the Five Mile Woods remained. They were all owned by private individuals or families: Michael Sadowski, Charles Guzikowski, Rita and Cyril Banko, Mary and Michael Banko and Laura and James Foulds.

THE PATRON SAINT OF THE WOODS

The efforts to save the Five Mile Woods by the local citizenry is a remarkable story and took a sustained effort in the face of critics, apathy, and the momentum that developers had in their favor. Opponents of unregulated development were outgunned on many fronts but citizens were concerned about the loss of farmland, and the need for open space and recreational assets. The hard work that created the Five Mile Woods Preserve was successful in the end because its advocates had engaged Township residents, convinced them of the rightness of their cause, and who, by large margins, supported their efforts in two public surveys and one referendum. The project also reflected a microcosm of a national trend occurring in many communities across the country at the time.

This was all accomplished under difficult time constraints and the fear that the Woods would be carved up for development, before a plan to save it could be implemented. This was a real threat at the time. It took the hard work of many people, over a period of six years, to save the most significant portions of it. But first it needed a visionary willing to take the lead and guide the efforts.

All such endeavors usually begin with the inspired vision of one person. And so it was with the saving of the Five Mile Woods and the dedicated work of Donald Formigli. Formigli was relatively new to the Township as he, his wife Ursula, and their children, Brent and Lynn moved into a house on Forrest Road, in a development, in Lower Makefield Township in 1967. It was not far from where he worked in Trenton. Having worked his way up to the position of General Foreman at U.S. Steel's Trenton Rope Mill, he went on to become a Sales Engineer. The mill was sold to Bridon American Corporation in 1984. Formigli retired from Bridon two years later to pursue a career in the financial services sector.[55]

Formigli had many interests including wild plants, botany, gardening and, most notably, the general quality

Courtesy Five Mile Woods Preserve
Donald Formigli Collection
Donald Formigli standing atop the Fall Line in the Five Mile Woods in 1977.

of life in the community in which he lived. From those interests came a passion for the Five Mile Woods that was located not far from where he lived. Because the Woods was then privately owned, he parked his car along Big Oak Road and walked into the large tract and began to explore it more. As he did, he discovered a remarkable world of rare plants, fascinating geology and a place of solitude. He often took family members and friends there for hikes.[56]

After he moved to Lower Makefield, he began attending Planning Commission meetings that focused on the Township's open space and recreation needs. Soon he realized the Township was not addressing those pressing concerns although he also knew development could not be legally stopped. It could only be managed. As a result of listening to the discussions at those meetings, Donald created an ad-hoc Lower Makefield Open Space Committee and served as its president. He designed the Township's *Bikeway Master Plan* and participated in tree surveys, including one undertaken in 1979 to inventory trees that dated back to William Penn's time.[57]

Active in the Republican party, he was a member of the Republican Club and was appointed to serve on the Lower Makefield Park and Recreation Board in 1973-74. He became its chairman in 1975, and served in that position until 1980. He also served on the Save Our Woods Committee. In 1979, Formigli was elected to the Township's Board of Supervisors. He later served on the board of directors of Open Space, Inc, a not-for-profit dedicated to preserving Bucks County's rural landscape.[58]

The Five Miles Woods effort required a major commitment of time and effort. Formigli's long struggle to save open space would not conclude until almost seven years later when the Five Mile Woods Preserve was dedicated in the fall of 1981. By that time, he had moved out of the Township.[59]

Most of the Five Mile Woods came to be preserved either by purchase, or by the use of planning tools available at the time. It was Donald Formigli and his vision, more than any other single individual, who was responsible for this remarkable achievement. To be sure, there were many other supporters, and people who volunteered to help along the way, including other members of the Open Space Committee and the Save Our Woods Committee, Township officials, the solicitor and other organizations. However, if there is a patron saint of the Woods it is certainly Donald Formigli.

LAYING THE GROUNDWORK

The successful effort to save the Five Mile Woods was the result of a complicated, yet well thought out and reasoned, plan. But the plan was also flexible because, as Formigli was soon to learn, the journey to save the Woods took many twists and turns. This plan focused on several strategic actions that included finding people of like mind in the Township, garnering support from citizens, reaching out to well-known figures and experts in the botanic and geological world, working with important county organizations and agencies, and coordinating the efforts of the Township's Board of Supervisors, and the Park and Recreation Board. In addition, and perhaps most importantly, he, along with others, developed a way to fund the acquisition of the Woods.

Formigli laid the groundwork by compiling the findings of his study of the Woods, and its plants, wildlife, and geology, and drafting a report which described why it was important, and how he and others could save it. By the time the effort was fully underway, he was an expert on the Woods and was its single most important promoter. In addition, he was careful to document each aspect of the project's progress.

Formigli then began enlisting the support of area residents and assembled a team of talented and savvy Township residents from a variety of backgrounds. Formigli and his partners engaged in a bipartisan effort to garner support from all the town's residents. He contacted some of the region's best-known experts and solicited letters of support for his efforts. He began to contact other groups, both regional and national, to see how the property could be saved and acquired. Formigli researched funding sources and how the ownership of the property could be accomplished without purchasing it, especially since, when he first started, Township officials were reluctant to accept ownership.

The effort to save the Woods was not an easy one, and in fact, was long and complicated. As with all such endeavors, some of the work of the supporters led to dead ends, but at the project's conclusion most of those efforts turned out to be fruitful but required determination, grit and patience. But first they had to decide what the future of the Woods might look like, ascertain if the community would support the project, and how to guide the effort through a complicated acquisition process.

THE STRATEGY TO SAVE THE WOODS

When the idea of saving the Woods was first proposed, there were a number of challenges. The first piece of this complex puzzle was to determine which parts of the Woods could be saved from development by using zoning tools, and which parts could be acquired. They also needed to decide which parts of the Woods might be expendable in order to save other parts.

Advocates needed to deal with the fact that developers already had plans on the table in the Five Mile Woods. To preserve those outlying areas of the Woods where development was under way would require using the leverage of the open space laws already on the books.

The next challenge was to decide which parts of the Woods needed the special protection afforded by acquisition. At a meeting of the project's most important advocates in early 1976, a determination was made that the two strategic parcels at the center of the Woods would need to be acquired. These were the Penn Central tract and adjacent Cutler tract. Another related issue was how the property would be managed after its acquisition, whether it be by a non-profit or a local government agency.

Most critically, however, there needed to be a way to fund the efforts because, as was ultimately borne out, the purchase of the land became an expensive proposition. At the time, there were a number of potential funding sources available but they all were extremely competitive, and required complicated application processes. For example, a federal grant program required that its funding be matched by a state or locality. There was also the Commonwealth's Project 70 and Project 500 grant funding that was available to develop recreational resources during this time. There was however, a local funding alternative that existed and which allowed the Township's Board of Supervisors to levy a local tax specifically for recreational purposes.[60]

When the efforts began in 1973-74, the Township's supervisors did not want to own the Woods, instead thinking that national, state, or county agencies were better equipped to handle such a task. They did not believe Lower Makefield Township had the financial capability to purchase them. The Township's supervisors believed that the local taxpayers should not be burdened with paying for the land purchase. In time, the membership of the Board of Supervisors changed its position and the citizenry expressed their approval for the acquisition of Five Mile Woods on three different occasions. This included overwhelming support demonstrated in two different surveys, and one voting referendum, held in 1978, which included authorizing a bond issue to purchase the Woods which also called for raising local taxes. More funding was found through a federal land program.

All of these complicated issues were intertwined and required a flexible strategy of dealing with the challenges that needed to be managed, in some cases with immediate action, and in others with long range thinking.

NOBODY REALLY KNOWS BECAUSE IT'S NOT REALLY BEEN TRIED

While the practice of preserving important natural and historic sites was long established, there were a variety of ways to save them for future generations. The first method was to purchase the property outright by either a government agency or not-for-profit organization or a combination thereof. While attractive, and offering the best protection, this could be and often was, prohibitively expensive. In Bucks County, this was particularly the case because land values rose rapidly due to the development pressure. For most small municipalities, the idea of purchasing open space was an onerous proposition because of the need to also worry about maintaining the property in the future. This was the case in Lower Makefield Township.[61]

During the early 1970s, innovative tools became available to community activists to preserve special places that did not require purchase. One example was the transfer of development rights from a developer, or property owner, to a government entity or non-profit organization. This was a new and untested idea in 1972, but became a common method to save open space and farmland after 1975. Instead of owning the land directly, a conservation easement was placed on the property and the owner was paid to not develop the property. This was considerably cheaper to accomplish and allowed the property to stay on the tax rolls, even if at a lower assessed value. Also, the owner could continue his use of the property. For example, a farmer could continue farming his land with the easement in place, a desired outcome.[62]

Another option was for a developer to give up all or some of his rights on one property and transfer them to another in the Township where a zoning change might be needed. This tool was not without critics who believed that this only forced undesired higher density development. Some planners supported this technique as a means to encourage the preservation of open space and limit sprawl.[63]

Another strategy used, and this was the case in Lower Makefield's land development ordinance, required builders to set aside a certain percentage of open space when developing a property. The Township adopted, with the PRB's support, a *fee-in-lieu-of payment* system that developers paid to the Township if they did not have areas of open space to set aside. The monies were placed into the Township's maintenance fund for future recreational projects and facilities. Previously, only developers who were building townhouses or multifamily projects needed to do this. But, in 1976, a revision of the fee-in-lieu-of payment ordinance was passed that included all subdivisions. This tool was used not only in Bucks County, but elsewhere the Commonwealth where residential and commercial development was heating up.[64]

A final option was that a landowner could simply donate his land to a non-profit organization or government agency and receive a federal tax deduction.[65]

But first, supporters had to determine how much the Woods were worth, based on assessed values. Early on, the group did not even know what the values were of most critical parcels of the Woods. Lloyd Klatzkin, a Township Supervisor, said as much when asked how much it would cost to purchase those parcels at a meeting. At the time, in 1974, he estimated the land might be worth a half million to a million dollars. He also suggested:

That's a guess. Nobody really knows because nobody's really tried.[66]

The third hurdle, and perhaps the most difficult challenge to overcome, was the simple fact of money. At the time the project was first conceived in late 1974, the Township's supervisors did not know whether local taxpayers even supported the purchase of open space and whether they would be willing to increase their taxes to accomplish the preservation of it. This issue, of how to fund the acquisition of the Woods, was a difficult one to overcome. It took many hours of meetings, contacts, discussions, and even a referendum before it was finally resolved.

WE ENDORSE YOUR ACTIVITIES

Several prominent and significant supporters were enlisted in the effort to save the Five Mile Woods. They wrote letters of support, lobbied agencies, and lent their voices to the effort. They included, among others; Dr. Edgar Wherry, a botanist with a national reputation; Robert Pierson, the executive director of the Bucks County Conservancy; Oliver Stark, the Pennsylvania Historical and Museum Commission's (PHMC) botanist at the Bowman's Hill Wildflower Preserve (BHWP); George Carmichael, the president of the Bucks County Audubon Society; U.S. Congressman Peter Kostmayer; and James Wright, an influential member of the Pennsylvania House of Representatives.

One of the first support letters was written by Oliver Stark. He was a professionally trained botanist, and during a long career at Washington Crossing, worked at the Bowman's Hill Wildflower Preserve (BHWP). His tenure was marked by his ability to successfully straddle the worlds of both the PHMC and the BHWP. He was a well-regarded and effective leader who served as the park's botanist from 1966-84. He served as the acting site administrator of the Crossing park in 1979 and 1980.[67]

Stark wrote the following, in his official capacity as the park's botanist and assistant superintendent, on April 25, 1974:

Five Mile Woods (is) a prime example of mature coastal plain oak-beech forest. To our knowledge it is only one of two remaining in Lower Bucks County. As such it is the undisturbed habitat for rare, herbaceous plants, particularly the pink lady slipper orchid and the whorled pogonia. Also in this area is a rare sphagnum moss habitat . . . It is our belief that unique habitats such as this need to be preserved for their representative natural plant and animal life.[68]

Another person with a tie to the Bowman's Hill Wildflower Preserve who was helpful in the Woods effort was David Benner. He was Oliver Stark's predecessor, having served as the Preserve's botanist from 1956-66. It was through his professional connections that he introduced Dr. Edgar Wherry to Donald Formigli. Benner also prepared a short report of his views of the Woods.[69]

Dr. Edgar Wherry was the most significant ally of these early efforts to gather support. His professional reputation was one of a regional, statewide and national stature. Dr. Wherry had been the Professor of Botany at the University of Pennsylvania and had a productive and remarkable career that included a prolific legacy of books and articles. He was one of America's premier naturalists. Not only did he have expertise in the area's geology, but he was also well-versed in the region's plants.[70]

His interests led him into a variety of careers as an educator, mineralogist, crystallographer, horticulturist and museum curator. Wherry received a degree in chemistry and then went on to earn a doctorate in mineralogy. One of the founders and a past president of the American Mineralogical Society, he served as editor of *The American Mineralogist*. In addition, he was a self-taught botanist.

He had many honors bestowed upon him and his discoveries included three species of plants that bear his name: the *Tiarella wherryi*, *Spilene wherryi*, and the *Dryopteris wherryi*, a fern. He also discovered the mineral Wherryite. During his long career, he had even worked with Thomas Edison, and by the time he arrived to help the cause of the Five Mile Woods, he had led a noteworthy life.[71]

Locally, he also played a critical role in the creation of the Bowman's Hill Wildflower Preserve in 1934. He was one of the five founding members of the Preserve that became the inspiration for many others across the nation. He served as the chairman of the executive committee that provided the necessary leadership and technical assistance when it was created in the 1930s and would remain involved for decades after that.[72]

During the decade of the 1950s, three hundred species had been established in the BHWP. Bowman's Hill even began to create mini-environments by placing bathtubs in the ground and filling them with various kinds of soil. The idea, a brainstorm of Dr. Wherry, was brought to realization in 1963 when eleven

Courtesy Five Mile Woods Preserve
Donald Formigli Collection

Dr. Edgar Wherry at the Five Mile Woods in 1975.

bathtubs were given to the Preserve to create these special planting habitats. Today his legacy remains in the form of the Wherry Trail, and his portrait that still hangs in the Headquarters Building.[73]

His support letter for the Five Mile Woods of December 20, 1974 was an important one. He wrote:

In the course of my botanical-ecological research, I have explored that area (the Five Mile Woods) thoroughly and have been impressed by the large number of rare and otherwise notable trees, shrubs, and lesser native plants growing there. It constitutes about the only remaining considerable-sized area where Coastal-plain vegetation remains in

Pennsylvania, and its loss would be a scientific-conservation tragedy.[74]

Wherry visited the Woods in the summer of 1975 with Donald Formigli. At the time his health was not good, and so Formigli went to a nursing home in Philadelphia to pick him up, and brought Wherry back after their meeting. It was probably his last visit to the Woods before his passing in 1982.[75]

George Carmichael became another advocate for the Woods. He had previously published two articles in the December 1974 and the February 1975 issues of the Bucks County Audubon Society's newsletter entitled *A Natural History of Lowest Bucks County.* They provided data that assisted the preservation efforts, and even today, remain a classic piece of research still cited.[76]

Carmichael, representing the Bucks County Audubon Society, penned an important letter of support on April 3, 1975. He wrote:

It is with considerable pleasure that in the name of the Bucks County Audubon Society I endorse your activities, in concert with the Bucks County Conservancy, to preserve the remnants of the Five Mile Woods ecosystem.[77]

Another local expert and supporter of the efforts to save the Woods was Dr. Ann Rhoads, a resident of Lower Makefield Township. At the time, she was working at the Morris Arboretum of the University of Pennsylvania, having started in 1976. She was responsible for the editing and publication of the *Atlas of the Flora of Pennsylvania* by Dr. Wherry, Jack Fogg and Herbert Wahl. She initiated the Pennsylvania Flora Database project and as a result published *The Vascular Flora of Pennsylvania, Annotated Checklist and Atlas* along with William Klein. In the years that followed she had a distinguished career with many accomplishments.[78]

Two other important and early advocates central to finding funding at the federal level included Peter Kostmayer, U.S. Congressman and Democrat from Bucks County. He supported the purchase of the Woods, and helped to procure part of the funding that was used for acquiring parts of the Preserve in 1980-82. Representative James Wright, a member of the Pennsylvania House of Representatives was another important supporter of the cause, and a powerful member of the House. Wright was an important advocate for a variety of programs including cultural, historic sites and historic preservation sponsored by the Pennsylvania Historical and Museum Commission.

THE CITIZENS SPEAK

It was clear from the letters of support that the experts who had knowledge about the importance of the geological and natural features of the Woods agreed on the necessity to save it. The next step was to ascertain whether that interest extended to the community that would have to pay for it, and in fact, support the entire recreation effort that was being considered. A survey was developed by the Open Space Committee that asked seven questions and solicited additional commentary. These were put into the form of a questionnaire and were handed out at five polling places in the Township on May 20, 1975, a primary election day.[79]

After the election, the results were tabulated and an overview was sent to the Board of Supervisors, and a number of groups who had been supporters, and advocates along with the regional media. Almost twelve hundred residents filled the forms out. The results were revealing as 87% of the respondents believed that the Township should have a parks and recreation program. Voters overwhelmingly thought that the Township should take ownership of natural areas like streams and floodplains. The most important priorities according to the survey were the creation of bicycle trails, acquisition of open space, tennis courts, a swimming pool, playgrounds and hiking trails.[80]

Numbers that proved critical to the Five Mile Woods effort was that 84% of those who responded thought that the Township should acquire open space, and 86% said it should provide recreational facilities. An overwhelming percentage also believed that the Township should accept land that was given to it by developers and maintain it. Almost 80% stated that they would vote for a Park and Recreation tax of two mills, or $25 per house assessed at $50,000.[81]

Several months after the survey three work groups were formed to address the needs that were revealed in the results of the survey. A bike path group was created to develop a plan, another to consider the building of tennis courts and managing them, and a third for open space.[82]

On the political level, by 1975, a decidedly anti-development sentiment became the central campaign issues for the fall elections. Candidates at all levels - local, county, and state - supported open space policies. In Lower Makefield this was welcome news because one of the candidates, Thomas Cowen, a Republican, offered a platform which stated that the Open Space Committee should come up with an open space master plan, encourage developers to set aside 20% of their land for open space, promote gifts of land, and have the township manager provide a report on various programs dealing with open space by the various government agencies.[83]

MARSHALLING THE EFFORT FORWARD

In addition to reaching out to prominent experts in the field and getting the views of the residents of Lower Makefield, Formigli began contacting various advocacy groups to enlist their support and advice including the National Wildlife Foundation, the Audubon Society, The Nature Conservancy, and the Bucks County Conservancy.

The Bucks County Conservancy was originally created in 1958 as the Bucks County Park Foundation with its main purpose to accept donations of land that

LOWER MAKEFIELD OPEN SPACE COMMITTEE

(A Non-Profit Organization of Concerned Lower Makefield Citizens)

1. Presently, with the exception of the ball fields across from the Township Bldg., all tennis courts and ball fields are provided by the public schools. Recent township budgets have allocated nothing to Parks & Recreation. Do you believe there should be a Parks & Recreation program in the township?

   _87%_ Yes   _11%_ No   _2%_ No opinion   _Total Responses = 1191_

2. What are your priorities for a Parks & Recreation program in Lower Makefield? Please limit your choice to 3 items.

   _646_ Bicycle trails   _122_ Meeting center   _474_ Acquire open space

   _297_ Hiking trails   _450_ Tennis courts   _191_ Ice skating rink

   _186_ Ball fields   _335_ Swimming pool   _33_ Absolutely nothing

   _287_ Playgrounds   ___ Other ___   _17_ Other ___

3. Many proposed developments in Lower Makefield have areas of streams and adjacent flood plains which cannot be built on. These areas are sometimes offered to our Township at no cost other than annual maintenance. They could be kept as natural wild areas. Do you think our township should accept ownership of this type of area?

   _86%_ Yes   _7%_ No   _7%_ No opinion   _Total Responses = 1194_

4. Do you think facilities and open space provided by developers should be owned and maintained by our township for use by every resident, or should they be owned and maintained by a neighborhood association and restricted for their use only?

   _57%_ Township owned   _35%_ Neighborhood owned   _8%_ No opinion   _Total Responses = 1140_

5. Would you favor our township budget including money for:

   a. acquiring open space? _84%_ Yes   _16%_ No _Total Responses = 1046_

   b. providing recreational facilities? _86%_ Yes   _14%_ No   _Total Responses = 1030_.

6. How much does your family spend per year on recreation at local private facilities? Please specify the type of facility.

7. Township supervisors presently have authority to levy a tax of up to 2 mils for Parks & Recreation. A 2 mil tax is $25 on a home selling for $50,000 and would provide approximately $76,000 per year on the present tax base. Would you vote for a referendum for a Parks & Recreation tax? _79%_ Yes _21%_ No   _Total Responses = 1138_

8. Additional comments and/or suggestions are welcomed on the back of this sheet. Thank you.

   (If you are interested in becoming active in the Lower Makefield Open Space Committee, please write your name, address and phone number on the back of this sheet.)

Courtesy Five Mile Woods Preserve
Donald Formigli Collection

The final tally from the voter survey conducted on May 20, 1975.

were to be preserved. By 1978, it was four hundred members strong and was the most important preservation organization in the county. It had taken control of five hundred acres of land. Led by Robert Pierson, its executive director, the offices of the organization were located at 33 West Court Street in Doylestown. At the time of the Woods efforts, Pierson, previously a paid executive, was working as a volunteer executive director. Prior to that, he was the executive director of the Bucks County Park Board during the 1950s and 1960s.[84]

The group's initial interest was in land preservation, but Pierson expanded its focus to include saving historic structures. The group established the Bucks County Register of Historic Places in 1974. Research discovered that the county had as many as twelve thousand historic sites that were one hundred years or older. Of those, two hundred and fifty were listed on the county register and then nominated to the National Register of Historic Places. Seven historical organizations were brought into existence with the Conservancy's guidance. Other environmental groups used the Conservancy's legal standing.[85]

In late 1974, Formigli established a partnership with the Bucks County Conservancy that would serve the Woods project well. This organization was his single most important non-profit ally. That November, Lloyd Klatzkin, a Township supervisor, Donald Formigli, Dan Rattigan and Robert Pierson met to discuss the Five Mile Woods. In addition, they talked about a twenty-five acre parcel of property along the Sandy Run Creek near a Toll Brothers residential development project. With that meeting began a productive relationship.[86]

Working with the Conservancy from 1975-76, Donald Formigli prepared a report on the Five Mile Woods for the organization with the help of George Carmichael, David Benner, John Lovrinic and Jean Seglem. Entitled *Five Mile Woods, Lower Makefield & Falls Townships Bucks County, Pennsylvania: A Brief Summary of the Natural Features and a Proposal to Protect the Area*, this twenty-three page report provided detailed information about the Woods' natural significance along with maps, land ownership, soil and water data, and a listing of animals and birds. It also included the support letters he had previously received from Edgar Wherry, Oliver Stark and George Carmichael and his two-part series of articles entitled *A Natural History of Lowest Bucks County*.[87]

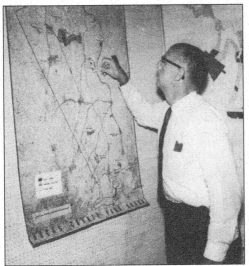

Courtesy Heritage Conservancy
Robert Pierson
1961

The report was an important promotional piece for the Woods and its preservation. It was distributed to a variety of individuals and organizations involved in open space preservation. All of the neighboring developers, township managers, Bucks County Planning Commission, and libraries received copies. The regional media were sent copies of the report. It was also sent to the officials of the Penn Central as they were considering its options regarding its tract.

Articles regularly appeared in the Conservancy's newsletters, and soon, Robert Pierson was contacting various groups to garner support and assistance. In reflecting on the project at one point in 1976 he believed, as some others did in Lower Makefield, that the Bucks County Conservancy was actually best suited to own the land, but unfortunately, they did not have the financial resources to do so.[88]

Another important ally to the project, which had been made possible by Pierson's wide range of contacts, was The Nature Conservancy. This organization had been involved in saving many significant parcels across the country since 1951. It had a national reach and a large membership, and its president, Patrick Noonan, attended a Bucks County Conservancy dinner in 1975 during which the Woods were discussed. At the dinner, he assured Lloyd Klatzkin that it could be saved. The Woods project came under the jurisdiction of the Eastern Regional Office, and its director, Bradford Northrup. Like Pierson, he used his contacts and offered important advice to move the project forward. He attended several important meetings and toured the property even though his office was in Boston.[89]

The Bucks County Audubon Society, while providing a letter of support, also sent representatives to meetings and tours of the property.

Word spread about the ongoing effort to save the Woods. On December 1, 1976, Robert Rodale, the president of Rodale Press in Emmaus, Pennsylvania, received a letter from a realtor, William Veitch. Veitch wrote that he understood the significance of the Woods and was inquiring if there might be some way that the property be acquired and saved given its unique characteristics. He was searching for a way to have an individual or corporate donor purchase the property, take it off the market and give it to a non-profit organization such as the Lehigh Valley Conservancy. A copy of the letter was sent to Formigli by the Lehigh Valley organization.[90]

A Powerful Advocate: The Park and Recreation Board

It was the Lower Makefield Township's Park and Recreation Board (PRB) that proved to be the most powerful advocate for the Woods. Because of Donald Formigli's position as the chairman, he and his board members had the responsibility, on behalf of the Township, to review development plans, determine how much open space was needed to be set aside for each project, and to make recommendations to the Lower Makefield Township Board of Supervisors as part of a typical project's approval. They closely coordinated their activities with the Board of Supervisors and representatives attended their meetings.[91]

The fight to save the Woods went on against a backdrop of many projects coming before the PRB for review, a myriad of recreation issues to settle, and finally planning for the Township's future recreation needs. On one night alone, November 3, 1977, at the height of the development boom, the PRB had eleven subdivision plans on its agenda. Despite all those concerns, the preservation of the Woods became an important priority and the board made a concerted effort to save the Woods from being broken up and developed piecemeal. Between 1976 and late 1978, when the first parcel of the Woods was purchased by the Township, the PRB undertook a number of actions in support of saving the Woods through its regulatory power.[92]

For example, in early 1976, as the Makefield Oak, Inc. residential development project was making its way through the planning process, the PRB wanted to preserve the portion of the Woods that was situated within its boundaries. This parcel was particularly important because it included the headwaters of the Queen Anne Creek that lay on the northern side of the Big Oak Road. There was added concern because at the time it was thought by advocates that it may have been a habitat for the bog turtle, an endangered species. A meeting was held with Herbert Burstein, the developer, and his engineers, and the headwaters, along with additional open space, was preserved, protected by a conservation easement. It remains undeveloped today as a wetland.[93]

There were negotiations with representatives from William Shender, Inc., the Cutler family, and Arthur Doyle, representing Independence Development, in an effort to save as much of the Woods as possible. With a final agreement and approval for Doyle's plans pending at the end of 1978, the PRB requested that it be allowed to remove endangered plants from the Independence Square lots before construction began there. The development endured several delays, and was not built until years later.[94]

The move to create the Township ordinance related only to the Woods, began in late 1976 with assistance from the Bucks County Conservancy and culminated with the passage of the Conservation Cluster Ordinance on July 25, 1977. The ordinance allowed developers to donate land for open space and in turn build at a higher density, and more specifically, was directed towards the Cutler parcel and the deal that the Township was trying to negotiate with the developer.

As the various development projects came closer to being approved, it looked like the Penn Central parcel would be developed. Ragan and Stein Associates, a planning firm representing the railroad company, presented a proposal to the PRB in the fall of 1977 to create a Five Mile Woods Preservation Zone so that the company's property development rights could be sold by the company. This might save the Woods, but would also create increased density in R1 and R2 zones elsewhere in the Township.[95]

The Township's Board of Supervisors took another critical step on March 28, 1978 when it downzoned parts of the Woods from R-3 to R-1. This lessened the density with which the parts of the Woods not already under development could be accomplished. It also lessened the value of the developer's lands including Penn Central's and the Cutlers. While it was believed by some that this ordinance to limit how many houses could be built in the Woods would be challenged in court, its more immediate impact was that it delayed any project in the most critical sections of the Five Mile Woods and bought the Township more time. Indeed, the action did create legal challenges for the Township as lawsuits were filed.[96]

When They Say, it is not About the Money, It's About the Money

The biggest hurdle, after deciding who was going to own the critical parcels of the Woods, and under what circumstances, was to find the money to purchase it if the tracts were to be owned by the Township. It quickly became apparent in meetings between the Bucks County Conservancy and other like-minded groups that there was little easily obtained grant funding available for such an acquisition at any level of government. During a series of meetings with officials of the Bucks County Audubon Society, The Nature Conservancy, and Bucks County Conservancy, it was also revealed that none of groups had the ability to buy the property. The Nature Conservancy however offered a loan to purchase the property. This necessitated Lower Makefield Township having to pay the loan back within three years, and to create a plan that assured the funding could be raised locally. It was clear that the community was going to have to raise the money itself to purchase the Woods by either donations or raising taxes.[97]

The consortium of the various individuals at the Township, county and regional levels, labored on. Formigli gave tours of the site for various officials of organizations who had been contacted. Consideration was given to having a new development zone created for the Woods. Robert Pierson met with, and then suggested to the regional office of the Pennsylvania Department of Community Affairs, that the Bucks County Conservancy formally apply for acquisition monies.[98]

In late 1976, Pierson reported to the Department of Community Affairs that he had compiled a preliminary estimate of the values of the properties that included the Woods. For the first time since the effort began, there were finally figures to demonstrate what amount of funding was needed, what properties might be reasonably acquired, and what parcels might be donated and given to the Conservancy.

The 1976 values for each property are listed in the chart that follows:

Tax Parcel Number	Owner FT – Falls Township LMT – Lower Makefield Township	Acres	Price per Acre	Cost
13-3-9-5	Penn Central (FT)	37.60	$4,000	
20-32-45	Penn Central (LMT)	115.33	$4,000	-
13-3-8	Penn Central (FT)	9.69	$4,000	$650,480
20-32-46	Cutler (LMT)	45.23	$12,000	$542,760
13-3-10	Guzikowski (Partial) (FT)	35.00	$5,000	$175,000
20-32-47	Shendor (Partial) (LMT)	5.00	$12,000	$60,000
20-32-28	Broadnix (LMT)	5.00	$12,000	$60,000
20-32-29, 32, 33, 35	Independence Development (LMT)	20.00	$12,000	$240,000
20-32-30	Deas (LMT)	5.00	$12,000	$60,000
20-32-31	Conrad (LMT)	5.00	$12,000	$60,000
20-32-34	Hicker (LMT)	4.84	$12,000	$58,000
13-10-1	Sadowski (FT)	20.00	$10,000	$200,000
	Total	307.69		$2,106.240 [99]

At the time that Pierson compiled his report, he wrote that the Cutler tract owners along with William Shendor, Inc., had agreed to donate parcels of land and that the Independence Development, and the Guzikowski and Sadowski families were also considering donating land to the Conservancy. Two other property owners, Mary Banko, a property owner along Big Oak Road (Tax Parcel Number 20-32-43) and Laura and James Foulds, owners of the neighboring property, (Tax Parcel Number 20-32-44) were approached by Dan Rattigan, a Township Supervisor, to see if they might be interested in preserving their land with conservation easements. Both lots were small but the Woods extended across the southern half of each of them.[100]

As this potential deal was beginning to form, Pierson wrote:

The Five Mile Woods offers the opportunity for two townships to cooperate in a venture not only to purchase land but to maintain it and carry on outdoor recreation programs there. The Cutler tract could be used for this purpose.[101]

Unfortunately, Pierson's estimated values were far lower than what Penn Central actually wanted for its land which complicated the possibilities of acquisition considerably. On May 22, 1976, a sign was posted on the Penn Central property by BAC Realty located in Morrisville, listing the 162 acres at $12,500 an acre or $2,025,000 for the whole parcel.[102]

Whatever the actual value of the Penn Central property, the fate of the Woods project still hinged on what would happen with that parcel. If that could not be acquired, the rest of the deal would probably come apart.[103]

Pierson pushed on with contacts at the Bureau of Outdoor Recreation, a federal agency, which resulted in what, in hindsight, turned out, to be a critical strategy meeting on April 14, 1977. At the meeting were officials from the Bucks County Conservancy, The Nature Conservancy's Eastern Regional office, Lower Makefield Township officials, Falls Township officials, representatives of the U.S. Bureau of Outdoor Recreation, the Pennsylvania Department of Community Affairs, and a representative of U.S. Congressman, Peter Kostmayer. Kostmayer had a long-standing interest in the activities of the Conservancy and would play an important role in preserving the Woods. [104]

It was the most important meeting held to date because all of the principals were represented. Among the items discussed, was the need to have a local fundraising component used as a match to obtain federal revenue sharing funds through the Bureau of Outdoor Recreation. There was also a need to get a price from Penn Central for their land. It was a number that was central to the calculus of purchasing as much of the Woods as possible.[105]

Prior to the meeting, representatives of the Bucks County Conservancy met with representatives of the Victor Palmieri and Company, the agents for the Penn Central Transportation Company, where it was revealed that Penn Central was having the value of the property assessed at the same time.[106]

Pierson was determined to move the project forward, and made regular contact with the agencies and various individuals involved. He continued to work with the Pennsylvania Department of Community Affairs. It was that contact that ultimately led to the receipt of a major grant for the acquisition of a part of the Woods by Lower Makefield Township.[107]

FOR SALE: THE WOODS

In 1973, the Penn Central Transportation Company hired Victor Palmieri and Company to create plans to lease, sell, or develop its myriad listing of properties. The company, based in Los Angeles, made millions of dollars resolving the complicated web of the railroad's non-operating properties including the Five Mile Woods. It hired Lower Makefield resident Rick Ragan, an architect with the firm of Ragan and Stein Associates, to evaluate the Five Mile Woods tract for possible development. He had served as a consultant on other local projects including a natural resource inventory.[108]

The final study concluded that Penn Central could build four hundred and thirty units of housing on the property. A conceptual drawing was created that included two named streets: Penn Treaty Drive and Queen Anne Circle.[109]

Courtesy Five Mile Woods Preserve
Donald Formigli Collection

Two of the most important parcels within the Five Mile Woods were located at its center. They were the Penn Central and Cutler tracts. Combined, the development of these two properties had the potential for 600 new homes.

In the spring of 1976, Penn Central Transportation Company, through its agent, Victor Palmieri and Company, placed *For Sale* signs on the property. This raised alarm bells for the various stakeholders who wanted to see the property preserved, including Robert Pierson. Pierson wrote a letter to Judge John Fullam of the United States District Court in Philadelphia appealing to him to find a way to let the property be preserved. Fullam was overseeing the dispersal of the bankrupt company's assets, large and small. Unfortunately for those supporting the project, the bankrupt company's assets could not be donated; they had to be sold. Pierson met with Allan Lipsky, Regional Vice President and Administrator for Victor Palmieri and Company to discuss the situation.[110]

Once again in the summer of 1977, new *For Sale* signs went up on the property. Representative Peter Kostmayer wrote to the U.S. Secretary of Transportation to see if an environmental impact statement would be required. This new posting again raised concerns among the stakeholders after the important April 14 meeting as a grand deal seemed to be within the grasp of the leaders of

THE FIVE MILE WOODS PRESERVE: A HISTORY

the Woods preservation efforts. In late 1977, representatives from Penn Central and the adjacent Cutler property owners met to discuss the Woods with the Park and Recreation Board. PC's agents proposed they be given development rights elsewhere in the Township. For that, the company would pay a fee that would go into a trust fund to purchase the railroad's land.[111]

Of the proposal, Township supervisor Lloyd Klatzkin said:

I think Penn Central is going out of their way to save the Woods.[112]

However, the company's development plans proceeded forward because of continued pressure from the bankruptcy court to shed its assets. At the February 2, 1978 Park and Recreation Board meeting, the company's plans for the development were placed on the agenda for the first time. The sketch plan included not only the Lower Makefield tract but the Falls tracts and included 288 single attached family homes (duplexes) and 124 detached family homes. One month later, they submitted a sketch plan that showed four hundred and thirty building lots for single family houses. This was probably done in part to put the Township on notice that, if it did not act in a timely way, the company would move forward with its plans.[113]

WE RESOLVE TO PURCHASE THE WOODS

The effort to save the Woods reached a critical point in late 1977 and early 1978 that required decisions be made that would finally resolve the impasse that had developed. Once again, the Park and Recreation Board turned to the citizens to get their opinion on how much they were willing to pay for the services that a previous poll said that they wanted. On November 8, 1977, the *Park and Recreation Board Citizen Survey Forms* were collected at various polling booths by Pennsbury High School students. The survey asked local citizens to prioritize the recreational needs of the Township.

When the voting was tallied, the highest vote getter was the protection of the Five Mile Woods, followed by the preservation of streams and woodlands, bike paths, a Township swimming pool, tennis courts and ball fields. The results showed that six hundred families were willing to pay an annual fee of $125 for the use of a community pool and one thousand voters were willing to pay between $25 and $50 annually for a tennis court fee. In all, twenty-eight hundred forms were turned in. With that impressive support, the Park and Recreation Board resolved to implement their action plan.[114]

On January 5, 1978, the PRB voted to make a series of formal recommendations to the Township's Board of Supervisors to acquire the File Mile Woods and rezone it. The draft report, prepared by Chairman Donald Formigli, proposed that the Township acquire one hundred and eighty acres. Included in the report was the rationale behind each purchase. The largest purchase was the Penn Central tract (Tax Parcel Number 20-32-45) of one hundred and fifteen acres. This tract included sections of both the Piedmont Plateau and Coastal Plain, the Fall Line, Queen Anne Creek, unusual and rare plants, and the eighteenth century Dark house foundation. The resolution also recommended that a moratorium be placed on the pending development plans, and that the Woods be rezoned to a lower density.[115]

There were two other smaller tracts that Penn Central owned but were not considered for acquisition because they were in Falls Township. The first of those tracts, Falls Township Tax Parcel Number 13-9-5, contained an open field and abutted the yet unfinished Route 1. The second tract, designated Tax Parcel Number 13-9-8, was a sliver of land that also abutted Route 1 and included a short section of the Fall Line. These Falls Township tracts included a total of forty-seven acres.[116]

The next major proposed acquisition was the Cutler Tract (Tax Parcel Number 20-32-46, 46-1, 46-2, 46-3, 46-4) which included five parcels totaling forty-five acres. It included a house, a sphagnum moss wetland, the Queen Anne Creek, an oak-beech forest, and rare and endangered plants. Four other parcels were included in the listing (Tax Parcel Number 20-32-28, 20-32-29, 20-32-30 and 20-32-31) that were each five acres in size and included parts of the Fall Line. At the time, they were vacant and had previously been used as wood lots.[117]

Included in the recommendation was additional information on the Cutler tracts, which was sandwiched between the Penn Central tract and Cambridge Estates. Its purchase was considered necessary because if only ten of the forty-five acres were developed as proposed, the runoff from the homes created the potential for damage in the neighboring microenvironment.[118]

There were two reports that supported the purchase of these one hundred eighty acres including the Bucks County Conservancy plan (1975), and a more recently completed study of the Penn Central tract by Ragan and Stein Associates. It demonstrated the importance of the tract as a natural resource. Another important justification cited was the Pennsylvania State Constitution that enabled local Townships to protect their natural resources.[119]

The PRB's recommendation asked the Township manager to draw up a plan to purchase the property, and that a moratorium on development plans for those one hundred eighty acres be put in place. A third recommendation was that the Woods, or at least those one hundred eighty acres, be rezoned for low density housing at one house per acre. While the board realized that it was likely to be challenged in court, it was hoped that a solution to the future preservation of the Woods could be found before then.

Lastly, the board recommended that the plans for the Cutler tract on the north side of the Big Oak Road be approved. While there had been a complicated relationship with the Cutlers, it was also believed that the size of the acreage on the northern side was not as critical to save as the land on the south side. To the PRB, this trade-off was worth it as it required that the Cutlers enter into an agreement with the Bucks County Conservancy for the lands on the south side of Big Oak Road. This allowed their development plans for the northern side to move ahead.[120]

After more than four years of debate, discussions, meetings, planning and negotiations, a viable plan for a nature preserve which would include more than half of the Five Mile Woods, was on the table. The saving of the Woods had come to a critical point as almost all of the parcels included in the Woods were in some stage of development. It was now or never for the Township to purchase the property outright or make some other accommodation. The PRB felt that to purchase the property was the only way left to proceed and the resolution passed unanimously.

Chairman Formigli, in reflecting on the importance of the action, said:

After four years of trying this is our first real chance to save the Woods. And with all other means of preserving the Woods having proved unworkable, this may well be the only chance we'll ever get.[121]

One month later Formigli put forth a draft document called *Planning for the Future of the Woods* which was approved by the PRB and sent to the Supervisors.

THE VOTERS SPEAK AGAIN

Just eleven days after the PRB's recommendation of January 5, 1978 was presented to the Township supervisors, the governing body agreed to put the proposal to referendum. The date for the vote was scheduled for May 16, 1978. The board also authorized the Township manager to begin negotiations with the property owners, on behalf of the Township, to acquire their land and to have all of the details regarding the purchase available to the public before the referendum. Just two weeks later, *For Sale* signs appeared on the Penn Central property which played into the hands of the advocates to purchase the property.[122]

Immediately afterward, a group of residents established an ad hoc group called the Save Our Woods Committee. It immediately swung into action promoting the purchase of the Woods, building on the goodwill and support that had been previously garnered. The group first met on January 29, 1978, and Paul Rhoads and Carol Dubois agreed to serve as co-chairmen. In a gesture to make the effort bipartisan, Rhoads represented the local Democratic Committee and Dubois represented the local Republican Committee.[123]

The organizers of the effort to save the Woods, begun four years earlier, were savvy to the ways of the media and there was a constant stream of newspaper

Courtesy Five Mile Woods Preserve
Donald Formigli Collection

The Save Our Woods committee had a special logo created that it used on bumper stickers, t-shirts and brochures. The logo, designed by Harry Casterlin, continues to be used.

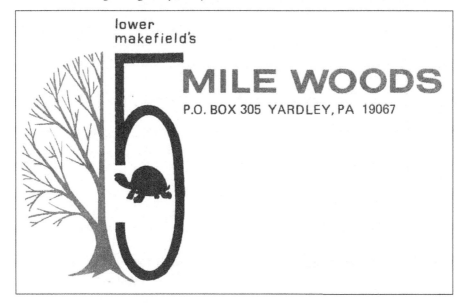

articles reporting on their activities. This was a critical component of the success of the venture. They began by meeting with various civic groups to gather information, create support and accept donations. At one of those meetings a survey was conducted with 75% of the those in attendance indicating they would pay more in taxes, averaging $25 on a $50,000 home, for open space and recreational facilities including bike trails and tennis courts.[124]

Armed with the knowledge they had of the community's support, the group pressed on. Their efforts took on many forms including guided walks of the Woods, traveling slide show programs that were given to a variety of civic, school, fraternal and religious organizations, a voter survey, participation in the political process, and media releases. A branding package was created that included a new distinctive logo, created by Harry Casterlin, a graphic designer and commercial

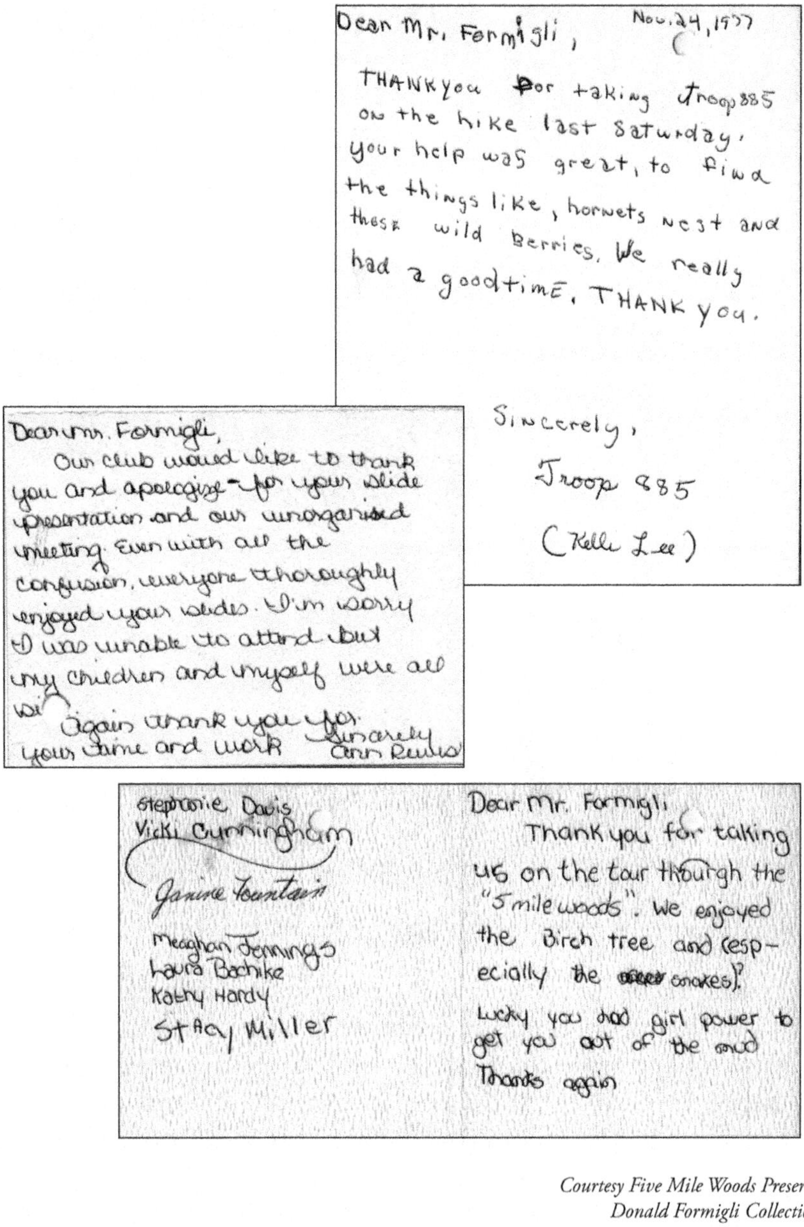

Dear Mr. Formigli,   Nov. 24, 1997

THANK you for taking Troop 885
on the hike last Saturday,
your help was great, to find
the things like, hornets nest and
these wild berries. We really
had a good time, THANK you.

Sincerely,

Troop 885

(Kelli Lee)

Dear Mr. Formigli,
    Our club would like to thank
you and apologize for your slide
presentation and our unorganized
meeting. Even with all the
confusion, everyone thoroughly
enjoyed your slides. I'm sorry
I was unable to attend but
my children and myself were all
sick. Again thank you for
your time and work   Sincerely
                       Ann Rewis

Stephanie Davis
Vicki Cunningham

Janine Fountain

Meaghan Jennings
Laura Bachike
Kathy Hardy
Stacy Miller

Dear Mr. Formigli,
    Thank you for taking
us on the tour through the
"5 mile woods". We enjoyed
the Birch tree and esp-
ecially the snakes!
Lucky you had girl power to
get you out of the mud
Thanks again

Courtesy Five Mile Woods Preserve
Donald Formigli Collection

In an effort to generate support to save the Five Mile Woods, public programs as well as hikes, were given to area organizations.

artist, which was used for bumper stickers and brochures supporting the referendum. A wine and cheese benefit was sponsored on April 9, 1978 to raise funds, in addition to 5K races, called the *5000 Meter Fun Run*. This program included a running event, bike ride, and walks in the Woods. Participants received t-shirts emblazoned with the Five Mile Woods logo.[125]

Between 1974-78, almost twenty-five presentations were made to organizations in Lower Makefield, Yardley, and Morrisville for young and old alike. These included the Democratic Club, the Republican Club, the Business and Professional Women's Club, the Yardley-Makefield Jaycees, Welcome Wagon, Questers, the Morris Arboretum, and the American Association of University Women (AAUW). Members of the AAUW came to be important advocates for the Woods.[126]

Guided walks were given regularly to promote the site and to allow local residents the ability to experience the Woods, and see why it was important to save. It was said that as a result of the walks at least one new discovery was made during each walk that added to the inventory of knowledge about the Woods. The walks were initially led by Don Formigli, and then by members of the Save Our Woods Committee.[127]

Courtesy Five Mile Woods Preserve
Donald Formigli Collection
Regularly scheduled hikes were given in the Five Mile Woods to generate support in saving it. At that time there were no formal trails or bridges built and so fording the Queen Anne Creek could be a little tricky for hikers.

Courtesy Five Mile Woods Preserve
Donald Formigli Collection

Area Scout groups took advantage of a new place to go hiking as the Save Our Woods Committee members led hikes on the Penn Central property. Volunteers provided not only excellent programs for the participants, but also helped to build local support. This hike took place in 1975.

Several slide programs were created for use in different settings. They were created by Formigli, Carol Dubois and Lynn Sims, and included slides taken at the Woods that illustrated what the Township was trying to save. There was a succinct narrative that also included a musical component. The slides featured beautiful and striking images of the Woods taken by Formigli.[128]

A Yardley and Morrisville native, Sims had been writing and performing songs about Bucks County and its beauty for years. A talented writer and performer, she came to be known as the *Bucks County Balladeer* with two albums to her credit. Sims's folk music, with its evocative lyrics, were always well received. The proceeds of the sales of her albums were donated to the Bucks County Conservancy. Sims taught geography and history at the high school level and had grown up in the county.[129]

Her popularity and the beauty of her albums caught the attention of Don Formigli, who in typical fashion, tried to reach her numerous times. Finally, he was successful and after having a discussion over dinner, along with a visit to the Woods, Sims was inspired to write two songs about the Woods.

In 1981, she recalled that in writing the first song that it was:

. . . a moving experience to walk through the Woods. I didn't sleep well that night. The next day I sat in that chair over there and wrote the song.[130]

The song, entitled *The Five Mile Woods*, became a theme song for the referendum efforts to promote and acquire the Woods and was performed for the first time on October 7, 1977 at the Township building.[131]

THE FIVE MILE WOODS
by
Lynn Sims

I walked last evening thru the quiet woods.
I saw the orchids rise above the leaves;
Watched the frogs lep o'er the stream,
And the deer go running through the green
Of the Five Mile Woods.

Oh why can't the orchids bloom forever.
Why can't the forest grow untouched.
But in the distance you can hear
The hammers and the dozers near.

There was a stream meandering upon its way
Beside the trees reaching to the sky;
Such lovely trees to walk beneath or
Sit beneath or dream beneath,
Now all concrete!

Oh rise ye sleeping people rise.
Oh speak ye silent people speak.
For then your words someone will hear,
And this woodland shall not disappear.

Then the orchids they shall bloom forever.
And the forest grow a century more,
And always there shall be this place
Of solitude and subtle grace.
This Five Mile Woods.
This Five Mile Woods.[132]

The second song written by Sims was entitled *The Queen Anne Creek* and its lyrics follow:

THE QUEEN ANNE CREEK
By
Lynn Sims

In Five Mile Woods as rain drops fall,
around the trees.
From springs and bogs the channels form,
Moving through the deep.
Cross under roadway waters leap,
and so begins the Queen Anne Creek.

The water snakes a twisting path
in soil as hard as clay.
In places wide and narrow,
and under fallen tree.
Water swelling, rising, spreading,
beyond the bounds of the Queen Anne Creek.

Spring banks are lined with flowers,
baneberry, daisies and ferns,
bright trout lilies, pale spring beauty.
Jack-in-the-pulpit and violets too.
Summer shade brings bright green grasses,
in Five Mile Woods, the Queen Anne blue.

Onward, southward moves the stream,
rocky ravine cut deep.
Here the creek cuts through the fall
dropping fifty feet.
Deep within the Five Mile Woods,
a trail along the Queen Anne Creek.[133]

For the Save Our Woods Committee and supporters of a preserve, the issue centered on money. In the referendum, the voters were asked if they would pay $25 more a year in taxes to preserve the Woods. At the time, Hank Miiller, a Township supervisor, published a Township newsletter that helped to promote the Woods, and included a financial analysis of the Woods acquisition. In appealing to the public, the committee and Miiller offered a detailed analysis of what the development would cost if it were allowed to proceed. While supporters of its development generally argued that it would be good for jobs, the community, the tax base, and the rights of private property owners to do what they wanted with their property, the figures revealed that the development would actually cost taxpayers more in the long run.[134]

If just two thousand of the proposed units in the R-3 zone were built, there would be almost nine hundred and fifty more students in the local schools and the need for thirty-one more classrooms. These were not one time expenses, but would have to be funded in the future as the expenses of building, maintaining the infrastructure and the hiring of teachers would only increase. The argument was made that it was cheaper to purchase the land for open space than to let it be developed, an argument that remains valid to this day. That did not even consider the intangible factor of the importance of open space to the community.[135]

A study, completed in the 1960s by Upper Makefield Township resident, Dr. Charlotte Dyer, showed that:

(Over a twelve-year period) a 115-acre farm, under the tax rate in Central Bucks County at the time generated enough taxes to result in a $6,480 surplus, but that 200 homes built on that land with an average of 2.7 children per family, meant a budget deficit of more than $3.9 million.[136]

As to the increase of $25 in one's annual tax bill, the committee engaged young people in the schools to make posters to be hung on clotheslines outside the polls on election day. One such poster featured what came to be known as the Oreo Cookie analogy. School children could make the sacrifice by eating one less pack of Oreo cookies a month for the year to make up the $25. Pictures of these and similar analogies, reminded voters that this was an investment in the future.[137]

As can be imagined, there was opposition to the proposal to buy the Woods. Those who did not want to see

Courtesy Five Mile Woods Preserve
Donald Formigli Collection

The southwestern corner of Lower Makefield Township, including the Five Mile Woods, was zoned R-3, or Residential, Single Family High Density. This could include single family homes or townhouses and there could be as many as four units per acre, a feature which was particularly attractive to developers. If the shaded areas were built out completely, there would be as many as 2,768 units of new housing.

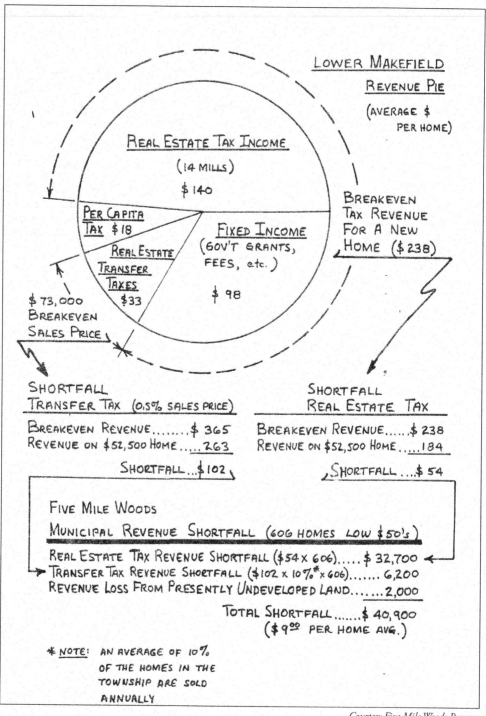

LOWER MAKEFIELD
REVENUE PIE

(AVERAGE $
PER HOME)

REAL ESTATE TAX INCOME
(14 MILLS)
$140

PER CAPITA
TAX $18

REAL ESTATE
TRANSFER
TAXES
$33

FIXED INCOME
(GOV'T GRANTS,
FEES, etc.)
$98

BREAKEVEN
TAX REVENUE
FOR A NEW
HOME ($238)

$73,000
BREAKEVEN
SALES PRICE

SHORTFALL
TRANSFER TAX (0.5% SALES PRICE)

BREAKEVEN REVENUE.......$365
REVENUE ON $52,500 HOME.....263

SHORTFALL...$102

SHORTFALL
REAL ESTATE TAX

BREAKEVEN REVENUE.....$238
REVENUE ON $52,500 HOME.....184

SHORTFALL...$54

FIVE MILE WOODS

MUNICIPAL REVENUE SHORTFALL (606 HOMES LOW $50's)

REAL ESTATE TAX REVENUE SHORTFALL ($54 x 606).....$32,700
TRANSFER TAX REVENUE SHORTFALL ($102 x 10%* x 606).......6,200
REVENUE LOSS FROM PRESENTLY UNDEVELOPED LAND.........2,000

TOTAL SHORTFALL.......$40,900
($9.00 PER HOME AVG.)

* NOTE: AN AVERAGE OF 10%
OF THE HOMES IN THE
TOWNSHIP ARE SOLD
ANNUALLY

Courtesy Five Mile Woods Preserve
Donald Formigli Collection

A comprehensive analysis of what a typical development actually cost the taxpayers was prepared by the Save Our Woods Committee and used in its public educational efforts.

the land purchased, described it as the *Green Elephant*. They believed that the Township was better off investing in a community park. The Woods would create delays in implementing the more broadly based recreation program. Their flyer stated that voters should *Stay Out of the Woods* and a letter to the editor made the same arguments. They also believed that all the possible options had not been explored.[138]

The supporters of the Woods effort also created their own flyers laying out the argument of why the bond should be passed including the arguments against development. On the reverse side of the flyer was the drawing of the proposed development of the Penn Central and Cutler tracts. They also answered criticisms from the opponents, that they had not looked for funding from other sources. These concerns were also answered in a letter to the editors of the local newspapers signed by Donald Formigli, Pat Fair, and Gail Hardesty eight days before the election.[139]

After months of lobbying and promoting the cause by the Save Our Woods Committee and its supporters, the residents of Lower Makefield Township went to the polls on May 16, 1978 to decide this question:

Should debt not to exceed the sum of $1,850,000 for the purpose of financing the acquisition of approximately 200 acres of ground known as The Five Mile Woods for use as park, recreation and open space areas be authorized to be incurred as debt approved by the electors of Lower Makefield Township? [140]

The citizenry voted overwhelmingly to approve the referendum to purchase the most critical tracts that made up the Five Mile Woods. Seventy percent voted in the affirmative. Bonding for the purchase was to be arranged after the election. What was equally remarkable about the passage of the referendum was that it had passed at the same time that the *People's Initiative to Limit Property Taxation*, or, California's *Proposition 13*, passed overwhelmingly just three weeks later on June 6, 1978.[141]

A Time to Celebrate

Negotiations with Palmieri began after the May referendum was approved by the voters. The land deal included not only the Lower Makefield tract, but the two Falls tracts as well. To implement the property transfer a complicated process requiring extended negotiations commenced as each part of the transaction was approved by the Trustees of Penn Central Transportation Company, the Township's solicitor, William Carlin, and the Lower Makefield Board of Supervisors. In addition, the approval of Judge John Fullam and the United States District Court in Philadelphia was needed. Fullam was overseeing the dispersal of the bankrupt company's assets, large and small.[142]

At long last, a sales agreement for the property was signed in November 1978 and an indenture for the tract, along with a quit claim deed, was agreed to between the two entities on December 11, 1978. The Penn Central Corporation, with its subsidiary, the Manor Real Estate Company, deeded 164.6 acres to Lower Makefield Township for $1,250,000. (Manor Real Estate was the same company that had put together the land transactions for U.S. Steel's Fairless Works in 1948-50.) A Resolution of Condemnation was passed by the Township's Board of Supervisors on January 2, 1979, and the purchase agreement was signed in February 14, 1979.[143]

The bond issue to purchase the Woods went on sale on February 5, 1979 and included the funding needed to purchase the Cutler tracts and build the municipal swimming pool. The thirty-year bond, amounting to $2.6 million, was ultimately paid off. The tax rate to support the debt was, as the members of the PRB and the Save Our Woods committee predicted: 2.50 mills.[144]

While Falls Township had not participated financially in the purchase of the Penn Central tract, it had supported the effort. Almost fifty acres of the Penn Central property was in Falls Township, and without its purchase by Lower Makefield, the parcels would have been landlocked. Penn Central also wanted to sell the entire tract and not still own those fifty acres. Falls Township had been working on its own open space programs for some time before this.

After three years of hard work by a group of community leaders, volunteers, not-for-profits, elected officials, and two townships, the most significant section of the Five Mile Woods was saved. From this initial acquisition, and subsequent purchases, came the Preserve that exists today.

On February 4, 1979, a little less than two months after the sales agreement was signed by Penn Central and the Township, there was a celebratory program sponsored by Lower Makefield Park and Recreation Board. It featured all the major players in the effort to date and was a time to celebrate. Attendees of the program saw an exhibition of photographs taken by local residents of the Woods over several years. The exhibit was coordinated by Hank Miiller, a Township supervisor, and Pat Fair, a member of the Township's PRB. Among the other features of the day was a musical program presented by Lynn Sims and coordinated with a slide show. She sang her ballads about the Five Mile Woods to begin and end the program.[145]

Consultant Rick Ragan spoke because of his interesting connection to the Preserve property. Carol Dubois and Paul Rhoads, the co-chairmen of the Save Our Woods Committee, presented a special painting of the Woods to the citizens of Lower Makefield thanking them for their approval of the referendum. The painting, by George Ivers, still hangs in the Township building.[146]

Gail Hardesty, who soon became the first president of a successor organization called the Friends of the Five Mile Woods, spoke about her group's plans.

John Carson closed the program out with a presentation that considered the Preserve in a larger regional context.[147]

While there was much to be happy about, remarks by Donald Formigli that day made clear that there was still lots to be done. Other challenges were now requiring solutions. The next hurdle was that the Township's PRB had to develop a management plan for the Five Mile Woods. There were two other tracts that were being sought, both five acres in size and located along the sliver of the Penn Central land (Tax Parcel Number 13-9-8) adjacent to the Route 1 right-of-way. In addition, the Township was also trying to acquire the Cutler tracts, (Tax Parcel Number 20-32-46-1, 2, 3, 4) which included forty-five acres. At that time the Township was in litigation with the owners.[148]

WHAT IF THE CONCERNED CITIZENS HAD BEEN TOO BUSY

About the time of the referendum the Bucks County Conservancy, in announcing a new natural areas survey, opined in its newsletter:

Thanks to the foresight of voters in Lower Makefield Township and the dedicated perseverance of the Save Our Woods Committee, the continued existence of the Five Mile Woods has been assured. We can be certain that the tireless public education effort by the Committee did much to influence the outcome of the referendum. But what would have happened had this handful of concerned citizens been unable or too busy to commit themselves to preserving a very special forest from the bulldozer blades? [149]

The Conservancy also presented two awards to those who had led the effort to Save Our Woods at its annual dinner in the fall of 1978 including its Conservation Award to Donald Formigli.[150]

THE WOODS ARE SAVED

With the acquisition of a significant portion of the Five Mile Woods soon to become a reality the next step was to create a plan for its preservation and guidelines for the use of the property. It was clear that there was also a need to hire a resident manager to guide the effort forward. In addition, a new headquarters was needed that would serve as the center of the Preserve's operations and public outreach programs.

In the years that followed, programs were developed that became annual traditions like the Earth Day Open House and the Fall Open House. The Friends of the Five Mile Woods took on a critical role in guiding the Township and providing assistance to maintaining the property and for lobbying for further land acquisitions. The Township also expanded its land holdings considerably after that initial acquisition in 1979. The dream of so many activists, volunteers, civic leaders, and environmental organizations to save the Woods had came to fruition.

COMMON BEECH

COMMON BEECH

Chapter 6

FULFILLING THE MISSION

There was a lot of chess playing on the Township's part.[1]
RICHARD McBRIDE
LAWYER REPRESENTING THE DEVELOPERS OF THE CUTLER TRACT

The Woods should be left in their natural state to provide opportunities for education, research and inspiration.[2]
PLANNING FOR THE FUTURE OF THE WOODS
1978

A Preserve is a state of mind, an attitude, protecting more than just the acreage it encompasses, it exposes all to an alternative relationship with the land.[3]
GUIDE FOR THE PRESERVATION OF THE PRESERVE
1979

As the supporters of the Five Mile Woods celebrated the success of the purchase of the Penn Central tract, planning was already underway to balance the need for public access and to protect the natural resources located in the Preserve. Before the Penn Central land transfer was finalized, Donald Formigli was working on a plan to administer the property. A series of studies were undertaken that provided a data base of what was there, what could be done and how the property could be managed. All of that planning culminated in the creation of a master plan written by Rick Mellon that has guided the destiny of the Preserve. On November 21, 1981, the Five Mile Woods Preserve was formally dedicated and opened to the public.

There was also a change in the leadership of the Woods efforts as Formigli, who had been elected to the Board of Supervisors, left the Township in 1981, just weeks before the Preserve was dedicated. Pat (Fair) Miiller became the chairman of the Park and Recreation Board in a seamless transition and continued the board's vision of creating a recreation and open space program for the Township.

With the Preserve now open to the public, the services of a resident naturalist were required to build on the work that had been done. Rick Mellon, the author of the *Master Plan for the Five Mile Woods Preserve,* was hired in 1981 and he served at the helm of leadership until 1995. Some have described his tenure as the *Preserve's Glory Years* as much was accomplished and many of the programs he initiated have continued. His successor was Bonnie Tobin who served for one year, followed by John Heilferty who has been the part-time Preserve Manager since 1997. He has also continued with regular programing, work days, and more recently, developing a deer management program. All three worked well with the volunteer support organization, the Friends of the Five Mile Woods. The Friends continued to partner with the Township to help maintain the property and provide programs for the public.

The last thirty-five years have been expansive ones for the Preserve. A number of parcels were acquired through a series of transactions that have almost doubled the size of the Preserve and saved more of the Woods. Trails have been constructed, facilities built and improved, and programs prepared for the public.

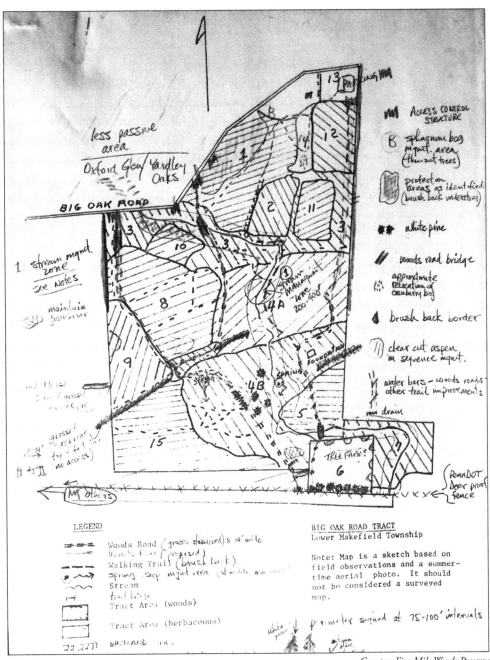

Courtesy Five Mile Woods Preserve
Pat Miiller Collection
District Forester's Report

In 1978 the first inventory of the Preserve's resources was prepared by District Forester Maurice Hobaugh in a report made for Lower Makefield Township.

These efforts have been recognized regularly with awards made by the state and various organizations over the years.

PLANNING FOR THE PRESERVE'S FUTURE

In the time leading up to the purchase of the Preserve, and during its formative years, a number of plans and studies were undertaken to guide the destiny of the property and various agencies were consulted. They addressed a multitude of issues including uses, access and managing the property. All of those early studies culminated with the creation of the *Master Plan for the Five Mile Woods Preserve* prepared by the first Resident Naturalist Rick Mellon in 1981.

The first working document to lay out a management and interpretive plan for what was then a proposed *Five Mile Woods Preserve* was prepared by Donald Formigli. He compiled the working document entitled *Planning for the Future of the Woods* in early 1978. Once it was approved by the Park and Recreation Board, it was sent to the Bucks County Park Board, the Bucks County Planning Commission and the Lower Makefield Board of Supervisors for review and approval.[4]

While the document was in an outline format, it did provide a foundation on which future planning documents would rest. It pointed out the unique qualities of the Preserve as well as some of the more practical concerns like uses and issues that would need to be resolved. The two principles that began the short document and have guided the use of the Preserve ever since are:

The Woods should be left in their natural state to provide opportunities for education, research and inspiration.

Hiking trails may be developed to follow existing trails at little to no cost through volunteer community efforts.[5]

This first principle was the one that ultimately guided the management of the Preserve because it clearly stated that it was not a park, and should not be developed for active recreational activities such as ball fields or playgrounds. The Preserve was a place, as its name said, where nature would be preserved in its unmanaged state. This differentiation was not one of semantics alone but also of a very real and practical concern for its future.

Other administrative issues included: blocking off vehicular access, establishing the Woods as a Wildlife Protection Area, the organization of a friends group, creating an endowment fund, consulting with Falls Township about plans, and having the Township police regularly check on the property.[6]

Even as these documents were developed, the Park and Recreation Board needed to come up with short term policies to protect the Preserve's natural resources from being damaged by visitors while allowing them to appreciate the

Woods. In 1979, a set of *Guidelines for Hikers* was prepared to assist volunteer leaders conducting hikes.

With the approval of the referendum in May 1978, the PRB began to reach out for advice immediately. A number of groups and agencies were contacted and given a chance to offer input as was the general public.[7]

The Department of Environmental Resources' District Forester Maurice Hobaugh offered to make recommendations with a forest management plan. He prepared a written report after a visit to the Woods on June 29, 1978 and submitted it in December.[8]

His proposed management plan included five goals:

To maintain (the Preserve) as a recreational and education area
To regulate stocking and growth of woodland to the full capacity of the site, thereby
increasing the value of the woodland
To maintain habitat for wildlife
To harvest timber in order to maintain the woodland in a healthy, vigorous condition
To prevent and/or control the hazards of insects, disease, fire, and erosion [9]

The overall theme of the report and its recommendations were to manage the site intensively including logging some of the timber which would create revenue for the Township and thinning out undesirable trees. Hobaugh divided the Preserve into fifteen distinct tracts and wanted to see the large and healthy trees as a centerpiece. He also suggested regular and selective cutting to increase the food supplies for wildlife. He proposed that an active planting regimen be undertaken as well as improving wildlife habitat. Another important recommendation was the creation of firebreaks, access roads, and a plan of action in the event of a forest fire. One of the most interesting recommendations was the relocation of the cranberry bog, presumably the one located on property owned by Independence Development, Inc., to the Preserve.[10]

The district forester's report represents in microcosm the major debate that has occurred for more than a century between the preservationists, who want to leave natural spaces undisturbed and to develop on their own, and the conservationists, who want to take advantage of the resources that exist and manage them wisely. The report remains a valuable resource because it provides a professional's observations of the Woods at the time, and provides the first contemporary map of the Preserve with its man-made and natural features noted.[11]

The state's Soil and Conservation Service agency also conducted a review of the property in 1978 but a copy of it could not be found. Two conclusions the agency reached were that fire access roads were not necessary, and that emergency access was not required because the interior of the Preserve was readily accessible by foot. The agency also concluded that the risk of fire was not an important one.[12]

The Academy of the Natural Sciences in Philadelphia conducted a Township-wide inventory and prepared a report entitled *Vegetation and Stream Survey: Lower Makefield Township, Bucks County, Pennsylvania (Report 78-50)* in 1978. The report provided an important and detailed overview of the Township's natural resources and was a valuable resource for planners. The Academy also assisted with an Environmental Impact Assessment when Makefield Oak, Inc.'s project was making its way through the review process at the same time. In addition, the Academy created a listing of rare plants in the Woods after several field trips.[13]

A GUIDE FOR THE PRESERVATION OF THE PRESERVE

By August 28, 1978, a draft of the Preserve's first detailed management plan was being considered and recommendations were accepted. The plan was a detailed operational document and covered all the management issues required to run such an entity including administrative rules, the role of the Friends of the Five Mile Woods, along with a variety of issues including signage, surveillance of the property, access, walking trails, visitor control, public relations, prohibited activity and educational and scientific uses. It also called for the hiring of a preserve manager and having that person occupy the stone house that stood on the property, now known as the Brelsford House.

The draft led to the creation of a final operating plan adopted by the Park and Recreation Board. This new document, created by Steve Wharton, was entitled *Five Mile Woods Preserve: Guide for Preservation* and dated June 7, 1979.

Wharton, a park and recreation planner, was hired in April 1978 and began working for the Township's Park and Recreation Board under a federal employment program called the Comprehensive Employment and Training Act. Wharton, a resident of Lower Makefield, had a degree from Penn State University in agronomy and worked on several projects with which the PRB was then engaged, including creating a parks and recreation comprehensive plan, drafting a set of rules governing the use of the parks and open space, and preparing grant applications for different opportunities for the Township.[14]

The new *Guide for Preservation* built on the work of the previous documents. The author went into great detail outlining the philosophies and ethics that governed the management of such a place. The plan's purposes were outlined as follows:

The objectives of the Five Mile Woods Preserve Stewardship Program are twofold. The primary objective is to maintain the area so that it sustains species, communities, and natural features that make significant contributions to the conservation of natural diversity. The second objective is to determine and promote land uses that are compatible with the preservation of natural diversity within the Preserve, in order to foster local support and recognition by the community of the values of natural diversity preservation.[15]

As stated in the plan, the Preserve's Stewardship Philosophy was as follows:

A Preserve is a state of mind, an attitude, protecting more than just the acreage it encompasses, it exposes all to an alternative relationship with the land.

Of basic concern is the need of protecting areas previously uninfluenced by man and maintaining these areas in their natural condition. However, it must be recognized that many of the areas within the Preserve already reflect some human disturbance, either through direct or indirect influence. In many cases, this influence is subtle, such as lowering the water table of the stream valley, removal of a predatory species from the entire region, or the substitution of introduced flora that replace native forbs and grasses. Yet, this slightly modified natural state is the closest representative we have to a primeval condition and therefore must be protected.

Although the natural world is not static, human activities can disturb and permanently alter both the short and long term patterns and processes of the natural systems. We must identify and monitor the ecological requirements of the Preserve and continually insure that the area receives the care and protection needed to sustain it.

The ownership of land generally involves problems, and trying to leave nature undisturbed can add a surprising array of difficulties. The philosophy which follows sets a direction for progress and establishes a framework for decision making to address these unforeseen difficulties. Read the philosophy carefully, weigh it, and consider it.[16]

The document laid out in great detail the operational aspects of the Preserve including many of the issues considered in the previous draft document. Ultimate responsibility for the property fell to the Township Supervisors with the Friends of Five Mile Woods serving as:

. . . an intermediary between the community and the Township . . . to foster local support and recognition by the general public of the values of natural diversity conservation.[17]

The *Guide for Preservation* further discussed permitted and prohibited activities and spelled out needs including a boundary survey, public relations, admissions, fees, annual reporting, hazards, signage, and the use of herbicides and pesticides. It also called for the development of a master plan by the end of the second year that the Township owned the land. The guide was adopted by the Township's Board of Supervisors on July 9, 1979. Since the adoption of the plan and its various components, the document has guided the destiny of the Preserve.[18]

The next document created as the result of the *Guide for Preservation's* goals was a master plan prepared within two years of the Preserve being opened. This task fell to Rick Mellon, the owner of Mellon Biological Services who began the task in January 1980. The master plan examined all the aspects of the Preserve including recording its many species along with analyzing its various habitats in great detail, and providing recommendations and guidance for its use and preservation as the Township moved forward with opening it to the public. It was a comprehensive document, more than one hundred pages long, and remains one of the most important reports ever created for the township on the property.[19]

Mellon also made a series of recommendations related to security and access. One of these included having a fence installed around the perimeter to control access. This was an important item because at the time snowmobilers, motorcycles, horseback riders, dirt bikers and even timber thieves had easy access to the Preserve's acreage. During the time when the Township planned for the management of and then opened the Five Mile Woods, various acts of vandalism were committed. In March 1979, it was reported that about fifty trees had been cut and stolen from the Preserve. In addition, there was concern about the boundary line along the southeastern corner of the property.[20]

The issue of emergency access was raised and Mellon believed that access roads should be built using established and existing woods roads and farm roads. This would require some construction and improvement projects to create three different access lanes.[21]

As part of the effort to create access and promote the educational function of the Preserve, a trail system was proposed that incorporated all the important features of the Preserve but not the most environmentally sensitive. Boardwalks, waterbars and new policies were to be developed to minimize the damage by users, especially in wet areas. Trails were to be marked with color coded markers and would be built to a certain size for various uses, like group hikes or individual hikers. Each trail would have a border of deadfall along its edges.[22]

To go with the trail network, an educational program needed to be created. While most visitors would use the trail network, other groups, such as local biology classes, would need more flexibility if they wanted to study artificially designated areas. All of this would be subject to a set of guidelines and partnerships with the teachers of the various school groups.[23]

Another issue that the biologist raised was noise intrusion. At the time, noise came from Big Oak Road and it was recommended that an earthen berm be erected beginning at the western boundary to where the road was straightened. Mellon also foresaw the severe noise that would come from Route 1 when it was opened and how the lower end of the Preserve, particularly below the Fall Line, would be especially affected by the traffic. For this problem, it was suggested that a wall at ten foot high wall be constructed, and along some parts of the highway that it should be fifteen feet in height.[24]

Other concerns included the dropping water table caused by the development that had gone on around the Preserve and was continuing. In addition, water was being drained directly from Cambridge Estates into the Five Mile Woods Preserve along its eastern boundary. Mellon proposed a solution for that problem, and suggested that a planned detention basin on the north side of Big Oak Road for the development being built by Makefield Oak, Inc. have a retention basin instead. These were built to his specifications.[25]

Mellon also called for habitat management that included maintaining the former fields, which still existed, as open space by undertaking annual maintenance cuttings. At the time, only 8% of the Preserve was open space but the plant diversity in those areas was still remarkable. If the areas were not managed, he suggested, the forest would take over and the habitat of those special areas would be lost. However, whatever management of habitat he suggested was not on the level that had been previously suggested by the district forester, Maurice Hobaugh.[26]

Another suggestion with regard to the habitat was to create an impoundment of about one acre in size south of the Preserve's headquarters. One of Mellon's hopes was to move the cranberry bog to the east of the Preserve's western boundary line.[27]

One of the results of the use of the land for agriculture was the digging of drainage ditches which lowered the water table. This made the land more useful for farmers. The report suggested that the Township should remove the drainage ditches, or that the clearing of the ditches be ended.[28]

Mellon called for regular testing to be done of the water and soil along with regularly gathering data on artificially created quadrants to maintain a database of information. Finally, he proposed that a part of the Guzikowski farm, located in Falls Township and to the east of the Preserve's eastern boundary, be acquired. This property would protect the Preserve and included a section of the Woods. The report concluded with a section on the significant areas that should not be publicized for fear of vandalism by plant collectors.[29]

A draft of the *Master Plan* was submitted on March 10, 1981, to the Park and Recreation Board. The final plan was due by the end of the month when it was presented to the Board of Supervisors. The Friends of the Five Mile Woods objected to several features of the new master plan including the construction of access roads and the two small areas that Mellon had called for to be managed more intensely. However, they ultimately approved the plan and its various components.[30]

Two other reports were completed in 1981, including one from The Nature Conservancy that provided guidance on the construction of trails, plantings, maintenance of open areas, and education programming. The report also included suggestions for the main entrance area. The second report was entitled *Report on the Hydrology of Five Mile Woods* and was written by Thomas Tyler Moore As-

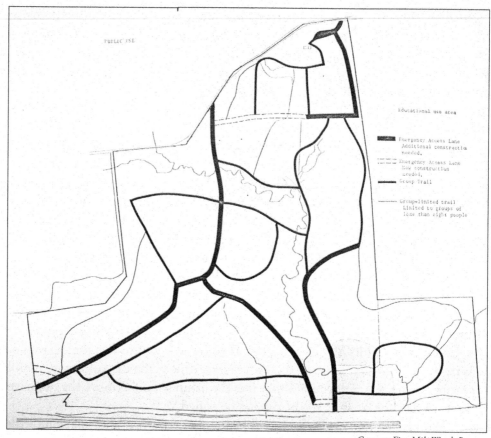

PUBLIC USE

Educational use area

Emergency Access Lane
Additional construction
needed.

Emergency Access Lane
New construction
needed.

Group Trail

Group-limited trail
Limited to groups of
less than eight people

Courtesy Five Mile Woods Preserve
Master Plan for the Five Mile Woods Preserve: Lower Makefield Township Pennsylvania
A series of access roads and a trail network were proposed in the 1981 Master Plan for the Preserve.

sociates of West Trenton, New Jersey for the Township. The report was written in response to the development going on outside of the borders of the Preserve. Of interest was how those properties and the water that drained from them, would affect the Preserve and how that impact could be mitigated.[31]

THE WOODS ARE WORTHY OF FEDERAL SUPPORT

With the purchase of the Penn Central tract complete and as the guide to managing the property and a master plan finished, advocates continued with their mission of trying to save as much of the Woods as possible. To undertake new land purchases, and to build the necessary infrastructure to open the facility to the public, the group began to pursue additional funding.

One of the results of the partnership with the Bucks County Conservancy was the contact made with the Pennsylvania Department of Community Affairs

(DCA) by Robert Pierson. This statewide agency, created in 1966, maintained relationships with a variety of other government agencies to help the Common-wealth and local governments apply for and manage grants in many different areas of interest including conservation and recreation. The part of the agency charged with those programs was the Bureau of Outdoor Recreation.[32]

The discussions to search for funding to purchase the Woods began with a variety of contacts made by Robert Pierson in late 1976. He contacted Bradford Northrup, the director of the Eastern Region of The Nature Conservancy, along with the staff at the DCA. Pennsylvania House of Representatives member James Wright, a prominent and important member, aided with research into possible funding sources. With those various discussions and correspondence began a long and complicated effort to obtain other funding to purchase part of the Woods.[33]

There was already a relationship established between the DCA and Lower Makefield Township, as it had received grant funding from the U.S. Bureau of Outdoor Recreation's program that passed through the DCA. In 1975, the federal agency awarded $650,000 to Bucks County for the purchase of land for parks and to build new facilities. Lower Makefield had applied for, and received, a $14,804 grant. Other grants were received from the agency after that so a relationship had

Courtesy Five Mile Woods Preserve
Donald Formigli Collection

U.S. Congressman Peter Kostmayer, pictured here in the center, along with his aide Peter Peyser on the right, and an unidentified aide on the left, was a major supporter of the Preserve and assisted with obtaining the Land and Water Conservation Fund grant in 1979.

been established.[34]

While the effort to find funding to purchase the Woods through the efforts of the DCA did not help with the purchase of the Penn Central tract, it created an opportunity to set up the pivotal meeting of April 14, 1977, when all the major stakeholders met and developed a strategy to preserve the Woods. Although the Penn Central tract was ultimately acquired with funding raised by the Township's bond, efforts continued to acquire additional parcels using federal funds.

Those involved with the Woods effort, and the DCA, focused on the United States Department of Interior's National Contingency Reserve Funds for special projects that passed through the Land and Water Conservation Fund (LWCF). This fund was created by the Congress as a vehicle to preserve natural areas, water resources and heritage sites. The financial underwriting came from offshore oil and gas royalties paid by oil companies. It was previously used for national parks, forests, refuges, with matching grants for park and recreation projects in the states and various localities.[35]

A formal application for funding an environmental impact study, was prepared by the Township's park and recreation planner Steve Wharton, Gail Hardesty, and the DCA. It requested $900,000. In late 1978, U.S. Congressman Peter Kostmayer wrote a letter to the Bureau of Recreation and Conservation in support of the application that was sent to the federal government's Department of Interior. He also lobbied the federal agency directly. The Bucks County Planning Commission passed a resolution to support Lower Makefield's efforts. Its 1977 *Comprehensive Plan* of Bucks County had designated the Woods as an area of natural importance.[36]

On June 11, 1979, Congressman Kostmayer announced that a $310,860 grant was awarded from the LWCF to be used to purchase additional land for the Preserve. However, at the time the funding was announced, Steve Wharton had left the Township's employ, something that created concern for the DCA since the application and implementation would take a great deal of work.[37]

As important as this achievement was, it still required additional paperwork and administrative work to bring

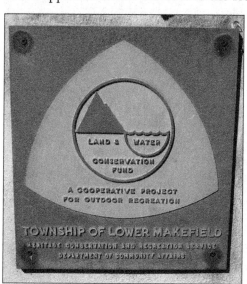

Courtesy Peter Osborne

An important component of the funding used to purchase the land to create the Preserve was a $300,000 grant from the Land and Water Conservation Fund which was managed by the U.S. Department of Interior. This plaque is located on the Headquarters building.

the grant to fruition. The first part of the application was submitted to the Department of Interior on October 4, 1979. To obtain the funding, the Township was required to have the Cutler tracts surveyed and assessed. Without a Township planner to assist her, Gail Hardesty, the first president of the Friends of the Five Mile Woods, began to deal with the grant's oversight that required a number of revisions to the original paperwork.[38]

After a complicated process, the funding was finally procured. Most of the grant went towards reimbursing the Township for the purchase of the Penn Central property and the remainder was used for the Cutler parcels.[39]

The Cutler Tract

The Cutler parcel had been on the radar screen of advocates who wanted to save the Woods from the very beginning. In fact, in 1977, it was believed that the Cutler tract would actually be acquired before the Penn Central property. In the end that was not to be. The property was split in two by Big Oak Road: the northern section being thirty-eight acres, the southern section forty-five acres. In total, it included eighty-three acres located entirely within the Piedmont Plateau. The lower tract was home to several rare species of plants. The acquisition of the southern parcel complemented the 1978 Penn Central acquisition, as it abutted the Penn Central property to the northeast. It also included a private residence that could be used for a Preserve headquarters and residence for the naturalist.[40]

This parcel's history, like that of the Dark tract, is an interesting one. It was entirely within a large land patent that had adjoined the Dark tract to the north. Originally owned by William and Charles Biles, it was more than double the size of the Dark property, and included almost six hundred acres. The Biles were among the earliest European settlers to come to Bucks County. William Biles was one of the founders of the Falls Meeting at Fallsington along with William Dark, and, in fact, the first meeting of the group was held in the Biles home. As an important landowner with large holdings, he played a significant role in the administration of the colony.[41]

The family's heritage is remembered today because Biles Island is located in the Delaware River to the southeast of the Preserve. He owned two parcels along the river in Falls Township and Samuel Dark was one of his neighbors. Biles's riverfront properties were not far from the Mannor of Penns-berry and family descendants were witness to the activities of George Washington and his army in 1776-1777, the famed crossings, and the Hessian occupation of the eastern shore of the Delaware River in southwestern New Jersey.[42]

Once the Biles tract passed out of the family's ownership, it was subdivided into smaller tracts over the years, and owned by many people, similar to what happened with the Satterthwaite tracts. Among the later owners were the Palmer and Brelsford families, both of whom had long ties to Lower Makefield Town-

Courtesy Library of Congress
Geography and Map Division
Library of Congress Control Number 2012587544

At least three structures were located on the Cutler tract (formerly the G. H. Rhoads tract) in the 1870s, including a stone house, now the Preserve's headquarters, a large barn that collapsed in the 1960s but whose foundation is still there, and a smaller building that was near the present-day open air auditorium.

ship. The property adjoining the Cutler property to the east was formerly owned by Richard Hough, another large landowner in Penn's colony.[43]

In searching through the deeds, there are a number of early transactions related to this property that are difficult to unravel. However, by the mid-nineteenth century, the land transactions become much simpler to follow. The 1850 Bucks County atlas map of Lower Makefield Township shows a T. P. Spencer living on the Cutler tract and the 1858 *Farm Map: Lower Makefield Township Bucks County, Pennsylvania* shows the property lines as they still existed one hundred and twenty years later, in 1978. In 1867, Thomas Nelson, having purchased the property from Thomas Spencer, sold the tract to George H. Rhoads. Going through several more transfers, in 1911, Paul and Elinor Cseplo purchased the property. Dolores Simpson and Judith and Paul Kraska and Gustave and Isabella Cseplo owned the property until 1962 when they sold it to Ruth and Herbert Reedman. The Cutlers purchased the property from Herbert Reedman in 1968 for speculation. The configuration of the property has remained the same, since at least, 1858.[44]

Most of the Cutler tract was previously used for agriculture, and as so many other farmers of the region, the Cseplos grew tomatoes and carrots for the Campbell Soup Company located in Camden, New Jersey. They also grew potatoes in the Preserve's present day parking area. In nearby fields, they grew hay and corn and leased additional farmland. In addition, there was an orchard behind the house, and on the opposite side of Big Oak Road, where apples and pears were grown. They also operated a fruit stand. The orchards appear on aerial photographs from the 1930s, but there is no evidence of the fruit trees surviving in the Preserve today. Ditches for draining the fields can be seen when walking on the trails near the Preserve headquarters.[45]

Over time, there were several buildings constructed on the Cutler tract. Only one of those buildings survives today, the others were lost to time. This is the stone building that served as the resident naturalist's home and Preserve headquarters. Today it serves as a private residence for a tenant but continues its role as Preserve headquarters.

THE BRELSFORD HOUSE

The old stone house has a mysterious past that is not easily revealed as it has been subject to several renovations and updates over the last two hundred and fifty years which makes dating it difficult. To determine its age and the succession of changes made to it would require an in-depth study by an architectural historian. That said, the general range of construction dates of the stone structure is believed to be from approximately 1780-1810.[46]

The western end of the house appears to be a typical Bucks County three bay wide stone house. The first-floor window and door configuration appear to be

Courtesy Peter Osborne

The Brelsford House
2016

original, the exterior walls are eighteen inches thick with hand-cut square beams in the basement to support the first floor. The stone is believed to have come from the Fall Line. The staircase leading from the first floor to the second may be original to the house. The first floor of this part of structure could date from as early as the 1780s but may be even later. The eastern wing of the house was probably added later, yet, as with the western half, the windows are not symmetrically placed, which indicates that there may have been changes.[47]

On the second floor, the windows are not symmetrically placed as is typical of houses of the late eighteenth or early nineteenth century. It has been suggested that the second story may have been added later, or altered as a result of an event or series of events that happened, such as a fire, that damaged the entire structure or that perhaps its elevation was raised. Parts of the building may be of wood frame construction.[48]

Another feature of the house as it existed when the Township acquired it, was the large roof overhang that had been added to the front of the building. This was done during the Reedman ownership of the building from 1962-68.[49]

Based on the deed research, and speculation about the construction of the house, it is believed that it was built by a Brelsford family member: either Issac or Abraham. (The family's name is also spelled Brelsfoard on one survey.) It is known for example, that in 1798, Abraham Brelsford owned the property on which the stone house stood. In the *List of Taxes Upon Dwelling Houses* in the same year Abraham owned a dwelling house that was valued at more than $100, as did Issac

Brelsford, who owned an adjoining parcel to the east.[50]

However, Paul Rhoads, an important advocate not only for the Woods but for the preservation of the house when the Township was deciding what to do with it, and considered demolishing, it has a different view. He believes it was built even earlier, possibly between 1730-1750. Perhaps the eastern wing was built first and the western wing added later. His view is important because he was the only person interviewed for the book who was in the structure before it was renovated by the Township. If his view is correct then it should be called the Palmer House as the Palmer family owned the tracts that included the Cutler parcels during this time.[51]

In the end the author has chosen to call it the Brelsford House, and not the Cutler House, as it has been since the late 1970s. While the Cutlers owned the house for a little more than a decade they did not have any historical association with the house. The Brelsfords may have built or enlarged it, and could have lived in it.

The house first appears on a map of Lower Makefield Township in the 1850 Bucks County atlas. Thomas Spencer is shown as living there and owning what came to be known as the Cutler tract. The 1876 and 1891 map of Lower Makefield shows the farm, now owned by George Rhoads, to include three buildings clustered together and located along a farm road that exited Big Oak Road. They were located just to the south of the Preserve's parking area.[52]

The same map shows a large L-shaped building along with another small building and the stone house. This building was a two-level stone Pennsylvania bank barn, an impressive structure, almost three stories tall and probably dates from the nineteenth century, although its construction date may have been sometime before 1876. It was similar to a barn on the nearby farm currently owned by Sandy Guzikowski (2016). It is known that in the 1950s the Cseplos kept six

Courtesy Five Mile Woods Preserve
Donald Formigli Collection

This photograph shows how the Brelsford House appeared in 1978 when the area around the structure was still open fields.

cows here. The use of the other two buildings is not identified on maps, but they were still standing in 1938. The barn deteriorated over time and probably collapsed in the 1960s.[53]

The two other buildings on the site included a carriage shed, and a chicken house. By the 1970s, there was no evidence of any of those buildings in aerial photographs. Today, only the foundation of the bank barn remains, along with the earthen ramp that led to the second floor of the building. The area where the buildings stood is covered with brambles and brush and is difficult to access.[54]

Courtesy Sharon Guzikowski Stewart

A photograph could not be found of the barn that stood on the Cutler tract but the Guzikowski barn, now owned by Sandy Guzikowski and just a short distance from the Preserve is similar in shape and design. At the Preserve, the barn would have looked like this when viewing it from the headquarters building.

A CRITICAL ACQUISITION

Beginning in 1974, Donald Formigli, representing the Open Space Committee and later the Township, and the Cutler representatives were involved in a complicated set of discussions, negotiations, and then legal actions over the property. Michael Cutler, of City Wide Realty in Philadelphia, served as the representative for the owners, Victor and Milton Cutler, who were from Jenkintown. He had presented the plans to subdivide and develop the property to the Township.[55]

Initially, the Cutlers were cordial and were willing to negotiate over the limits of development on their property after walking the property with Donald Formigli. They made a proposal to donate a portion of the Woods (the property on the southern side of Big Oak Road) if they were allowed higher densities on the tract opposite it. The Township accommodated this proposal with the passage of the Conservation Cluster Ordinance in the summer of 1977. This donation would allow the Township to match any future funding prospects with in-kind land. Meetings continued and on January 5, 1978 there was a meeting with the Cutler representatives; PRB representatives; Hart Rufe, the president of the Bucks County Conservancy; and Robert Pierson, its executive director. However, the Cutlers changed course and decided that they needed about seven acres on the southern side of Big Oak Road to make the project work for them. After several years of negotiations with the Township, PRB and the Conservancy, the deal seemed to be unraveling.[56]

These negotiations, which on several occasions seemed to be coming to a successful conclusion, ran into legal challenges over the value of the land because of the change in zoning. As a result, the Cutlers sued the Township. It all ended when an agreement was made between the Township and the Cutlers in the spring of 1979 and a series of transfers began on September 18, 1980 when Victor and Milton Cutler sold what is now the park's headquarters and parking area to the Township. This included Tax Parcel Number 20-32-46-1 and 2. Not long before the closing, there had been tenants in the Brelsford House but by the time of the closing it was empty.[57]

The next parcel was sold in 1981 and included the 7.8 acres that abutted the former Penn Central property, Tax Parcel Number 20-32-46-4. The final parcels of the remaining Cutler tracts were sold to Lower Makefield in March 1982 when a 7.3-acre parcel along Big Oak Road, and twenty-one acres behind the headquarters building, Tax Parcel Number 20-32-46 and 3. The value of all the transactions was almost $400,000 and payments were staggered over two years to accommodate the Cutlers desire to spread their capital gains taxes over several years. However, the Township was given the use of entire property after the first transfer. The tract was originally purchased for $187,000 in 1968.[58]

The deeds included a clause that stated:

This land was acquired for open space and public recreation purposes with grant and aid assistance under the Federal Land and Water Conservation Fund Act of 1965.[59]

The northern parcel, thirty-eight acres in size, was subsequently developed and called Big Oak Bend. Long before, the advocates of the Woods had determined that this parcel was not as significant as others because it was on the northern side of Big Oak Road, did not include any of the Woods, and would create administrative issues for the Township if it did own it.[60]

There are features that remain from the Cutler's ownership and the result of their efforts to develop the property. For example, south of the Brelsford House, there are several large holes and piles of dirt that are the result of percolation tests that were undertaken by engineers. They were dug out by large earth moving machinery and were never filled in.[61]

Courtesy Five Mile Woods Preserve
Donald Formigli Collection

After the purchase of the Cutler tract for inclusion in the Preserve, the Brelsford stone house was renovated for use as the Preserve's headquarters and privately leased residence by Lower Makefield Township.

The Preserve Headquarters

In the first draft of the planning document for the future of the Preserve in 1978, it was suggested that the Brelsford House, or as it was previously called, the Cutler House or the Manor House, be used as a residence for a part-time or full-time resident naturalist. Once the purchase of the first two Cutler tracts was completed, plans were made for the renovation of the house that also included a new headquarters for the Preserve, an exhibit area, and rest room facilities. Because the naturalist would be living on the site, an extra measure of security was provided to the Township.[62]

Bids for renovating the house were received in early 1981, and after a recommendation by the Park and Recreation Board, the Board of Supervisors entered into a contract to renovate the house. The historic stone house, with a large two story porch of recent construction, was completely gutted and upgraded. Unfortunately, whatever remained of the historic interior fabric of the building, aside from the staircase, was lost. The work cost, including soft and hard expenses, almost $200,000, and was completed by William C. Cox, Inc. The house was remodeled again in 1993.[63]

A new parking area was created at the entrance to the Preserve on Big Oak Road, and different ideas were submitted by design firms for the Preserve's entrance area. A plan was finally adopted and constructed. After the building was occupied, a long berm was created that ran directly in front of the Brelsford House along Big Oak Road. The berm was created to block the original road into the property and was said to have cut down on traffic noise. It remains to this day. [64]

At the same time the PRB also considered options for leasing the building, and hiring a resident naturalist. Initially the board considered the title of park ranger but that was rejected in favor of resident naturalist. With the position's title resolved, in 1981, the Township hired its first manager for the Five Mile Woods Preserve, Rick Mellon. [65]

DEDICATION OF THE PRESERVE
NOVEMBER 21, 1981

Almost eight years after the first discussions began about preserving the Woods, a dedication and ribbon cutting ceremony officially opening the Five Mile Woods Preserve was held on Saturday, November 21, 1981. Donald Formigli, who had overseen so much of the effort to preserve the Woods, cut the ribbon at 11:30 a.m. to formally open the facility to the public. He had just resigned his position on the Township's Board of Supervisors on October 10 because he had moved out of the Township. [66]

In the months leading up to the grand opening, renovation work was completed on the Brelsford House, and Rick Mellon moved in with his wife and family. A series of trails were built in the Penn Central and Cutler tracts and identified with trail markers. This network originally included the Sphagnum, Sweetgum, Creek, Crossing, 5-Mile, Fall Line, and Heath Trails. Boardwalks were constructed over wet areas by many local Boy Scouts and Girl Scouts.

About eighty people were present to participate in the ribbon cutting. They included Gail Hardesty, representing the Friends of the Five Mile Woods; Preserve advocates; local citizens; members of the Board of Supervisors; members of the Park and Recreation Board, Bruce Dorbian from the Bureau of Recreation and Conservation and the Department of Community Affairs; and a representative from the National Park Service, Robert Johnson. Johnson said:

The results here show that a few dedicated leaders can galvanize government into action. You are fortunate to have the park board and sympathetic community leaders that you have, but it's you, the people, that deserve the commendation for your efforts. [67]

Rick Mellon said on the special occasion:

The Woods is not meant to be a museum. It is here as a place where everyone can feel at peace and relax. It's to be enjoyed and cared for by all. [68]

5 Mile Woods Preserve

OPENING DAY CEREMONIES

5 Mile Woods Preserve
Township of Lower Makefield
Opening Ceremonies

November 23, 1981
11 a.m.

Introductions	Patricia R. Miiller, Chairman, Lower Makefield Township Park and Recreation Board
Speakers	William Queale, Chairman, Lower Makefield Township Board of Supervisors
	Bruce Dorbian, Regional Supervisor, Bureau of Recreation and Conservation, Department of Community Affairs, Commonwealth of Pennsylvania
	Robert Johnson, National Park Service, Mid-Atlantic Region
	Gail Hardesty, President, Friends of the Woods
Ribbon Cutting	Donald O. Formigli (at main trail entrance)

Guided Walks at 11:30 a.m., 12:00 p.m., and 1:00 p.m.

Courtesy Five Mile Woods Preserve
Donald Formigli Collection

Program for Opening Day
November 21, 1981

LOWER MAKEFIELD TOWNSHIP

Board of Supervisors
William Queale, Chairman
Grace M. Godshalk
Lloyd H. Klatzkin
Henry S. Miiller
William T. Bueltman

Park and Recreation Board
Patricia R. Miller, Chairman
Robert Gift
Philip R. Orwick
Charles Gravener
Mary Borkovitz
J. Robert Dinon
Ann Rhoads

Friends of the Woods
Gail Hardesty
Fred Gusz
James Westwater
Vincent Wright

Richard Mellon, Resident Naturalist

Courtesy Five Mile Woods Preserve
Donald Formigli Collection

Program for Opening Day
November 21, 1981

Courtesy Five Mile Woods Preserve
Donald Formigli Collection

Donald Formigli cut the ribbon during the opening ceremonies for the Five Mile Woods Preserve.

Courtesy Five Mile Woods Preserve
Donald Formigli Collection
Donald Formigli (left) and Michael Fair (center) inspect the bog on Opening Day at the Preserve.

The headquarters and nature center were opened and tours of the Preserve were led by members of the Friends who had been conducting them regularly for several years. The effort of so many hard-working volunteers had come to a successful conclusion, and the first phase of the effort was complete.[69]

MANAGING THE PRESERVE

The Lower Makefield Township's Board of Supervisors decided at the beginning that a resident manager would be required to oversee the Preserve's day-to-day operations. Since the creation of the Preserve, there have been three administrators who worked for the Township overseeing the management of the property. They came from different backgrounds, and brought a variety of experiences to the position. Each has made their own contribution to promote the Preserve, and save it for future generations. Each has left a unique legacy.[70]

The first person hired as the Resident Naturalist was Rick Mellon. He was well acquainted with the Preserve having written the first, and only, master plan to guide the Township in its management of the property. Beginning on April 1, 1981, with the completion of the *Master Plan,* he became the first professional to manage the property and he served until 1995. He was a graduate of Penn State University with a degree in biology, and had worked for Oliver Stark at the Bowman's Hill Wildflower Preserve. Mellon was an environmental consultant and the owner of Mellon Biological Services. His company conducted surveys and created plans for areas with threatened and endangered species, avian protection, open space and master plans for habitat mitigations. In addition, Mellon taught in college and university settings, and owned a tour business that took him all over the country.[71]

His time as the Preserve's site administrator was particularly fortuitous because he was involved in mitigating issues created by the nearby developments, including Big Oak Woods and Yardley Oaks. His expertise proved to be helpful to the Township. Because of all that he did to establish the Preserve, and create the foundation on which its many programs would be started and then continued, Rick Mellon's tenure came to be called the *Preserve's Glory Years*. He left the Preserve in 1995 after a controversy with the Township. The Friends of the Five Mile Woods gave him a recognition dinner in May 1996 to honor his service. After leaving the Woods, he turned his focus to promoting a successful consulting business that has completed many successful projects throughout the region.

Bonnie Tobin succeeded Rick Mellon as a part-time Naturalist/Facilities Manager in 1996. She continued in her position as the Environmental Educational Specialist at Tyler State Park located just outside of Newtown. Originally from Reading, Pennsylvania, she earned a degree from Penn State in wildlife science with an emphasis on environmental resource management. At the time, she lived in housing at Tyler State Park. Tobin had previously been associated with the Roving Nature Center, a program that would become a part of the Preserve's education outreach. Her tenure was a short one, as she left the position in January 1997.[72]

Following Tobin's departure in 1997, the Township hired John Heilferty as the Naturalist and Preserve Manager. Heilferty serves in that position to this day, and has been the longest serving Naturalist at the Preserve. At the time of his hiring, Heilferty was employed full time as a wetlands/wildlife biologist in the New Jersey Department of Environmental Protection (DEP), and as a Lower Makefield Township resident, was also volunteering on the Township's Environmental Advisory Council. He had previously held a part-time position as the Yardley Borough zoning officer. He earned his degree in biology at the University of Scranton focusing on environmental studies. Heilferty currently supervises the DEP's Endangered and Nongame Species Program within the Division of Fish and Wildlife. In that capacity, he works with a wide variety of wildlife species, primarily the amphibians and reptiles, but he also does some specific work with avian species, including efforts to band bald eagle chicks.[73]

Because of his job responsibilities, he was familiar with the various biological

Courtesy Five Mile Woods Preserve
Bonnie Tobin
1996

Courtesy Five Mile Woods Preserve
Rick Mellon
c. 1993

Courtesy Peter Osborne
John Heilferty
2016

and geological features of the Preserve, and he had experience with the Ashland Nature Center's education programs for young people including its Junior Naturalist program. Since his appointment to the position he has continued to oversee the Preserve, provided regular programming, overseen workdays, and develop a Township deer management program for the Preserve.[74]

TAKING THE MISSION FORWARD:
FRIENDS OF THE FIVE MILE WOODS

With the success of the Save Our Woods Committee in getting the 1978 referendum passedt, this group of volunteer advocates decided to continue to support the efforts to preserve the Woods as a community-based organization. In the first two draft plans for the operation of the Preserve, there was a provision made for a friends group to be created that would assist with the management of the Preserve. They would serve as an advisory group to the Township with a member of the Park and Recreation Board serving as an ex-officio member and liaison with the Township. This group was to be called the *Friends of the Five Mile Woods*. Many of its founding members were either members of the PRB or the Lower Makefield Board of Supervisors.[75]

The group's first official annual meeting took place on February 4, 1981, and they were formally chartered in 1984. In 1987 they applied for, and received, a Federal Employer Identification Number from the Internal Revenue Service. It is believed that the Friends subsequently received tax-exempt status from the IRS.[76]

The Friends remain an active partner with the Township today, more than thirty years later. These volunteers have one annual meeting and quarterly meetings when they plan the activities for the coming year. These activities include providing assistance in maintaining the Preserve with scheduled work days from March to November, and

Courtesy Peter Osborne

John Lloyd has faithfully served as the president of the Friends of the Five Mile Woods for more than twenty years. He can often be found giving tours to visitors like this one of the Preserve's small cranberry bog in the northwestern corner of the property. Here he shows visitors what a cranberry plant looks like.

program support such as guided and themed hikes, open houses, and public outreach activities. Work days are often followed by special programs. Membership is
open to the public and there are no restrictions to join the organization. In 2016
the group has a mailing list of one hundred and sixty recipients and there are currently a small number of dedicated Friends. They produce occasional newsletters
distributed or articles written for the Township newsletter and the group also
submits press releases to the area newspapers to inform the public of its activities.
The Township maintains a web page for the Preserve and its address is: *www.lmt.
org/park-fivemilewoods.*[77]

MUSHROOMS, BATS AND A ROVING NATURE CENTER
Since the Preserve opened more than thirty-five years ago, it has been a place
of much activity including work projects, programs, lectures and hikes. During
Rick Mellon's tenure, many of his programs and projects have become part of
the regular scheduled activities at the Preserve ever since. Volunteers, led by Rick
Mellon, completed numerous projects at the Preserve. A network of trails criss-
crossing the Preserve were developed and maintained, boardwalks crossing over
wet areas were built, waterbars installed, signboards erected, repairs made, trees
and brush were pruned and junk was removed that was dumped there for years
before the Township's purchase of the property. Over time the Preserve's entire
outer perimeter was fenced. When new land acquisitions were made, the new

Courtesy Peter Osborne

*The trails of the Preserve have been marked since its opening. Different trail markers have been used
over time. Today many of the sign posts include an "HQ" to show where the Preserve's headquarters are
in case hikers get lost on the trail.*

parcels were incorporated into the Preserve and new trails built in those areas. As a way of thanking volunteers, Mellon arranged for field trips to other interesting sites.[78]

Boy Scouts and Girl Scouts have long been active at the Preserve. They have conducted programs on site, and completed many service projects to address maintenance needs. Numerous Scouts have earned their advancement to higher ranks, including Eagle Scout. In addition, service groups, from corporations like the FMC Corporation came to the Preserve to help.[79]

Summer educational programs for children, and regularly scheduled guided walks, were part of the annual calendar. School classes, scouts, community organizations, college classes (University of Pennsylvania) and other area institutions, use the site as an outdoor classroom. Teachers were invited to the Woods to develop programs for getting students from the Pennsbury schools to the Preserve. George Carmichael did water studies with students in the Woods. Natural history site brochures, and trail brochures were developed along with training for volunteers to serve as guides.[80]

Rick Mellon also created nature courses held at the Preserve that included field trips, like the *The Fascinating World of Nature: An Environmental Awareness Study Group*. Some of the programs that were offered included *Owl Walks*, *Rare Plants of Bucks County*, *Birds of the Five Mile Woods*, *Orchids of the Five Mile*

Courtesy Five Mile Woods Preserve
Pat Miiller Collection

The Preserve hosted a fifth anniversary celebration of its opening in 1986.

Woods, Acid Rain and its Impact on Forests, and *Wildflowers of the Crowfoot Family.* Regularly scheduled tours were continued, as they had been before the Preserve was created, along with guided group tours.

One of the more creative programs hosted at the Preserve was the Roving Nature Center, a summer educational program which operated on a *fully mobile basis* as described in one promotional piece. Based in Bath, Pennsylvania, this popular program was hosted by five other sites and the Preserve. Beginning in 1989, it operated for about twenty years. The Center provided the counselors and environmental-related activities, and moved people from site to site to provide a variety of programs for children aged four through twelve.[81]

The Preserve celebrated the fifth anniversary of its opening in 1986. The event included a birthday cake, gifts, prizes and a scavenger hunt. Along with remembering the effort to save the Woods, there was a program to honor the volunteers who assisted with administering the Township's property and programs. In 1991, a tenth anniversary program was held. Other programs included face painting, coloring, and paper making.

When John Heilferty assumed the position of Naturalist and Preserve Manager in 1997, he continued to sponsor many of the popular programs and added more. These included *Family Fun Walks at Five Mile Woods, Bats in Your Back Woods,* the *Annual Five Mile Woods Frog and Salamander Walk,* the *Lower Makefield Township Frog Squad* and maple syrup demonstrations. The headquarters displays were redesigned to include a collection of turtles, frogs and salamanders. A special YouTube presentation called *Five Mile Woods Mushrooms* was created by Anthony and Emily Townsend during this time too.

Lectures and demonstrations are regularly sponsored, and regularly sched-

Courtesy Peter Osborne

Volunteers and friends of the Preserve (left to right) Collin Stuart, John Lloyd, and Jim Puzo clear out growth at the entrance to the Preserve during the June 2016 workday. Workdays are regularly scheduled throughout the year.

A new waterbar was installed across the Creek Trail during the June 2016 workday. Waterbars help to prevent trail erosion. Here, from left to right, Larry Miller, Ayden Boccamsuso, Steve Myers, Chris Myers, Chloe Myers and Tyler Rugarber all lend a hand installing it. The Myers family members belong to Boy Scout Troop 10 in Lower Makefield Township and Chloe is a member of Brownie Troop 2098 in Yardley.

uled work days continue. Guided tours continue to be given by Heilferty and members of the Friends and the Preserve. It is open from dawn to dusk and a trail map is distributed at the trailhead which allows for self-guided walks. The Friends and Preserve staff participate in local events including the annual Earth Day Open House and provide an exhibit for the annual Harvest Day in Yardley followed by another Open House at the Preserve. To allow for greater access, the Township purchased a Landeez wheelchair, a special device that allows those with physical challenges to use the Preserve's trails and facilities.[82]

The only program related to the history of the Preserve took place on October 16, 1997 when Lower Makefield Historical Society's past president, Ralph Thompson, made a presentation on the history of the Preserve. At the joint meeting of Preserve's Friends and the historical society, Thompson presented his important findings on the people who had originally settled it and farmed it. It was the first time that a detailed look at the history of the property was ever presented and the first time that the Friends and historical society had ever made a joint presentation.[83]

As has been the case for more than thirty years, the work of clearing and maintaining the trails continue along with regular trash and litter clean ups. A number of Scouting projects have been completed that included laying out and constructing new boardwalks and bridges, building two new trails, blazing trails, creating an outdoor classroom, building bulletin boards, installing signage, re-building the storage shed, generating aerial maps of the Preserve, and more recently constructing a new bat house. [84]

A long-standing tradition at the Preserve includes the regularly scheduled workdays that take place on the second Saturday of the month from May to November. During a typical workday in the spring of 2016, for example, John Heilferty oversaw the installation of a waterbar on one of the trails and gave a short lecture on erosion, and how waterbars work. At the same time, work was undertaken at the front entrance to cut back of some of the vegetation covering fences and trees in the entrance area. [85]

Since 1981, visitors to the Preserve have mainly come from Lower Makefield Township, Yardley, Morrisville and Levittown and places even further away. There is a regular stream of visitors who come to walk, look for birds or plants, or simply to commune with nature.

CONTROLLING THE DEER HERDS

One of the most important challenges that has confronted the Township at the Preserve, is the herds of deer both within and around the Preserve. Even before the Township acquired the Five Mile Woods, there were frequent traffic accidents as deer crossed Big Oak Road and struck passing automobiles. In 1978, Police Chief Charles Ronaldo testified at a Park and Recreation Board Meeting that there were herds of deer roaming throughout the Township and that as open space and farmland was being lost along with a reduced food supply, the impact of deer on residential housing streets and yards was growing. He estimated that about twelve deer were killed by cars on Big Oak Road every year and that sixty were killed in Lower Makefield annually. His suggestion was to open the Woods to hunting for a two-month period every year. [86]

When the district forester Maurice Hobaugh prepared his report in 1978, he too saw the potential problem with deer as they had no natural enemies. His final recommendation was to sell hunting permits for a limited open season for bow and arrow, or buckshot. In 1981 when Rick Mellon prepared his *Master Plan* he, too saw a growing problem as deer became more dependent on the Preserve for food. [87]

The guiding mission of the Preserve was to leave any management of its resources to a minimum. In the early years, hunting was prohibited, and the property was posted. One of the challenges faced by those administering the property, was that the area had previously been a place where local hunters had been active. When the Independence Development lots were acquired on the west side of the Preserve, the Township adopted a policy that hunting was strictly prohibited and prosecuted hunters when necessary. Even in the mid-1980s, hunters were occasionally seen on the property although the sightings were fewer and fewer.[88]

However, by the early 1980s, it was clear that the deer were beginning to have an impact on the plants and trees there. When development was completed on three sides of the Preserve (Route 1 being the southern boundary) the deer migrated into the Preserve. By 2003, the problem had become so severe that John Heilferty contracted an aerial infrared imaging survey of the deer to estimate the approximate size of the population. The 2004 aerial count showed forty-nine deer in the Five Mile Woods.[89]

Over time, John Heilferty considered several solutions including the use of a professional sharpshooter and non-lethal methods. A sharpshooting company, White Buffalo, was used for one year, but the Township ultimately settled on controlling the deer herd in Lower Makefield by establishing a partnership with Big Oak Whitetail Management Association (BOWMA), a group advocating the use of bow hunting. While there were challenges in conducting the hunt, in the end, the overall endeavor proved to be successful as the effort to control the deer meant trying to balance the needs of those who regularly used the Preserve with the hunters, and those who opposed any kind of hunting program. The solution that has proved to be the most successful and least controversial was to sponsor a special hunting season in the Preserve and Township during the regular deer season. The property is posted and the hunt advertised.[90]

The success of the program not only in the Preserve, but throughout the Township was clear. By 2014, 370 deer had been removed from Lower Makefield with little opposition from Township residents. In 2016-17, only three deer were taken in the Preserve, and thirty-six in the Township. The establishment of the deer management effort was an important accomplishment of Heilferty's time as the Preserve manager.[91]

To show the effects of damage that the deer wrought at the Preserve, Heil-

Courtesy Five Mile Woods Preserve
Donald Formigli Collection

The deer population in the Preserve is controlled through an annual hunt that begins in the early fall and continues until mid-winter.

ferty erected several fenced-in areas, thirty foot by thirty foot, that show how the deer impact the environment. Inside the fenced areas where deer are excluded, the growth of vegetation is much denser than outside of them. Fencing was also erected to protect some of the rare orchids.[92]

Another challenge that the Preserve faces, as does the surrounding region, is from the invasive plants that crowd out native plants. This is a major problem, and one that almost defies solving. However, Heilferty and the Friends have taken measures to address removal of Japanese knotweed.

THE PRESERVE EXPANDS

The Friends and the Township were always looking for ways to expand the Preserve after the opening of the Preserve and as a result, Lower Makefield acquired several more significant properties, to expand and protect the core of the Preserve. By 1996, Lower Makefield Township owned 285 acres outright of the Five Mile Woods.

THE HIBBS LOTS

In the 1980s, a series of smaller parcels also came to be included in the Preserve. These parcels, the Hibbs Lots, as they are collectively known, had originally been one parcel of sixty-five acres that extended from the western end of the Giles Satterthwaite (1818-1897) farm, all the way to Oxford Valley Road. These lots were in the southwestern corner of the Five Mile Woods and several bounded Route 1. They had been part of the original Dark parcel.

Sarah (1810-1895) and Jacob Hibbs (1806-1870) purchased this parcel some time before 1858. After Jacob's death in 1870, the property was variously labeled as the *Jacob Hibbs Estate* or the *Hibbs Estate* on the township maps. They came to be called the *Hibbs Lots*. Between 1876 and 1891, a large parcel was sold to Huston Wright on the western end.[93]

The remaining parcel was broken up into five acre parcels with one given to seven of the nine children of Sarah and Jacob. These parcels included a right-of-way along the southern end of the lots from the Oxford Valley Road for access, and a second right-of-way along the northern end of the lots. They were described in one deed as the *Joseph and Samuel Hibbs Woodland* and apparently were used for harvesting wood into the 1930s. Joseph (1833-1912) and Samuel (1840-1927) were two of the sons. All the lots passed into the twentieth century intact, and remained in the possession of various family members or their descendants.[94]

Ruth and John Deas sold their lot, Tax Parcel Number 20-32-30 to 5-Mile Square, a Pennsylvania partnership from Doylestown, on October 1, 1979. Marion Conrad, who owned an adjacent lot, Tax Parcel Number 20-32-31, also sold her parcel to 5-Mile Square on the same day. (The partnership was owned by Deas and Conrad.) Both parcels came into the Township's possession on March 31,

1983 under eminent domain proceedings.[95]

The remaining five Hibbs parcels were incorporated into the Preserve in another series of transactions between a developer, Arthur Doyle, the president of Independence Development, Inc. of Newtown, Pennsylvania and the Township. The final transaction were concluded on November 13, 1985 when Lower Makefield acquired fifty-five acres from Independence Development.[96]

Jacqueline and Eugene Hieber sold their parcel, Tax Parcel Number 20-32-34 to Lower Makefield Township on December 22, 1988. This inholding was the last of the Hibbs Lots to come into the Preserve, and a water storage tank was erected on the northern end of the parcel.[97]

THE INDEPENDENCE DEVELOPMENT LOTS

Between 1968-78, Independence Development purchased seven parcels, large and small, for a planned residential development. Several of the previous owners had been Hibbs descendants and another was Henry, Dick and Ike Associates, a development partnership. Of those seven lots, six of the parcels included parts of the Woods. Two of the lots were open fields. Four of the seven Hibbs tracts were included in these series of acquisitions. Almost all the parcels were within the boundaries of the original Dark tract. Just the northwestern corner of Tax Parcel Number 20-32-42 was in the former Biles tract and like the Dark and Satterthwaite parcels had been broken up and sold off. Together, Independence's inventory in this part of Lower Makefield Township at that time included Tax Parcel Numbers 20-32-28, 29, 32, 33, 35, 38-1, and 42.[98]

These properties bordered the former Penn Central tract on the east, Big Oak Road on the north, Oxford Valley Road to the west, and the partially completed Route 1 to the south. While the developer's original plan in 1978 had been to build sixty-eight new homes, a series of events caused delays including a moratorium on sewer connections. In 1982, Independence Development filed a plan that called for commercial development of the western part of the property with the remaining property being used for residential development. The property along Oxford Valley Road was zoned commercial, and the land to the east of it was zoned R-3, residential. Because of disputes with the township, the proposed project found itself in litigation.[99]

As with the Cutler tract, a number of these parcels were of interest to those who wanted to save the Woods. The Bucks County Conservancy had been focused on the donation of several of the tracts to either its organization or the Township as part of its larger effort. The most significant piece in the tract, Tax Parcel Number 20-32-42, was also the largest. It had been owned by Elaine and Samuel Willard, Jr. and included their home, a stone house, which was located on a farm lane back from Big Oak Road. There was also a large barn, dating perhaps from the 1920s or 1930s, near the house. They were deeded the property by

Willard's father in 1956 and sold it to Henry, Dick and Ike, Inc, a developer, in 1966.[100]

Willard Jr., an arborist, owned the Penn Tree Company, developed an evergreen nursery on the property that maintained a stock of thousands of junipers, boxwood, blue spruce, Norway spruce, hemlocks, Scots, and white pine trees. The nursery benefited by its proximity to Levittown as people came from there and other developments to purchase Christmas trees and to buy trees to landscape their properties. After the sale of the property in 1966, the family continued to operate Christmas tree retail operations around the region.[101]

Today, the Preserve's Evergreen Trail passes through the middle of the former nursery and some of the trees that Willard planted still survive. However, as the decades have gone by, native trees have begun to take over the area again. Evidence of the former nursery also remains with oddly shaped evergreens that had previously been cut for Christmas trees. There are occasional circular holes in the ground that are evidence of trees being excavated for sale. The driveways that separated the nursery into sections can still be seen. Another unique feature located in this section of the Preserve is the small cranberry bog created in relatively

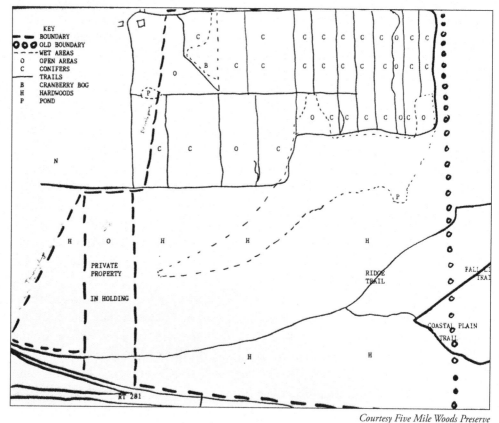

Courtesy Five Mile Woods Preserve
This 1985 map of the western part of the Preserve shows the layout of the former Willard Nursery.

recent times, an accident of nature. It is located near where Willard burned his brush and garbage, and at one time was planted with evergreen trees. Prior to the Willard's ownership, it is believed that the property may have had been used for a dairying operation.[102]

All of these newly acquired properties combined, allowed for the trail network to be expanded along with the Preserve's other programs. In addition, more of the Woods were protected.[103]

Like the Cutler negotiations, the discussions about the Independence Development lots also had difficult episodes as the township, which required that open space be set aside, required even more acreage set aside for this project, most of which included parts of the Woods. Independence Development even purchased five more acres, one of the Hibbs lot owned by Helen and Russell Broadnix (Tax Parcel Number 20-32-28), to be used for open space. The developer wanted to build 158 townhouses and 68 single family homes and was willing to make some concessions to the Township but finally came to a point where his project would not be viable and unable to proceed.[104]

Courtesy Peter Osborne

Sam Willard, as well as later owners, sold Christmas trees to Levittowners and area residents. Here, the stump of a Christmas tree sprouted new branches after it was cut.

The developer ultimately changed course and decided to build a shopping center along Oxford Valley Road in a C-2 zone, Commercial – Highway Services. However, to get the project through to completion both sides made concessions. The Township granted approval for the shopping center to be built and which would be located next to the Preserve. In addition, Independence Development, as part of the deal, agreed to sell more than fifty acres to the Township for inclusion in the Preserve. This was the land that Independence Development had originally planned for residential housing. These decisions were not without controversy as one of the Lower Makefield

Township's Board of Supervisors, Grace Godshalk said:

I just feel that to take more than $500,000 of the taxpayer's money to buy land that will be bordered by Route 1 and a shopping center is unnecessary.[105]

In the summer of 1985, the attorneys representing the developer and the Township agreed to a stipulation that settled pending litigation, allowed the commercial portion of the development to continue forward, and provided the way for the Township to purchase the land that was going to be used for residential development. On November 13, 1985, Independence Development, Inc. sold fifty-five acres to Lower Makefield Township. The agreement ended litigation between

Courtesy Peter Osborne

After the land transfer was completed by Independence Development, a fence was erected by the township around the perimeter of the property which still marks the boundary line except for the more recent acquisitions. One of the access roads to the various lots of trees planted and harvested by Sam Willard can be seen next to the fence.

the company and Township after the Township had made a zoning change to part of the property. Independence Development was also required to landscape the corner and fence the boundary between the Preserve and the shopping center. At the same time, Independence Development was negotiating with another developer to sell the property.[106]

The transaction included the following restriction that was attached as a rider to the deed:

All the aforementioned premises being conveyed to Lower Makefield Township shall be utilized as part of the Five Mile Woods Preserve, for active or passive recreation, or any other uses similar thereof or necessary to maintain the aforementioned permitted uses. If any other use shall be made of these premises in violation of the restrictions, any resident of Lower Makefield Township may petition the Court of Common Pleas of Bucks County, which said Court, if after hearing, finds that Lower Makefield Township has violated these restrictions, shall order the property be conveyed to a conservation organization within the discretion of the court.[107]

THE BANASEK PARCEL

On February 28, 1986, Lower Makefield acquired a small sliver of land, 0.56 acres in size, that was bounded on the east by the former Penn Central tract (Tax Parcel Number 13-3-8), to the north by three of the Hibbs lots and to the south by Route 1. The property became available when the estate of Stephen Banasek was being settled by his wife, Bessie. Banasek had acquired the property in the 1940s. The parcel (Tax Parcel Number 13-3-7-1) was part of a larger parcel of more than thirty acres to the south, but was cut off from it because of the taking of land for the construction of the new Route 1, and the exit ramp at Oxford Valley Road.[108]

The larger Banasek tract (Tax Parcel Numbers 13-4-2, 13-3-6, 13-3-7), along with one of the Penn Central parcels (Tax Parcel Number 13-3-8) in Falls Township, had previously been owned by the Moons, a prominent area family who had lived in Bucks County for many years. Those parcels had also abutted the former William Satterthwaite Jr. farm on the east. This transaction completed the acquisitions of all the properties that bounded Route 1.[109]

PRESERVED FOREVER

Two land transactions were undertaken during this era by Lower Makefield Township as it acquired another parcel of the Woods. More importantly, it received a grant from the Bucks County Open Space program that in turn began a process which placed a conservation easement on the entire Preserve property, essentially protecting it for the future. With this last acquisition, Lower Makefield Township now owned 295 acres.

THIS IS A NICE ADDITION

Two additional parcels were purchased in 2004 by Lower Makefield Township and incorporated into the Five Mile Woods Preserve. The acquisitions came about because of several factors. The first was that the owners had recently signed an agreement with a developer to buy the property which bordered the northern edge of the Preserve and was critical to protecting the Woods. Soon it became known that the property would be developed and a *For Sale* sign was placed on it. With that, the Friends of the Five Mile Woods and the Township's Environmental Advisory Committee swung into action.[110]

Another factor that played into the purchase was that the parcels were listed as Priority 1 tracts in the 1999 *Natural Areas Inventory of Bucks County* prepared by Ann Rhoads and the Morris Arboretum of the University of Pennsylvania. The inventory had listed 115 significant properties that included some of the county's most important natural habitats. Several other nearby tracts that included the Five Mile Woods were also listed.[111]

Courtesy Peter Osborne

Throughout the Preserve, there are reminders of the property's distant past, including this section of fence that once ran along the boundary between the Willard and Banko properties.

The Banko tracts, as they were called, included Tax Parcel Numbers 20-32-43, and 20-32-43-1, and were 3.8 acres and 7.7 acres, respectively. Both were located along Big Oak Road. The first parcel was owned by Rita and Cyril Banko and purchased by the Township on June 9, 2004 for $225,000. The second parcel was purchased from Cyril's parents, Michael and Mary, on the same day for $525,000.[112]

After the transaction was completed, Board of Supervisors member, Pete Stainthorpe said:

This is a nice addition. It ensures that the whole length of Big Oak Road in that area is preserved. It will add an additional thirteen acres to our Preserve, it prevents more housing and it keeps Big Oak natural.[113]

The two parcels were located within the former Dark/Satterthwaite tract. Located on the property was a mid-

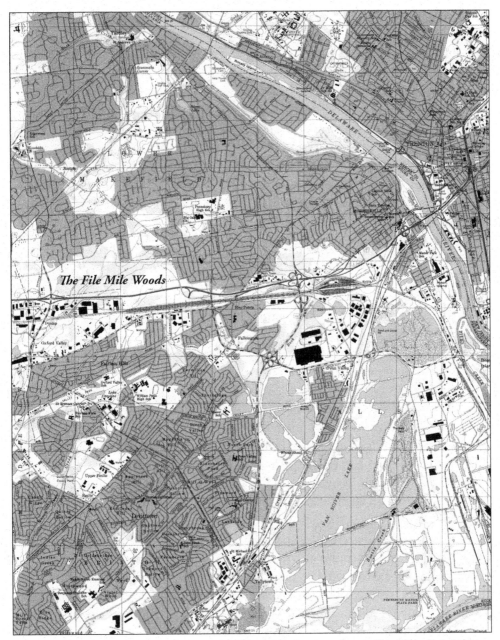

Courtesy United States Geological Survey

By 1995, when this USGS topographic map (Trenton West, NJ, PA) was created, residential and commercial development almost surrounded the Five Mile Woods Preserve. The new Route 1 had been opened, but the shopping mall was not yet completed to the west of the Preserve. As can be seen most of the surrounding area had been built out.

nineteenth century vernacular wood
frame house along with several outbuildings which were all subsequently
demolished. The foundation of their
barn can still be found. The Bankos
were farmers and are believed to have
leased some of the Pennsylvania Railroad's adjoining land to grow hay and
pasture their cows. They also leased out
their land to area farmers. The Bankos,
like the Cseplos and Guzikowskis, were
part of a larger emigration from Eastern Europe, including the countries
of Hungary and Poland. Many arrived
after 1910 pursuing agricultural interests.[114]

Courtesy Peter Osborne

*The Five Mile Woods Preserve was recognized by
Bucks County as being preserved open space. The
sign, placed on Big Oak Road, was erected to commemorate the designation.*

The purchase also represented a
major milestone as it was the first land
acquisition made by the Township in
several years and was made possible
because of funding that voters had approved in 1998 to buy open space. In

that year, they had voted to borrow up to $7.5 million dollars for land purchases.
Previously, the Township had prepared the *Lower Makefield Township Open Space
Plan* which inventoried its natural features, and created a listing of important
lands that needed to be acquired. In addition, the Bucks County Open Space's
Natural Areas Program provided $275,000 of the funding that was necessary.[115]

As part of the agreement to fund the purchase of the Banko property, Bucks
County placed a conservation easement on the entire property. While there were
deed restrictions on several of the parcels, this new restrictive covenant protected
the entire Preserve, except for the headquarters building and the property immediately around the water storage tank. The easement covered 292 of the 295 acres
(1.57 acres for the water storage tank and one acre for the Preserve headquarters).
It was probably the most significant land transaction since the original purchase
of the Penn Central property in 1979. The *Deed of Conservation Easement* from
Bucks County was implemented by the Bucks County Open Space program in
the spring of 2007. The creation of the easement satisfied the long-term concerns
of many that the Township might at some future date turn the Preserve into a
park with more active recreation activities than were allowed in the Preserve.[116]

The permanent restrictions were common ones: no industrial or commercial
activities were permitted on the property, pesticides that would impact water sup-

ply were forbidden, advertising was not allowed on the site, and the dumping of hazardous waste was forbidden. Additional restrictions included a no clear-cutting clause and specified that only trees posing a hazard could be cut, or for clearing utility right-of-way's. There was to be no planting of invasive plants and sound forest stewardship practices were to be implemented.[117]

While this easement was related to the Preserve's land owned by Lower Makefield Township, there were two other existing agreements previously made with developers. The first was with the owners of Cambridge Estates, and now called Big Oak Woods. In that covenant, the Township agreed to maintain the green spaces in between the rows of housing, adjacent to the Preserve, and along the eastern boundary of the Preserve. The second agreement was with the developer of the Yardley Oaks, and concerned the area where the headwaters of the Queen Anne Creek were located.[118]

MORE OF THE WOODS PROTECTED

Two other tracts of land containing parts of the Five Mile Woods were saved as open space. In 2000, the Sadowski farm in Falls Township (Tax Parcel Number 13-9-1), bordering on Stony Hill Road, was purchased by Falls Township. The acquisition funding included a grant from the Bucks County Open Space Program. These thirty-one acres included the section of the Woods that extended farthest to the east.[119]

In early December 2016, the Board of Supervisors of Lower Makefield Township voted to purchase the development rights of the Sandy Guzikowski farm (Tax Parcel Number 20-32-47). It contained a small portion of the Woods. While not contiguous to the Preserve, it saves another section of the Woods from development. The purchase of the Guzikowski development rights was the result of the successful floating of a bond by the Township in 2008 to save open space, along with another in 2016 for $15 million. There are now only two parcels left that contain parts of the Woods that have not been preserved.[120]

WATER STORAGE TANK CONSTRUCTION

Various residential development projects continued unabated into the 1980s and with that was the need for more water. In early 1986, the Keystone Water Company appeared before the Township's Planning Commission in its search for a location to place a water storage tank. The parent company, Pennsylvania American Water Company, had franchise rights to most of Lower Makefield Township. The company's manager requested a one acre lot in the area near the shopping center proposed by Independence Development. Because of the siting of the potential shopping center, it was thought that this was the best location.[121]

The fluted water storage tank was constructed at a cost of $1.2 million and was 135 feet high, seventy-five feet in diameter, and could hold one million gallons of water. Built on northern end of the Hibbs lot formerly owned by Eugene and Jacqueline Hieber (Tax Parcel Number 20-32-34), the land was leased by the water company from the Township for ninety-nine years. The one-acre lot was fenced and posted allowing only limited access. The rest of the property was incorporated into the Preserve.[122]

Courtesy Peter Osborne

The Shoppe Oxford Oaks Shopping Center finally opened after many delays. The water storage tank can be seen in the background on the right-hand side of the photograph.

SHOPPE OXFORD OAKS SHOPPING CENTER

The Independence Development Company had originally proposed to build a large residential community at the western end of the Woods in 1978 but was stopped in the late 1970s with the institution of a moratorium on additional sewer hook ups. By 1985, with the approval of a zoning change, Independence Development moved forward with plans to sell its holdings to another developer. Ultimately the shopping center, with a Kohl's as its anchor store, was opened in 1997. More recently, a new Shop Rite was opened in 2014.[123]

A PLACE OF NATIONAL NATURAL SIGNIFICANCE

Once the Preserve was established, it was the recipient of numerous awards in recognition of what had been accomplished. In 1978, the Bucks County Conservancy presented Donald Formigli with its Conservation Award for his efforts to save the Woods. The Bucks County Audubon Society also recognized his hard work with a service award in 1978. In 1991, the Conservancy again honored Don, and his work at the Preserve, with an award.[124]

In 1987 the Friends of the Five Mile Woods were the recipient of the *Take Pride in Pennsylvania* award from the Commonwealth's Department of Environmental Resources. The award honored groups that promoted the natural resources in several categories. The Friends received recognition in the Civic and Citizen organization category. The group was then nominated to take part in the national *Take Pride in America* program. The Preserve and the Friends received the *Com-*

munity Preservation Award for outstanding service from the Lower Makefield Historical Commission in 2002 during National Historic Preservation Week.[125]

In 2003, Lower Makefield Township, the Friends of the Five Mile Woods and Preserve staff submitted an evaluation of the Five Mile Woods Preserve to the National Park Service for consideration to participate in its National Natural Landmark program. The application for the prestigious listing was first recommended for consideration by Preserve supporter, Dr. Ann Rhoads, in 1988. Dr. Rhoads was active in the efforts to save the Woods in the late 1970s, served on the Lower Makefield Township Park and Recreation Board, and worked for the University of Pennsylvania's Morris Arboretum in Philadelphia. She was the author of several books on the flora of Pennsylvania and was involved with numerous field surveys with the Commonwealth's Department of Conservation and Natural Resources. Rhoads was also a former member of the Bucks County Planning Commission where she helped create a natural areas plan.[126]

While the designation did not bring any funding, it was prestigious as there were no other sections of the Fall Line listed on the NPS Landmarks inventory. Begun in 1962, by 1989 there were almost six hundred other natural landmarks around the country. In Pennsylvania, only two state parks carried the designation, Hickory Run State Park and Rickets Glen State Park.[127]

After discussing the potential listing with the National Park Service and the Township, Rhoads compiled the forty-page evaluation report. In addition, she created a comprehensive listing of resources for the nomination, sought support letters and submitted the first nomination in 1989. But just as it arrived a ten-year moratorium was placed on the program and with that the nomination was placed on hold. It was not until 2003 when it was submitted again. This time the effort was assisted by John Heilferty; John Lloyd, Jan McFarlan, who represented the Friends of the Preserve; Terry Fedorchak, Lower Makefield Township's Manager; who wrote a letter of support; and Wayne Bergman, Falls Township's Manager. The 1989 and 2003 nominations were valuable beyond the potential for designation. Equally important was that for the first time since Rick Mellon's *Master Plan* of 1981, a significant report was compiled about the resources at the Preserve.[128]

The evaluation also looked at the Fall Line from a larger context, rather than just a statewide view. Dr. Rhoads contacted officials in Delaware and New Jersey to see if sites that were similar in size to the Preserve existed in either state. They did not. In the end, she concluded that the Preserve could be designated a National Natural Landmark. The proposed boundary of the Natural Landmark would have included the entire Preserve.[129]

As part of her review, Rhoads reviewed four other sites that had been considered in a study of potential landmark sites. Curiously, the Great Falls of the Potomac were not listed, and they are probably the best surviving example of the Fall Line in the United States. However, as the nomination went through the review process in 2003, it was put on hold by the Washington office of the National Park Service, as the Bush administration in Washington was not promoting the program at the time. The application has not been submitted since.[130]

FAREWELLS

As time has gone by, many of the early leaders and advocates of the Woods project have passed on. One of the Preserve's important supporters and a nationally known scholar died on May 19, 1982 at the age of 96. Dr. Edgar Wherry was an important advocate for the preservation of the Woods. His letter of support was included in the report that was prepared for the Bucks County Conservancy and sent to the board of directors of the Penn Central Corporation, when their assistance was sought for the purchase of their part of the Woods.[131]

At the Bowman's Hill Wildflower Preserve, his memory was preserved with a trail named in his honor. His portrait hangs in the organization's headquarters building. [132]

Another important supporter, George R. Carmichael Jr., a teacher with extensive knowledge of Bucks County natural and geological history died in 2016. He too had supported the effort to save the Woods. He was 86. He authored a significant article about the county's geology for the Bucks County Audubon Society newsletter that was included in the first official report on the Five Mile Woods prepared by the Bucks County Conservancy. At the time of the article's publication, he was the Education Chairman of the Bucks County Audubon Society.

Professionally, Carmichael was chair of the science department at Pennsbury High School West and was the first summer naturalist at the Silver Lake Nature Center where he helped reintroduce many native plants. He was also a member of a number of many environmental groups.[133]

Other leaders of the effort who are gone include: Robert Pierson, the leader of the Bucks County Conservancy for many years, Lloyd Klatzkin, and Dan Rattigan, both former Lower Makefield Township supervisors.

Another sort of farewell took place on August 8, 1991, when the Fairless Works officially closed. The closure happened forty years after the ground breaking on March 1, 1951. At one time, ten thousand people worked at the site. On the day the plant ended operations, there were only eight hundred and fifty employees left. Its construction had begun a process that transformed lower Bucks County and whose effect spread across the region.[134]

A VISION FOR THE COMMUNITY REALIZED

The success of the Five Mile Woods project was only one part of a well-thought-out long-term strategy to provide recreational resources for Township residents and to plan for preserving open space at a time of intense development pressure. The grander strategy that was developed years earlier based on the 1975 survey of Township residents, was ultimately and successfully implemented step-by-step.

A new bike path ordinance and a master plan establishing a system of bike paths was completed. The first section was constructed from the Township building to Oxford Valley Road and dedicated in August 1978 by four of the most important advocates for recreation and open space in the Township: Donald Formigli, Gail Hardesty, Hank Miiller and Pat (Fair) Miiler. It continued to be expanded in years to come.[135]

In June 1978, a plan was unveiled for the construction of a multifaceted community park located next to the Township building on Edgewood Road. The plan for active recreation facilities met the wishes of the Township residents as expressed in the 1975 survey. It included a bike path, picnic grove, tennis courts, nature trails, ball fields, playground, and a user-fee swimming pool. The funding came from the fee-in-lieu-of payments made by developers. Ultimately, like the Five Mile Woods, the community park, and pool, came to pass and the park opened on May 16, 1981. The Preserve opened six months later.[136]

The Township also approved zoning that was far reaching in its impact. Hank Miiller, a former member of the Board of Supervisors, said that the ordinance was:

. . . probably the most technical ordinance we've ever had in the Township, possibly the most technical in the county.[137]

A farmland preservation ordinance, another important community goal, was developed and became Township policy when it was passed in 1986. The Lower Makefield Farmland Preservation Corporation created a method for developers to save farmland by building higher density housing, and dedicating the open space to agriculture.[138]

Pat (Fair) Miiller later recounted:

Even as development continued in Lower Makefield Township, there was a vision to control development and preserve natural resources and this was simultaneously realized.[139]

Even with these successes, residential developments continued to be built around the county. In the summer of 1978, a newspaper reported that twelve thousand new homes and apartments were either planned or being built on the

Route 413 corridor in Newtown, Middletown and Northampton Townships. It was the largest series of development projects in the county since the construction of Levittown.[140]

JOB WELL DONE

The Five Mile Woods Preserve, a dream to its founders in 1974, continues to provide benefits of all kinds. People from the Township and around the region continue to visit, hike its trails, partake of its programs and enjoy its solitude. The hard work of so many through all the years, unknown to those who use it today, is remembered here, with a sense of gratitude and amazement about how the journey has progressed.

Courtesy Peter Osborne

John Heilferty, the Preserve Manager, gives a tour of the Queen Anne Creek to visitors on Earth Day 2016.

COMMON BEECH

COMMON BEECH

Chapter 7

A WALK IN THE FIVE MILE WOODS

From its inception, the Five Mile Woods preservation effort has been an example of imagination and intelligent planning. The Woods stand as a living monument to what dedicated Township officials and concerned citizens can accomplish, given a common goal.[1]

BUCKS COUNTY COURIER TIMES

JUNE 13, 1979

FIVE MILE WOODS PRESERVE BROCHURE

Special places need special efforts.[2]

JEFFREY MARSHALL

PRESIDENT

HERITAGE CONSERVANCY

I HAVE SPENT ABOUT ONE YEAR AT THE PRESERVE, walking its trails, observing its wildflowers, traipsing along the Fall Line, attending its programs, meeting its volunteers and supporters, and researching about it in various archives. Unfortunately, most of my time writing this book was spent looking at a computer screen or being inside a room reviewing collections at various archives.

While researching is my first professional love, my favorite thing to do when undertaking a project like this is to spend my time exploring and wandering all over the property. I often see things that most do not because they do not have the trained eye to look for old foundations, former woods roads, stands of certain types of trees, the remains of former orchards, lilac bushes, patches of asparagus, and unusual rock formations. I found myself looking at the Preserve with a very different set of eyes than most.

When I walked through the Preserve I was peeling back the layers of history that happened there: What was life like here for the Dark family? What did the landscape look like at different times? How did that ditch get there? Why is a trail located where it is? When did a boardwalk get built?

Then there are the interviews, meetings and walks with a variety of individuals that give me additional insights and provide new information. All these pieces of information and insights come together and allow me to tell a story in book form. This is my mission. Therefore, the story of the Five Mile Woods Preserve is a collection of various legacies including a natural one, an historical one, a legacy of service, and one of vision.

A SEASON FOR ALL THINGS

The primary legacy of the Preserve is a natural one. It is a place of wonderment and natural beauty and each season reveals a variety of nature's forces at work. Like all places in nature, there is a season for all things. And so it was when this project began. As the year passed, the Preserve's appearance gradually changed with the seasons. Spring had not arrived at the Preserve and it still had its winter appearance when I first visited. But each time Don Formigli and I walked on a trail to explore the place, something new was coming up. As the weeks went by there were carpets of spring beauty, pockets of trout lilies, May apples, and periwinkle. Then the trees began to leaf out including the dogwoods, the sweet gums, and the beautiful beeches, some of which had been damaged by thoughtless vandals carving their initials into their bark over the decades.

By the time summer had arrived, it was difficult to find things that could be so readily seen when the woods were still barren. In the fall, the Preserve was this magical place of color and beauty. During the last months of the year it had shed its color and was a steel gray, revealing once again its interesting topography and remnants of its historic past.

In walking the Preserve with people like Don, John Heilferty and John Lloyd on different occasions I was struck, as many have been for two generations, by the remarkable array of plants, wildflowers and trees that grow there. Of the three, Don was the most romantic, if you will, in describing them. In a slide program that he and his colleagues used in the late 1970s to garner support for the Five Woods preservation efforts there were occasional whimsical phrases contained in the text that was read.

For example, he described several features of the Woods:

Spring is a special time in the Five Mile Woods when all of its wonders can be seen. It is unique for the great variety of wild flowers most of which bloom in the spring. The Pink Lady Slipper Orchid is the showiest of our native orchids.[3]

Both Johns are scientists and experts at the plant life and they are more scientific in their descriptions. Their depth of knowledge is remarkable and it was well worth taking a walk with them as I saw different kinds of plants that I might never have noticed or appreciated even if I had.

Each day there were people coming to hike on the trails, jog or take leisurely strolls on the various pathways. Some were serious students of the plants and trees of the Preserve, others were interested in its frogs and turtles, and still others had a special reason for being there. For example one day there was family visiting to help a son work on requirements for a Boy Scout merit badge. Some of the visitors had come for years; others had only recently moved to the Township and were walking the Preserve's trails for the first time.

The geological history of the Five Mile Woods Preserve is what helped to save it and remains at the center of the interpretive efforts. The Fall Line, Atlantic Coastal Plain and the Piedmont Plain and their meeting in Lower Makefield relatively undisturbed is an amazing accident of geology and geography. This is particularly unique because in neighboring Delaware and New Jersey there are few places like the Woods in terms of acreage devoted to the preservation of the Fall Line. It is the most remarkable of the Preserve's legacies.[4]

THE HISTORICAL LEGACY AT THE PRESERVE

The second important legacy of the Preserve is the recorded history of the people who have lived there and their impact upon the land. While no documented Native American sites have been found within the Preserve's current boundaries, it is also worth noting that no archaeological testing has ever been conducted there. It seems likely that those early peoples passed through at various times during their thousands of years of habitation in the greater Delaware Valley. It is known, for example, that there were two Native American sites found not far from the southwestern corner of Lower Makefield, where it meets Falls and Middletown Townships.

The connection of the Dark family to the Preserve is an interesting one, especially given that they played a role in the administration of William Penn's *Holy Experiment* and the Falls Meeting. Their significance to the county's history has been largely forgotten. By the first part of the eighteenth century, most of the grandchildren of William (c.1629? -1716?) and Allis (1617-1687) Dark, had left Bucks County and migrated to Virginia. Today the family's legacy survives in various legal and property records including a deed illustrated earlier in this book. And there is the house foundation within the Preserve near the Queen Anne Creek that is believed to have been built by them. The Satterthwaite family, however, has a different legacy as the descendants of its various branches continue to reside in Lower Makefield and Falls Townships, and the surrounding region. Unlike the Darks, they did not play a role in the colonial or county's government. However, they were farmers and merchants and their names can be seen on various maps of the region over the last two centuries. Some, who still carry the family name, live within a short distance of Fallsington. Female descendants continue to pass the family's legacy forward although their names have been changed with their marriages.[5]

One of the Satterthwaite houses, associated with the family's plantations within and near the Preserve, still stands. Home to, and once owned by, William Satterthwaite, Jr. (1775-1859), it became the center of the family's farming operations and from records we know it was also the scene of family weddings. The Satterthwaites had acquired the property in 1774 from Sarah and Robert Lucas.[6]

The Satterthwaite house is located today between Business Route 1 and the former Pennsylvania Railroad's Trenton Cut-off. The historic house is now home to several businesses. It is hard to imagine it being at the center of all the William Satterthwaite family's holdings and extensive farming operations as it does not seem to have any relevance to the Preserve. While it is just a short distance away as the crow flies, its importance seems distant because of all the various transportation corridors, commercial buildings, and homes that have been built nearby.

The stone structure's various architectural features have been changed over time, new window casings and sash were installed, and the exterior wall on the

Courtesy Peter Osborne

The home of William Satterthwaite, Jr. survives and stands on Business Route 1 in Falls Township. While it may seem like a long distance from the Preserve, the northern end of this tract of land bordered the section of his large farm that now is included in the Preserve.

eastern side was stuccoed over. This feature was typical of the era as it protected damp and cold air from penetrating into the building. There are several types of pointing on the front and back sides of the building that reflect repairs from different eras. The western section of the house is thought to be the oldest. However, the basic stone structure, home to several generations of the Satterthwaites still stands.[7]

There is some debate about its date of construction, some say it was built in 1702, which seems early, but the Falls Township commemorative history states it was constructed in 1773, which seems more likely. The book also calls it the *former Sherman Titus House*. Titus was the owner during the mid-twentieth century. The addition on the back side is said to have been added in the 1960s.[8]

The foundation of the Dark/Satterthwaite home near the Queen Anne Creek is all that survives within the Preserve boundaries of their occupancy along with the traces of two roads that once crossed the property. Buried near the house site are probably artifacts that would reveal more about their lives.

The heritage of both the Dark and Satterthwaite families also survive in other legal records in Doylestown, the Falls Meeting, and finally, in the three graveyards at Historic Fallsington. The early generations were probably buried near the Meeting House. The earliest generations of both families are probably buried in unmarked graves, as was Quaker custom from the late 1600s to the 1850s. Mem-

Courtesy Peter Osborne

Historic Fallsington is just a little more than two miles southeast of the Five Mile Woods Preserve in Falls Township. The Satterthwaite connection to this place was strong as was the Dark family's connection. The early Satterthwaites were probably buried here in the Falls Friends Meeting Cemetery in unmarked graves, as was the custom, in the rear section of the cemetery.

Courtesy Genealogy of the Satterthwaite Family

This 1775 octagonal schoolhouse, at the corners of Oxford Valley and Big Oak roads, was built with the help of the Satterthwaite family and their neighbors. The building survived in good condition until well into the 20th century. This is how it appeared around 1910. Today, there is nothing left but ruins.

bers of later generations of Satterthwaites can be identified in the Fallsington graveyards because of their small but simple inscribed headstones. The remains of persons in the four Quaker cemeteries, some of whom were Satterthwaites, were moved to Fallsington because of the construction of the Fairless Works.[9]

Fallsington was a place that was central to the lives of these two families. The small hamlet, located at the crossroads of several important roads, was a religious center, a regional gathering place, and later a stagecoach stop. It was one of the earliest settled communities in the Commonwealth and central to the history of the Quaker community in America. The Darks would have heard William Penn speak at the Mannor of Penns-berry when he was there from 1682-84 and 1699-1701 or worshipped with him when he attended the Falls Meeting. They may have helped with the construction of the first Meeting House in 1690.[10]

The Satterthwaites also had a long history with the Meeting as they played a part in the construction of three of the Meeting's buildings and the group's long and eventful history. Their farms neighbored the community and spread northward to include what is now the Five Mile Woods Preserve. Members of the various generations of the William Satterthwaite families could go to Meeting by traveling entirely on their farms or plantations as they called them.

A schism between two doctrines of Quakerism, the Orthodox and Hicksites, in 1841 necessitated having two Meeting buildings at Fallsington. When Lewis Satterthwaite (1886-1941) and Mary Satterthwaite (1887-1976), each representing the different factions, married in 1910, a process began that ultimately healed the rift between the two groups and the Falls Meetings were reunited in 1945. Lewis and Mary were from two different lines of the family. Lewis was the son of Henry Satterthwaite, the final owner of the Satterthwaite property now included within the Preserve.[11]

Historic Fallsington, Inc., created in 1953, saved the remarkably well-preserved village just as the residential developments in Fairless Hills and Levittown were being built along with Fairless Works. Those projects were in close proximity to this remarkable collection of buildings and sites. The preservation organization came to own six historic landmarks. There, at the center of the historic community, many of the buildings that generations of Satterthwaites walked by, still stand. Several would have been familiar to the Darks including the Moon-Williamson log cabin.

At least one of the houses still standing in Historic Fallsington was built by a member of the large family. Now in private ownership, the house Thomas Satterthwaite built in 1852 is located at 57 Main Street. Other Satterthwaites also owned businesses or homes in Fallsington. In all, ninety significant buildings were included within the historic district. The distinctive Quaker legacy lives on at the Falls Meeting. The Friends still meet on Sundays, just as they have done since 1683.[12]

Another place with which the Darks and Satterthwaites would have been familiar was the Mannor of Penns-berry or as it is better known today, Pennsbury Manor. It is located about four miles from Fallsington. Today the plantation, reconstructed in the 1930s, is located on the site where the original manor stood on the Delaware River. In walking the grounds, a visitor can still experience what it might have been like in those days of long ago. One can imagine William Dark walking down the main pathway, and presenting himself to William Penn so he could obtain the patent and survey of his land. At that time, the manor house was still being constructed.[13]

By the time that the Satterthwaites took possession of the Dark tract, Penn's home would have been in ruins. However succeeding generations of the Satterthwaite families did settle on the large tract of land that was once part of the original manor. A number of Satterthwaite homes were destroyed with the construction of U.S. Steel's Fairless Works, Fairless Hills and Levittown.[14]

Today the Quakers, who were so important to the founding of the colony of Pennsylvania and its early administration and the success of its economy, make up only 1% of the county's population.[15]

ADDRESSING THE SCARCITY OF KNOWLEDGE

As much as we know about the Native Americans and their time in the Delaware Valley and the Dark and Satterthwaite families, there is still much to be uncovered in the Preserve which would help with the interpretation of the role of these indigenous peoples, the Quaker families and their legacies.

The dearth of knowledge about the Native Americans at the Preserve, for example, and their association with the land for more than ten thousand years seems to call out for more research and perhaps some testing to be conducted at likely inhabitation sites within the Woods.

This is also the case with the Darks and Satterthwaites. The historical records from the late seventeenth and early eighteenth centuries that are available regarding the Dark family are very limited. While Ralph Thompson presumed that William Dark lived on the land now known as the Five Mile Woods Preserve, there is at least one other theory about his residency. Helen Heinz has suggested that the Dark and his wife may not have lived at what is now the Preserve. Perhaps, she thinks, they lived in Philadelphia County. This is based upon the fact that prior to coming to America, William Dark had been a glover in England. He may have continued with that occupation when he got to America. At this time, we cannot really know although the evidence still seems to point, as least as far as I am concerned, to him having lived in what is now the Five Mile Woods.

However, genealogical data from the second generation presents us with a scenario that supports Helen's theory. Genealogical records reveal a connection the Dark family had with Byberry Meeting as all of John and Jane Dark's children were registered there. Heinz suggests that the Darks may have leased the land at the Five Mile Woods out to another farmer, particularly after his father died and left him the remainder of plantation. On this I agree with Helen.[16]

Another mystery is that of the Dark/Satterthwaite house. It could not have been the only building sited there along the Queen Anne Creek. There must be more building foundations that have disappeared or been buried. We know that there were barns and other buildings to support the agricultural pursuits of the families living there as shown by the document that deeded half the property of William Dark to his son John in 1696. Certainly, this was the case with the Satterthwaites.[17]

In discussing this with Jeff Marshall, he suggested that one of the reasons that there may be no surviving foundations of other agricultural structures is that once the buildings were no longer used or perhaps destroyed by an event like a catastrophic fire, the remaining stone may have been removed and put to use elsewhere leaving no visual evidence of a building having been located there.[18]

In addition, remains of old orchards, gardens and livestock pens might be found as they have been at other historic sites around the country through archaeological excavations. Neighbor James Foulds, for example, remembers seeing a ring of stone at the Dark house site years ago, and believes that it was the remains of a well. This was confirmed by the District Forester's report written in 1978. Foulds also remembers several pedestals of rocks that may have been the remains of foundations for several out-buildings to the south of the Fall Line and near the Queen Anne Creek.[19]

The former Dark house site has long been of interest to those who were active in the affairs of the Preserve. In 1986, Rick Mellon proposed *The Ruins Project* in which he recommended further investigations. This included documenting what remained at the site, and encouraging volunteers to place the house site in a larger context of the region's history when conducting tours. This should still be given a high priority because when the Preserve was acquired there were still two chimney supports standing. Only a part of one remains today. Time is taking its toll on the site.

Another structure worthy of investigation is the Brelsford House along with the bank barn that stood nearby. While the house was probably built in the late eighteenth century further research might provide additional insights into the property's agricultural legacy and the inhabitant's lifestyles. Even though much work has been done on the house since its construction, there are still clues to be discovered with a more in-depth investigation.

Archaeological testing conducted at various locations within the Preserve would further expand the database of information. Certainly, the artifacts that were uncovered would provide additional insights into the lives of these people, both ancient and more recent inhabitants, and that of the land that now makes

Courtesy Donald Formigli

The author, John Lloyd and James Foulds discuss historic features near the Fall Line at the Preserve.

up the Preserve. They would also make for great exhibits.

The property certainly had farm roads that crossed it at various times aside from the Satterthwaite road shown on the 1828 survey or the Dark farm road that probably met another road that led to Fallsington. Rick Mellon's 1981 *Master Plan for the Five Mile Woods Preserve* includes a map that shows several woods roads that still existed at the time and were designated as potential access roads. Further research into the Bucks County road petitions might provide new information not only on the roads but also the buildings that were located near them. Another avenue of research might be the reports on the Division of Districts which might shed more light on the 1737 change in the boundary line between Falls and Lower Makefield Townships.[20]

As is often the case in projects like this, I find myself making suggestions to the managing agency because for the most part I am an outsider, a tourist if you will. I see the institutions with a different set of eyes, more clearly perhaps than the folks who are just trying to keep the doors open, the trails maintained and a myriad of tasks that need to be accomplished.

During my course of talking with visitors and hikers at the Preserve, it was clear to me that despite the heroic efforts of the staff and volunteers, many of those coming to the Woods do not understand its significance. They love the place, the solitude, the trails, the trees, the rare plants, and the views, but do not really know how special the place is or what its role was in the Commonwealth's development. While this book addresses some of those needs, not everyone who visits the Preserve will buy it.

There is a need for an interpretive plan for the Preserve which would include strategically placed signage along with QR codes so that visitors could use their phones to obtain more detailed information. This is an increasingly common tool at our nation's museums. For example, signage along the Fall Line would help visitors to understand its importance not only to the Preserve and its uniqueness to the region's geological past, but also its role in American history. The unique plants growing there need to be highlighted even if their exact locations are not revealed. The listing of the various species at the conclusion of this book might make a nice handout for visitors and could be converted into a checklist of things to find there.

There might be an interpretive panel, for example, that shows how the Woods have appeared over the years using aerial photographs and the various ways that the land has been used. When the visitors park their cars in the parking lot they might be interested to know that they are parked on a patch of land that grew prodigious amounts of potatoes for the Campbell Soup Company. Another area of interpretation might be how neighboring development affects the Preserve, including issues such as water distribution or endangered plants.[21]

The Dark/Satterthwaite house site needs to be interpreted not only because of its significance to the Preserve, but also for the roles that the families who occupied it played in the Commonwealth's history and the founding of American Quakerism. While care must be given so that the site is not vandalized or compromised, the site lends itself to interpreting the broader issues that affected the families who lived there and what their lives were like. Other aspects of the Preserve's architectural legacy that might be interpreted include the remains of the ruins of the bank barn and Preserve's headquarters.

Another area of interest to the author relates to the current status of the Preserve. Consideration should be given to preparing a new inventory and master plan for the Township. The plans that were created from 1978-82 have guided the destiny of the Preserve and its development now for almost forty years. Given that the Preserve is such a different place than it was in 1978, it seems an appropriate time to undertake another assessment of the resources.

This new study would reflect more recent developments such as the fact that today the Preserve is almost entirely covered by a forest which is different from when it was created in 1980 when there was still open space remaining within the Woods. Rick Mellon had originally called for the open spaces to be maintained knowing that if they were not that in a short amount of time the forest would take back those areas. On this he has been proven right.[22]

While those areas are beautiful forest now, it is clear that some of the unique plant species were lost as the succession of forest simply took over the open spaces in spite of early efforts to maintain them. For example, whereas 8% of the Preserve was once open space, today almost all of that is gone, and with it, some of the remarkable plant diversity. In 1980, there was a six-acre area south of the Preserve headquarters which was then an oldfield and several species of rare plants could only be found there. Today this area is completely wooded.[23]

It would also be revealing to see what plants are gone now because of the thick canopy or what plants are now growing in the Preserve because of these changes. Because the Preserve is now an oasis in the middle of a vast development, there must certainly have been some changes in the different species of birds, animals, reptiles and insects that inhabit the Woods. Finally, the database of information has been steadily growing since the early 1980s as is evidenced by the species listings in the Appendix. Even today, reading Rick Mellon's *Master Plan* is a fascinating exercise because of what he saw when he created the inventory but also because of his predictions of what would happen.

A new master plan would guide the Township into the future and provide ideas as to what could be done to enhance the property and allow it to continue serving as a model for scientific research. A new interpretive program would enhance ongoing programs and perhaps attract new visitors and scholars. Several funding sources could be pursued to undertake some of this work.

When the first parcels of the Preserve were purchased with money from the Township bond,and the grant from the Land and Water Conservation Fund, there were considerable financial resources that were used to establish and develop the Preserve. In the decades since, funding has been found to purchase additional land. However, on the operational side, while the Preserve has continued to receive Township support in terms of a budget, maintenance and staff, it has, like all agencies, been subject to budget cuts, freezes and challenges. Today the focus is essentially on maintenance of the property and the programs. It is here that the Friends organization might be able to assist the Township by seeking funding from sources that the Township cannot tap into for purposes such as preparing an interpretive plan or a new master plan.

Two final suggestions might be considered. This first is to reconsider the submittal of the National Natural Landmark application. While it was put on hold in 2003, it might be worth investigating to see if it is worth it to try again. Lastly, when the Preserve was first established, Route 1 had yet to be finished and so traffic noise was not a problem. However, after the highway was opened, it was clear that the noise diminished the environment at the Woods. Rick Mellon called for sound barriers to be erected but this was never accomplished. John Heilferty has explored this with the Department of Transportation officials who cited budget issues as the reason it cannot be done today. I still wonder if a concerted effort was made by the local state representatives to lobby the Pennsylvania Department of Transportation that it might yet be persuaded to undertake such a project given the heavy traffic now passing by on Route 1 and the significance of the Preserve. All along the region's major highways sound barriers are being installed.

The Ties that Bind Us

Historical connections fascinate me and I am always interested in documenting them when they involve a project on which I am engaged. On a beautiful June night in 2016 one of those interesting connections occurred at the annual Garden Party sponsored by the Heritage Conservancy in Doylestown. The event, held at the Aldie Mansion, was to honor volunteers and supporters of the organization. The mansion was once the home to William Mercer, the younger brother of Henry Mercer, a towering figure in Bucks County history.

The building was abandoned and in danger of being lost when the Conservancy stepped in and acquired the historic structure from the owners of the adjacent property in 1987. This generous donation from the developers of the shopping center, and Conservancy's subsequent restoration effort, returned the building to its former beauty. While the property is mostly screened from its neighbors, there was no small irony that this beautiful historic structure sits right next to a large shopping center. This paradox comes from the fact that for decades, the Conservancy has labored to preserve the county's heritage and its open space.[24]

One of the organization's projects recognized that evening was the Conservancy's beautiful annual calendar. Awards were given to honor the photographers who had taken pictures throughout Bucks and Montgomery Counties that helped to preserve and protect its distinctive natural and historic heritage. All the photographs were beautiful, inspiring, and made for a stunning 2017 calendar. One of those submitted was by none other than Don Formigli. He had taken the picture of a yellow trout lily in the crook of a beech tree on a day that we were walking through the Preserve just weeks before in April.

For me the evening was an interesting one as there were only a few people there who would have recognized the significance of that moment. As the program commenced, I remembered that the Conservancy had been a critical supporter of the early efforts to save the Preserve in the 1970s. Through the hard work of its first director, Robert Pierson, the effort was successful because he had assisted with crafting the strategy and making the connections that were ulti-

Courtesy Peter Osborne

The Aldie Mansion
Home to the Heritage Conservancy

mately successful in saving the Woods. He also set the course that would identify a critical and important source of funding for the project.

Pierson was a remarkable individual whose generosity and vision for Bucks County still benefits it. At one point when there were not enough funds to pay his salary, he volunteered in his position so another staff member could be paid. A landscape architect by training he was an early proponent of farmland preservation especially since he had witnessed the development that had happened so quickly in Falls Township and was spreading northward.[25]

The local efforts to save the Woods had been recognized by the group when it presented its Conservation Award to Don in 1978. The citation on the award reads:

For his perseverance and devoted service in preserving the Five Mile Woods, and for his example that one individual can make a big difference.[26]

Once again, the organization was recognizing the Woods project by honoring Don and using his photograph for the month of April 2017. Another person who remembered that effort of long ago was Jeff Marshall, now president of the organization. Jeff arrived at the Conservancy in 1980 as an assistant researcher and was familiar with the Woods efforts.[27]

Marshall, in reflecting on all the projects that the organization was honoring that evening, said:

Special places need special efforts.

Conservation efforts reflect an optimism about the future.[28]

Afterwards Jeff, Don, John Heilferty, and I discussed what would have seemed like ancient history to some. Yet, what struck me was that after all these years, Don was still making a contribution to the Preserve he had been instrumental in helping to create. *The Patron Saint of the Woods,* as I have called him elsewhere in this book, had once again brought the Five Mile Woods Preserve public recognition.

Courtesy Gary Street

The Heritage Conservancy, originally incorporated as the Bucks County Park Foundation in 1958, and later the Bucks County Conservancy, has raced against development pressures and challenges for more than fifty years in a heroic effort to save the county's important natural and historic heritage. It has saved thousands of acres of farmland and unique places from development. To date it has preserved more than thirteen thousand acres through outright acquisition, purchase of development rights or working through a variety of partnerships. The Five Mile Woods Preserve is one of the many projects that the organization either initiated or assisted with that came to fruition. It has taken a lead in creating an inventory of the county's historic properties and documenting them.

Don Formigli with his award winning photograph at the Heritage Conservancy's annual recognition program in 2016.

The board, staff, volunteers, and donors continue to fulfill its mission successfully. Today, the organization provides environmental educational programs, assists with preserving the county's history using a variety of techniques, and works with various stakeholders. The Conservancy has five hundred members and two hundred business members and looks to the future with optimism as it has for more than five decades.

There are other fascinating connections that have some tie to the Preserve. When Don Formigli began seeking counsel about the importance of the Preserve in the late 1970s, he contacted a number of people. Many of them were the leading botanists of their day both regionally and nationally. Even today their names can bring a sense of awe to those who have an interest in the subject. First and foremost, among them was Dr. Edgar Wherry. He was one of the founders of the Bowman's Hill Wildflower Preserve in the 1930s, one of the first preserves in nation, and also the only preserve to receive WPA funding in the entire country during the New Deal era. The Bowman's Hill group provided inspiration to many of the early wildflower sanctuaries, and then in 1974, Wherry, along with Oliver Stark, provided letters of support for the Woods project. While that may not mean much to a current generation of users of the Preserve, those letters proved that the Woods were unique and worth saving.

One of the humorous connections was the naming of the Penn Central's plan to develop their acreage in the Woods. The firm called it Penn Treaty Woods, a play on the description of the Five Mile Woods and the connection to the place where Penn had originally signed a treaty to purchase the land from Native Americans. Little could the person who named the development have known that the Woods had been owned by one of Penn's original patent holders who would have been at least vaguely familiar with that treaty.

Finally, there are unanswered questions remaining that need further study. For example, Rick Mellon offered a different interpretation of how the Queen Anne Creek got its name from mine. He suggested that rather than honoring the queen, the naming of the Creek was an insult to her because of its insignificance. That have been a very politically incorrect thing to do at the time however. And one final mystery. Who put a Rambler automobile on what became the Independence Development's lot that bordered the Banko property (Tax Parcel Number 20-32-42) just off of the Evergreen Trail? And, who later dragged it off the property given that it was knee deep in mud and that the wheels were rotted? [29]

LOYAL FRIENDS WHO ARE KEEPING THE PROMISE

The third legacy of the Preserve is the service that has been given to it by its naturalists, its volunteers, the Township's Board of Supervisors, managers and the taxpayers. One of the most important stakeholders in the effort are the Friends of the Five Mile Woods. They have been in existence since the acquisition of the Penn Central tract was completed in 1978. Many of the founders of the Friends were members of the original Save Our Woods Committee.

Over the decades, the Friends have played a significant role at the Preserve and the Township has relied heavily on this group to maintain the Preserve, to conduct the programs, and support the naturalists and managers over the years. There have been occasional rough patches as there are in all human endeavors. It can be imagined that there were times when the Friends were frustrated with the Township or vice versa. Surely there have been times when the issues were bedeviling. For many years, the group has tried to expand their volunteer base with modest success.

They have coordinated regular monthly workdays beginning in March and continuing until November. They undertake work projects such as cutting small trees that have fallen, keeping the trails clear and picking up litter and various other work projects. The Friends and the Preserve Naturalists have sponsored various activities over the years including open houses, lectures, education programs and tours. They also help to maintain the Preserve headquarters and create plans for future maintenance needs. The organization holds an annual meeting in February where members discuss plans and their concerns.

During the writing of this book there were regular work days when volunteers came to assist in the maintenance of the Preserve. Some were residents of Lower Makefield Township, others came from Yardley or Levittown. Some had volunteered there for a few years and others had been coming for decades. Most were retired and wanted to give back to their community. Everyone felt passionate about this special place.

Typical of the programs sponsored by the Preserve Manager John Heilferty and the Friends was the annual Earth Day program that took place at the Preserve on April 24, 2016. There were visitors of all ages who came from a variety of places including Lower Makefield Township, Levittown and Falls Township. Members of the Friends, and John, gave tours and shared their love of the place with visitors. Listening in on one of the tours, the guides had a wealth of knowledge, were insightful and particularly adept at engaging young people.

On October 9, 2016, the Preserve sponsored its annual Fall Open House, but unfortunately Hurricane Matthew was playing havoc with the weather and so the attendance was not as good as it might have been. However, by the end of the day as the clouds receded, area residents stopped by to visit.

Two of the visitors were Connor Gray and Dominick Fantano along with their mothers Jaclyn and Jarry. Connor was eight years old and a regular on the Preserve's Frog Squad, participating in *Frog Walks*. Because of his participation in the program he was given a copy of the *Peterson Guide to Reptiles and Amphibians* which he proudly carried that day. He loved to flip rocks and look for salamanders, frogs and spring peepers. His friend, Dominick, tagged along and liked to walk in the Preserve. John Heilferty engaged them, discussing their interests and encouraging them to continue to make new discoveries.

Another visitor that day was Arden Williams, an Administrative Assistant at the Silver Lake Nature Center, and her daughter Aaron. They were out for a ride and wanted to see the Preserve. The new Silver Lake facility is a beautiful one, opened in 1991, and located across the road from the Delhaas Woods. Recently new exhibits were built at the center that are beautiful, impressive and informative. The Silver Lake Nature Center is worth a visit.

On another day, while walking on one of the trails, I came upon a young family and they asked me about the trail system. We got talking further about the Preserve, and as it turned out, it was their first time there. The family had just moved into the Township and were looking for places to get outdoors. The father was sure they had found a place that they would begin to use regularly. In thinking about that conversation and countless others that have taken place since the Preserve was created, I could not help but think of those founders and how pleased they would be.

THE FIVE MILE WOODS TODAY

A final legacy of the Preserve is remembering the visionaries who created it and were part of a larger national conservation movement that was going on at the time. The story of the Five Mile Woods and its creation and preservation reveals a complicated effort that was involved in saving this unique property. To have honored those who blazed that trail so long ago has been a very satisfying pursuit for the last year. Many have continued to remain active in a variety of causes elsewhere.

Today there is only one other large woodland tract left in lower Bucks County aside from the Five Mile Woods. It is the Delhaas Woods, and it too was saved by visionaries including the lead agency, Bucks County Department of Parks and Recreation. While it was, and still is, promoted as being a unique woodland, which it is to be sure, it is a relatively young forest. In fact, during World War II, the site was used for ammunition storage. Since the 1940s, a new forest has reclaimed the land. It is now a beautiful place for a walk and is part of an impressive facility which includes a nature center and parkland managed by Bucks County.

The second tract is of course the Five Mile Woods Preserve. It has remained, for the most part, an undeveloped tract over the last three hundred years. While there has been a succession of agricultural uses, none have changed the physical landscape in a significant way. Except for the steady succession of forest and the construction of a few buildings and roads, which have largely disappeared, the general topography has remained undisturbed. If one eliminates the noise from the traffic on Route 1 and imagines most of the land without trees and as a farm or plantation, it is a view that most of its occupants have seen for many of the last three hundred years. For the native peoples who passed through here for thousands of years there was probably a combination of open fields and forests that changed regularly over time depending on the occurrence of natural events like fire or disease.[30]

When the Preserve opened, it was not that long ago that a significant amount of the acreage had been used for agriculture. In the decades before the efforts to save the Woods began, and as the uses of the land changed, rare plants could be found in the Woods. In addition, activists who preserved the Woods thought the endangered bog turtle was present. Since the 1981 dedication of the Preserve, the land has reverted to forest and the combination of pastures, farm fields and orchards have all disappeared.

There have been other events in recent decades that have impacted the Five Mile Woods. In the late 1940s, there was a forest fire that raced through parts of the Woods including the Preserve. A significant number of oak trees were destroyed by the gypsy moth infestations of the early 1980s. This was made even worse by several droughts at the same time. In 1996 an unusually strong storm passed through the area that dropped between eight and eleven inches of rain in four hours. The volume of water in the Queen Anne Creek was so powerful that the stream's channel was lowered by three feet as it came through the Fall Line.[31]

When one looks at an aerial view of the Five Mile Woods today, surprisingly, aside from a couple sections that were not preserved but developed, its unique shape can still be seen. In 2003, it was estimated that about four hundred acres of the Woods remained in contiguous parcels and that 295 acres were protected as they were owned outright by the Township. Three other easements have also saved portions of the Woods.

Some of the Woods were lost with the building of Cambridge Estates (now Big Oak Woods) to the east. As part of the approval process for the development, a small portion was saved because of a conservation easement with the Township. This includes the five wooded medians on the western side of the development and the land right at the Preserve's eastern boundary. A large parcel, which included a part of the Woods, on the northern side of Big Oak Road, across from the Preserve, was also saved. This is the source of the headwaters of Queen Anne Creek. This easement was negotiated as part of the approval for the construction of Yardley Oak and Oxford Glen developments.

The far western end of the Dark tract was developed as a commercial center called Shoppe Oxford Oaks Shopping Center after the plans for a residential development were delayed. None of the Woods was lost here. While it was largely developed, a significant part of the Woods was protected as the result of some of those critical planning decisions and compromises made earlier by Lower Makefield Township as the center was going through the planning process. As part of the approval process, the Township purchased more than fifty acres of the Woods that were added to the Preserve.

Finally, there is the vision of several farmers and their families who continue to maintain their properties as open space or active farms and have not yet sold to developers including the Foulds, Guzikowski and Sadowski families. In 2000, one of those families, the owners of the Sadowski farm in Falls Township (Tax Parcel Number 13-10-1), bordering on Stony Hill Road, sold their land to Falls Township through the Bucks County Open Space Program. These thirty-one acres include the section of the Woods that extend farthest to the east.[32]

Michael Sadowski, the owner, reflected on the state of development when he said:

I remember when there was nothing in this area but farms.[33]

In the closing weeks of 2016 it was announced that the development rights to the Sandy Guzikowski farm (Tax Parcel Number 20-34-132) had been purchased by Lower Makefield Township, funded partly by Bucks County Open Space funds. It contains a small section of the Woods and while not contiguous to the Preserve, another piece of the Woods had been preserved.[34]

At this point, there are just two parcels that include parts of the Woods which are not protected by either conservation easement or outright ownership by Lower Makefield or Falls Townships. The first is about forty acres in size and lies within the Guzikowski farm in Falls Township (Tax Parcel Number 13-3-10). The farm is approximately 141 acres. This property abuts the Preserve on its east. The last property is owned by the Foulds family on Big Oak Road in Lower Makefield Township (Tax Parcel Number 20-32-44). While the Woods do not extend all the way to the road, there are parts of the Woods located here. This property is bounded by the Preserve on three sides and the Township has discussed acquiring the property. All in all, it is quite remarkable that in the end, so much of the Woods was saved using a variety of techniques. No one could have ever foreseen this thirty-five years ago.[35]

In looking back at the vision of the founders of the Preserve, and more expansively, the developers of the Lower Makefield recreational system, along with the Bucks County park and recreational system, time has proven them all correct. For example, in Lower Bucks County, in 1970, 6% of the land was dedicated to parks, recreational facilities and open space. By 2009, the figure stood at 13%. The amount of land that was undeveloped or dedicated to agriculture made up about 44% of the land in Lower Bucks County in 1970 but by 2009 the amount had declined to 11%. Across the entire county in 1965, 65% of the land was used for agricultural purposes or was undeveloped. By 2009, that amount had declined to 35%.[36]

Today the Township, and Bucks County, can be proud of the fact that despite the intense development that has taken place over the last six decades, and will continue, many acres of open space have been preserved, in addition to many historic sites. At the time that county officials began making the clarion call to save open space and create recreational spaces in the 1950s, there were some who probably questioned the wisdom of that vision. They believed that the county would remain rural. But now, six decades later, it is clear those leaders in the open space movement were extraordinarily prescient.

THE VISION AND LEGACY: FORTY YEARS LATER

The introduction for this book began with a discussion of dreamers who have created many of our prized natural and cultural resources. While this book's main focus was the Five Mile Woods Preserve, it is important to remember that the Lower Makefield Township's Park and Recreation Board, which was so instrumental in saving the Woods, was incredibly busy with a myriad of responsibilities. New residential developments kept coming to it for review, other projects were being undertaken and special events were being held. The PRB was also creating a vision for the community's future needs.

That vision called for the preservation of open space and farmland, the building of a community park that included a playground, picnic area, tennis courts, a pool and ballfields. In addition, a bike path system and performing arts program were envisioned. In the end, all their efforts came to pass. The Township has a recreational program that is the envy of many. Those devoted volunteers, the various Board of Supervisors and the taxpayers can all be proud of the legacy that they created. Most people who use those facilities today probably have no knowledge of those early efforts or the dedicated efforts of those citizen activists.

Pat Miiller often reminded me of the fact that the Preserve was the result of a grass-roots effort that started with the local citizenry's desire to save this unique parcel of land with such a fascinating geological, cultural and historic legacy. She believed that it may have been the first such effort in Bucks County where local citizens not only wanted something but volunteered time, expertise, and skill to achieve and maintain their vision. It certainly was an inspiring endeavor.

Working my way through many pages of documents, plans, interviews, and discussions I was reminded regularly that the Five Mile Woods Preserve is typical of many similar efforts across the country over the last one hundred and fifty years. These are the places that we the people have saved, often against all the odds. The Preserve was saved by people who had a strong passion for the place.

In 1937, a superintendent of Washington Crossing Historic Park reflected on what was needed to carry that park's mission forward and his comments are just as relevant to the Woods today.

He said:

Public interest and support is necessary. You and your friends can do much to help. [37]

In reflecting upon that, and thinking about the contributions and hard work of those who have gone before us, I am reminded of the famed John Muir quote about mountains calling, and to paraphrase it here, let me say:

The Five Mile Woods are calling and I must go.

Courtesy Five Mile Woods Preserve
Donald Formigli Collection

Boardwalks allow hikers to cross wet areas in the Five Mile Woods Preserve. This is a typical view along one of the numerous trails at the Five Mile Woods Preserve.

COMMON BEECH

COMMON BEECH

Chapter 8

REFLECTIONS
AND
A PASSION FOR THE PLACE

The principal obligation of the Preserve is to hold all the Preserve flora, fauna, and their habitats in trust for the preservation of natural diversity.[1]

GUIDE FOR THE PRESERVATION OF THE PRESERVE

1979

IN 2016, THE FIVE MILE WOODS PRESERVE celebrated its thirty-fifth birthday, having opened its facilities and most its trails in the late fall of 1981. In 2018, it will celebrate the fortieth anniversary of the purchase of the Penn Central tract which established this jewel in a crown of the various recreational facilities in Lower Makefield Township. With these two special anniversaries, its seems only right to have several volunteers and staff reflect upon the history of the Woods, their relationship with it and what they thought that the future might hold for it.

There have been three site managers since the Preserve opened in 1981 and five chairmen of the Friends of the Five Mile Woods who have faithfully served the Woods. A good team needs good leadership and the Preserve's various leaders have often provided those skills to carry out the vision. The following is a list of the Preserve's leadership since its creation.

FIVE MILE WOODS PRESERVE MANAGERS
Rick Mellon, Resident Naturalist (1981-1995)
Bonnie Tobin, Naturalist (1996-1997)
John Heilferty, Preserve Manager (1997-Present)

CHAIRMEN OF THE FRIENDS OF THE FIVE MILE WOODS
Gail Hardesty – 1981- 1984
Ron Montgomery - 1985-1995
Ron Montgomery, Co-Chair - 1995
Jan McFarlan, Co-Chair - 1995
John Lloyd – 1996 - Present

As part of the commemorative nature of this book, the author asked several people who have been involved with the Preserve for a long period of time to reflect on their time working there. The essays, which include the book's Preface, reveal the deep feelings that these friends, supporters and its current manager have about the Preserve and the remarkable legacy that was saved and can now be enjoyed by visitors.

To begin, Jeff Marshall, the President of the Heritage Conservancy, provided excerpts from an article written by Robert Pierson in 1962. Pierson was the first director of the Bucks County Conservancy and played a significant role in saving the Five Mile Woods. He was remarkably prescient as he foresaw the critical challenges that had to be addressed at that moment if the Bucks County was to retain its character. Then there is an essay by Pat Miiller who was the chairman of the Lower Makefield Township's Park and Recreation Board, John Lloyd who is the current chairman of the Friends of the Five Mile Woods, and John Heilferty who is the current manager of the Five Mile Woods Preserve.

To conclude this collection Jeff provided an essay that speaks to a theme that the entire book reflects upon, which is that essence of history is remembering, particularly of those who led the way in preserving this special place. The following essays are their thoughts in their own words.

Courtesy Peter Osborne

The Fall Line

James Carr (L) and Robert Pierson (R) reviewing subdivision plans in 1957.

How Can These Green Belts Be Preserved?
By Robert Pierson
Former Executive Director, Bucks County Conservancy

What will Bucks County look like ten, twenty or even fifty years from now? When we talk about our increasing population for the years 1980 or 2010, many of today's young people will actually be part of this population. The real fact is that the kind of communities we build during our period of rapid expansion will set the pattern for all time and the kind of living these young people will have the rest of their lives.

We have inherited an area justifiably famous for its natural beauty and its liability. And, of course, time doesn't stop in 1980 or 2010. Those of us living here in Bucks County have a real responsibility to our children and their children as well as to our own enjoyment of life for we are but the custodians of the land we use.

Situated as we are between Philadelphia and New York, the great squeeze will continue and Bucks County can either be a vast monotonous sea of asphalt and shingles or it can be a number of well planned communities surround and interlace with green belts.

But how can these green belts be preserved? How can we make sure that our stream valleys, our mountains, the deep gorges and the magnificent wooded area will continue to delight and refresh the people?

Parks are not primarily structures of concrete, stone, and paving. Parks are basically open green spaces where people can get out and enjoy a change from the pressures of everyday living, where kids can play in a stream, play ball or just hike through the woods.

But the opportunities are so vast in Bucks that public agencies cannot do the whole job. Out of the concern to preserve more open spaces the Bucks County Park Foundation (now the Heritage Conservancy) was formed as a private non-profit corporation to encourage and receive gifts of land for future park lands and facilities. Its purpose further states that it will receive land for the protection of the streams, valleys, lakes and ponds in Bucks County, and for the setting aside of other lands in Bucks County necessary to assure present and future generations an adequate amount of open land, thus to provide a means for preserving such land for the recreation, exercise, and education of the public.

Courtesy Five Mile Woods Preserve
Donald Formigli Collection

Hart Rufe, a former president of the Bucks County Conservancy, observes a wounded bat while on a tour of the Five Mile Woods Preserve in 1976.

Courtesy Five Mile Woods Preserve
Donald Formigli Collection
Pat Miiller at the victory celebration after the overwhelming passage of the referendum to purchase the most important tracts of the Five Mile Woods in the spring of 1978.

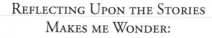

REFLECTING UPON THE STORIES
MAKES ME WONDER:
WHAT MORE CAN BE LEARNED FROM THE WOODS?
By
Pat Miiller
Former Chairman of the Lower Makefield Township Recreation and Park Board

History is a Greek word which means, literally, just investigation.
ARNOLD TOYNBEE

This quote sums up so much of what this book and The Five Mile Woods Preserve are all about. When Don Formigli engaged Peter Osborne to write a book about the Woods Preserve, he set afoot an investigation not only of how the Woods has been preserved but deeper searches about the stories of the land itself. As a detective, Peter has unearthed much about the early history of what is now Lower Makefield Township.

Investigation is also the opportunity the Woods itself provides for current and future generations. My personal involvement in saving the Woods stemmed from my firm belief that nature and trees and rocks and woods offer unique and vital opportunities to inspire curiosity, to explore, and to dream. As land is developed and society becomes more complex, I believe kids need – we all need – natural places to ground and inspire us.

I was born in Bristol and experienced firsthand the rapid development and change in the nearby rural areas along with the disregard for natural areas and prime farmland that Peter discusses. Living in Lower Makefield in the 1970's, I wanted to make a positive difference in how the area was developed. We worked to be proactive in achieving our vision. Continuing to live in the area, I have enjoyed seeing how our dreams became reality shaping Lower Makefield and its quality of life. As I recalled our work to save the Woods in Chapter 5, the work in which I was so directly involved years ago, I was reminded of another quote:

Study history, study history.
In history lies all the secrets of statecraft.
Winston Churchill

Thanks Don and Peter for the opportunity to be directly involved in this book. Digging a little deeper and reflecting upon the stories makes me wonder – what more can be learned from the Woods?

I Hope to See You Soon in the Woods
By John Lloyd
Chairman, Friends of the Five Mile Woods

I have been asked to reflect on my experience as a member and leader of the Friends of Five Mile Woods over the last twenty-five or more years. I became interested in Five Mile Woods through my sister Jan McFarlan who was a past chairman. She and I went to a meeting nearly thirty years ago, and were greeted warmly by the membership and we have both stayed active ever since. This was around the time when the Preserve was celebrating its five-year anniversary. As presented earlier, the Friends played a key role in the initial preservation of Five Mile Woods. So many of the early Friends played multiple roles in that story. In addition, Don Formigli, Gail Hardesty, Ann Rhoads, Pat Miiller and others were members of the Park Board or were LMT supervisors but they were all truly Friends of Five Mile Woods. They were all able to work together to save a wonderful place for our Township and our region. What they achieved was difficult and I am proud to be able to continue as a member and leader of such a remarkable group.

The work of the Friends has evolved from that of an organization of activism, trying to save Five Mile Woods from the bulldozer and urban sprawl, to an organization of stewardship to maintain and preserve this place for generations to come. A key part of the Friends stewardship role is education. Each year we stage numerous events where we try to spread the message of Five Mile Woods and the importance of preservation of open space in our community. We host two open house events each year where we provide nature displays and guided walks for the public. It has been a real privilege to lead these walks. We show people the fall line and explain its geological and human significance. Adults almost always show that moment of understanding that is the reward for any good guide.

Courtesy Peter Osborne

John Lloyd, doing what he does best, revealing the fascinating natural wonders of the Woods to visitors in 2016.

Our school age visitors often present the most curiosity. They often ask the kind of questions that we can't answer and will have to look up when we get back to the nature center. The youngest visitors are happy to collect leaves and learn that they have different shapes and colors. And we always remind visitors of the importance of Five Mile Woods and of having such a unique nature preserve in their neighborhood.

In addition to education, the Friends continue the mission of preservation, maintenance and enhancement of Five Mile Woods. We have seen several properties added to the Preserve since it was originally founded and have been watchful for additional opportunities to preserve contiguous or nearby open space. The Independence Square property, home of the Evergreen Trail, was added in the 1980s. About ten years ago, we added the Banko property and, in 2017, an agricultural easement was obtained on the nearby Guzikowski farm. All these acquisitions have helped to buffer and protect the core area of Five Mile Woods and the Friends have helped to monitor the availability of these properties and bring them to the attention of Township officials. Our most visible core mission is in the maintenance of the Woods for the enjoyment of our visitors. Our monthly workdays provide an opportunity for community service for our members and many others. Scout troops, religious organizations and school groups have all contributed to our workdays. We welcome all who have an interest in nature and service. Even though many times we spend much of our time talking about the Woods we still manage to do some trail maintenance too.

I hope this book has convinced you that Five Mile Woods is a unique wildlife habitat and that it was preserved by the farsighted commitment of civic minded neighbors. Please come to Five Mile Woods and enjoy the many trails and the beautiful scenery. It is a great place to visit in any season. And if you appreciate it like the Friends of Five Mile Woods do, then maybe you would like to join us in our work to preserve and protect this wonderful place. We are always happy to welcome new members. I hope to see you soon in the Woods.

Courtesy Peter Osborne

John Heilferty installing a waterbar along a trail in the Five Mile Woods.

MY JOURNEY IN EXPLORATION AT THE FIVE MILE WOODS PRESERVE
By John Heilferty
Five Mile Woods Preserve Manager

My journey in exploration at the Five Mile Woods Preserve began a mere 20 years prior to Peter Osborne researching and documenting this amazing story of how the Preserve came to be. And as is evidenced by the remarkable history Peter has uncovered, mine is but a very small part in the events which have shaped the Preserve as we know it today. Having recently married, and with our first child on the way, my wife and I ushered in 1992 with the task of selecting a community within which to purchase our first home and begin raising our family. We were both happy to find that Lower Makefield Township addressed all of the important variables that couples consider when making such a decision – good schools, abundant amenities, a diverse and welcoming community, and proximity to both of our jobs. Yet I was also impressed by the availability of open spaces, both within and immediately surrounding the Township. This had significant appeal to me, both as a wildlife biologist working full-time for New Jersey's Department of Environmental Protection as well as an individual whose primary recreational interests take place outdoors. My visits to the Preserve in those early years were admittedly infrequent, as the demands of raising a new and constantly growing family happily consumed most of my free time. But I still recall my personal "discovery" of the Five Mile Woods Preserve as having been one of thankful amazement.

Not long after moving to the Township, I interviewed for a volunteer opportunity on the Township's Environmental Advisory Committee, or "EAC." It seemed a useful way I could give back to the community, allowing me to take some of the workplace skills and experiences I utilized daily protecting natural resources in New Jersey, and employ them right here in my own back yard. Among the projects the EAC was undertaking at that time was the identification of undeveloped parcels throughout the Township that might potentially be investigated for acquisition using County open space monies. This included properties in the vicinity of the Preserve. My involvement with the EAC led to my meeting Scott Fegley, who served on the Board of Supervisors at that time and was the Board's liaison to the EAC. Scott was a passionate and energetic advocate for the Township's natural resources and open spaces. We eventually discovered a shared concern regarding the impact increasing development was having upon the Township's wetlands and stream corridors. Scott proposed that we pool our complimentary knowledge on the issue, and together we drafted, proposed and had adopted the Township's first wetlands buffer ordinance.

Through the appearances those efforts required before the Board of Supervisors and the coordination that was necessary with Township Manager Terry Fedorchak, the Township staff and governing body became very familiar with my background and experience. This served me well when, in 1997, I learned that the Township was in search of a qualified candidate to manage the Five Mile Woods Preserve. I was not aware of what specific responsibilities were entailed and was already managing a full-time job. But seeing as Terry Fedorchak and the Board had become a familiar audience, I decided it could not hurt to interview for the position, if only to see what this position might involve, how much time it actually required, and inquire as to "what" or "who" they were looking for ...

Well, twenty years later, I remain privileged to serve my community as the Naturalist at the Five Mile Woods Preserve. As was confirmed during my discussions with the Township Manager back in 1997, the "Naturalist" position involves part-time responsibilities managing the (approximately) 300-acre property, organizing programs or events that are run or hosted by the Township, acting as the Township's liaison with tenants renting the single-family residence located on site, and coordinating with the "Friend's" group chartered to help maintain and advocate for the Preserve.

Stewardship of the Preserve is guided by a "Guide for Preservation" prepared by Rick Mellon, the original manager of the Preserve. The Guide for Preservation memorialized the general philosophy of the Preserve - that the Preserve is intended for passive, recreational use by the public in a manner that does not compromise or inhibit the properties main purpose, that being the preservation of the natural communities and biological diversity that existed on the property at the time of its acquisition. The Guide for Preservation did not advocate for widespread management of existing habitats or communities within the Preserve, either in attempt to restore them to some condition that might have existed historically or to one which might presently be considered more desirable. For example, no effort was to be undertaken to "enhance" or "improve" the Preserve's wildflower communities via supplemental plantings or propagation. In fact, very little management of specific ecosystems was recommended at all. Despite being primarily "forested" since its inception, no forestry practices were identified or recommended to manage forest stand quality or succession within the Preserve. These decisions were less an opinion on the benefits or disadvantages of such practices. Rather, they reflected the belief that the Preserve had value exactly as it existed, without need to aspire to a former or future state. It also acknowledges that – as much as *preserving* the Woods was in fact the goal - it was in fact unrealistic to believe that through active or constant management, it could be preserved in time. The reality the Guide for Preservation embraced was that the Five Mile Woods Preserve has been, and will continue to be shaped by the anthropogenic influences which surround it.

There were, of course, some minor management exceptions. When the property was acquired in the early 1980's, portions of the Preserve were in early successional states such as fields or meadows, and these were encouraged to be maintained (these efforts faltered). The Guide also briefly mentions the impacts which invasive plant species might have upon the Preserve's ecosystems, and even more briefly mentioned deer browse. No management plans were ever established, though concerns grew on one of those fronts and would soon take up a significant amount of my time. In short, the Guide for Preservation is as much a directive on what activities should *not* occur within the Preserve as it is a mandate for aggressive management that should be performed.

Much of the time I spent at the Preserve during my early years was happily consumed with meeting and coordinating events with the "Friends" organization that was chartered to assist with stewardship of the Woods since its earliest day. Among the earliest Township decisions concerning the preservation of the Five Mile Woods was the creation of a group of Township residents who would volunteer to assist in stewardship decisions concerning the Preserve. The "Friends of Five Mile Woods" I met over 15 years after the group's founding quickly impressed me as a proactive, passionate and hard working group of volunteers, many of whom were actively involved in the original preservation effort Peter Osborne so meticulously details herein. Yet there were as many "new" volunteers who, not unlike I did in 1992, "discovered" the Preserve some time after its creation, but to their credit *also* discovered that they could not only enjoy the Woods as a frequent visitor but also as an active advocate.

Much of what I learned about the Preserve in those early years, I learned from the Friends. Among the group I found a collection of birders, botanists and outdoor enthusiasts who were every bit as fluent and knowledgeable as I – and in some areas proving to be more so. But there were also friends who were unashamedly indifferent to Carl Linneaus' dictate that "Latin must fill the air" if one is to partake in the study or enjoyment of wildlife. There are Friends who attended every volunteer workday, held once a month from March through November, and others who might make even *greater* personal effort simply to attend one. There are Friends who prefer instead to staff our public events, greeting visitors at our twice-annual open houses, or even Friends who's forte is merely delivering fresh baked brownies for our many visitors at those events. They are an enjoyable group with which to coordinate, and I've learned not to underestimate their talents, generosity, or the amount they can accomplish in a 3-hour workday. They are good people and better friends, and the Preserve and Township as a whole are better for their service.

The Friends hold an annual meeting where we set goals and objectives for the coming year, openly discuss maintenance or upkeep concerns, and plan workdays when most all of the trail maintenance and repairs will occur. The main purpose for this, of course, is to make the Preserve safe and inviting for the general public. With a few exceptions discussed below, the Preserve is open for use by the public every day from dawn to dusk. However, "public use" of the Preserve has also historically included nature camps run throughout the summer and geared towards 6 through 12 year olds. When I took on the Naturalist position in 1997, the Township hosted summer camps that routinely attracted as many as 30 children in the morning, and 30 more in the afternoon, for nature-themed programs that excited and inspired. By making Township facilities available to a reputable contractor who provided quality programs at a very reasonable price, the Township was able to subsidize a unique experience for our residents, and one that the Preserve was uniquely capable of delivering. The programs were developed and managed by a local organization, and were instructed by professional teachers who frequently returned summer after summer. This delighted the many "returning campers," who would commonly be greeted by first name as they walked in the nature center doors on the first day of "camp." I presided over many successful years when parents primary concern was getting their children enrolled before classes filled, not whether their children would enjoy the program or want to return on "day two".

Over the years, the Township *also* excelled at delivering sports opportunities for Township residents, providing abundant athletic fields which in turn spawned corresponding athletic organizations. While certainly an equally valuable amenity for Township children, week-long *sports* camps become both more popular *and* more abundant. Unfortunately, they appear to have doomed the summer camps that for so many years had kids exploring "out in the woods," notwithstanding hot sticky afternoons, guaranteed bug bites and the occasional run-in with poison-ivy. Before long, the competition from other "camp" opportunities started to affect nature camp attendance, and enrollment numbers certain weeks became economically unsustainable. Classes with only a few campers enrolled would occasionally need to be cancelled last minute, rescheduled or combined. Frustrations with the resulting uncertainty only further hindering enrollment in subsequent years, and as a result, for the past few summers, we have not been able to host cost-effective nature camps at the Preserve. The allocation of Township staffing does not facilitate programs led by professional "Township" staff either, and so for the past few years, summers within the Woods have not been as full of the sounds of childhood wonder.

Thankfully, my responsibilities as liaison between tenants renting the single-family dwelling on side have only gotten easier over time. Where my early years were fraught with frequent tenant turnover and were at times not without concerns, the Township is presently fortunate to have not only a very stable arrangement in place, but one which has in fact benefitted the Preserve with unsolicited care and stewardship of the property beyond that which is required by our mutual agreements.

As far as oversight of the Preserve itself was concerned, one of the management issues I decided did warrant concerted action was the issue of over-abundant deer. By the mid-2000's, it was becoming clear to myself and the Friends of Five Mile Woods that the Preserve was experiencing significant damage due to deer browse. Many other trained biologists shared that concern, including nationally recognized botanist Dr. Ann Rhoads of the University of Pennsylvania. The evidence was not lacking if you knew what you were looking for, which in the case of deer browse is what you do *not* see. In many portions of the Preserve, one could see hundreds of feet thought the understory - early evidence that deer were completely consuming all vegetation within their reach. Further, by merely hiking through the Preserve around dawn or dusk, it was becoming easier and easier to document both the abundance and ambivalence of deer.

Around 2004, I started actively discussing these issues with the Friends of Five Mile Woods, and eventually with Township Supervisor Terry Fedorchack. Taking any action at all to address the problem would require the approval of the Board of Supervisors, under the close direction of the Township Manager. Among the realities I needed to make clear to both parties was that successfully addressing the matter would likely take time, money and will-power. The latter would not be insignificant. I was transparent in sharing my understanding that some form of lethal management would likely prove to be required. Unfortunately, societal realities in communities such as Lower Makefield Township essentially guaranteed that some percentage of our residents would respond adversely to any such proposal.

To document the Preserve's deer problem, myself and the Friends of Five Mile Woods invited respected biologists from the region to walk the property, discussing and inspecting for the signs of over-abundant deer. The evidence was clear, wide spread, and alarming. I also arranged for a contractor to perform an actual deer population estimate, arrived at by analyzing infra-red video obtained while flying a Cessna aircraft in a grid patter over the Preserve during wintertime (leaf-off) conditions. As a biologist, I knew there was really no "magic number" for how many deer Five Mile Woods *should* contain or support. This is less a matter of numbers, and more a matter of *impacts*. Yet as I also accurately predicted, that would be among the most frequently asked questions I would need to address. A number of reliable, scientifically based studies, performed for the intended purpose of investigating the effect deer have on forest or ecosystem health, have concluded broadly that deer at densities over approximately 20 per square mile resulted in direct adverse impacts to forest health and composition, with resulting indirect adverse effects on all other forest wildlife. The population estimate we received from the flyover if Five Mile Woods and its immediate environs indicated *over 50* deer in the square mile surveyed. I also recommended the Township contract with a respected deer management biologist to independently assess the situation both within Five Mile Woods and in the Township as a whole. The Township retained and was well-served by Bryon Shissler of Natural Resource Consultants, Inc.. After a number of site visits and discussions with myself and Township officials, Bryon prepared a detailed report addressing the Township's deer population, documenting the impacts over-abundant deer were having township-wide, cataloging available management or mitigation alternatives, and discussing the effectiveness of each per his vast experience in the field of deer management. Bryon also attended many public meetings and helped formulate and guide implementation of the Townships initial deer management strategy.

Ultimately, Township leaders found it easy to accept that deer were in fact over-abundant throughout the Township. They also understood that this had very real impacts for Township residents: Deer adversely affect resident's gardens and landscaping and played a role in the spread of Lyme disease. Over-abundant deer also significantly increased the risk of deer-car collisions – there were over 70 reported to Township police during the final year this issue was being publicly debated, with 113 deer actually removed from Township roads. And they accepted *my* primary concern that deer were having unacceptable adverse impacts on the forest ecology within Five Mile Woods – the crown jewel of the Township's environmental stewardship legacy. After patiently holding many public meetings where residents were afforded the opportunity to voice their varied and often emotional opinions, Township officials agreed to take action.

The final recommendation of the Township's deer management consultant was to manage the deer population using trained, professional contractors to perform sharpshooting at select, appropriate sites throughout the Township. The consultant's recommendation to employ this methodology reflected several realities, some readily apparent, others less so. Managing the deer population merely by encouraging public hunting was not recommended, as it largely reflected the pre-existing conditions which had resulted in the problem in the first place. The degree of urbanization in our community simply rendered too much of the lands within the Township inaccessible to hunters. Further, only archery tackle is allowed in our region – a fact that was not intended as a knock against bow hunters, though some hunters unfortunately perceived it as such. Rather, it was an acknowledgement that per design, archery tackle is simply a challenging and inefficient means by which to harvest deer. The alternative of using professional sharpshooters had been demonstrated to be both safe *and highly effective* in communities very similar to Lower Makefield Township, such as Princeton, New Jersey (where sharpshooters continue to be employed to this day). And while some residents seemed incredulous that a rifle would be employed to manage deer in the Township, not a single safety incident regarding deer management via sharpshooting was (nor could be) aired in support of their perceived concern. The Township agreed to advance with such a proposal.

Unfortunately, the Pennsylvania Game Commission would not issue special use permits for a "stand-alone" sharpshooting program. Rather, they required that a public hunt first be employed by the Township before sharpshooting could commence. This continues to be a short-sighted yet firmly entrenched policy position that has no foundation in their concern regarding the success of urban deer management programs. Rather, it serves only to placate public hunters, who not only vehemently oppose sharpshooting but also fund the Game Commission via their license sale revenue. Unfortunately, requiring a public hunt before a sharpshooting effort exposes deer herds to the random, area-wide wounding of *individual* deer, educating the remaining population and causing them to become more wary. The Township's subsequent sharpshooting effort was therefore not as successful as might otherwise have been the case (the same contractor's removal rates in Princeton, NJ, as well as in other locales where there is no public hunt requirement, have consistently been more productive). Due to the failure to meet expectations and concern over the costs involved, sharpshooting was never again pursued by Township leaders, and to this day, only archery is employed to manage deer within the Township. While not a literal "cost," this has required that several "public" properties throughout the Township, including the Five Mile Woods Preserve, be made available for hunting during late summer, fall and early winter – periods when public use would ordinarily be at their height. To address safety and liability concerns which would otherwise have been associated with to true "public" hunting on these lands, the Township has since only contracted with a grass-roots hunter's organization, Big Oak Whitetail Management Association (BOWMA), which formed to provide a capably, safe and very low cost alternative to sharpshooting. The local group provides privately insured, organization-assessed individuals who agree to operate under additional management-oriented requirements imposed by the Township. These requirements are largely intended to incentivize each participant's removal of deer, requiring that they donate their first harvested deer to a local food bank before keeping one to supplement food for their family, and that they each harvest at least 4 does before being allowed to target a buck. Such requirements ensure that reduction of the deer population remains the primary objective. BOWMA also solicits permission to hunt on private lands, where that is possible, and this has expanded opportunities for deer removal within the Township beyond that which existed previously under "routine" public hunting.

Whether these efforts will satisfactorily address the affects over-abundant deer are having throughout the community remain to be seen. On average, BOWMA removes approximately 70 deer from the municipality each season – not an insignificant number. Yet less than one tenth of these are taken from the Preserve, and while there is indeed little monetary cost to that effort, there is certainly incidental "cost" at the Preserve in terms of having to close the Preserve to the public during hunting periods which could span as much as three months of the year. The issue has therefore pitted the two primary goals of the Preserve against themselves: my primary interests are in maintaining the ecological balance of the forest ecosystem, yet the public closures required preclude residents from accessing the Preserve during some of the most desirable seasons to be in the Woods. Generally low removal rates within the Preserve have resulted in my reducing the closure periods. Time will tell if this is an effective strategy to restore forest ecosystem balance, but it is clearly the only strategy that appears realistic in the near term.

One of the aspects of the Naturalist position I enjoy most is the opportunity it provides to teach members of the community about the Preserve and its many wonders. During portions of my tenure as Naturalist, the schedule of my full time job permitted me to do school programs. However, these opportunities largely involve weekend or evening scout programs or the regularly scheduled open houses or related events at the Woods. As a particular interest of mine is vernal pool ecology and the study of our native amphibian species, my favorite program is an evening frog and salamander walk I schedule early each spring where we visit a vernal pool near the nature center and observe the seasonal breeding activities of wood frogs, spring peepers and spotted salamanders. But each opportunity for me to share my passion and enjoyment of nature has brought with it great reward.

Of course, advocating for the Preserve will always be required. During my tenure as Naturalist, the Township has taken advantage of important opportunities to acquire or protect properties surrounding the Preserve that might otherwise have been further developed. Continued success on that front will depend upon the willingness of remaining landowners to accept the appraised value of their land, rather than the value a developer might be able to offer. This difference is not always significant, and we have had great success with landowners who place a high personal value on the environment and natural resource protection rather than merely getting every dollar out of their property that they can when they are ready to sell. I remain hopeful that we can prevail.

As I discovered myself 25 years ago, the Five Mile Woods Preserve is a remarkable oasis of nature in an otherwise highly urbanized setting. Its core area and location at the headwaters of Queen Ann's Creek have resulted in the remarkable retention of its natural processes. It has been a privilege to share that discovery over the past 20 years with other residents, and to advocate for the Preserve's continued health. One of the most frequent questions we are asked during our public events is "Why is it called the Five Mile Woods?" Honestly, that has always been a bit of a mystery, as the property was referred to as "the five mile woods" prior to its formal acquisition by the Township. The best explanation the Friends have been able to offer was that the property was likely once associated with a swath of natural forest that stretched around 5 miles in length, and so those who frequented those woods – notwithstanding their having been "private" property at the time - grew to refer to it in that fashion. The Five Mile Woods is obviously much smaller now. But thanks to the efforts of some very environmentally conscious residents back in the 1970's, these woods will forever harbor the very same flora and fauna that made those vast tracks of forest so special all those years ago. As this book reveals, many persons have had a hand in its preservation and continued protection. Just as the Preserve's name honors the landscape's past, so too is it appropriate to honor the history of the persons who were instrumental in the property's protection. It is indeed a remarkable story.

IN TWO HUNDRED YEARS, YOU WILL BE HEROES.
By Jeff Marshall
President, Heritage Conservancy

I was asked to be a reader of Peter Osborne's history of the Five Mile Woods. I immediately agreed. The book brings back fond memories of not only important events in the preservation of land in the county, but of people who helped write the story. Over the past forty years, I have been privileged to know many of the people named in the book from Peter Kostmayer, James Wright, Dr. Ann Rhoads and numerous Township officials. I had the great fortune and honor to have worked at the Conservancy under Bob Pierson's tenure.

This book affirms what I probably never took the time to absorb, that Margaret Mead, another Bucks County resident, was correct when she wrote:

Never doubt that a small group of thoughtful, committed citizens can change the world; indeed, it's the only thing that ever has. Always remember that you are absolutely unique. Just like everyone else. Never believe that a few caring people can't change the world. For, indeed, that's all who ever have.

Peter subsequently asked me to contribute an essay to be included with the book. Again, I immediately agreed. One of the things that resonated with me in the book was the passage that reads:

Despite the heroic efforts of the staff and volunteers, many of those coming to the (Five Mile) Woods do not understand its significance. They love the place, the solitude, the trails, the trees, rare plants and the views, but do not really know how special the place is or what its role was in the Commonwealth's development.

I would only add that they also do not understand the herculean efforts by so many people to make the impossible possible. I can only speak about Bob Pierson from the perspective of having worked with him every day. I think he would say that recognition for his work was not important.

Those who do this work are not in it for the recognition, we do it for our children and our children's children. I have been privileged to carry on the work at Heritage Conservancy that Bob started. When I worked for Bob Pierson I was fresh out of college and to me he was already an old man (although he may not have been much older than I am today).

Now when I think back on all of the conservation work Bob and others did when Bucks County was still very rural I think of the Greek proverb that goes:

A society grows great when old men plant trees whose shade they know they shall never sit in.

Bucks County was still very rural in the 1960s and 1970s. Men of vision could see the future. They knew if they did nothing, future generations would not sit in shade unless they planted the trees by protecting our special places.

I recently read somewhere that for people that embrace conservation as a defining purpose, there are opportunities for them to forge meaningful connections to the earth and each other. They embrace these opportunities because a true conservationist understands that beyond the conservation work itself is the importance of forging a community worth preserving. One act, like a stone in a pond, can have an enormous ripple effect.

The ripple effect of what one person can achieve is great when coupled with a love for the land. I recently spoke with Linda J. Mead, President and CEO of the D & R Greenway Land Trust in Princeton, New Jersey. She also worked with Bob at the Bucks County Conservancy.

She wrote:

My first experience with Bob Pierson was a three-hour interview for a volunteer job to serve as his land preservation assistant. I was impressed with the humble attitude of this man, who had acquired much of Bucks County's park system as the first county parks director, and who started the "Bucks County Conservancy" in his basement. His vision was profound, during a time when land was still untouched and plentiful throughout the county.

Bob and Linda visited landowners at kitchen tables to talk about conservation before open space became a common term. It was Bob's idea to start a Significant Natural Areas Preservation Program in 1986. Most people don't know that it was the people and accomplishments of that program that inspired the Bucks County Open Space Program, which over twenty years has protected fifty-five thousand acres of land.

The spark that Bob lit led to yet another twenty thousand acres of land in New Jersey and the Delaware River watershed that are preserved now and forever.

The work of land preservation does, in fact, live on well after the initial acquisition, and the value that it brings to people's lives can't be measured. I agree with Linda's comment that:

I've seen land preservation bring families together, heal bodies and spirits, inspire art and action for the greater good. Bob Pierson was an unsung hero whose accomplishments are celebrated every day by those who enjoy the lands protected by his hands and by his inspiration.

I know from a personal experience with another preservation success the feeling of what has recently become a catch phrase of pay it forward when someone remarked:

In two hundred years, no one will know who you were, but you will be heroes.

Those who preserve land for future generations are heroes. I am glad that with the telling of this story, people will know who the heroes were, and for those who are still around; thank them for their tireless efforts.

Courtesy Heritage Conservancy
Jeff Marshall
2016

COMMON BEECH

COMMON BEECH

APPENDIX

Acquisition Maps

While the Preserve is one single contiguous tract of land today, it was actually pieced together with various acquisitions over a period of several decades. The following maps illustrate how the Preserve's property boundaries have changed over time. They are approximations using a tax map and should not be used to determine the legal boundaries. The boundary lines were created by the author. The 2017 map also includes the conservation easements that extend the preservation of the Woods beyond just the tracts owned by the two townships.

Courtesy Peter Osborne

Former Banko property line, looking east

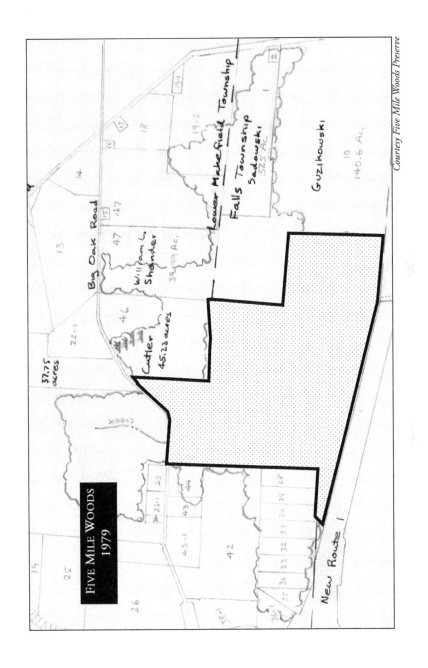

FIVE MILE WOODS
1979

Courtesy Five Mile Woods Preserve

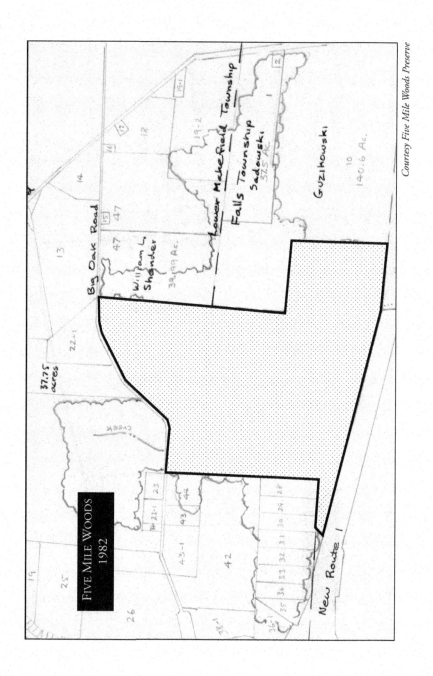

Courtesy Five Mile Woods Preserve

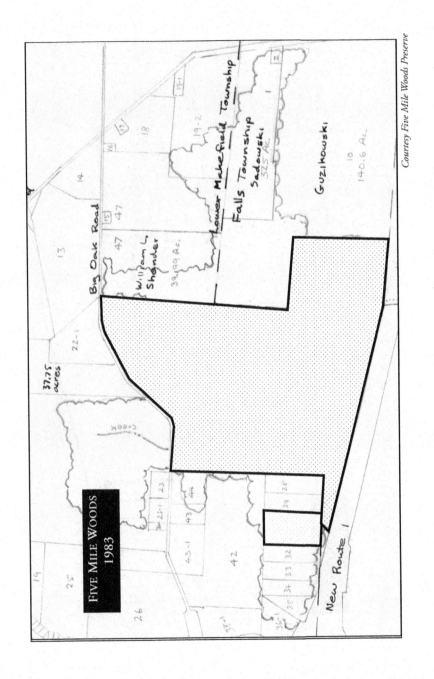

Courtesy Five Mile Woods Preserve

FIVE MILE WOODS
1983

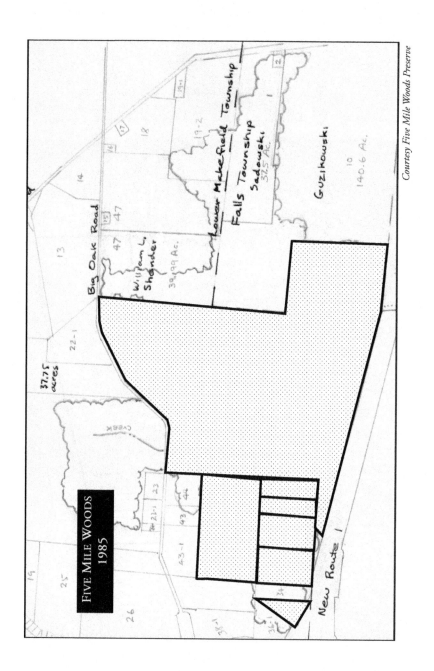

Courtesy Five Mile Woods Preserve

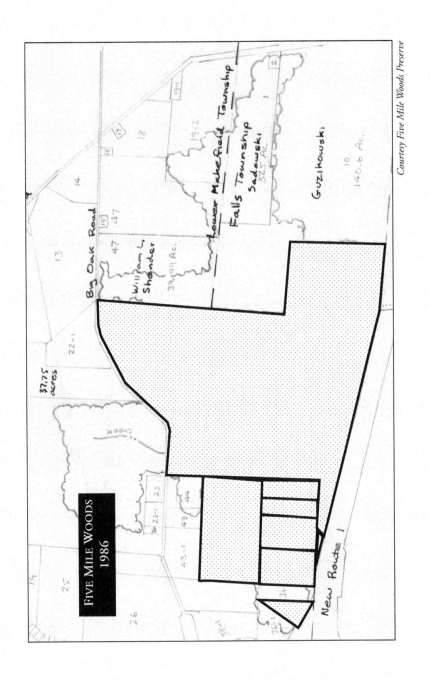

Courtesy Five Mile Woods Preserve

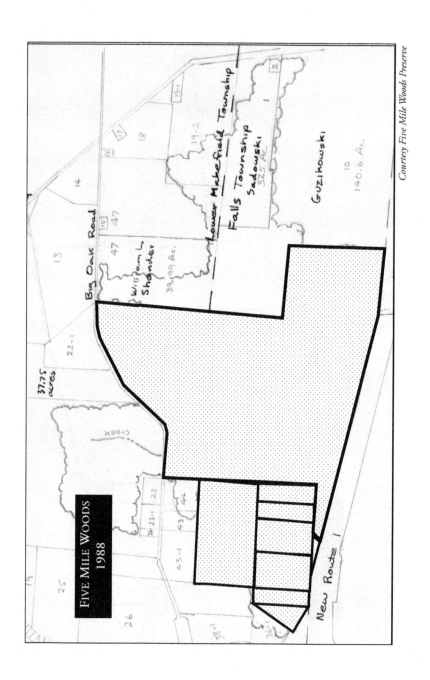

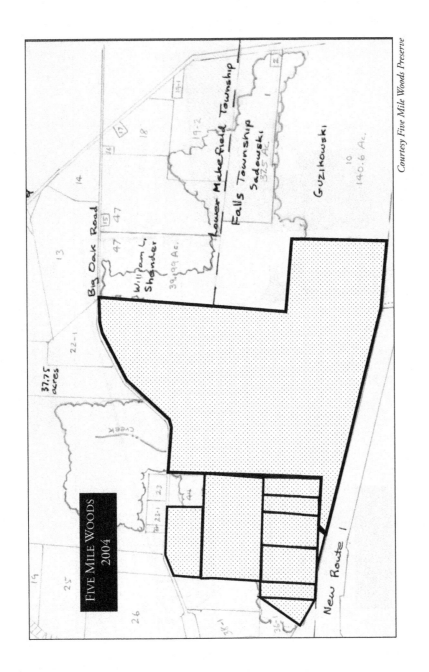

Courtesy Five Mile Woods Preserve

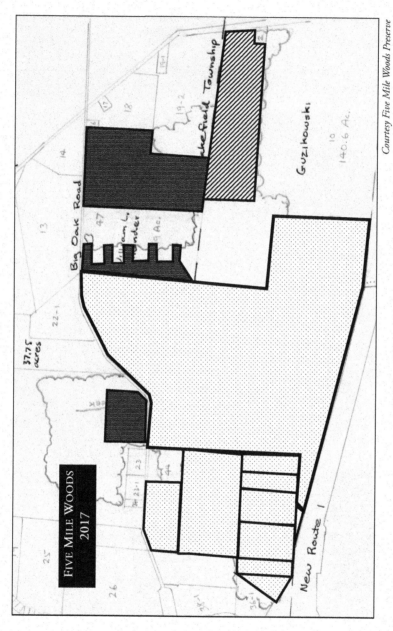

Courtesy Five Mile Woods Preserve

The Five Mile Woods Preserve - 2017
Lower Makefield Township owned parcels - Light shading
Falls Township owned parcel - Cross hatch
Conservation easements - Dark shading

TRAILS IN THE FIVE MILE WOODS

When the Preserve opened in 1981 the trail network only included the Penn Central and Cutler tracts. As the years went by and the Preserve expanded, so did the trail network. By 2002 there were ten trails within the Preserve which allowed visitors to see all of its fascinating geological, environmental and cultural history. They total about five miles in length. The trail map that has been included here is from 2004.[1]

Today the network includes the following trails:

5 Mile Trail – This is the Preserve's longest trail and travels almost all the way to Route 1 and allows a walker to see the various ecosystems and terrains contained within it, including the Piedmont Plain, Atlantic Coastal Plain, the Fall Line and the Queen Anne Creek.

Sphagnum Trail – Passing through the Preserve's vernal pools, this trail allows walkers to see mating grounds and hatcheries for the frogs and salamander who live here. It is a short trail for those who might not want to hike a long distance.

Creek Trail – The trail passes along the Queen Anne Creek, the meandering creek where some fish, salamanders and frogs can be found for most of the year. This trail passes near the base of the ridge where the Dark house foundation sits. It is hard to find it during the summer with trees and shrubs leafed out but during the rest of the year the stone foundation can still be seen. Please do not disturb this important site.

Heath Trail - This trail allows hikers to see the ridge line that separates the Coastal Plain and Piedmont Plateau. It passes near the Dark house foundation and is also a great place to see deer.

Fall Line Trail – On this pathway hikers will get to walk along a section of the Fall Line as well as see what the Dark and Satterthwaite farms would have looked like in an earlier time. This is also a place where one can see in microcosm how the Fall Line influenced American history and the development of the Eastern seaboard's towns and cities.

Ridge Trail – Providing walkers with a wonderful view of the Coastal Plain within the Preserve, it also turns at a corner in the southwest part of the Preserve, the farthest that one can go in a southwesterly direction.

Coastal Plain Trail – This trail allows walkers to see the Coastal Plain, which begins here and continues all the way to the Atlantic Ocean. At one time this was the edge of the ocean. For those in search of turtles this is an excellent place to do so.

Sweetgum Trail – This trail leads you through the Piedmont Plain. One of the characteristics of this zone is the abundance of sweet gum trees that can be identified by their unique seed, a round, ball-shaped and spiked receptacle. You will also find blueberries late in the summer.

Evergreen Trail – This is the Preserve's newest trail and it passes through the former nursery of Samuel Willard. Here one can still see the rows of pines, spruces and hemlocks that were once planted for wholesale and retail sale. Also, circular holes in the ground remain from a time when small trees and shrubs were removed and stumps where Christmas trees were once cut. One can also see the woods roads that divided the various sections of the nursery.

Trail Name	Length	Marker Color
5-Mile Trail	0.9	Yellow
Sphagnum Trail	0.2	Red
Creek Trail	0.5	Green
Heath Trail	0.4	Red
Fall Line Trail	0.5	White
Ridge Trail	0.3	Blue
Evergreen Trail	0.8	Green
Coastal Plan Trail	0.3	Orange
Sweetgum Trail	0.3	Blue
Crossing	0.1	Orange

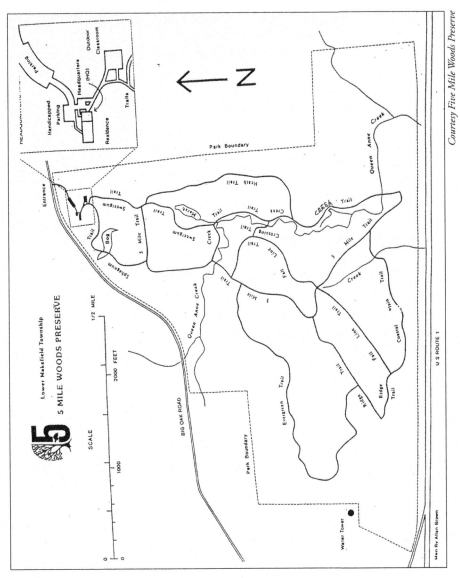

The trails in the Five Mile Woods Preserve
2004

Courtesy Five Mile Woods Preserve

SPECIES FOUND AT THE FIVE MILE WOODS PRESERVE

The following lists of plants, trees, mammals, reptiles, amphibians and birds found at the Preserve, and in the greater Five Mile Woods area, were compiled by a variety of sources of individuals and institutions. This list combines all the previous inventories created by Donald Formigli, Rick Mellon, John Heilferty, John Lloyd, David B. Long, Helen Heinz, Dr. Ann Rhoads, Edgar Wherry, and the Academy of Natural Sciences of Philadelphia.

The following sources were used, all of which can be found at the Preserve's headquarters:

Plant Life Identified on Cutler Property, Donald Formigli, 1974
Notes from Dr. Edgar Wherry – 1975
Five Mile Woods, Lower Makefield & Falls Townships Bucks County, Pennsylvania: A Brief Summary of the Natural Features and a Proposal to Protect the Area,
     Donald Formigli 1975-76
Animal Life Five Mile Woods Preserve , Donald Formigli, 1976-1978
Rare Plants of Five Mile Woods and *Five Mile Woods (Bucks County Pennsylvania) Revisited*, Alfred Schuyler, 1978-79 [2]
Plant Life Identified in Five Mile Woods, Donald Formigli, 1978-1981
Master Plan for the Five Mile Woods Preserve, Rick Mellon, c. 1981
An Evaluation of sites representing the Fall Line Zone in the Mid-Atlantic Region: For eligibility as a National Natural Landmark: Sites Evaluated Five Mile Woods Preserve, Dr. Ann Rhoads, 2003
The Birds of Five Mile Woods, c. 1990s
Bowmans Hill Plant Stewardship Index surveys, John H. Heilferty, 2009
The Birds of Five Mile Woods, David B. Long, 2013 [3]
Helen Heinz Interview, 2016

These various inventories were created at different times, and some of the items listed may no longer be found at the Preserve or more generally in the Woods because of the steady changes in the landscape that have occurred during the last forty years. The listings include the common names and scientific names. As of 2003, there were seven plants, three animals and a plant community that were considered either endangered, threatened or rare.

Plant Species Listing

The plant species listing includes growth habitat, whether the species is native to Pennsylvania, and state and PBS status. It should also be noted that the list of plants at the Preserve is not complete as research continues.

Plant Species List - Data Sources

Scientific and common names were updated using *The Plants of Pennsylvania, An Illustrated Manual,* Second edition, 2007, by Ann F. Rhoads and Timothy A. Block, University of Pennsylvania Press.

N/I = Native to Pennsylvania or Introduced from outside the state.
State status and PBS status from Pennsylvania Natural Heritage Program, Species list for plants. *http://www.naturalheritage.state.pa.us/Species.aspx*

Bird List

With respect to birding, the Preserve is considered among the best areas in Lower Makefield Township to observe birds as it is an important stop on the Delaware River flyway.

Courtesy Five Mile Woods Preserve
Donald Formigli Collection
Pink Lady Slipper Orchid

PLANTS

COMMON NAME	SCIENTIFIC NAME	GROWTH HABIT	N/I	ST	PBS
American beech	Fagus grandifolia	deciduous tree	N		
American chestnut	Castanea dentata	deciduous tree	N		
American elm	Ulmus americana	deciduous tree	N		
Apple	Malus pumila	deciduous tree	I		
Basswood	Tilia americana var. americana	deciduous tree	N		
Big-tooth aspen	Populus grandidentata	deciduous tree	N		
Bitternut hickory	Carya cordiformis	deciduous tree	N		
Black oak	Quercus velutina	deciduous tree	N		
Black or Sweet birch	Betula lenta	deciduous tree	N		
Black walnut	Juglans nigra	deciduous tree	N		
Black willow	Salix nigra	deciduous tree	N		
Choke cherry	Prunus virginiana	deciduous tree	N		
Crabapple	Malus sp.	deciduous tree	N/I		
Cucumber magnolia	Magnolia acuminata	deciduous tree	N		
Flowering dogwood	Cornus florida	deciduous tree	N		
Gray birch	Betula populifolia	deciduous tree	N		
Hornbeam; Ironwood	Carpinus caroliniana	deciduous tree	N		
Ironwood	Ostrya virginiana	deciduous tree	N		
Mockernut hickory	Carya tomentosa	deciduous tree	N		
Northern red oak	Quercus rubra	deciduous tree	N		
Peach	Prunus persica	deciduous tree	I		
Pear	Pyrus sp.	deciduous tree	I		

COMMON NAME	SCIENTIFIC NAME	GROWTH HABIT	N/I	ST	PBS
Persimmon	Diospyros virginiana	deciduous tree	N		
Pignut hickory	Carya glabra	deciduous tree	N		
Pin oak	Quercus palusrtris	deciduous tree	N		
Quaking aspen	Populus tremuloides	deciduous tree	N		
Red ash	Fraxinus pennsylvanica	deciduous tree	N		
Red maple	Acer rubrum var. rubrum	deciduous tree	N		
Sassafras	Sassafras albidum	deciduous tree	N		
Scarlet oak	Quercus coccinea	deciduous tree	N		
Shadbush	Amelanchier canadensis	deciduous tree	N		
Shagbark hickory	Carya ovata	deciduous tree	N		
Silver maple	Acer saccharinum	deciduous tree	N		
Sour cherry	Prunus cerasus	deciduous tree	I		
Sourgum, Blackgum, Tupelo	Nyssa sylvatica	deciduous tree	N		
Swamp white oak	Quercus bicolor	deciduous tree	N		
Sweet cherry	Prunus avium	deciduous tree	I		
Sweetgum	Liquidambar stryaciflua	deciduous tree	N		
Tuliptree	Liriodendron tulipifera	deciduous tree	N		
Umbrella-tree	Magnolia tripetala	deciduous tree	N	PT	PR
White ash	Fraxinus americana var. americana	deciduous tree	N		
White oak	Quercus alba	deciduous tree	N		
Wild black cherry	Prunus serotina	deciduous tree	N		
Willow oak	Quercus phellos	deciduous tree	N		

COMMON NAME	SCIENTIFIC NAME	GROWTH HABIT	N/I	ST	PBS
Yellow birch	Betula alleghaniensis	deciduous tree	N		
Sweetbay magnolia	Magnolia virginiana	semi-evergreen tree	N		
Norway spruce	Picea abies	evergreen tree	I		
Red cedar	Juniperus virginiana	evergreen tree	N		
Scots pine	Pinus sylvestris	evergreen tree	I		
Short-leaf pine	Pinus echinata	evergreen tree	I	N	PT
White pine	Pinus strobus	evergreen tree	N		
American elder	Sambucus canadensis	deciduous shrub	N		
American filbert or hazelnut	Corylus americana	deciduous shrub	N		
Amur honeysuckle	Lonicera maackii	deciduous shrub	I		
Black huckleberry	Gaylussacia baccata	deciduous shrub	N		
Black locust	Robinia pseudoacacia	deciduous shrub	N		
Black raspberry	Rubus occidentalis	deciduous shrub	N		
Blackhaw viburnum, blackhaw	Viburnum prunifolium	deciduous shrub	N		
Common blackberry	Rubus allegheniensis	deciduous shrub	N		
Dangleberry	Gaylussacia frondosa	deciduous shrub	N		
Deerberry	Vaccinium stamineum	deciduous shrub	N		
False indigo	Amorpha fruticosa	deciduous shrub	I		
Fetter-bush, Swamp dog-hobble	Leucothoe racemosa	deciduous shrub	N	TU	PR

COMMON NAME	SCIENTIFIC NAME	GROWTH HABIT	N/I	ST	PBS
Hearts-a-bursting, Strawberry-bush	Euonymus americanus	deciduous shrub	N		
Highbush blueberry	Vaccinium corymbosum	deciduous shrub	N		
Japanese barberry	Berberis thunbergii	deciduous shrub	I		
Linden viburnum	Viburnum dilatatum	deciduous shrub	N		
Lowbush blueberry	Vaccinium pallidum (V. pallidum)	deciduous shrub	N		
Maleberry	Lyonia ligustrina	deciduous shrub	N		
Maple-leaved viburnum	Viburnum acerifolium	deciduous shrub	N		
Meadow-sweet	Spiraea alba var alba		N		
Narrow-leaved Meadowsweet		deciduous shrub			
Multiflora rose	Rosa multiflora	deciduous shrub	I		
Northern arrowwood	Viburnum recognitum	deciduous shrub	N		
Pinxter-flower	Rhododendron periclymenoides	deciduous shrub	N		
Possum-haw	Viburnum nudum	deciduous shrub	N	PE	PE
Purple chokeberry	Aronia prunifolia	deciduous shrub	N		
Pussy willow	Salix discolor	deciduous shrub	N		
Red chokeberry	Aronia arbutifolia	deciduous shrub	N		
Red choleberry	Photinia pyrifolia (Pyrus arbutifolia)	deciduous shrub	N		
Silky dogwood	Cornus amomum	deciduous shrub	N		
Smooth winterberry	Ilex laevigata	deciduous shrub	N		
Southern arrowwood	Viburnum dentatum	deciduous shrub	N		
Spicebush	Lindera benzoin	deciduous shrub	N		
Staggerbush	Lyonia mariana	deciduous shrub	N	PE	PE

COMMON NAME	SCIENTIFIC NAME	GROWTH HABIT	N/I	ST	PBS
Staghorn sumac	Rhus typhina	deciduous shrub	N		
Steeple-bush; Hardhack	Spiraea tomentosa	deciduous shrub	N		
Swamp azalea	Rhododendron viscosum	deciduous shrub	N		
Swamp rose	Rosa palustris	deciduous shrub	N		
Sweet pepperbush	Clethra alnifolia	deciduous shrub	N		
Winterberry holly, Black alder	Ilex verticillata	deciduous shrub	N		
Witch-hazel	Hamamelis virginiana	deciduous shrub	N		
Bayberry	Myrica pensylvanica	semi-evergreen shrub	N		
American holly	Ilex opaca	evergreen shrub	N	PT	PT
Cranberry	Vaccinium macrocarpon	evergreen shrub	N	PT	
Mountain laurel	Kalmia latifolia	evergreen shrub	N		
Sheep laurel	Kalmia angustifolia	evergreen shrub	N		
Catbrier/ Glaucus Greenbrier	Smilax glauca	deciduous vine	N		
Fox grape	Vitis labrusca	deciduous vine	N		
Frost grape	Vitus vulpina	deciduous vine	N		
Hog peanut	Amphicarpaea bracteata	deciduous vine	N		
Poison-ivy	Toxicodendron radicans	deciduous vine	N		
Swamp dewberry	Rubus hispidus	deciduous vine	N		
Virginia-creeper	Parthenocissus quinquefolia	deciduous vine	N		

COMMON NAME	SCIENTIFIC NAME	GROWTH HABIT	N/I	ST	PBS
Catbrier, Greenbrier	Smilax rotundifolia	semi-evergreen vine	N		
Japanese honeysuckle	Lonicera japonica	semi-evergreen vine	I		
American bugbane	Actaea pachypoda	herbaceous	N		
American germander	Teucrium canadense	herbaceous	N		
Annual bluegrass	Poa annua	herbaceous	I		
Appalachian ironweed, Tawny ironweed	Vernonia glauca	herbaceous	N	PE	PE
Arrow-leaved tearthumb	Polygonum sagittatum	herbaceous	N		
Asiatic dayflower	Commelina communis var. communis	herbaceous	I		
Barnyard-grass, cockspur	Echinchloa muricata (E. pungens)	herbaceous	N		
Bartonia	Bartonia virginica	herbaceous	N		
Bee-balm, Oswego-tea	Monarda didyma	herbaceous	N		
Beechdrops	Epifagus virginiana	herbaceous	N		
Beggar's-lice; virginia stickseed	Hackelia virginiana	herbaceous	N		
Bellwort	Uvularia sessilifolia	herbaceous	N		
Bitter dock	Rumex obtusifolius	herbaceous	I		
Bittersweet, Oriental; Asian	Celastrus orbiculatus	herbaceous	I		
Black cohosh, Black snakeroot	Actaea racemosa (Cimicifuga racemosa)	herbaceous	N		
Bladder sedge	Carex intumescens	herbaceous	N		
Bladdernut	Staphylea trifolia	herbaceous	N		

COMMON NAME	SCIENTIFIC NAME	GROWTH HABIT	N/I	ST	PBS
Bloodroot	Sanguinaria canadensis	herbaceous	N		
Blue marsh violet	Viola cucullata	herbaceous	N		
Blue vervain, Simpler's-joy	Verbena hastata	herbaceous	N		
Blue wood aster	Symphyotrichum cordifolium	herbaceous	N		
Bluets, Quaker-ladies	Houstonia caerulea	herbaceous	N		
Boneset	Eupatorium perfoliatum	herbaceous	N		
Broad beech fern	Thelypteris hexagonoptera (Dryopteris hexagonoptera)	herbaceous	N		
Broom-sedge	Andropogon glomeratus	herbaceous	N		
Broom-sedge	Andropogon virginicus	herbaceous	N		
Bugleweed	Lycopus virginicus	herbaceous	N		
Bull thistle	Cirsium vulgare	herbaceous	I		
Bur-reed	Sparganium americanum	herbaceous	N		
Calico aster	Symphyotrichum lateriflorum	herbaceous	N		
Canada goldenrod	Solidago canadensis	herbaceous	N		
Canada mayflower	Maianthemum canadense	herbaceous	N		
Canada thistle	Cirsium arvense var. arvense	herbaceous	I		
Canadian sanicle/ Canada black snakeroot	Sanicula canadensis	herbaceous	N		
Canadian St. John's-wort	Hypericum canadense	herbaceous	N		
Cardinal-flower	Lobelia cardinalis	herbaceous	N		
Carrion-flower	Smilax herbacea	herbaceous	N		
Celandine, lesser	Ranunculus ficaria	herbaceous	I		

COMMON NAME	SCIENTIFIC NAME	GROWTH HABIT	N/I	ST	PBS
Christmas fern	Polystichum acrostichoides	herbaceous	N		
Cinnamon fern	Osmunda cinnamomea	herbaceous	N		
Clearweed	Pilea pumila	herbaceous	N		
Common blue violet	Viola sororia var. sororia	herbaceous	N		
Common burdock	Arctium minus	herbaceous	I		
Common dandelion	Taraxacum officinale	herbaceous	I		
Common milkweed	Asclepias syriaca	herbaceous	N		
Common mouse-ear chickweed	Cerastium vulgatum	herbaceous	I		
Common periwinkle	Vinca minor	herbaceous	I		
Common plantain	Plantago major	herbaceous	I		
Common wintercress	Barbarea vulgaris var. vulgaris	herbaceous	I		
Common woodrush	Luzula echinata	herbaceous	N		
Common yellow wood-sorrel	Oxalis stricta	herbaceous	N		
Cranefly orchid	Tipularia discolor	herbaceous	N	PR	
Creeping Bent-grass	Agrostis stolonifera	herbaceous	n/a		
Curly dock	Rumex crispus	herbaceous	I		
Cut-leaved grape fern	Botrychium dissectum	herbaceous	N		
Cutgrass/White grass	Leersia virginica	herbaceous	N		
Cypress Panic-grass	Dichanthelium dichotomum var. dichotomum	herbaceous	n/a		
Downy rattlesnake-plantain	Goodyera pubescens	herbaceous	N		
Dwarf cinquefoil	Potentilla canadensis	herbaceous	N		
Dwarf dandelion	Krigia biflora	herbaceous	N		

COMMON NAME	SCIENTIFIC NAME	GROWTH HABIT	N/I	ST	PBS
Dwarf ginseng	Panax trifolius	herbaceous	N		
Early goldenrod	Solidago juncea	herbaceous	N		
Ebony spleenwort	Asplenium platyneuron	herbaceous	N		
Emmons' sedge	Carex albicans var. emmonsii	herbaceous	n/a		
Enchanter's-nightshade	Circaea canadensis sp. Canadensis (C. lutetiana, C. quadrisulcata)	herbaceous	N		
Evening-primrose	Oenothera biennis	herbaceous	N		
False foxglove	Agalinus purpurea (Gerardia purpurea)	herbaceous	N		
False hellebore	Veratrum viride	herbaceous	N		
False nettle	Boehmeria cylindrica var. cylindrica	herbaceous	N		
False solomon's seal; Solomon's plume	Smilacina racemosa	herbaceous	N		
Field garlic	Allium vineale	herbaceous	I		
Field thistle	Cirsium discolor	herbaceous	N		
Field woodrush	Luzula multiflora	herbaceous	N		
Fireweed; Pilewort	Erechtites hieracifolia	herbaceous	N		
Forked rush	Juncus dichotomus	herbaceous	N	PE	PE
Fowl mannagrass	Glyceria striata	herbaceous	N		
Gall-of-the-earth	Prenanthes trifoliata	herbaceous	N		
Grass rush	Juncus biflorus	herbaceous	N	TU	PR
Grass-leaved goldenrod	Euthamia graminifolia var. graminifolia	herbaceous	N		
Gray goldenrod	Solidago nemoralis	herbaceous	N		
Ground ivy	Glechoma hederacea	herbaceous	I		

COMMON NAME	SCIENTIFIC NAME	GROWTH HABIT	N/I	ST	PBS
Hairgrass	Agrostis hyemalis	herbaceous	I		
Hairgrass/Long-awned Hair-grass	Muhlenbergia capillaris	herbaceous	N	PX	PX
Hairy bittercress	Cardamine hirsuta	herbaceous	I		
Halberd-leaf tearthumb	Persicaria arifolia	herbaceous	N		
Halberd-leaved tearthumb	Polygonum arifolium	herbaceous	N		
Hawkweed	Hieracium scabrum	herbaceous	N		
Hay-scented fern	Dennsteadtia punctilobula	herbaceous	N		
Heal-all, Self-heal	Prunella vulgaris var. lanceolata	herbaceous	N		
Heath aster	Symphyotrichum pilosum	herbaceous	N		
Henbit	Lamium amplexicaule	herbaceous	I		
Hoary tick-trefoil	Desmodium canescens	herbaceous	N		
Hollow Joe-pye-weed	Eurtrochium fistulosum (Eutrochium fistulosum)	herbaceous	N		
Hooked crowfoot	Ranunculus recurvatus	herbaceous	N		
Horse-balm, stoneroot	Collinsonia canadensis	herbaceous	N		
Hyssop skullcap	Scutellaria integrifolia	herbaceous	N		
Indian cucumber-root	Medeola virginiana	herbaceous	N		
Indian strawberry	Duchesnea indica	herbaceous	I		
Indian-hemp	Apocynum cannabinum	herbaceous	N		
Indian-pipe	Monotropa uniflora	herbaceous	N		
Indian-pipe	Monotropa uniflora	herbaceous	N		
Indian-tobacco	Lobelia inflata	herbaceous	N		
Interrupted fern	Osmunda claytoniana	herbaceous	N		

COMMON NAME	SCIENTIFIC NAME	GROWTH HABIT	N/I	ST	PBS
Jack-in-the-pulpit	Arisaema triphyllum ssp. pusillum	herbaceous	N		
Jack-in-the-pulpit	Arisaema triphyllum ssp. triphyllum	herbaceous	N		
Japanese knotweed	Fallopia japonica	herbaceous	I		
Japanese stiltgrass	Microstegium vimineum	herbaceous	I		
Jewelweed; Touch-me-not	Impatiens capensis	herbaceous	N		
Jumpseed	Persicaria virginica	herbaceous	N		
Lady fern	Athyrium filix-femina var. angustum	herbaceous	N		
Lance-leaved violet	Viola lanceolata var. lanceolata	herbaceous	N		
Lemon-balm	Melissa officinalis	herbaceous	I		
Little bluestem	Schizachyrium scoparium	herbaceous	N		
Long sedge	Carex folliculata	herbaceous	N		
Long-leaved panic grass	Panicum longifolium	herbaceous	N	TU	PE
Low smartweed	Persicaria longiseta	herbaceous	I		
Mad-dog skullcap	Scutellaria lateriflora	herbaceous	N		
Marsh fern	Thelypteris palustris	herbaceous	N		
Maryland meadow-beauty	Rhexia mariana	herbaceous	n/a		
Massachusetts fern	Thelypteris simulata	herbaceous	n/a		
Mayapple	Podophyllum peltatum	herbaceous	N		
Meadow-beauty	Rhexia virginica	herbaceous	N		
Mild water-pepper, Water smartweed	Persicaria hydropiperoides	herbaceous	N		
Moneywort	Lysimachia nummularia	herbaceous	I		
Netted chain-fern	Woodwardia areolata	herbaceous	N	N	PR

(translator name(s))

PENDIX

COMMON NAME	SCIENTIFIC NAME	GROWTH HABIT	N/I	ST	PBS
New York fern	Thelypteris novaboracensis	herbaceous	N		
Northern bracken fern	Pteridium aquilinum	herbaceous	N		
Northern swamp or marsh buttercup	Ranunculus hispidus var. carietorum (R. caricetorum)	herbaceous	N		
Orange daylily	Hemerocallis fulva	herbaceous	I		
Orchard Grass	Dactylis glomerata	herbaceous	I		
Ox-eye daisy	Leucanthemum vulgare (Chrysanthemum leucanthemum)	herbaceous	I		
Panic grass	Dichanthelium meridionale	herbaceous	N		
Panicled aster	Symphyotrichum lanceolatum ssp. lanceolatum (Aster simplex)	herbaceous	N		
Partridgeberry	Mitchella repens	herbaceous	N		
Path rush	Juncus tenuis var. tenuis	herbaceous	N		
Perfoliate bellwort	Uvularia perfoliata	herbaceous	N		
Pink lady's-slipper	Cypripedium acaule	herbaceous	N		
Pipsissewa; Spotted wintergreen	Chimaphilla maculata	herbaceous	N		
Pokeweed	Phytolacca americana	herbaceous	I		
Primrose violet	Viola primulifolia	herbaceous	N		
Purple-stemed aster	Symphyotrichum puniceum	herbaceous	N		
Purpletop	Tridens flavus	herbaceous	N		
Queen Anne's-lace, wild carrot	Daucus carota	herbaceous	I		

309

COMMON NAME	SCIENTIFIC NAME	GROWTH HABIT	N/I	ST	PBS
Ragweed	Ambrosia artemisiifolia	herbaceous	N		
Rattlesnake fern	Botrichium virginianum	herbaceous	N		
Reed canary grass	Phalaris arundinacea	herbaceous	I		
Reedgrass	Calamagrostis cinnoides	herbaceous	N		
Rice cut grass	Leersia oryzoides	herbaceous	N		
Round-leaved throughwort	Eupatorium rotundifolium	herbaceous	N		
Royal fern	Osmunda regalis	herbaceous	N		
Rue anemone	Anemonella thalictroides	herbaceous	N		
Sandplain yellow flax	Linum intercursum	herbaceous	N	PE	PE
Screwstem	Bartonia paniculata	herbaceous	N	N	PR
Sedge	Carex tribuloides	herbaceous	N		
Seedbox, False loosestrife	Ludwigia alternifolia	herbaceous	N		
Sensitive fern	Onoclea sensibilis	herbaceous	N		
Shinleaf	Pyrola elliptica	herbaceous	N		
Short-hair sedge	Carex crinita var. crinita	herbaceous	N		
Silver-rod, White goldenrod	Solidago bicolor	herbaceous	N		
Skunk-cabbage	Symplocarpus foetidus	herbaceous	N		
Small white aster	Symphyotrichum racemosum (Aster vimineus)	herbaceous	N		
Small-flowered crowfoot	Ranunculus abortivus	herbaceous	N		
Small-headed beak-rush	Rhynchospora capitellata	herbaceous	N		
Small-leaved Panic-grass	Dichanthelium dichotomum var.ensifolium	herbaceous	n/a		
Soapwort gentian	Gentiana saponaria	herbaceous	N	TU	PE

COMMON NAME	SCIENTIFIC NAME	GROWTH HABIT	N/I	ST	PBS
Soft rush	Juncus effusus var. Pylaei	herbaceous	N		
Soft rush	Juncus effusus var. solutus	herbaceous	N		
Solomon's seal	Polygonatum biflorum	herbaceous	N		
Solomon's-seal	Polygonatum pubescens	herbaceous	N		
Southern beech fern	Phegopteris hexagonoptera	herbaceous	N		
Southern lady fern	Athyrium filix-femina var. asplenioides	herbaceous	N		
Southern yellow wood-sorrel	Oxalis dillenii ssp. filipes	herbaceous	N		
Spike-rush	Eleocharis tenuis var. tenuis	herbaceous	N		
Spotted St. John's-wort	Hypericum punctatum	herbaceous	N		
Spreading sedge	Carex laxiculmis var. laxiculmis	herbaceous	N		
Springbeauty	Claytonia virginica	herbaceous	N		
Star-flower	Trientalis borealis	herbaceous	N		
Sundrops	Oenothera fruticosa	herbaceous	N		
Swamp milkweed	Asclepias incarnata	herbaceous	N		
Swan's sedge	Carex swanii	herbaceous	N		
Sweet everlasting	Pseudognaphalium obtusifolium	herbaceous	n/a		
Sweet white violet	Viola macloskeyi	herbaceous	N		
Sweet-scented bedstraw	Gallium triflorum	herbaceous	N		
Tall meadow-rue	Thalictrum pubescens	herbaceous	N		
Tearthumb, Scratch-grass	Persicaria sagittata	herbaceous	N		
Tickseed sunflower	Bidens polylepis	herbaceous	I		
Tickseed sunflower	Bidens trichosperma (Bidens cronata)	herbaceous	N		

COMMON NAME	SCIENTIFIC NAME	GROWTH HABIT	N/I	ST	PBS
Timothy	Phleum pratense	herbaceous	I		
Toothed wood fern	Dryopteris carthusiana	herbaceous	N		
Turtlehead	Chelone glabra	herbaceous	N		
Violet wood-sorrel	Oxalis violacea	herbaceous	N		
Water-plantain	Alisma triviale	herbaceous	N		
Weak rush	Juncus debilis	herbaceous	N	N	PT
White avens	Geum canadense var. canadense	herbaceous	N		
White snakeroot	Ageratina altissima	herbaceous	N		
White vervain	Verbena urticifolia	herbaceous	N		
White wood aster	Eurybia divaricata	herbaceous	N		
White-edged sedge	Carex debilis var. debilis	herbaceous	N		
Whorled loosestrife	Lysimachia quadrifolia	herbaceous	N		
Whorled-pogonia	Isotria verticillata	herbaceous	N		
Wild licorice	Gallium circaezans var. circaezans	herbaceous	N		
Wild licorice/ Lance-leaved Wild Licorice	Gallium lanceolatum	herbaceous	N		
Wild sarsaparilla	Aralia nudicaulis	herbaceous	N		
Wild strawberry	Fragaria virginiana	herbaceous	N		
Wood anemone	Anemone quinquefolia	herbaceous	N		
Wood lily	Lilium philadelphicum	herbaceous	N		
Wood reedgrass	Cinna arundinacea	herbaceous	N		
Wool-grass	Scirpus cyperinus	herbaceous	N		
Wool-grass	Scirpus rubricosus (see Scirpus cyperinus)	herbaceous	N		

COMMON NAME	SCIENTIFIC NAME	GROWTH HABIT	N/I	ST	PBS
Wrinkle-leaf goldenrod	Solidago rugosa	herbaceous	N		
Yarrow	Achillea millefolium	herbaceous	I		
Yellow flax	Linum medium	herbaceous	N		
Yellow Foxtail	Setaria glauca	herbaceous	n/a		
Yellow star-grass	Hypoxis hirsuta	herbaceous	N		
Yellow trout-lily	Erythronium americanum	herbaceous	N		
Deep-rooted running-pine (clubmoss)	Lycopodium tristachyum	clubmoss	N		
Flat-branched ground-pine (clubmoss)	Lycopodium obscurum	clubmoss	N		
Northern running-pine (clubmoss)	Lycopodium complanatum	clubmoss	N		
Running-pine (clubmoss)	Diphasiastrum digitatum	clubmoss	N		
Lesser duckweed	Lemna minor	aquatic plant	N		

REPTILES

COMMON NAME	SCIENTIFIC NAME
Black Rat Snake	Elaphe obsoleta obsoleta
Box Turtle	Terrapene carolina
Eastern Box turtle	Terrapene carolina carolina
Eastern Garter Snake	Thamnophis sirtalis sirtalis
Eastern Milk Snake	Lampropeltis triangulum triangulum
Northern Black Racer	Coluber constrictor constrictor
Northern Water Snake	Natrix sipedon
Spotted Turtle	Clemmys guttata

AMPHIBIANS

COMMON NAME	SCIENTIFIC NAME
American Toad	Anaxyrus americanus
Bullfrog	Lithobates catesbeianus
Eastern Redback Salamander	Plethodon cinereus
Green Frog	Lithobates clamitans
Northern dusky salamander	Desmognathus fuscus
Northern Red Salamander	Pseudotriton r. ruber
Northern slimy salamander	Plethodon glutinosus
Northern Spring Peeper	Pseudacris crucifer
Northern two-lined salamander	Eurycea bislineata
Spotted Salamander	Ambystoma maculatum
Wood Frog	Lithobates sylvaticus

Mammals

COMMON NAME	SCIENTIFIC NAME
Big Brown Bat	Eptisicus fuss
Eastern Cottontail Rabbit	Sylvilagus floridanus
Eastern Coyote	Canis latrans
Eastern Gray Squirrel	Sciurus carolinensis
Eastern Mole	Scalopus aquaticus
Eastern Red bat	Lasiurus borealis
Gray Fox	Urocyon cinereoargenteus
Hoary Bat	Lasiurus cinereus
Least Shrew	Cryptotis parva
Little Brown Myotis	Myotis lucifufus
Long-tailed weasel	Mustela frenata
Meadow Vole	Microtus pennsylvanicus
Muskrat	Ondatra zibethica
Northern Flying Squirrel	Glaucomys sabrinus
Opossum	Didelphis marsupialis
Racoon	Procyon lotor
Red Fox	Vuples fulva
Short-tailed Shrew	Blarina brevicaudata
Silver-haired Bat	Lasionycteris noctivagans
Starnose Mole	Condulura cristata
Striped Skunk	Mephitis mephitis
White-footed Mouse	Peromyscus leucopus
Whitetail Deer	Sylvilagus floridanus
	Odocoileaus virginianus

BIRDS

This list was compiled from source materials which varied regarding standards for species inclusion, and should therefore be considered a list of possible bird species that could inhabit the Five Mile Woods Preserve on a regular or seasonal bases, as well as a great number of additional species which might make only very brief appearances or fly-overs during east-coast migrations, might take refuge during severe storm events or which might occur merely as *vagrants*.

Bird's nest in the winter at the Five Mile Woods Preserve.

COMMON NAME	SCIENTIFIC NAME
Acadian Flycatcher	Empidonax virescens
Alder Flycatcher	Empidonax alnorun
* American Bittern	Botaurus lentigenosis
American Crow	Corvus brachyrhynchos
American Goldfinch	Spinus tristis
American Kestrel	Falco sparvernius
American Redstart	Setophaga ruticilla
American Robin	Turdus migratorius
American Tree Sparrow	Spizella arborea
American Woodcock	Philohela minor
American Woodcock	Scolopax minor
Bald Eagle	Haliaeetus leucocephalus
Baltimore Oriole	Icterus galbula
Bank Swallow	Riparia riparia
Barn Swallow	Hirundo rustica
Barred Owl	Strix varia
Bay-breasted Warbler	Dendroica castanea
Belted Kingfisher	Megaceryle alcyon
Bicknell's Thrush	Catharus bicknelli
Black Vulture	Coragyps atratus
Black-and-white Warbler	Mniotilta varia
Black-billed Cuckoo	Coccyzus erythropthalmust
Black-capped Chickadee	Parus atricapillus
Black-throated Blue Warbler	Setophaga caerulescens
Black-throated Green Warbler	Dendroica virens
Black-throated Warbler	Dendroica caerulescens
Blackburnian Warbler	Dendroica fuscus
Blackpoll Warbler	Dendroica striata
Blue Grosbeak	Passerina caerulea
Blue Jay	Cyanocitta cristata
Blue-gray Gnatcatcher	Polioptila caerulea
Blue-headed Vireo	Vereo solitarius
Blue-winged Warbler	Vermivora pinus
Broad-winged Hawk	Buteoe platypterus
Brown Creeper	Certha familiaris
Brown Thatcher	Toxostoma rufum

Brown-headed Cowbird	Molothrus ater
Canada Goose	Branta Canadensis
Canada Warbler	Wilsonia candensis
Cape May Warbler	Dendroica tigrine
Carolina Chickadee	Parus carolinensis
Carolina Wren	Thryothorus ludovicianus
Cedar Waxwing	Bombycilla cedrorum
Cerulean Warbler	Setophaga cerulea
Chestnut-sided Warbler	Dendroica pansylvanica
Chimney Swift	Chaetura pelagica
Chipping Sparrow	Spizella passerine
Chuck-wills-widow	Caprimulus carolinensis
Cliff Swallow	Petrochelidon pyrrhonota
Common Flicker	Colaptes auratus
Common Grackle	Quiscalus quiscalus
Common Nighhawk	Chordeiles minor
Common Redpoll	Carduelis flammea
Common Yellowthroat	Geothlypis trichas
Cooper's Hawk	Accipiter cooperii
Dark-eyed Junco	Junco hyemalis
Downy Woodpecker	Picoides pubescens
Eastern Bluebird	Sialia sialis
Eastern Kingbird	Tyrannus tyrannus
Eastern Phoebe	Sayornis phoebe
Eastern Screech Owl	Megascops asio
Eastern Wood Pewee	Contopus virens
European Starling	Sternus vulgaris
Evening Grosbeak	Hesperiphona vespertina
Field Sparrow	Spizella pusilla
Fish Crow	Corvus ossifragus
Fox Sparrow	Passerella iliaca
Golden-crowned Kinglet	Regulus satrapa
Golden-winged Warbler	Vermivora chrysoptera
Goldfinch	Carduelis firstus
Gray Catbird	Dumetella carolinensis
Gray-cheeked Thrush	Catharus minimus
Great Blue Heron	Ardea herodias

Great Crested Flycatcher	Myiarchus crinitus
Great Horned Owl	Bubo virginianus
Green Heron	Botaurus virescens
Hairy Woodpecker	Picoides villosus
Hermit Thrush	Catharus guttatus
Herring Gull	Larus argentatus
Hooded Warbler	Wilsonia citrina
House Finch	Carpodacus misicanus
House Sparrow	Passer domesticus
House Wren	Troglodytes aedon
Indigo Bunting	Passerina cyanea
Kentucky Warbler	Oporonis formosus
Killdeer	Chardarius vociferous
Least Flycatcher	Empidonax minimus
Lincoln's Sparrow	Melospiza lincolnii
* Long-eared Owl	Asio otus
Louisiana Waterthrush	Seiurus motacilla
Magnolia Warbler	Dendroica magnolia
Mallard	Anas platyrhynchos
Mourning Dove	Zenaida macroura
Mourning Warbler	Oporonis philadelphica
Nashville Warbler	Vermivora ruficapilla
Northern Cardinal	Cardinalis cardinalis
Northern Flicker	Colaptes auratus
Northern Harrier	Circus cyaneus
Northern Mockingbird	Mimus polyglottos
Northern Parula Warbler	Parula Americana
Northern Waterthrush	Seiurus noveboracensis
Orchard Oriole	Icterus spurius
Osprey	Pandion halisaetus
Ovenbird	Seiurus aurocapillus
Palm Warbler	Dendroica palmarum
Pileated Woodpecker	Dryocopus pileatus
Pine Siskin	Carduelis pirius
Pine Warbler	Dendroica pinus
Prairie Warbler	Dendroica discolor
Purple Finch	Carpodacus purpureus

Red-bellied Woodpecker	Melanerpes carolinus
Red-eyed Vireo	Vireo olivaceus
Red-headed Woodpecker	Melanerpes erythrocephalus
Red-shouldered Hawk	Buteo lineatus
Red-tailed Hawk	Buteo jamicaensis
Red-winged Blackbird	Agelaius phoeniceus
Ring -billed Gull	Larus delawarensis
Ring-necked Pheasant	Phasianus colchicus
Rose-breasted Grosbeak	Pheuctucus lodovicianus
Ruby-crowned Kinglet	Regulus calendula
Ruby-throated Hummingbird	Archilochus lolubris
Ruffed Grouse	Bonasa umbellus
Rufous-sided Towhee	Pipilo erythrophthalmus
Rusty Blackbird	Euphagus carolinus
Scarlet Tanager	Paraang loivcea
Sharp-shinned Hawk	Acceipiter striatus
Solitary Vireo	Vireo solitaries
Song Sparrow	Melospiza melodia
Swainson's Thrush	Catharus ustulatus
Swamp Sparrow	Melospiza georgiana
Tennessee Warbler	Vermivora peregrine
Tree Swallow	Tachycineta bicolor
Tufted Titmouse	Parus bicolor
Turkey Vulture	Cathartes aura
Veery	Cathraus fuscescens
Warbling Vireo	Vireo gilvus
White-breasted Nuthatch	Sitta carolinensis
White-crowned Sparrow	Zonotrichia leucophrys
White-eyed Vireo	Vireo griseus
White-throated Sparrow	Zonotrichia albicollis
Wild Turkey	Meleagris gallopavo
Willow Flycatcher	Empidonax traillii
Wilson's Warbler	Wilsonia pusilla
Winter Wren	Troglodytes troglodytes
Wood Duck	Aix sponsa
Wood Thrush	Hylocichla mustelina
Worm-eating Warbler	Helmitheros vermivorus

Yellow Warbler	Dendroica petechia
* Yellow-bellied Flycatcher	Empidonax flaviventris
Yellow-bellied Sapsucker	Sphyrapicus varius
Yellow-billed Cuckoo	Coccyzus americanus
Yellow-breasted Chat	Icteria virens
Yellow-rumped Warbler	Dendroica coronate
Yellow-throated Vireo	Vireo flavifrons

COMMON BEECH

COMMON BEECH

ENDNOTES

The following abbreviations have been used in both the endnotes and bibliography:
DFC
This designation is used for the Donald Formigli Collection.
PMC
This designation is used for the Pat Miiller Collection.
HHC
This designation is used for the Helen Heinz Collection
FMWPA
The designation is used for the Five Mile Woods Preserve Archives
LMHS
This designation is used for the Lower Makefield Historical Society

Notes to Manuscript

During this project, Donald Formigli, Pat Miiller, President of the Lower Makefield Historical Society, Helen Heinz, Lower Makefield historian, John Heilferty Preserve Manager and John Lloyd, Chairman of the Friends of the Five Mile Woods regularly read the manuscript and made corrections or added their insights. If the corrections were of a minor nature the author simply made them. If the corrections or insights were important and required citation, then the citation will appear in this form: (Heinz, Notes To Manuscript April 1, 2016)

All the draft manuscripts were given to the FMWP at the end of the project and identified if future researchers want to track down a source. This is also true of all the corrected versions of the final draft reviewed by the readers of the manuscript. They too were given to the FMWP and each labeled by the reader's name using the same format as listed above.

Interviews

During this project, various people were interviewed and the author's notes from those interviews were given to the FMWP at the end of the project and identified if future researchers want to track down a source. The citation will appear in this form: (Miiller 2016). The date of the interview will appear in the Bibliography.

Web Sites

All web sites that are cited were active at the time of publication.

ENDNOTES

INTRODUCTION

1 (Five Miles Woods project to get $300,000 grant 1979)
2 (Osborne, Where Washington Once Led: A History of New Jersey's Washington Crossing State Park 2012, 19)
3 (Osborne, No Spot In This Far Land is More Immortalized: A History of Pennsylvania's Washington Crossing Historic Park 2014, 98-99, 129-133)
4 (Osborne, No Spot In This Far Land is More Immortalized: A History of Pennsylvania's Washington Crossing Historic Park 2014, 590-592)
5 (Osborne, No Spot In This Far Land is More Immortalized: A History of Pennsylvania's Washington Crossing Historic Park 2014, 502)
6 (P. Miiller, Notes to Manuscript October 5, 2016)
7 (P. Miiller, Notes to Manuscript October 5, 2016)

CHAPTER I

1 (Ann Rhoads 2003, 16)
2 (Ann Rhoads 2003, 18)
3 (Bob Freitag, Susan Bolton, Frank Westerlund, Julie Clark 2009, 77) (Dalton 2006) (Huets 2013) (Ann Rhoads 2003, 32) (Great Falls Park, Virginia 2017) (Shafer April 15, 2003)
4 (Early Botanists of Bucks County n.d., 49-50) (Davis, W.W.H. 1876, Appendix, 3) (Early Botanists of Bucks County n.d., 49-50)
5 (Davis, W.W.H. 1876, Appendix, 3) (Early Botanists of Bucks County n.d., 49-50)
6 (Robertson 1971-1972, 1) (Philadelphia Botanical Club: Herbarium 2017) (Schuyler 1979)
7 (Ann Rhoads 2003, 2) (Ann Rhoads honored by Nature Conservancy 1987)
8 (Ann Rhoads 2003, 2) (Ann Rhoads honored by Nature Conservancy 1987)
9 (Richards 1956, 16-17)
10 (Carmichael 1974-1975, Part I (December 1974, Vol. 5, No. 7, Part II (February 1975, Vol. 6, No. 5)) (Richards 1956, 8-9)
11 (Roberts 1996, 47-49, 247-249, 342) (Richards 1956, 8)
12 (Watershed Restoration Action Strategy: State Water Plan Sub-basin 02E Pidcock Creek and Mill Creek and Tributaries to the Delaware River in Lower Bucks County, Pennsylvania 2004, 1) (Richards 1956, 8-9) (Roberts 1996, 47-49, 247-249, 342) (Carmichael 1974-1975, Part I (December 1974, Vol. 5, No. 7, Part II (February 1975, Vol. 6, No. 5)) (Formigli, The Five Mile Woods (DFC) 1975, 2)
13 (Berg 2004) (Richards 1956, 58) (Fossils of the Northeastern US: a brief review 2016, 92, 95)
14 (Carmichael 1974-1975, Part I (December 1974, Vol. 5, No. 7, Part II (February 1975, Vol.6, No. 5)) (Roberts 1996, 341-347) (Richards 1956, 20) (Falon April 19, 1979) (Benner 1932, 12,15)
15 (Carmichael 1974-1975, Part I (December 1974, Vol. 5, No. 7, Part II (February 1975, Vol. 6, No. 5)))
16 (Hughes, Farm Map Lower Makefield Township Bucks County, Pennsylvania 1858) (D. Formigli, Five Mile Woods Program and Nature Photography Show (DFC) February 4, 1979) (Heinz 2016) (Ann Rhoads 2003, 3) (Historic Fallsington: The Story of an Early Bucks County Village 1947, 2008, 1, 7)

17 (Carmichael 1974-1975, Part I (December 1974, Vol. 5, No. 7, Part II (February 1975, Vol. 6, No. 5)) (Richards 1956, 16, 24) (Formigli, The Five Mile Woods (DFC) 1975, 2) (Benner 1932, 13) (Heinz, Notes to Manuscript July 30, 2016) (Mellon, Master Plan for the Five Mile Woods Preserve 1981, 8)

18 (Mellon, Master Plan for the Five Mile Woods Preserve 1981, 8)

19 (J. Marshall 2017)

20 (John Lawrence, Brian Albright 2012, 2-5)

21 (Falon April 19, 1979)

22 (Falon April 19, 1979) (Carmichael 1974-1975, Part I (December 1974, Vol. 5, No. 7, Part II (February 1975, Vol.6, No. 5)) (Berg 2004)

23 (Benner 1932, 7) (Heilferty 2017)

24 (Bob Freitag, Susan Bolton, Frank Westerlund, Julie Clark 2009, 77) (Dalton 2006) (Huets 2013)

25 (Bob Freitag, Susan Bolton, Frank Westerlund, Julie Clark 2009, 77) (Dalton 2006) (Huets 2013) (Heilferty, Notes from Manuscript April 4, 2017, 22)

26 (Bucks County Planning Commission 2011, 73) (D. Formigli July 29, 2016) (Heinz 2016) (Miiller 2016)

27 (Osborne, Where Washington Once Led: A History of New Jersey's Washington Crossing State Park 2012, 30-31) (Bob Freitag, Susan Bolton, Frank Westerlund, Julie Clark 2009, 77) (Carmichael 1974-1975, Part I (December 1974, Vol. 5, No. 7, Part II (February 1975, Vol. 6, No. 5))

28 (Richards 1956, 8) (Geology - Franklin College 2016) (Winchester 2013, 170) (Roberts 1996, 242)

29 (Carmichael 1974-1975, Part I (December 1974, Vol. 5, No. 7, Part II (February 1975, Vol.6, No. 5)) (Bob Freitag, Susan Bolton, Frank Westerlund, Julie Clark 2009, 77) (Roberts 1996, 279, 298) (Winchester 2013, 170-171) (Heilferty 2017)

30 (Report on Roads and Canals, Communicated to the Senate April 4, 1808, 729)

31 (Ann Rhoads 2003, 32)

32 (Formigli, Text for Five Mile Woods Slide-Tape Program (DFC) 1979)

33 (D. Formigli, Five Mile Woods Program and Nature Photography Show (DFC) February 4, 1979) (Heilferty, Notes from Manuscript April 4, 2017, 24)

34 (Heilferty 2016) (D. Formigli, Five Mile Woods Program and Nature Photography Show (DFC) February 4, 1979) (D. Formigli, The Five Mile Woods (DFC) 1975, 9, 15) (Heilferty 2017) (Heilferty, Notes from Manuscript April 4, 2017, 24) (Watershed Restoration Action Strategy: State Water Plan Sub-basin 02E Pidcock Creek and Mill Creek and Tributaries to the Delaware River in Lower Bucks County, Pennsylvania 2004, 8) See the USGS maps for elevation information.

35 (Watershed Restoration Action Strategy: State Water Plan Sub-basin 02E Pidcock Creek and Mill Creek and Tributaries to the Delaware River in Lower Bucks County, Pennsylvania 2004, 2, 6, 8) (Noll 1891) (Bucks County Planning Commission 2014, Maps 2 & 3)The plan did not include designing the trail to begin at the Preserve or the headwaters of the Queen Anne Creek.

36 (Watershed Restoration Action Strategy: State Water Plan Sub-basin 02E Pidcock Creek and Mill Creek and Tributaries to the Delaware River in Lower Bucks County, Pennsylvania 2004, 8) (Formigli, The Five Mile Woods (DFC) 1975, 9) (Bucks County Planning Commission 2014) (Heilferty 2016) (Heilferty 2017) (Heilferty, Notes from Manuscript April 4, 2017, 24)

37 (Watershed Restoration Action Strategy: State Water Plan Sub-basin 02E Pidcock Creek and Mill Creek and Tributaries to the Delaware River in Lower Bucks County, Pennsylvania 2004, 3, 6)
38 (Bucks County Planning Commission 2014, 2, 6, 27)
39   (Bucks County Planning Commission 2014, Maps 2 & 3) The plan did not include any proposal to begin the trail at the Preserve or near the headwaters of the Queen Anne Creek.
40 (Thomas Holmes, Lloyd Smith c. 1705) (MacReynolds 1955, 324) (Espenshade 1925) (Heinz 2017)
41 (J. Scott 1876) (Hughes, Farm Map of Falls Township, Bucks County, Pennsylvania 1858)
42   (Heilferty 2017) To follow the route of the Rock Run see the Trenton West NJ/PA USGS maps which show it flowing southward in 1907. The 1995 map shows it flowing into the bodies of water that were created in the years after the Fairless Works was built. The author has chosen to use the historic name of Pennsbury Manor in the book rather than its current variation.
43 (Davis, W. W. H. 1876, 189-190)
44 (Bonomi 1998)
45 (Royal Family History 2016) (Davis, W. W. H. 1876, 189-190) (Pennsbury Manor: People at Pennsbury 2016) (Mary Dunn, Richard Dunn, editors 1982, Vol. 4, 187)
46 (Davis, W.W.H. 1876, 189-190) (Royal Family History 2016)
47 (Bonomi 1998, 15-16)
48 (Mary Dunn, Richard Dunn, editors 1982, Vol. 4, 187)
49 (Report - Road Leading from Newtown to Jenk's fulling mill July 7, 1696)
50 (Formigli, The Five Mile Woods (DFC) 1975, 1) (Formigli, Text for Five Mile Woods Slide-Tape Program (DFC) 1979) (Heilferty 2016) (Heilferty 2017) (J. Foulds 2016) (Mellon 2017) At the time of the efforts to save the Preserve supporters consistently described a small wetland near Big Oak Road as the sphagnum moss bog. Today, it is more correctly called a sphagnum moss wetland as a wetland does not meet the technical definition of a bog. Also, it was described as one of only two sphagnum bogs located in Bucks County at the time, which because of this change in definition is also not correct. The origins of this wetland is disputed. While Jim Foulds believed that the material excavated from this area was used for the berm in front of the Brelsford House, Rick Mellon and John Heilferty believe that the wetland had been in existence before the berm was created. There is also some disagreement as to whether it was man-made or a naturally occurring phenomenon.
51 (Heilferty 2017) (D. Formigli, The Five Mile Woods (DFC) 1975, 2, 5) (Carmichael 1974-1975, Part I (December 1974, Vol. 5, No. 7, Part II (February 1975, Vol. 6, No. 5)) (Heilferty 2016) (Mellon 2017)
52 (Heilferty 2017) (Heilferty 2016) (Heilferty, Notes from Manuscript April 4, 2017, 28)
53 (D. Formigli, The Five Mile Woods (DFC) 1975, 5) (John Lawrence, Brian Albright 2012, 2-6) (Carmichael 1974-1975, Part I (December 1974, Vol. 5, No. 7, Part II (February 1975, Vol.6, No. 5))) (Heilferty 2017)
54 (John Lawrence, Brian Albright 2012, 2-4 & 5) (Heilferty 2017)
55 (A. Rhoads April 7, 2017) (Edgar Wherry, John Fogg and Herbert Wahl 1979) (Ann Rhoads, William Klein 1993)
56 (Formigli, The Five Mile Woods (DFC) 1975, 5) (Heilferty, Notes to Manuscript December 31, 2016) (A. Rhoads April 7, 2017) (Lauren Poster, Ann Rhoads and Timothy Block 2013, 101-124)
57 (Heilferty 2016) (Heilferty, Notes to Manuscript December 31, 2016)

58 (Heilferty 2016) (Shandle 1985) (Academy of Natural Sciences of Philadelphia December 1, 1978, II, 12) (Mellon, Master Plan for the Five Mile Woods Preserve 1981, 72) (Heilferty 2016) (Mellon 2017)

59 (Heilferty 2016) (Shandle 1985) (Academy of Natural Sciences of Philadelphia December 1, 1978, II, 12) (Mellon, Master Plan for the Five Mile Woods Preserve 1981, 72) (Heilferty 2016) (Mellon 2017) (J. Marshall 2017)

60 (Penn Pilot: Historic Aerial Photographs of Pennsylvania 2016) The name attributed to the stone house over the years has been the Cutler House. It has been changed in this manuscript to reflect the historical data that is known about the house. It is now believed that it was built by a Brelsford family member, either Isaac or Abraham. Brelsford will be used in all future references to the house.

61 (Penn Pilot: Historic Aerial Photographs of Pennsylvania 2016) (Heilferty 2016) Don Formigli also took aerial photographs of the Woods in 1974.

62 (Formigli, Text for Five Mile Woods Slide-Tape Program (DFC) 1979)

63 (Heinz 2016) (Heinz 2016) (Heinz 2016) (A. Rhoads April 7, 2017)

CHAPTER 2

1 (Pennbury Manor: Plan Your Visit 2016)

2 (Lawmaking and Legislators in Pennsylvania: A Biographical Dictionary 1682-1709 1991, 311)

3 (Amos Satterthwaite, Elizabeth Satterthwaite 1910, 21)

4 (Benner 1932, 25)

5 (Check 1987)

6 (Check 1987) (Heinz, Notes to Manuscript April 7, 2017)

7 (The Township of Lower Makefield, Bucks County, Pennsylvania 2016) (Benner 1932, 5) (Atlas of Pennsylvania n.d., 108) (Visit Bucks County 2016)

8 (Atlas of Pennsylvania n.d., 85) (Fischer 2004) See Fischer's book for an extensive treatment of the famed Christmas Crossing and subsequent Battles of Trenton and Princeton.

9 (Clark 2006, 96-97) (Bucks County Planning Commission 2011, 266)

10 (Osborne, No Spot in This Far Land Is More Immortalized: A History of Pennsylvania's Washington Crossing Historic Park 2014, 39)

11 (Davis, W. W. H. 1876, 118-119) (J. H. Battle 1887, 440) (Thompson, Slate Hill Cemetery National Register of Historic Places Registration Form 1991)

12 (Davis, W. W. H. 1876, 118-119) (J. H. Battle 1887, 440) (Heinz, Notes to Manuscript July 30, 2016, 30) (Heinz 2016) (Thompson, Slate Hill Cemetery National Register of Historic Places Registration Form 1991) (Lower Makefield Historical Commission 1992, 11) The actual boundaries can be approximated by comparing Davis's description and the Holmes map of Bucks County.

13 (Davis, W. W. H. 1876, 101-103)

14 (Davis, W. W. H. 1876, 661)

15 (Atlas of Pennsylvania n.d., 76) (Osborne, Perseverance & Vigilance: The History of the Old Decker Stone House 2007, 5) (Native American Context – Digging I95 2016, 1-2)

16 (Atlas of Pennsylvania n.d., 76) (Native American Context – Digging I95 2016, 2-6)

17 (Atlas of Pennsylvania n.d., 76) (Native American Context – Digging I95 2016, 6-10)

18 (Jane Clark Shermayeff and Associates 2009, 9) (National Park Service 2016)

19 (White, When the Lenape ruled the land 1992) (Lower Makefield Historical Commission 1992, 2-3) (John Lawrence, Brian Albright 2012, i) This reports an excellent and detailed overview of the native peoples in the area from their arrival until their migrations west.
20 (Lower Makefield Historical Commission 1992, 3) (White, When the Lenape ruled the land 1992) (Heinz, Notes to Manuscript July 30, 2016)
21 (Osborne, Where Washington Once Led: A History of New Jersey's Washington Crossing State Park 2012, 36) (Wade Summer 2008, 1-4)
22 (White, When the Lenape ruled the land 1992)
23 (White, When the Lenape ruled the land 1992) (Lower Makefield Historical Commission 1992, 4) (Deed of Indians to William Biles 1737)
24 (Heinz, Notes to Manuscript July 30, 2016, 32)
25 (Penn Treaty Museum 2016)
26 (Satterthwaite 1945, 2) (William Penn's Country Estate Pennsbury Manor 2016) (Penn Treaty Museum 2016) (Lawmaking and Legislators in Pennsylvania: A Biographical Dictionary 1682-1709 1991, 797)
27 (Satterthwaite 1945, 2) (William Penn's Country Estate Pennsbury Manor 2016) (Penn Treaty Museum 2016)
28 (Satterthwaite 1945, 2-3) (Pennsbury Manor: People at Pennsbury 2016) (S. Snipes 2001, 14)
29 (Thompson, Historic Sites in & adjacent to Five Mile Woods (Revised edition) 1997, 6) (The Founding of the Quaker Colony of West Jersey 2016) (Lower Makefield Historical Commission 1992, 5) (Heinz, Notes to Manuscript July 30, 2016)
30 (Heinz, Notes to Manuscript July 30, 2016)
31 (Mark Reinberger, Elizabeth McLean July 2007, 272-273, 277-278)
32 (William Penn's Country Estate Pennsbury Manor 2016) (Lloyd 2016) (Mark Reinberger, Elizabeth McLean July 2007, 293)
33 (William Penn: Seed of a Nation Exhibit 2016) (Lawmaking and Legislators in Pennsylvania: A Biographical Dictionary 1682-1709 1991, Vol. 1, 14)
34 (Heinz, Notes to Manuscript July 30, 2016) (J. Marshall, Notes to Manuscript April 7, 2017)
35 (Davis, W. W. H. 1876, 38) (J. H. Battle 1887, 674) (William Dark Genealogy 2016) (Lawmaking and Legislators in Pennsylvania: A Biographical Dictionary 1682-1709 1991, Vol. 1, 311-312)(Thompson, Historic Sites in & adjacent to Five Mile Woods (Revised edition) 1997, 6-7) (Thomas Holmes, Lloyd Smith c. 1705) (P. Lea Thomas Holmes 1687) The author has used several sources for the Dark genealogical information including various Family Tree Maker files, *Lawmaking and Legislators in Pennsylvania,* the *History of Bucks County* by W. W. Davis and a BCHS paper entitled *Bucks County Pioneers in the Valley of Virginia.* While some of the information presented in these sources agrees, on other matters they do not agree. For example, *Lawmaking and Legislators* believes that William Dark was born c. 1629 while most of the family genealogists have used a 1642 date and Davis has it as 1622. The author has tried to the best of his ability to sort this out and thinks that the date c. 1629 seems most probable. If his wife Honor was of the age suggested by the various sources, she would have been beyond her childbearing years when they married. Other records, such as the Index to Estates, Bucks County, Pennsylvania, spell son John Dark's name with an "e" as does his will.
36 (Lawmaking and Legislators in Pennsylvania: A Biographical Dictionary 1682-1709 1991, Vol. 1, 311-312) (J. H. Battle 1887, 116) (Lower Makefield Historical Society, The Township Historical Commission, The Historical Architectural Review Board 1998)
37 (Thompson, Historic Sites in & adjacent to Five Mile Woods (Revised edition) 1997, 2) (Davis, W. W. H. 1876, 37-38) (Deed Book 1, Page 301 1690) (Deed Book 2, Pages 94-95 1696)

38 (Mark Reinberger, Elizabeth McLean July 2007, 272) (Davis, W. W. H. 1876, 720) (Thompson, Historic Sites in & adjacent to Five Mile Woods (Revised edition) 1997, 3-4, 6)

39 (The Township of Lower Makefield, Bucks County, Pennsylvania 2016) (Lower Makefield Historical Society, The Township Historical Commission, The Historical Architectural Review Board 1998) (Thompson, Historic Sites in & adjacent to Five Mile Woods (Revised edition) 1997, 3) (William Dark Genealogy 2016) (Davis, W. W. H. 1876, 37-38) (Deed Book 1, Page 301 1690) (Thomas Holmes, Lloyd Smith c. 1705) (Thompson, Lower Makefield Township Bucks County, Pennsylvania Map of Original Grantees 1988) (Heinz, Notes to Manuscript July 30, 2016, 30) (Heinz 2016) In one version of his report Thompson says that the patent included 325 acres but this could just have been a typo because it is clear that he saw the deeds which state 235 acres. In a second version, he reports that a later survey shows that it was 290 acres in size.

40 (Thompson, Historic Sites in & adjacent to Five Mile Woods (Revised edition) 1997, 3-4, 6) (Thompson, Lower Makefield Township Bucks County, Pennsylvania Map of Original Grantees 1988)

41 (Heinz 2016) (Terry McNealy and Francis Waite 1982, 1)

42 (William Dark Genealogy 2016) (Lawmaking and Legislators in Pennsylvania: A Biographical Dictionary 1682-1709 1991, Vol. 1, 311-312) (Davis, W. W. H. 1876, 37-38)

43 (Lawmaking and Legislators in Pennsylvania: A Biographical Dictionary 1682-1709 1991, Vol. 1, 311) (Davis, W. W. H. 1876, 37-38) Davis reports that he was a grocer and not a glover.

44 (Lawmaking and Legislators in Pennsylvania: A Biographical Dictionary 1682-1709 1991, Vol. 1, 31, 63, 311-312) (Report - Road Leading from Newtown to Jenk's fulling mill July 7, 1696)

45 (William Dark Genealogy 2016) (Lawmaking and Legislators in Pennsylvania: A Biographical Dictionary 1682-1709 1991, Vol. 1, 311-312) (Davis, W. W. H. 1876, 37-38) (Smyth Vol. 4, 454)

46 (Lawmaking and Legislators in Pennsylvania: A Biographical Dictionary 1682-1709 1991, Vol. 1, 311-312)
(Report - Road Leading from Newtown to Jenk's fulling mill July 7, 1696) (Lawmaking and Legislators in Pennsylvania: A Biographical Dictionary 1682-1709 1991, Vol. 1, 311-312) (Davis, W.W.H. 1876, 37-38).

47 (Thompson, Historic Sites in & adjacent to Five Mile Woods (Revised edition) 1997, 6) (William Dark Genealogy 2016) (Davis, W. W. H. 1876, 105) (Sheppard 1970, 146) (Historic Fallsington: The Story of an Early Bucks County Village 1947, 2008, 2) (G. Smyth Vol. 4, 450-453) (Lawmaking and Legislators in Pennsylvania: A Biographical Dictionary 1682-1709 1991, Vol. 1, 311-312) (Mary Dunn, Richard Dunn, editors 1982, Vol. 4, 102) (Thompson, Slate Hill Cemetery National Register of Historic Places Registration Form 1991) (Satterthwaite 1945, 1, 3-4)

48 (William Dark Genealogy 2016) (Davis, W.W.H. 1876, 37-38) (Thomas Holmes, Lloyd Smith c. 1705) (Thompson, Lower Makefield Township Bucks County, Pennsylvania Map of Original Grantees 1988) (Lawmaking and Legislators in Pennsylvania: A Biographical Dictionary 1682-1709 1991, Vol. 1, 309-311)

49 (Mary Dunn, Richard Dunn, editors 1982, Vol. 4, 99, 100, 102) (Lawmaking and Legislators in Pennsylvania: A Biographical Dictionary 1682-1709 1991, Vol. 1, 309-311)

50 (Thompson, Historic Sites in & adjacent to Five Mile Woods (Revised edition) 1997, 7) (Formigli, Text for Five Mile Woods Slide-Tape Program (DFC) 1979) While most of the stonework was indeed laid up without mortar, there is some mortar in the foundation suggesting that repairs might have been made at a later date.

51 (Thompson, Historic Sites in & adjacent to Five Mile Woods (Revised edition) 1997, 7) (Heinz 2016) (J. Marshall 2017)

52 (Formigli, Text for Five Mile Woods Slide-Tape Program (DFC) 1979)

53 (Historic Fallsington: The Story of an Early Bucks County Village 1947, 2008, 5-6) (S. Snipes 2001, 28-29) (J. Marshall, Notes to Manuscript April 7, 2017)

54 (William Dark Genealogy 2016) (Lawmaking and Legislators in Pennsylvania: A Biographical Dictionary 1682-1709 1991, Vol. 1, 311-312)

55 (Deed Book 2, Pages 94-95 1696) It is worth remembering that this descriptive language was often used in early deeds.

56 Notes attached to Ralph Thompson's research files in the possession of Helen Heinz.

57 (Pennsylvania, Wills and Probate Records, 1683-1993 2015) (Thompson, Historic Sites in & adjacent to Five Mile Woods (Revised edition) 1997, 8) (Heinz, Notes to Manuscript July 30, 2016) (Heilferty, Notes from Manuscript April 4, 2017)

58 (Lower Makefield Historical Society, The Township Historical Commission, The Historical Architectural Review Board 1998)

59 (Pennsylvania, Wills and Probate Records, 1683-1993 2015) (William Dark Genealogy 2016) (G. Smyth Vol. 4, 450-454) (Heinz, Notes to Manuscript April 7, 2017)

60 (Thompson, Historic Sites in & adjacent to Five Mile Woods (Revised edition) 1997, 8) (Cary Family Genealogy 2016) (Heinz, Notes to Manuscript September 24, 2016) (Snipes 2017) (J. Marshall, Notes to Manuscript April 7, 2017) Curiously the boundary change, an important piece of county and township history, has had very little written about it.

61 (Amos Satterthwaite, Elizabeth Satterthwaite 1910, 5)

62 (Amos Satterthwaite, Elizabeth Satterthwaite 1910, 3)

63 (J. H. Battle 1887, 984)

64 (J. H. Battle 1887, 983)

65 (Davis, W.W.H. 1876, 646, 754-755) (William Satterthwaite Genealogy 2016) (W. W. Davis Vol. 1, 126-127) (Kenderine 1918, 100-101, 141-147,163)

66 (Davis, W. W. H. 1876, 755)

67 (Davis, W. W. H. 1876, 755)

68 (Amos Satterthwaite, Elizabeth Satterthwaite 1910, 21, 23) (Heinz, Notes to Manuscript July 30, 2016) (Thompson, Historic Sites in & adjacent to Five Mile Woods (Revised edition) 1997, 8)

69 (Amos Satterthwaite, Elizabeth Satterthwaite 1910, 23) (William Satterthwaite Genealogy 2016) (Thompson, Historic Sites in & adjacent to Five Mile Woods (Revised edition) 1997, 8)

70 (Thompson, Historic Sites in & adjacent to Five Mile Woods (Revised edition) 1997, 8) It is worth noting that Samuel Cary died in 1766 and William Satterthwaite Sr. and Jr. were witnesses to his will indicating that there had been a relationship that was not just one based on a property purchase.

71 (Amos Satterthwaite, Elizabeth Satterthwaite 1910, 48a)

72 (Amos Satterthwaite, Elizabeth Satterthwaite 1910, 48a) (Thompson, Historic Sites in & adjacent to Five Mile Woods (Revised edition) 1997, 8) (J. Marshall 2017)

73 (Terry McNealy and Francis Waite 1982, 60) (Will of William Satterthwaite Jr. 1786) (Williams, Richard and Mildred 1973, 79) (J. Marshall, Notes to Manuscript April 7, 2017)

74 (Janet Brittingham n.d., 44) (J. Marshall, Notes to Manuscript April 7, 2017)

75 (Thompson, Historic Sites in & adjacent to Five Mile Woods (Revised edition) 1997, 8) (Amos Satterthwaite, Elizabeth Satterthwaite 1910, 23) (Will of William Satterthwaite Jr. 1786) The Satterthwaite genealogy by Amos Satterthwaite disagrees with Ralph Thompson on William Sr.'s death date. The former proposes 1788, the latter 1787.

76 (Will of William Satterthwaite Jr. 1786)

77 (Will of William Satterthwaite Jr. 1786) (Heinz, Notes to Manuscript April 7, 2017)

78 (Amos Satterthwaite, Elizabeth Satterthwaite 1910, 23-24) (J. H. Battle 1887, 983) (National Society, Sons of the American Revolution 2016)

79 (Deed Book 401, Page 447 1918) (Thompson, Lower Makefield Township Bucks County, Pennsylvania Map of Original Grantees 1988) (Thompson, Historic Sites in & adjacent to Five Mile Woods (Revised edition) 1997, 8) (Lower Makefield Historical Commission 1992, 7) (Osborne, Property Research Records 2017) Helen Heinz has in her collection a copy of a survey showing the northern line of the Satterthwaite tract and the small fourteen-acre Palmer tract that was sold to him. The survey probably dates from the late eighteenth century.

80 (Thompson, Historic Sites in & adjacent to Five Mile Woods (Revised edition) 1997, 8) (William Satterthwaite Genealogy 2016) (Amos Satterthwaite, Elizabeth Satterthwaite 1910, 23) (Bucks County Tax Records: Lower Makefield, Roll 40)

81 (Thompson, Historic Sites in & adjacent to Five Mile Woods (Revised edition) 1997, 8) (Hughes, Farm Map Lower Makefield Township Bucks County, Pennsylvania 1858) (Bucks County Tax Records: Lower Makefield, Roll 40)

82 (Amos Satterthwaite, Elizabeth Satterthwaite 1910, 26-27) (Quaker Genealogy, Vol. II n.d.) Some of the dates used by the Satterthwaite genealogy contradicted Falls Meeting records and so the data from the Falls Meeting was used instead.

83 (Amos Satterthwaite, Elizabeth Satterthwaite 1910, 26-27, 35) (William Satterthwaite Genealogy 2016) (Deed Book 401, Page 447 1918)

84 (William Satterthwaite Genealogy 2016) (Thompson, Historic Sites in & adjacent to Five Mile Woods (Revised edition) 1997, 8)

85 (Wandling, Peering into the Past 1978) (William Satterthwaite Genealogy 2016) (Snipes 2017) (Deed Book 401, Page 447 1918)

86 (J. H. Battle 1887, 984)

87 (Deed of Indians to William Biles 1737)

88 (Historic Fallsington: The Story of an Early Bucks County Village 1947, 2008, 7-8) (The Religious Society of Friends 2016)

89 (Thompson, Research Report on the Octagonal Schoolhouse n.d.) (Lower Makefield Township Historical Commission 1998) There is some discrepancy regarding the construction of the building. It is not clear which Moon designed the building, the father or the son. At least one source, Henry Mercer, believed that the building dated to the early nineteenth century while others have argued that the interior may date from that time but that the exterior walls probably date to the time of construction in 1775. In addition, W. W. H. Davis wrote in his history of Bucks County that: *In olden times the children from the vicinity of Yardleyville went to school down to the Oxford school-house. But in course of time an eccentric man, named Brelsford, a famous deer hunter of that section, built an eight-square on the site of the present Oak Grove school-house, on a lot left by Thomas Yardley for school purposes.* It is also curious that the school is not designated on the county atlases from 1850-91 although there is one shown in Oxford.

90 (Lower Makefield Township Historical Commission 1998) (Heinz 2016) (Bucks County Planning Commission 2003, 7)

91 (Neeld Octagonal Schoolhouse Files n.d.) (Heinz, Notes to Manuscript July 30, 2016)

92 (Thompson, Research Report on the Octagonal Schoolhouse n.d.) (Edmond Cocks Volume 7) (Map of the Vicinity of Philadelphia: Lower Makefield Township section 1860) (Hughes, Farm Map Lower Makefield Township Bucks County, Pennsylvania 1858) (Heinz 2016) (White, Historian seek preservation of Octagonal Schoolhouse 1987) (S. Snipes 2001, 187)

93 (Thompson, Research Report on the Octagonal Schoolhouse n.d.) (Edmond Cocks Volume 7, 48-56) (Map of the Vicinity of Philadelphia: Lower Makefield Township section 1860) (Hughes, Farm Map Lower Makefield Township Bucks County, Pennsylvania 1858) (Heinz 2016) (White, Historian seek preservation of Octagonal Schoolhouse 1987) (LaVo 2016)

94 (Hughes, Farm Map Lower Makefield Township Bucks County, Pennsylvania 1858)

95 (Willard 2017) (Penn Pilot: Historic Aerial Photographs of Pennsylvania 2016)

96 (Heinz, Notes to Manuscript July 30, 2016)

<h2 style="text-align:center">CHAPTER 3</h2>

1 (Winchester 2013, 241)

2 (Lower Makefield Historical Commission 1992, 18)

3 (Bucks County Planning Commission 2011, 210)

4 (Heinz 2016) (Davis, W. W. H. 1876, 738-739) (J. H. Battle 1887, 181) (J. Marshall, Notes to Manuscript April 7, 2017)

5 (J. H. Battle 1887, 336) (Lower Makefield Historical Society, The Township Historical Commission, The Historical Architectural Review Board 1998) (J. Marshall, Notes to Manuscript April 7, 2017)

6 It is important to point out that the 1696 count was for taxable individuals because the Dark family, for example, had five family members alone by that point and son John had seven children. (The Township of Lower Makefield, Bucks County, Pennsylvania 2016) (Lower Makefield Historical Society, The Township Historical Commission, The Historical Architectural Review Board 1998) (J. Marshall, Notes to Manuscript April 7, 2017)

7 (The Township of Lower Makefield, Bucks County, Pennsylvania 2016) (Davis, W. W. H. 1876, 262, 712-713)

8 (The Township of Lower Makefield, Bucks County, Pennsylvania 2016) (Lower Makefield Historical Commission 1992, 19) (Lower Makefield Historical Society, The Township Historical Commission, The Historical Architectural Review Board 1998) (Heinz, Notes to Manuscript December 11, 2016)

9 (Benner 1932, 9)

10 (J. Marshall, Notes to Manuscript April 7, 2017)

11 (Dale 2003, 35) (Fackenthal 1932, 132-135, 136-138) (Heinz, Notes to Manuscript September 24, 2016) (Davis, W. W. H. 1876, 247)There is some disagreement in the various sources whether Thomas Yardley was the son of Thomas Yardley or his nephew.

12 (W. W. Davis, The Two Makefields Vol. 2, 12-13)

13 (Jack and Lorraine Seabrook 2000, 91)

14 (Dale 2003, 7-8, 35) (Davis, W. W. H. 1876, 661)

15 (Heinz 2016) (White, When the Lenape ruled the land 1992) (J. H. Battle 1887, 185) (Heinz, Notes to Manuscript December 11, 2016) (Helen Heinz to Peter Osborne December 13. 2016)

16 (Heinz, Notes to Manuscript April 7, 2017)

17 (Ely Vol. 5)

18 (J. H. Battle 1887, 334) (Davis, W. W. H. 1876, 740)

19 (J. H. Battle 1887, 184) (Davis, W. W. H. 1876, 740) (Faris 1917, 285)

20 (Heinz 2016) (P. Miiller, Notes to Manuscript October 5, 2016) (Helen Heinz to Peter Osborne October 3, 2016) (Bucks County Planning Commission 2003, 7) (Helen Heinz to Peter Osborne January 16, 2017) (Helen Heinz to Peter Osborne December 13. 2016) (Lower Makefield Historical Commission 1992, 14)

21 (Steil 2016, 1) (The Township of Lower Makefield, Bucks County, Pennsylvania 2016) (Check 1987)

22 (J. Marshall, Notes to Manuscript April 7, 2017)

23 (Davis, W.W.H. 1876, 740) (Helen Heinz to Peter Osborne December 13. 2016)

24 (J. Marshall, Notes to Manuscript April 7, 2017)Helen Heinz has in her collection a copy of a survey showing the northern boundary line of the Satterthwaite tract and the small fourteen acre Palmer tract that was sold to him. The survey probably dates from the late 18th century.

25 (Steil 2016, 1) (Deed Book 401, Page 447 1918) (Snipes 2017)

26 (Steil 2016, 1) (Deed Book 401, Page 447 1918) (Snipes 2017) (Lower Makefield Roads January 2014, 3)

27 (S. Snipes 2001, 38) (Helen Heinz to Peter Osborne December 13. 2016)

28 (J. Marshall, Notes to Manuscript April 7, 2017)

29 (J. Marshall, Notes to Manuscript April 7, 2017)

30 (Mellon, Master Plan for the Five Mile Woods Preserve 1981)

31 (D. Formigli, Five Mile Woods Program and Nature Photography Show (DFC) February 4, 1979)

32 (Rivinus 2004, 6-7)

33 (Rivinus 2004, 6-8)

34 (Rivinus 2004, 7) (Zimmerman 2002, 9-10)

35 (Rivinus 2004, 6-7) (Johnston 2005, 77) (Friends of the Delaware Canal 2017)

36 (H. Miiller, Notes to Manuscript April 7, 2017)

37 (H. Miiller, Notes to Manuscript April 7, 2017)

38 (Rivinus 2004, 6-8) (Osborne, Where Washington Once Led: A History of New Jersey's Washington Crossing State Park 2012, 45-50)

39 (Rivinus 2004, 6-7)

40 (Clark 2006, 57)

41 (Strausbaugh 2006, 19-20)

42 (Strausbaugh 2006, 19-20)

43 (Strausbaugh 2006, 19-20)

44 (Kiscaden 1973, 6) (Strausbaugh 2006, 19-20)

45 (Davis, W. W. H. 1876, 748) (Treese 2012, 13-14) (Carson 1960, 65-66) (Bell April 7, 2017)

46 (Treese 2012, v) (Railroad History: An Overview of the Past 2015)

47 (Treese 2012, 2) (Deed Book 401, Page 447 1918)

48 (PHMC Historic Resource Survey Form: Pennsylvania Railroad Morrisville Line; Trenton Cutoff 2010, 34, 37) (Taber 1987, 425) (Bell April 7, 2017)

49 (W. W. H. Davis, Edited by Warren Ely and John Jordan 1992-2002, 212-213) (Taber 1987, 425) (Messer 1999, 252) (Bell April 7, 2017)

50 (Railway Review No. 59, 1916, 746) (PHMC Historic Resource Survey Form: Pennsylvania Railroad Morrisville Line; Trenton Cutoff 2010, 34, 37) (Bell April 7, 2017)

51 (Oscar Sanodval, Thomas Carroll and Lewis Morgan 2005) (Bell April 7, 2017)

52 (Stockham 2017) (Bell April 7, 2017)

53 (Deed Book 401, Page 447 1918) (Osborne, Property Research Records 2017) (William Satterthwaite Genealogy 2016)

54 (Spivey 2001, 2) (Bell April 7, 2017)

55 (The Philadelphia Chapter of the National Railway Historical Society 2016) (Bell April 7, 2017)

56 (The Township of Lower Makefield (Bucks County, Pennsylvania) 2016) (Davis, W. W. H. 1876, 749) (Spivey 2001, 2) (Lower Makefield Historical Commission 1992, 18) (Lower Makefield Historical Society, The Township Historical Commission, The Historical Architectural Review Board 1998)

57 (Heinz, Notes to Manuscript December 11, 2016) (Heinz, Notes to Manuscript April 7, 2017)

58 (Steil 2016, 1, 3)

59 (Winchester 2013, 241-242) (E. W. James on designating the Federal-aid system and developing the U.S. numbered highway plan 2016) (Route 1, John H. Ware III Memorial Highway 2016)

60 (Heinz, Notes to Manuscript September 24, 2016) (Richman 2005, 86-87)

61 (Route 1, John H. Ware III Memorial Highway 2016) (Lower Bucks County Street and Road Map 1972) (Mellon 2017) (Osborne, Property Research Records 2017) (Pasko April 7, 2017)

62 (Route 1, John H. Ware III Memorial Highway 2016)

63 (Lincoln Highway Heritage Corridor 2016) (Lincoln Highway Association 2016)

64 (Lincoln Highway Heritage Corridor 2016) (Lincoln Highway Association 2016) (Michael Williamson and Michael Wallace 2007, 3-4, 37, 39, 41) (Pasko April 7, 2017)

65 (Bucks County Planning Commission 2011, 32)

66 (Route 13 2016)

67 (Heinz 2016)

68 (Delware River Joint Toll Bridge Commission 2007, 7) (Delaware Expressway: Historic Overview 2016) (Interstate 95 2016) (Steil 2016, 5) (Heinz, Notes to Manuscript September 24, 2016)

CHAPTER 4

1 (Davis, W.W.H. 1876, 875)

2 (H. Scott 1951)

3 (David Amers and Linda McClelland 2002, 16) (Spivey 2001, 2) (Yardley Historic District 2016) (Farkas 2012-2015)

4 (David Amers and Linda McClelland 2002, 16) (Spivey 2001, 2) (Yardley Historic District 2016) (Farkas 2012-2015)

5 (Pennsylvania Turnpike 2017) (National Interstate and Defense Highways Act 2017)

6 (Heinz 2016) (Viriginia and Lee McAlester 1984, 320-370, 416-429) (Lower Makefield Historical Commission 1992, 20) (Heinz, Notes to Manuscript September 24, 2016, 73)

7 (Miiller 2016)

8 (S. Snipes 2001, 200-205)

9 (The Township of Lower Makefield (Bucks County, Pennsylvania) 2016)

10 (P. Rhoads 2017)

11 (S. Snipes 2001, 137-139) (P. Rhoads, Pennsbury Manor to Fairless Works of U.S. Steel Corporation: A Chronology 1998)

12 (S. Snipes 2001, 137-139) (P. Rhoads, Pennsbury Manor to Fairless Works of U.S. Steel Corporation: A Chronology 1998)

13 (S. Snipes 2001, 137-139) (Snipes 2017) (Stockham 2017) (P. Rhoads, Pennsbury Manor to Fairless Works of U.S. Steel Corporation: A Chronology 1998)

14 (S. Snipes 2001, 139)

15 (S. Snipes 2001, 139)

16 (S. Snipes 2001, 155, 204)

17 (S. Snipes 2001, 139-141)

18 (Heinz, Notes to Manuscript September 24, 2016)

19 (H. Scott 1951) (Mullaney 1951)

20 (Gold 1995) (Bucks County Planning Commission 2014, 1)

21 (S. Snipes 2001, 212) (Bucks County Planning Commission 2011, 231) (Miiller 2016) (Living Places - Fairless Hills 2016)

22 (S. Snipes 2001, 212) (Bucks County Planning Commission 2011, 231)

23 (H. Scott 1951) (S. Snipes 2001, 155) The author confused Fairless Hills with Levittown, hence the mistake in the statistics.

24 (S. Snipes 2001, 202)

25 (S. Snipes 2001, 204)

26 (S. Snipes 2001, 204) (Miiller 2016) (Richard and Amy Wagner 2010, 7) (The Most Perfectly Planned Community in America: Levittown, Pennsylvania 1997-2015) (Miiller 2016) (Snipes 2017) (Stockham 2017)

27 (S. Snipes 2001, 202) (Bucks County Planning Commission 2011, 245) (Richard and Amy Wagner 2010, 7) (The Most Perfectly Planned Community in America: Levittown, Pennsylvania 1997-2015)

28 (Heinz 2016) (Heinz, Notes to Manuscript September 24, 2016)

29 (The Township of Lower Makefield (Bucks County, Pennsylvania) 2016) (Benner 1932, 5-6) (Bucks County Planning Commission 2011, 231)

30 (Lower Makefield Historical Commission 1992, 20) (75 Years of Service to Customers and Communities: Annual Report 2009, 16) (Pennsylvania Highways 2017)

31 (Lower Makefield Open Space Committee 1973)

32 (The Township of Lower Makefield (Bucks County, Pennsylvania) 2016) (Benner 1932, 5-6) (Davis, W. W. H. 1876, 735) (Lower Makefield Historical Commission 1992, 11) (Forstall 1990, 136-137) (Bucks County Population Figures 2010) (Bucks County Planning Commission 2003, 7)

33 (Bucks County Planning Commission 2011, 12, 246)

34 (Miiller 2016)

35 (Bucks County Planning Commission 2011, 271)

36 (The Township of Lower Makefield (Bucks County, Pennsylvania) 2016) (Miiller 2016)

37 (Sesame Place 2017) (Heinz, Notes to Manuscript April 7, 2017)

38 (Osborne, No Spot in This Far Land Is More Immortalized: A History of Pennsylvania's Washington Crossing Historic Park 2014, 320-332)

39 (Mullaney 1951) (Miiller 2016)

40 (O'Brien 1988, 84)

41 (Bucks County Planning Commission 2014, 21) (Historic Bolton Mansion 2016)

42 (Township of Falls, Bucks County, Pennsylvania 2016) (Heinz, Notes to Manuscript April 7, 2017)

43 (Historic Fallsington: The Story of an Early Bucks County Village 1947, 2008, 19)

44 (Bucks County Planning Commission 2011, 5) (Bucks County Park Board 1958) (Nyholm 1978)

CHAPTER 5

1 (Cohn 1978)

2 (Cohn 1978) (Seasons Greetings 1977)

3 (Ronald Chase to Don Formigli (DFC) November 6, 1978)

4 (Heinz, Notes to Manuscript December 11, 2016)

5 (Bucks County Park Board 1958) (Dyer 1978)

6 (Miiller 2016) (Bucks County Planning Commission 2003, 1)

7 (Lower Makefield Historical Commission 1992, 24) (Bucks County Planning Commission 2003, 78) (Heinz, Notes to Manuscript December 11, 2016)

8 (Lower Makefield Historical Commission 1992, 33) (Heinz, Notes to Manuscript December 11, 2016)

9 (Bucks County Park Board 1958) (Lower Makefield Open Space Committee 1973) (Formigli, 1976 Park and Recreation Board Budget Request (DFC) 1975) (Manegold 1981)

10 (Bucks County Park Board 1958) (Lower Makefield Open Space Committee 1973) (Formigli, 1976 Park and Recreation Board Budget Request (DFC) 1975) (Manegold 1981) (Lower Makefield Historical Commission 1992, 21) (Miiller 2016) (Proposed Park and Recreation Program for Lower Makefield (DFC) 1976)

11 (Lower Makefield Township Resolution No. 466, Bill No. 682 (DFC) January 4, 1982) (Lower Makefield Historical Commission 1992, 21) (Miiller 2016)

12 (Miiller 2016)

13 (Lower Makefield Historical Commission 1992, 26) (Miiller 2016)

14 (D. Formigli September 15, 2016) (Donald Formigli: The need to preserve natural resources December 1977, 15)

15 (Hondras, Citizen's unit works for open space 1974) (Areas of Interest for Open Space (DFC) Undated)

16 (Formigli, Text for Five Mile Woods Slide-Tape Program (DFC) 1979) (D. Formigli, Notes for News Article (DFC) c. 1974) Hank Miiller points out even though the township might have thought the Woods a special place it was still zoned R-3 with R-4 being the highest density.

17 (Penn Pilot: Historic Aerial Photographs of Pennsylvania 2016)

18 (Penn Pilot: Historic Aerial Photographs of Pennsylvania 2016)

19 (Ann Rhoads 2003) According to the National Natural Landmark nomination, it is the only cranberry bog still left in Bucks County.

20 (MacReynolds 1955, 425)

21 (Heinz 2016) (Snipes 2017) It is important to note that Sam Snipes' recollection is the only one that predates the 1950s. Also, see Donald Formigli's archives which includes all of the early documentation about how the Woods were saved.

22 (L. J. Foulds 2016) (Nazzaro 1979) (Five Mile Woods: A Forest Preserve c. 1983) (Heilferty, Notes from Manuscript April 4, 2017) (H. Miiller, Notes to Manuscript April 7, 2017)

23 (J. Marshall 2017) (Snipes 2017) (Mellon 2017)

24 (Formigli, The Five Mile Woods (DFC) 1975, 1) (Heilferty, Notes from Manuscript April 4, 2017)

25 (Slide Program - What's Worth Preserving in Lower Makefield as Open Space (DFC) c. 1975)(Heinz 2016) (Five Mile Woods 1974)

26 (Heilferty, Notes from Manuscript April 4, 2017)

27 (Mellon 2017) (Heilferty, Notes from Manuscript April 4, 2017)

28 (Formigli, Land Parcels of Five Mile Woods (DFC) 2016) (Property Owners (Five Mile Woods) (DFC) 1974) (Heilferty, Notes from Manuscript April 4, 2017)

29 (Treese 2012, v) (Heinz, Notes to Manuscript April 7, 2017)

30 (Alexander November 1995, 16) (A Chronology of American Railroads January 1962)

31 (Pennsylvania Railroad Rolling Stock Thematic Resource Nomination to the National Register of Historic Places November 28, 1979)

32 (Interpretive Panels, History Museum, Steamtown National Historic Site 2015) (Cupper 2002, 17)

33 (Treese 2012, 7)

34 (Mergers and Bankruptcies, Railroads: The 1960s and 1970s 2015)

35 (Cupper 2002, 17)

36 (Treese 2012, 7) (Bell April 7, 2017)

37 ((Interpretive Panels, History Museum, Steamtown National Historic Site 2015)

38 (Cupper 2002, 16)

39 (Treese 2012, 185)

40 (Treese 2012, 7)

41 (Railroad History, An Overview of the Past 2015)

42 (Railroad History, An Overview of the Past 2015) (Mergers and Bankruptcies, Railroads: The 1960s and 1970s 2015)

43 (Emerson 1989, 6)

44 (Emerson 1989, 6) (Stoffer 1979)

45 (Alan Lipsky to Robert Pierson February 23, 1977)

46 (Penn Pilot: Historic Aerial Photographs of Pennsylvania 2016)

47 (Lower Makefield Township June 1977, 5-6) (Wise 1979)

48 (Formigli, The Five Mile Woods (DFC) 1975, 1) (D. Formigli, Notes for News Article (DFC) c. 1974)

49 (Thomas Tyler Moor Associates 1981, Plate 2)

50 (Formigli, Land Parcels of Five Mile Woods (DFC) 2016) (Silkwood 1977) (Thomas Tyler Moor Associates 1981, Plate 2) (B. Nyholm, Rare orchid stands in way of development 1978)

51 (Minutes, Lower Makefield Park and Recreation Board (DFC) November 2, 1978) (Minutes, Lower Makefield Park and Recreation Board (DFC) September 8, 1977)

52 (Formigli, Land Parcels of Five Mile Woods (DFC) 2016)

53 (Formigli, Text for Five Mile Woods Slide-Tape Program (DFC) 1979, 3) (Formigli, Land Parcels of Five Mile Woods (DFC) 2016)

54 (Formigli, Text for Five Mile Woods Slide-Tape Program (DFC) 1979, 3) (Formigli, Land Parcels of Five Mile Woods (DFC) 2016)

55 (Formigli September 15, 2016) (Donald Formigli: The need to preserve natural resources December 1977, 15) (Donald Formigli to Peter Osborne October 23, 2016)

56 (Formigli September 15, 2016) At the time, there was someone living in the house on the Cutler tract that ultimately became the current Preserve's headquarters.

57 (Formigli September 15, 2016) (Donald Formigli: The need to preserve natural resources December 1977, 15) (Nyholm, Arbor Day: Conservancy searching for rare, old trees 1979) (Lower Makefield Township Resolution No. 466, Bill No. 682 (DFC) January 4, 1982) (Township Newsletter, Lower Makefield February 1977) (Donald Formigli to Lower Makefield Board of Supervisors (DFC) June 20, 1975)

58 (Formigli September 15, 2016) (Lower Makefield Township Resolution No. 466, Bill No. 682 (DFC) January 4, 1982) (Formigli resigns post in L. Makefield Township 1981)

59 (Formigli September 15, 2016) (D. Formigli July 29, 2016)

60 (Lower Makefield Open Space Committee 1973) (Proposed Park and Recreation Program for Lower Makefield (DFC) 1976)

61 (Bird 1974) (Gale 1975)

62 (Bird 1974) (Rinehart 1974)

63 (Bird 1974) (Rinehart 1974)

64 (Township Newsletter, Lower Makefield Fall 1976) (Lower Makefield Historical Commission 1992, 21) (Miiller 2016)

65 (Bird 1974)

66 (Hondras, Citizen's unit works for open space 1974)

67 (Osborne, No Spot In This Far Land is More Immortalized: A History of Pennsylvania's Washington Crossing Historic Park 2014, 379, 502)

68 (Oliver Stark to Donald Formigli (DFC) April 25, 1974)

69 (Robert Pierson to Donald Formigli (DFC) January 5, 1975)

70 (Osborne, No Spot In This Far Land is More Immortalized: A History of Pennsylvania's Washington Crossing Historic Park 2014, 252,441-442) (Richards 1956, 7) (Pennsylvania Geological Survey 1982, 12)

71 (Mr. Edgar Wherry, 96 of Germantown 1982)

72 (Osborne, No Spot In This Far Land is More Immortalized: A History of Pennsylvania's Washington Crossing Historic Park 2014, 29)

73 (Osborne, No Spot In This Far Land is More Immortalized: A History of Pennsylvania's Washington Crossing Historic Park 2014, 340, 441-442)

74 (Edgar Wherry to Donald Formigli (DFC) December 20, 1974)

75 (D. Formigli September 15, 2016)

76 (Carmichael 1974-1975)

77 (George Carmichael to Donald Formigli April 3, 1975)

78 (Ann Rhoads to Peter Osborne April 14, 2017)

79 (Lower Makefield Open Space Committee - Report on 1975 Survey (DFC) June 30, 1975) (Lower Makefield Questionaire (DFC) April 1975)

80 (Lower Makefield Open Space Committee - Report on 1975 Survey (DFC) June 30, 1975) (Donald Formigli to Lower Makefield Board of Supervisors (DFC) June 20, 1975)

81 (Lower Makefield Open Space Committee - Report on 1975 Survey (DFC) June 30, 1975) (Donald Formigli to Lower Makefield Board of Supervisors (DFC) June 20, 1975)

82 (Progress Report - Lower Makefield Open Space Committee (DFC) October 1975)

83 (Open space plan urged by Cower 1975) (H. Miiller, Notes to Manuscript April 7, 2017)

84 (Nyholm 1978)

85 (Bucks County Register of Historic Places October 1975)

86 (Sill 1974) (D. Formigli September 15, 2016)

87 (D. Formigli, Five Mile Woods: Lower Makefield and Falls Townships, Bucks County, Pennsylvania 1975)

88 (Robert Pierson to Juliann Whelan (DFC) August 10, 1976)

89 (Bradford Northrup to Lloyd Klatzkin (DFC) January 5, 1976) (Lloyd Klatzkin to Patrick Noonan April 22, 1975)

90 (William Veitch to Robert Rodale (DFC) December 1, 1976)

91 (Five Mile Woods November 1976) (Township Newsletter, Lower Makefield Township February 1978)

92 (Minutes, Lower Makefield Park and Recreation Board (DFC) November 3, 1977)

93 (Minutes, Lower Makefield Park and Recreation Board (DFC) June 30, 1976) (Minutes,

Lower Makefield Park and Recreation Board (DFC) March 4, 1976) (Minutes, Lower Makefield Park and Recreation Board (DFC) August 5, 1976)

94 (Minutes, Lower Makefield Park and Recreation Board (DFC) November 2, 1978) (Minutes, Lower Makefield Park and Recreation Board (DFC) January 6, 1977) (Minutes, Lower Makefield Park and Recreation Board (DFC) December 7, 1978)

95 (Minutes, Lower Makefield Park and Recreation Board (DFC) September 8, 1977)

96 (D. Formigli, Dates to Remember (DFC) 1981) (Minutes, Lower Makefield Park and Recreation Board (DFC) January 6, 1977) (B. Nyholm 1977) (B. Nyholm, Woodlands rezoning approved 1978) (P. Wandling, Woods rescue remains priority 1978) (H. Miiller, Notes to Manuscript April 7, 2017)

97 (Five Mile Woods 1976)

98 (Five Mile Woods November 1976) (Robert Pierson to Bruce Howard December 7, 1976)

99 (Robert Pierson to Bruce Howard (DFC) December 7, 1976)

100 (Open Space Meeting (DFC) November 19, 1974)

101 (Robert Pierson to Bruce Howard (DFC) December 7, 1976)

102 (Robert Pierson to Bruce Howard (DFC) December 7, 1976) (William Veitch to Robert Rodale (DFC) December 1, 1976) (D. Formigli September 15, 2016)

103 (Robert Pierson to Bruce Howard (DFC) December 7, 1976)

104 (Five Mile Woods June 1977)

105 (Five Mile Woods June 1977)

106 (Five Mile Woods June 1977)

107 (Minutes, Lower Makefield Park and Recreation Board (DFC) January 6, 1977)

108 (Barrett 2016) (Developer's Plan for the 5 Mile Woods (DFC) c 1977) (Minutes, Lower Makefield Park and Recreation Board Minutes (DFC) February 3, 1977) (Minutes, Lower Makefield Park and Recreation Board (DFC) January 5, 1978)

109 (Developer's Plan for the 5 Mile Woods (DFC) c 1977) (Minutes, Lower Makefield Park and Recreation Board Minutes (DFC) February 3, 1977)

110 (PHMC Historic Resource Survey Form: Pennsylvania Railroad Morrisville Line; Trenton Cutoff 2010, 37) (Robert Pierson to John Fullam (DFC) June 8, 1976) (D. Formigli, Five Mile Woods Program and Nature Photography Show (DFC) February 4, 1979)

111 (Minutes, Lower Makefield Park and Recreation Board (DFC) December 1, 1977) (Minutes, Lower Makefield Park and Recreation Board (DFC) January 5, 1978) (Minutes, Lower Makefield Park and Recreation Board (DFC) September 8, 1977) (Township Newsletter, Lower Makefield June 1977) (Peter Kostmayer to Martin Convisser (DFC) July 20, 1977)

112 (Walker 1977)

113 (Minutes, Lower Makefield Park and Recreation Board (DFC) December 1, 1977) (Minutes, Lower Makefield Park and Recreation Board (DFC) January 5, 1978) (Minutes, Lower Makefield Park and Recreation Board (DFC) February 2, 1978)

114 (Minutes, Lower Makefield Park and Recreation Board (DFC) December 1, 1977)

115 (Minutes, Lower Makefield Park and Recreation Board (DFC) January 5, 1978) (Township Newsletter, Lower Makefield February 1978) (D. Formigli, Dates to Remember (DFC) 1981) (P&R Board Recommendation on the Five Mile Woods (DFC) January 5, 1978)

116 (Deed Book 2325, Pages 1104-1106 1978) (Minutes, Lower Makefield Park and Recreation Board (DFC) January 5, 1978)

117 (Minutes, Lower Makefield Park and Recreation Board (DFC) January 5, 1978)

118 (Minutes, Lower Makefield Park and Recreation Board (DFC) January 5, 1978)

119 (Minutes, Lower Makefield Park and Recreation Board (DFC) January 5, 1978)

120 (Minutes, Lower Makefield Park and Recreation Board (DFC) January 5, 1978)

121 (A Woods That Goes On For Miles Spring 1978)

122 (Township Newsletter, Lower Makefield February 1978) (D. Formigli, Five Mile Woods Program and Nature Photography Show (DFC) February 4, 1979) (Cohn 1978)

123 (Township Newsletter, Lower Makefield February 1978) (D. Formigli, Five Mile Woods Program and Nature Photography Show (DFC) February 4, 1979) (Cohn 1978) (D. Formigli, Dates to Remember (DFC) 1981) (A.-P. Rhoads 2017) (Dubois 2017)

124 (Hondras, Citizen's unit works for open space 1974) (Miiller 2016)

125 (P. Miiller, Notes to Manuscript November 11, 2016) (A.-P. Rhoads 2017)

126 (P. Miiller, Notes to Manuscript October 5, 2016) (Formigli, Text for Five Mile Woods Slide-Tape Program (DFC) 1979) (Formigli, Programs Presented (DFC) 1979)

127 (Formigli, Text for Five Mile Woods Slide-Tape Program (DFC) 1979)

128 (P. Miiller, Notes to Manuscript October 5, 2016) (D. Formigli, Text for Five Mile Woods Slide-Tape Program (DFC) 1979) (Falon, These ballads are tuned into Bucks County 1981)

129 (Falon, These ballads are tuned into Bucks County 1981) (D. Formigli, Text for Five Mile Woods Slide-Tape Program (DFC) 1979)

130 (Falon, These ballads are tuned into Bucks County 1981)

131 The minutes of the P&R Board state that Don Formigli wrote the song but they are incorrect as is another press account that says that he wrote it. In discussing this with Lynn Simms the author confirmed that she had written it. (Minutes, Lower Makefield Park and Recreation Board (DFC) October 6, 1977) (Simms 2017)

132 Reprinted with the author's permission.

133 Reprinted with the author's permission.

134 (Henry Miiller to Peter Osborne January 2, 2017)

135 (Draft of Letter from Lower Makefield Park and Recreation Board (DFC) 1974-1975) (Henry Miiller to Peter Osborne January 2, 2017)

136 (Schaffhausen 1978)

137 (Miiller 2016) (Henry Miiller to Peter Osborne January 2, 2017)

138 (Think! Then Vote No on the Five Mile Woods Question in the May 16 Primary (DFC) May 1978)

139 (To the Editor from Donald Formigli, Pat Fair, Gail Hardesty (DFC) May 8, 2016)

140 (Insert in April 1978 Lower Makefield Township Newsletter: Five Mile Woods Question on May 16 Primary Ballot (DFC) April 1978)

141 (Minutes, Lower Makefield Park and Recreation Board (DFC) January 5, 1978) (Township Newsletter, Lower Makefield June 1978) (Dubois 2017)

142 (PHMC Historic Resource Survey Form: Pennsylvania Railroad Morrisville Line; Trenton Cutoff 2010, 37) (Robert Pierson to John Fullam (DFC) June 8, 1976) (D. Formigli, Five Mile Woods Program and Nature Photography Show (DFC) February 4, 1979)

143 (Deed Book 2325, Pages 1104-1106 1978) (D. Formigli, Five Mile Woods Program and Nature Photography Show (DFC) February 4, 1979) (Minutes, Lower Makefield Park and Recreation Board (DFC) February 1, 1979) (Township Newsletter, Lower Makefield June 1979) (B. Nyholm, Makefield signs deal to buy 5 Mile Woods 1978)

144 (D. Formigli, Five Mile Woods Program and Nature Photography Show (DFC) February 4, 1979) (Minutes, Lower Makefield Park and Recreation Board (DFC) February 1, 1979) (Township Newsletter, Lower Makefield June 1979) (B. Nyholm, Makefield signs deal to buy 5 Mile Woods 1978)

145 (Falon, These ballads are tuned into Bucks County 1981) (D. Formigli, Text for Five Mile Woods Slide-Tape Program (DFC) 1979) (D. Formigli, Five Mile Woods Program and Nature Photography Show (DFC) February 4, 1979)

146 (D. Formigli, Five Mile Woods Program and Nature Photography Show (DFC) February 4, 1979)

147 (D. Formigli, Five Mile Woods Program and Nature Photography Show (DFC) February 4, 1979)

148 (D. Formigli, Five Mile Woods Program and Nature Photography Show (DFC) February 4, 1979)

149 (Natural Areas Survey 1978)

150 (Minutes, Lower Makefield Park and Recreation Board (DFC) October 5, 1978)

CHAPTER 6

1 (Woestendiek, They'll be strolling woods, not a development 1981)

2 (D. Formigli, Planning for the Future of the Five Mile Woods 1978)

3 (Five Mile Woods Preserve: Guide for Preservation June 7, 1979, 2-1)

4 (Minutes, Lower Makefield Park and Recreation Board (DFC) February 2, 1978) (D. Formigli, Planning for the Future of the Five Mile Woods 1978)

5 (D. Formigli, Planning for the Future of the Five Mile Woods 1978)

6 (D. Formigli, Planning for the Future of the Five Mile Woods 1978)

7 (D. Formigli, Five Mile Woods Program and Nature Photography Show (DFC) February 4, 1979) (Minutes, Lower Makefield Park and Recreation Board (DFC) October 5, 1978)

8 (Minutes, Lower Makfield Park and Recreation Board (DFC) June 1, 1978) (Hobaugh 1978)

9 (Hobaugh 1978, 2)

10 (Hobaugh 1978, 5-12)

11 (Hobaugh 1978)

12 (Five Mile Woods Management Plan August 28, 1978, 3)

13 (D. Formigli, Five Mile Woods Program and Nature Photography Show (DFC) February 4, 1979) (Minutes, Lower Makefield Park and Recreation Board (DFC) December 7, 1978) (Minutes, Lower Makefield Park and Recreation Board (DFC) July 7, 1978) (Schuyler 1979)

14 (Five Mile Woods Preserve: Guide for Preservation June 7, 1979) (Township Newsletter, Lower Makefield Township April 1978) (Minutes, Lower Makefield Park and Recreation Board (DFC) February 1, 1979)

15 (Five Mile Woods Preserve: Guide for Preservation June 7, 1979, 1-1)

16 (Five Mile Woods Preserve: Guide for Preservation June 7, 1979, 2-1)

17 (Five Mile Woods Preserve: Guide for Preservation June 7, 1979, 1-2)

18 (Minutes, Lower Makefield Board of Supervisors Meetings July 9, 1979)

19 (Mellon, Master Plan for the Five Mile Woods Preserve 1981, 3)

20 (Minutes, Lower Makefield Park and Board Meeting March 1, 1979) (Mellon, Master Plan for the Five Mile Woods Preserve 1981, 101-103)

21 (Mellon, Master Plan for the Five Mile Woods Preserve 1981, 101)

22 (Mellon, Master Plan for the Five Mile Woods Preserve 1981, 102-103)

23 (Mellon, Master Plan for the Five Mile Woods Preserve 1981, 104)

24 (Mellon, Master Plan for the Five Mile Woods Preserve 1981, 91-93)

25 (Mellon, Master Plan for the Five Mile Woods Preserve 1981, 95)

26 (Mellon, Master Plan for the Five Mile Woods Preserve 1981, 98-99) (Minutes, Lower Makefield Park and Recreation Board (DFC) March 10, 1981)

27 (Mellon, Master Plan for the Five Mile Woods Preserve 1981, 98-99) (Minutes, Lower Makefield Park and Recreation Board (DFC) March 10, 1981)

28 (Mellon, Master Plan for the Five Mile Woods Preserve 1981, 100)

29 (Mellon, Master Plan for the Five Mile Woods Preserve 1981, 95)

30 (Minutes, Lower Makefield Park and Recreation Board (DFC) December 4, 1980) (Hardesty March 22, 1981)

31 (The Nature Conservancy Recommendations to the Five Mile Woods Preserve 1981)

32 (RG-34. Records of the Department of Community Affairs 2016) (Bruce Dorbian to Lloyd Klatzkin (DFC) June 22, 1979)

33 (Robert Pierson to Bradford Northrup (DFC) February 17, 1977)

34 (Bucks towns urged to seek park funds 1975)

35 (Bucks County Planning Commission 2014, C1)

36 (B. Nyholm, L. Makefield asks $900,000 to buy Woods 1978) (Five Miles Woods project to get $300,000 grant 1979)

37 (D. Formigli, Dates to Remember (DFC) 1981) (Bruce Dorbian to Lloyd Klatzkin (DFC) June 22, 1979)

38 (Minutes, Lower Makefield Park and Recreation Board (DFC) August 2, 1979)

39 (Fred Owen to William Carlin (DFC) November 3, 1980)

40 (Formigli, Land Parcels of Five Mile Woods (DFC) 2016) (Nyholm, Makefield to vote on Woods plan 1977)

41 (Satterthwaite 1945, 3) (Thompson, Lower Makefield Township, Bucks County, Pennsylvania: Map of Original Grantees 1998)

42 (Satterthwaite 1945, 3) (Davis, W. W. H. 1876, 128)

43 (Thompson, Lower Makefield Township, Bucks County, Pennsylvania: Map of Original Grantees 1998) (Thompson, Lower Makefield Township, Bucks County Pennsylvania: Historical Map 1798 1988) (Hughes, Farm Map Lower Makefield Township Bucks County, Pennsylvania 1858) (Osborne, Property Research Records 2017)

44 (Osborne, Property Research Records 2017) (Deed Book 365, Page 5 1911) (Deed Book 1693, Page 187 1963) (Deed Book 1911, Page 102 1968) (Rhoads c. 1978)

45 (Penn Pilot: Historic Aerial Photographs of Pennsylvania 2016) (L. J. Foulds 2016)

46 (J. Marshall 2017) (Heinz 2017) (P. Rhoads 2017)

47 (Heinz 2017) (J. Marshall 2017) (J. Marshall 2009) (P. Rhoads 2017) (Helen Heinz to Peter Osborne January 16, 2017)

48 (Helen Heinz to Peter Osborne January 16, 2017)

49 (A. and P. Rhoads 2017) (P. Rhoads 2017) (Helen Heinz to Peter Osborne January 16, 2017)

50 (Thompson, Lower Makefield Township, Bucks County Pennsylvania: Historical Map 1798 1988) (Rhoads c. 1978) A survey map in the collection of the Bucks County Historical Society, shows Issac Brelsford owning the Cutler tract. The survey dates to sometime after 1790.

51 (P. Rhoads 2017)

52 (Penn Pilot: Historic Aerial Photographs of Pennsylvania 2016) (Osborne, Property Research Records 2017)

53 (Hertkom 2016) (Penn Pilot: Historic Aerial Photographs of Pennsylvania 2016) (L. J. Foulds 2016) (Osborne, Property Research Records 2017)

54 (L. J. Foulds 2016) (Penn Pilot: Historic Aerial Photographs of Pennsylvania 2016)

55 (Sill 1974) (Donald Formigli to Michael Cutler July 17, 1974) (Open Space Meeting (DFC) November 19, 1974) (Osborne, Property Research Records 2017)

56 (Minutes, Lower Makefield Park and Recreation Board (DFC) December 1, 1977) (Minutes, Lower Makefield Park and Recreation Board (DFC) January 5, 1978) (Nyholm 1978) (Walker 1977) (Minutes, Lower Makefield Park and Recreation Board (DFC) April 28, 1977) (Woestendiek 1981) (B. Nyholm 1977) (B. Nyholm, Builder modifies Woods Offer 1977)

57 (Deed Book 2458, Page 709-711 1982) (Deed Book 2417, Page 1169-1171 1981) (Deed Book 2398, Page 0609-0611 1980) (Deed Book 2398, Page 0612-0614 1980) (Deed Book 2458, Page 0706-0708 1982) (Osborne, Property Research Records 2017) (Fred Owen to Patricia Delmar (DFC) October 11, 1979) (Land Price reached in Makefield 1979)

58 (Deed Book 2458, Page 709-711 1982) (Deed Book 2417, Page 1169-1171 1981) (Deed Book 2398, Page 0609-0611 1980) (Deed Book 2398, Page 0612-0614 1980) (Deed Book 2458, Page 0706-0708 1982) (Deed Book 1911, Page 102 1968) (Osborne, Property Research Records 2017) (5 Mile Woods Financial Balance (PMC) January 1,1981) (Henry Miller to Peter Osborne January 21, 2017)

59 (Deed Book 2458, Page 709-711 1982)

60 (Deed Book 2458, Page 709-711 1982) (Osborne, Property Research Records 2017) (Sill 1974) (Formigli, Land Parcels of Five Mile Woods (DFC) 2016)

61 (J. Foulds 2016)

62 (Five Mile Woods Management Plan August 28, 1978, 7)

63 (Minutes, Lower Makefield Park and Recreation Board (DFC) February 5, 1981) (5 Mile Woods Financial Balance (PMC) January 1,1981) (Notes, Lower Makefield Township Meeting April 3 1995)

64 (Minutes, Lower Makefield Park and Recreation Board (DFC) September 4, 1980) (J. Foulds 2016) (Mellon 2017) Jim Foulds believed that the dirt for the berm came from the excavation of the sphagnum bog. Rick Mellon remembered the berm being built during his time and that the bog was already in existence.

65 (Minutes, Lower Makefield Park and Recreation Board (DFC) February 5, 1981)

66 (D. Formigli, Dates to Remember (DFC) 1981) (Hill 1981)The program mistakenly states that the opening date was November 23.

67 (Hill 1981)

68 (Hill 1981)

69 (Chesner 1981)

70 (Jan McFarlan and Ron Montgomery 1995)

71 (Rick Mellon 2017) (Colletti n.d.)

72 (Stanton 1996) (Nature at its best in LMT: A Visit to 5 Mile Woods Winter 1996-1997, 4) (Watson 1996) (Gilbert 1997)

73 (Gilbert 1997) (Resume of John Heilferty 1997) (John Heilferty to Terry Fedorchak May 30, 1997) (Heilferty, Notes from Manuscript April 4, 2017)

74 (Resume of John Heilferty 1997)

75 (Five Mile Woods Management Plan August 28, 1978, 1) (D. Formigli, Planning for the Future of the Five Mile Woods 1978, 1)

76 (Friends of the Five Mile Woods - Incorporation Files 1987) (Minutes, Five Mile Woods Business Meeting April 1, 1987) (Mellon 2017) (Jeffrey Garton to James Dillon (DFC) February 14, 1984)

77 (Nature at its best in LMT: A Visit to 5 Mile Woods Winter 1996-1997, 4)

78 (Lower Makefield Historical Commission 1992, 27) (Nature at its best in LMT: A Visit to 5 Mile Woods Winter 1996-1997, 4) (Selda 1987)

79 (Lower Makefield Historical Commission 1992, 27) (Heilferty, Notes from Manuscript April 4, 2017)
80 (Minutes, Lower Makefield Park and Board Meeting June 7, 1979) (P. Miiller, Notes to Manuscript October 5, 2016) (Robinson 1986) (Township Newsletter, Lower Makefield Township March 1987)
81 (Nature at its best in LMT: A Visit to 5 Mile Woods Winter 1996-1997, 4)
82 (Gilbert 1997) (Werner, At Five Mile Preserve, they're ready to roll: All-terrain wheelchair helps disabled hit the trail 1998) (Heilferty 2016)
83 (LMT historians showcase township's forest preserve 1997) (Thompson, Historic Sites in & adjacent to Five Mile Woods (Revised edition) 1997)
84 (Heinz, Notes to Manuscript September 24, 2016, 105)
85 (Friends of the Woods receive state commendations 1987)
86 (Minutes, Lower Makefield Park and Recreation Board (DFC) February 1, 1979)
87 (Hobaugh 1978, 11) (Mellon, Master Plan for the Five Mile Woods Preserve 1981, 32)
88 (Selda 1987) (Township Newsletter, Lower Makefield Township March 1987)
89 (Ann Rhoads 2003, 25) (English 2007) (L. Davis December 23, 2004)
90 (Big Oak Whitetail Management Association 2014)
91 (Big Oak Whitetail Management Association 2014) (Heilferty 2016)
92 (H. Miiller, Notes to Manuscript April 7, 2017)
93 (Jacob Hibbs Genealogy 2016)
94 (Deed Book 2655, Page 0797-801 1985) (Osborne, Property Research Records 2017)
95 (Deed Book 2358, Page 843 1979) (Deed Book 2358, Page 840-845 1979) (Deed Book 2497, Page 1066-1066 1983)
96 (Deed Book 2655, Page 0797-801 1985) (Osborne, Property Research Records 2017)
97 (Deed Book 13, Page 926-928 1988)
98 (Deed Book 2655, Page 0797-801 1985) (Osborne, Property Research Records 2017) The Henry, Dick and Ike Associates was a partnership of Richard Winn, Richard Goldberg, Henry Feinberg and Rose Feinberg whose legal address was Philadelphia. They had owned most of the parcels for several years.
99 (Deed Book 2655, Page 0797-801 1985) (Osborne, Property Research Records 2017) (J. Foulds 2016) (Stipulation for Agreed Order of Court - Independence Development Corp v. Lower Makefield Township July 24, 1985)
100 (Deed Book 2655, Page 0797-801 1985) (Osborne, Property Research Records 2017) (Deed Book 1919, Page 643 1968) (Deed Book 1828, Page 145 1966) (Willard 2017) (Penn Pilot: Historic Aerial Photographs of Pennsylvania 2016) (Deed Book 4010, Page 1941-1943 2004) (J. Foulds 2016) (J. Foulds 2016)
101 (J. Foulds 2016) (Willard 2017)
102 (Osborne, Property Research Records 2017) (Deed Book 2655, Page 0797-801 1985) (L. J. Foulds 2016) (J. Foulds 2016) (Ann Rhoads 2003, 19) (Willard 2017)
103 (Thompson, Historic Sites in & adjacent to Five Mile Woods (Revised edition) 1997) (Osborne, Property Research Records 2017)
104 (P. Wandling, 5-Mile Woods battle is seen at impasse 1977) (B. Nyholm, Independence Square buys five acres for open space 1977)
105 (L. A. Miller, Mall, park deal approved by L. Makefield 1985) (Stipulation for Agreed Order of Court - Independence Development Corp v. Lower Makefield Township July 24, 1985)
106 (L. A. Miller, Mall, park deal approved by L. Makefield 1985)
107 (Deed Book 2655, Page 0797-801 1985)

108   (Deed Book 2662, Page 50-54 1986) (Deed Book 2207, Page 0252 1976) (Osborne, Property Research Records 2017) (Stockham 2017)

109   (Deed Book 2662, Page 50-54 1986) (Stockham 2017)

110   (Deed Book 4002, Page 1591 2006) (L. J. Foulds 2016) (Deed Book 4010, Page 1941-1943 2004) (Werner, Land Purchase adds acreage to preserve 2004) (Lloyd 2016) (Lloyd 2016)

111   (Report of the Bucks County Open Space Task Force June 20, 2007, 4) (Minutes, Friends of the Five Mile Woods January 9, 2004)

112   (Deed Book 4002, Page 1591 2006) (L. J. Foulds 2016) (Deed Book 4010, Page 1941-1943 2004) (Heinz 2016) (Werner, Land Purchase adds acreage to preserve 2004) (Pickering, Corts & Summerson April 28, 2004)

113   (Werner, Land Purchase adds acreage to preserve 2004)

114
 (Deed Book 4002, Page 1591 2006) (L. J. Foulds 2016) (Deed Book 4010, Page 1941-1943 2004) (Heinz 2016) (Snipes 2017)

115   (Werner, Land Purchase adds acreage to preserve 2004) (Minutes, Friends of the Five Mile Woods January 9, 2004) (Natural Areas Program: Grant Application Review April 28, 2004) (Lower Makefield Township Open Space Plan April 1998) (Voters to sav if Preserve branches out 1998)

116   (Bucks County 2007) (Deed Book 5324, Page 1848 2007) (Minutes, Friends of the Five Mile Woods January 9, 2004) (Long 2017)

117   (Bucks County 2007) (Deed Book 5324, Page 1848 2007)

118   (Heilferty 2016)

119   (Falls Township Board of Supervisors March 24, 2000)

120   (Hellyer 2016)

121   (Bucks County Planning Commission 2003, 45) (Robert Gray to James Dillon March 13, 1986)

122   (Deed Book 13, Page 926-928 1988) (Stanert 1987)

123   (L. A. Miller 1985) (Werner, Land Purchase adds acreage to preserve 2004) (Shop Rite 2017) (Heinz, Notes to Manuscript April 7, 2017)

124   (Minutes, Lower Makefield Park and Recreation Board (DFC) October 5, 1978)

125   (Friends of the Woods receive state commendations 1987) (Marthaler 2002)

126   (Ann Rhoads honored by Nature Conservancy 1987) (Minutes, Friends of the Five Mile Woods June 15, 1988)
 (Ann Rhoads 2003, 2)

127   (Werner Unknown) (Ann Rhoads 2003, 5)

128   (Ann Rhoads 2003) (Michelle Batcheller to Terry Fedorchak August 10, 2001)

129   (Werner Unknown) (Ann Rhoads 2003, 2, 13, 24, 34)

130   (Shafer April 15, 2003)

131   (Osborne, No Spot in This Far Land Is More Immortalized: A History of Pennsylvania's Washington Crossing Historic Park 2014, 252, 268, 441, 442) (Pennsylvania Geological Survey October 1982, 12)

132   (Osborne, No Spot in This Far Land Is More Immortalized: A History of Pennsylvania's Washington Crossing Historic Park 2014, 252, 268, 441, 442) (Pennsylvania Geological Survey October 1982, 12)

133   (Falon April 19, 1979) (George R. Carmichael Jr. June 26, 1929 - April 27, 2016 Summer 2016) (George Carmichael 2016) (Lloyd, Notes to Manuscript November 21, 2016, 144)

134   (Fleishman 1991)

135 (Lower Makefield cuts ribbon for bikeway opening 1978)
136 ($127,500 Lower Makefield park plan unveiled 1978) (Minutes, Lower Makefield Park and Recreation Board (DFC) March 10, 1981)
137 (Martellaro 1980)
138 (Lower Makefield Historical Commission 1992, 21) (Bucks County Planning Commission 2003, 19) (Schlatter 1986)
139 (P. Miiller, Notes to Manuscript November 11, 2016, 123)
140 (Newill 1978)

CHAPTER 7
1 (Five Mile Woods: A Forest Preserve (Brochure) 1982)
2 (J. Marshall, The Garden Party, Aldie Mansion, Doylestown, Pennsylvania June 8, 2016)
3 (Formigli, Text for Five Mile Woods Slide-Tape Program (DFC) 1979)
4 (Ann Rhoads 2003)
5 (Heinz 2016)
6 (Deed Book 401, Page 447 1918) (Heinz, Notes to Manuscript April 7, 2017)
7 (J. Marshall, Notes to Manuscript April 7, 2017)
8 (S. Snipes 2001, 133)
9 (Lower Makefield Township Historical Commission 1998, 77) (Various Site Visits by Peter Osborne 2016) (Lower Makefield Historical Society, The Township Historical Commission, The Historical Architectural Review Board 1998) (Snipes 2017) (A.-P. Rhoads 2017)
10 (Historic Fallsington: The Story of an Early Bucks County Village 1947, 2008, 1)
11 (S. Snipes 2001, 31) (Mark Reinberger, Elizabeth McLean July 2007, 271, 275, 282) (William Satterthwaite Genealogy 2016)
12 (Historic Fallsington Walking Guide 2016) (S. Snipes 2001, 32-33)
13 (William Penn's Country Estate Pennsbury Manor 2016) (Mark Reinberger, Elizabeth McLean July 2007, 272)
14 (Mark Reinberger, Elizabeth McLean July 2007, 305-306)
15 (Snipes 2017) (Stockham 2017)
16 (Heinz, Notes to Manuscript April 7, 2017)
17 (J. Foulds 2016) (Deed Book 401, Page 447 1918) (Thompson, Historic Sites in & adjacent to Five Mile Woods (Revised edition) 1997) (Hobaugh 1978)
18 (J. Marshall 2017)
19 (J. Foulds 2016) (Deed Book 401, Page 447 1918) (Thompson, Historic Sites in & adjacent to Five Mile Woods (Revised edition) 1997) (Hobaugh 1978)
20 (J. Marshall 2017)
21 (J. Foulds 2016)
22 (Mellon 2017)
23 (Mellon, Master Plan for the Five Mile Woods Preserve 1981, 98-99)
24 (J. Marshall, Notes to Manuscript April 7, 2017)
25 (Simms 2017)
26 (Bucks County Conservancy Conservation Award October 13, 1978)
27 (Donald Formigli to Peter Osborne December 15, 2016)
28 (J. Marshall, The Garden Party, Aldie Mansion, Doylestown, Pennsylvania June 8, 2016)
29 (Mellon 2017)
30 (Academy of Natural Sciences of Philadelphia December 1, 1978, II, 3)
31 (J. Foulds 2016) (Lempert 1986) (Mellon 2017) (Mellon, Notes to Manuscript April 7, 2017)

32 (Falls Township Board of Supervisors March 24, 2000) (Long 2017) (J. Marshall, Notes to Manuscript April 7, 2017) David Long relayed how the property came to be sold to Falls Township. He said he had met with the owners and convinced them to sell the farm to the township which happened after this conversation.

33 (Fisher 2000)

34 (J. Marshall, Notes to Manuscript April 7, 2017)

35 (J. Marshall, Notes to Manuscript April 7, 2017) (Heilferty, Notes from Manuscript April 4, 2017)

36 (Bucks County Planning Commission 2011, 46)

37 (Osborne, Where Washington Once Led: A History of New Jersey's Washington Crossing State Park 2012, 407)

Chapter 8

1 (Five Mile Woods Preserve: Guide for Preservation June 7, 1979)

Appendix

1 (Ann Rhoads 2003) (5 Mile Woods Report Spring 2002)

2 This data is a compilation from Benner's work on Bucks County plants and the Academy of Natural Sciences herbarium and field work, and several letters written between 1978-1980 which reside in the digital collection of the Academy materials in the FMWP collection.

3 (D. B. Long 2010-2013)

Bibliographic Essay

1 (Leslie 1976, xii)

2 (Leslie 1976, xii)

3 (Schuyler 1979, 1)

4 (Schuyler 1979, 1)

Acknowledgements

1 (Seasons Greetings 1977, 15)

2 (Lower Makefield Township Resolution No. 466, Bill No. 682 (DFC) January 4. 1982)

3 (Lower Makefield Historical Society, The Township Historical Commission, The Historical Architectural Review Board 1998)

COMMON BEECH

COMMON BEECH

BIBLIOGRAPHIC ESSAY

URING THE COURSE OF CREATING THIS BOOK the author consulted a wide variety of sources and used the *Chicago Manual of Style* (as interpreted by Microsoft's Office Word program) in citing them. That said, the author likes what an old colleague and fellow author, Vernon Leslie, said long ago in the foreword to his classic work, *The Battle of Minisink: A Revolutionary War Engagement in the Upper Delaware Valley*, with regard to sourcing. He wrote:

Where there are deviations (of style) and there are several in regard to footnotes, bibliographical citations, intertextual references, etc., they arise from personal preferences on the part of the author which he has every right to indulge.[1]

And so has this author, who might also add another quote from Vernon's foreword to the same book:

It is hoped that this volume will be judged not only on its own merits, but also against a background of what has previously appeared on the subject.[2]

This is of particular interest with regard to the heavy sourcing of the book. The author believed that a detailed paper trail be left for future researchers. The author begs the forgiveness of the reader with regard to the many endnotes. The bibliography contained herein is the most extensive ever created for the Preserve.

Researching the Five Mile Woods Preserve
Digital Archives and Inventory

At the conclusion of this project, the author's entire collection of notes, photocopies, files and photographs were placed in the archives of the Preserve along with a digital version of the most significant resources. As the author proceeded with the project he met a number of individuals who willingly shared information, documents and photographs and those items have all been donated to the Preserve.

There are a number of collections of materials that proved to be especially valuable to this effort and include important resources regarding the Preserve, its history, and its special geological and natural features. They are included in the following listing.

Archival Collections
Donald Formigli Collection

The Donald Formigli Collection includes a comprehensive assortment of materials related to the geological and natural aspects of the Preserve, photographs, organizational paperwork, correspondence, media releases, promotional literature and land acquisition records. These date from the genesis of the original vision for the Preserve in 1974 and proceed until Don left the Township in the fall of 1981. There are a few items from the 1990s and 2000s.

This remarkable legacy assisted the author in no small measure and includes four binders and one large container of files and other resources. In 2015-16, Don scanned the most important parts of his collection and the author scanned additional materials from the collection. The collection remains in his possession.

Preserve Archive

Prior to the writing of this book the Preserve only had a small archive of materials relating to the property's history and its institutional history. There are very few annual reports that survive for example. During this project, the author compiled many digital files that tell the story not only of the preservation and operation of the Preserve but also reveal the fascinating history of the land before the creation of the Preserve. All the major reports that were created over the years for the Preserve are now available digitally. Hundreds of photographs were graciously given to the Preserve by Donald Formigli. The author also donated the photographs he took. This effort will dramatically expand their collection for future researchers, staff and volunteers.

The complicated series of land transactions that are illustrated in the Appendix, and the various records located in the Bucks County Recorder of Deeds Office reveal fascinating information about the property dating back more than three hundred years. Copies of all the deeds, property reports and mapping data are all included. There are also several county planning documents and resources that provide additional context for why the Preserve was created and what its future might be. All of the sources cited are now in either a digital format or printed in hard copy.

Friends of the Preserve Archives

John Lloyd inherited many of the Preserve's records when he became chairman of the organization. He continues to maintain that collection which is very valuable in relaying the story of the Preserve beginning in the mid-1980s and continuing into the 1990s with some materials from the 2000s.

Lower Makefield Historical Society Archives

An excellent collection of local history materials resides at the Lower Makefield Historical Society (LMHS) archive located in the Township center. The historical society has been an important advocate for preserving the community's heritage since its creation in 1978. The society's web page (*www.lowermakefieldhistoricalsociety.com*) is also an important source of information about the history of the community.

One of the most valuable resources that the author found in this collection was a paper entitled *Historical Sites in and Adjacent to Five Mile Woods* by Ralph Thompson. The report, the first ever written detailing how many of the early property transfers came about, includes information on most of the various owners. Mr. Thompson was a remarkable and accomplished Township historian and his *Map of Original Patents* and the *Historical Map: 1798* are remarkable works of research. His detailed reports on various aspects of the town's history will remain the best source of information for many years to come. The binders that he created are now kept at the LMHS and his original notes were archived and given to Helen Heinz.

Pat Miiller Collection

Pat Miiller has retained many critical documents relating to the early history of the creation of and early years of the operation of the Preserve. She became the chairman of the Park and Recreation Board in 1980 and served for several years after that, and was involved with the opening of the Preserve and purchase of the Cutler tracts.

Her collection includes a copy of Rick Mellon's *Master Plan for the Five Mile Woods Preserve: Lower Makefield Township Pennsylvania*, the report entitled *Hydrology of Five Mile Woods: Lower Makefield Township, Bucks County, Pennsylvania* by Thomas Tyler Moore Associates, and the Department of Environmental Resources' *Forest Management Report* for the Preserve. She also has Township newsletters, minutes of Township meetings and correspondence from the 1980s.

Helen Heinz Collection

Helen Heinz maintains a large collection of materials related to the Township's past. She has focused on land transactions but is also conversant with its cultural and genealogical past and maintains Ralph Thompson's original collection research notes. In particular, she has copies of eighteenth century survey maps of the Preserve area.

David B. Long Collection

David Long has a number of documents that relate to the recent history of the Five Mile Woods Preserve including a copy of the Township's 1998 *Open Space Plan* and the paperwork for the 1989 National Natural Landmark nomination. He shared both with the author.

Bucks County Historical Society

The Bucks County Historical Society in Doylestown owns a remarkable collection of archival materials. They have an impressive number of family genealogies, atlases, maps, histories and primary sources including tax and census records. A number of those sources were used for this project including various papers that were delivered to the membership of the BCHS over the last one hundred years. Their archives maintain materials related to the history of both Lower Makefield and Falls Townships.

The BCHS also owns several interesting primary documents that are related to the Preserve including an original 1696 road survey to which William Dark was a witness along with a transcription of a deed of land purchased from the area's Native Americans and was witnessed by William Satterthwaite. They also possess a surveying lesson book that was used by William Satterthwaite IV.

Bucks County Land Records

The Bucks County Recorder of Deeds is the repository of the land records for the county including those of the Preserve. The county also retains the wills that were probated, including those of the Dark and Satterthwaite families. The tax assessment cards proved to be very valuable in sorting out the chain of titles and various deeds for the tracts that now make up the Preserve.

Pennsbury Manor

Pennsbury Manor, managed by the Pennsylvania Historical and Museum Commission, is a remarkable place in spite of its controversial reconstruction in the 1930s. To walk down the road leading to the Manor and then stand on the shoreline is to walk into the Commonwealth's ancient but important past. The staff maintain an extensive and comprehensive collection of books and files that covers a wide variety of topics including crafts and lifestyles of the seventeenth century and William Penn including a copy of the *Papers of William Penn,* an important source of information about the administration of the colony of Pennsylvania. The staff at the site is well-versed in the history of the Manor, William Penn and the period.

Native Americans

The story of the region's Native Americans is told extensively in the *Data Recovery Archaeological Investigation Report: River Road Site: I-95 Scudder Falls Bridge Improvement Project*. The archaeological reports that were completed for the Scudder Falls Bridge project are fascinating and provide the most recent insights into the Native Americans who lived in the area. A concise overview of Native American history called, *Digging I-95: An interactive report about the archaeology of Northern Liberties, Kensington-Fishtown, and Port Richmond, along the Delaware River waterfront in Philadelphia* can be found at *http://diggingi95.com/projectinformation/prehistoriccontext*.

Family Genealogy

The author's research into the two main families who lived in the Five Mile Woods Preserve, the Darks and the Satterthwaites, was given to the Preserve's archives at the end of the project. While the Darks have had just a few short articles written about them, the Satterthwaites were the study of a comprehensive family genealogy that was printed in 1910. In addition, there are still many family members living in Falls and Lower Makefield Townships. Dark and Satterthwaite genealogical materials can be found at the Bucks County Historical Society and Pennsbury Manor.

Photographs

The photographs and graphics used in this book come from a variety of sources which are cited under each graphic. The Donald Formigli Archival Collection includes not only photographs of various events and programs that have taken place at the Preserve but an impressive collection of pictures taken of the various wildflowers and natural resources there. The author has given all of the digital photographs he created during the course of the project to the Preserve. When another photographer provided an image, the author has acknowledged that person in the text.

The Natural History of the Five Mile Woods

There are a number of important sources of information on the environment, flora and fauna in the Five Mile Woods and in Bucks County in general. Walter Benner's seminal work, *Flora of Bucks County,* is an excellent source and remains a classic work. It is also believed that he collected in the general area of the Preserve. However, it is worth remembering that his book was written in 1932, when more than 90% of Bucks County was still agricultural. Many profound changes have swept over the county and the Five Mile Woods since then.[3]

George Carmichael, the chair of the science department of Pennsbury High School West, wrote an important article entitled *A Natural History of Lowest Bucks*

County which appeared in two parts in the Bucks County Audubon Society's newsletter in 1974-75. It was frequently cited by early supporters of the Woods preservation effort and by this author. However, its information is also dated and new research has been conducted and written about since then.

An important inventory of what existed in the proposed Five Mile Woods Preserve and how it should be managed was prepared by Department of Environmental Resources District Forester Maurice Hobaugh in 1978. The *Woodland Management Plan for the Five Mile Woods* provides an interesting view of how the Preserve could have been developed. It also provides researchers with the first map of the resources that existed at the time in the proposed Preserve.

In 1978, the Division of Limnology and Ecology of the Academy of Natural Sciences of Philadelphia prepared a report entitled *Vegetation and Stream Survey: Lower Makefield Township, Bucks County, Pennsylvania (Report 78-50)*. This study remains an important one in reviewing the natural history and subsequent development in the Township.

One year later, a field trip to the Woods led by Dr. Alfred Schuyler, the Associate Curator in the Department of Botany for the Academy led to a short but important report of the plants that were seen at that time. Entitled *Five Mile Woods (Bucks County, Pennsylvania) Revisited*, Dr. Schuyler documented what they had found there and compared those findings to what Bayard Long, an important Bucks County botanist, found in the vicinity of the Woods fifty years before. Long had previously turned over his specimens to the Academy.[4]

The most significant study ever undertaken of the Five Mile Woods Preserve was completed in 1981 by the Resident Naturalist of the Preserve, Rick Mellon. Mellon prepared a comprehensive inventory of the property entitled *Master Plan for the Five Mile Woods Preserve: Lower Makefield Township Pennsylvania*. It inventoried all the natural features of the Preserve including the geology, soil, plant life, animal life and some historical data. However, like the previous sources mentioned, much has happened and changed at the Preserve since then.

Two other studies have been prepared that provide more data on the Woods and the Preserve including *Geologic Investigation: Five Mile Woods* by Alex McPhee and Leslie Keers and the *Report on the Hydrology of Five Mile Woods, Lower Makefield Township, Bucks County, Pennsylvania* in 1981.

The most recent study of the Preserve was prepared by Dr. Ann Rhoads and entitled *An Evaluation of sites representing the Fall Line Zone in the Mid-Atlantic Region: For eligibility as a National Natural Landmark: Sites Evaluated Five Mile Woods Preserve* in 2003. This evaluation was intended to nominate the Preserve to the official listing of the nation's Natural Landmarks maintained by the National Park Service. This study not only looks at the entire Atlantic Coastal Fall Line along with the section contained within the Preserve, but also its plants, trees, geology and management. It also includes an extensive list of valuable references.

With regard to the area's geology the author relied on two other sources including a fascinating study of the area's geological history, and probably one of the most detailed ever published, entitled the *Geology of the Delaware Valley*. It was written by Horace Richards in 1956. Finally, there is David Roberts *Geology: Eastern North America* which is part of the well-known Peterson Field Guide series.

Additional Resources

Online newspapers were a useful resource to document some of the events that took place at the Preserve and provide a larger context for what was going on regionally and statewide with regard to its history. For this, the author occasionally used the services of *www.genealogybank.com*, *www.newspaperarchives.com* and the online archives of the *New York Times*. The author used *FamilyTreeMaker* and *www.ancestry.com* to build on the work done by Ralph Thompson and his report on the historic structures located on the Preserve's land. There were a number of newspaper clippings found in various collections that also provided information.

Finally, there are the many people that the author informally interviewed including current Preserve and Friends staff, a former site administrator, and Preserve advocates, all of whom are listed in the bibliography.

About Context

The creation of the Five Mile Woods Preserve did not happen in a vacuum nor did its subsequent development. The Preserve fits into a larger context of what was happening regionally and nationally with regard to the preservation of open space. For example, the pressure of development, which was an essential factor in the creation of the Preserve, was happening throughout the region at the time, not only in Bucks County but in the Commonwealth and neighboring New Jersey. As a result, many other preserves, parks and forests were saved or enhanced during this time with various sources of funding from the federal, state, county and local governments. The Preserve is a typical example of what happened and how a successful project could be completed. All in all, the author tried to provide a larger context to better understand the Preserve's history.

It is also worth stating that the author was a site administrator for many years and came to this book looking at the Preserve and its history through that lens. His view is from a manager's perspective, with a larger and broader vision of what is going on. However, for some who have worked or served the Preserve over the years, they have a different view of things. In interviewing staff and volunteers, it was interesting to listen to those different views.

New Frontiers to be Explored

During the course of this project, the author reviewed many files of materials and spoke with a number of people about the Five Mile Woods. One of the conclusions he drew is that there is still additional archival material available in various locations that could be culled and compiled into other research projects. With as much information as has been included within these pages, there are still new frontiers to be explored. It is hoped that this book will lay the groundwork for new research and inspire the next generation of Preserve volunteers and staff to delve further into its past.

COMMON BEECH

COMMON BEECH

BIBLIOGRAPHY

Jane Clark Shermayeff and Associates. 2009. *Abbott Farm National Historic Landmark Interpretive Plan.* Trenton, New Jersey: Mercer County Planning Division.

2016. *Native American Context – Digging 195.* July 14. Accessed 2016. http://diggingi95.com/projectinformation/prehistoriccontext/.

January 1,1981. "5 Mile Woods Financial Balance (PMC)."

Spring 2002. *5 Mile Woods Report.* Friends of the Five Mile Woods.

2009. *75 Years of Service to Customers and Communities: Annual Report.* New Hope, Pennsylvania: Delaware River Joint Toll Bridge Commission.

January 1962. "A Chronology of American Railroads." *Association of American Railroads.*

Academy of Natural Sciences of Philadelphia. December 1, 1978. "Vegetation and Stream Survey: Lower Makefield Township, Bucks County, Pennsylvania."

Advance of Bucks County. 1978. "Lower Makefield cuts ribbon for bikeway opening." August 17.

Alan Geyer, William Boles. 1987. *Outstanding Geological Features of Pennsylvania.* Harrisburg, Pennsylvania: Department of Resources Management.

February 23, 1977. "Alan Lipsky to Robert Pierson."

Alexander, James. November 1995. "Where History and Magic Converge." *FRM Milepost.*

Amos Satterthwaite, Elizabeth Satterthwaite. 1910. *Genealogy of the Satterthwaite Family: Descended from William Satterthwaite Who Settled in Bucks County, Pennsylvania.* Philadelphia: Franklin Printing Company.

April 14, 2017. "Ann Rhoads to Peter Osborne."

Ann Rhoads. 2003. "An Evaluation of sites representing the Fall Line Zone in the Mid Atlantic region: For eligibility as a National Natural Landmark: Site Evaluated: Five Mile Woods."

Ann Rhoads, William Klein. 1993. *The Vascular Flora of Pennsylvania, Annotated Checklist and Atlas.* Philadelphia: American Philosophical Society.

Undated. "Areas of Interest for Open Space (DFC)."

Barrett, Wayne. 2016. "Behind the Seventies-Era Deals that Made Donald Trump." *Village Voice,* July 20.

Bell, Kurt. April 7, 2017. "Notes from Manuscript."

Benner, Walter. 1932. *The Flora of Bucks County.* Philadelphia: Published by the author.

Berg, Christian. 2004. "School of hard rocks." *The Morning Call,* July 11.

Big Oak Whitetail Management Association. 2014. "Lower Makefield Township Deer Management Proposal."

Bird, Maryann. 1974. "Townships told of tools to help protect open land." *Bucks County Courier Times,* May 6.

Block, Ann Rhoads and Timothy. 2007. *The Plants of Pennsylvania, An Illustrated Manual.* 2nd edition. Philadelphia, Pennsylvania: University of Pennsylvania Press.

Bob Freitag, Susan Bolton, Frank Westerlund, Julie Clark. 2009. *Floodplain Management: A New Approach for a New Era.* Washington, D.C.: Island Press.

Bonomi, Patricia. 1998. *The Lord Cornbury Scandal: The Politics of Reputation in British America.* Chapel Hill: University of North Carolina Press.

January 5, 1976. "Bradford Northrup to Lloyd Klatzkin (DFC)."

June 22, 1979. "Bruce Dorbian to Lloyd Klatzkin (DFC)."

October 13, 1978. "Bucks County Conservancy Conservation Award."

Bucks County Conservation News. Spring 1978. "A Woods That Goes On For Miles."

Bucks County Courier Times. 1975. "Bucks towns urged to seek park funds." July.

Bucks County. 2007. "Deed of Conservation Easement and Declaration of Restrictive Covenants, Bucks County Natural Areas Program." Doylestown, Pennsylvania, March 12.

Bucks County Park Board. 1958. *Park and Recreation Areas of Bucks County, Pennsylvania.* Doylestown, Pennsylvania: Bucks County Board of Commissioners.

Bucks County Planning Commission. 2011. *Bucks County Comprehensive Plan 2011.* Doylestown, Pennsylvania: Bucks County, Pennsylvania.

Bucks County Planning Commission. 2014. *Mill-Queen Anne-Black Ditch Creeks: Trail Feasibility Study.* Doylestown, Pennsylvania: Bucks County Planning Commission.

Bucks County Planning Commission. 2003. *Township of Lower Makefield: Comprehensive Master Plan Update.* Lower Makefield Township.

2010. *Bucks County Population Figures.* Doylestown, Pennsylvania: Bucks County Historical Society.

October 1975. "Bucks County Register of Historic Places." *Conservation News.*

n.d. "Bucks County Tax Records: Lower Makefield, Roll 40."

2016. "Bucks County, Pennsylvania Tax Records, 1782-1860." *Ancestry.com.* Accessed August 25, 2016. www.ancestry.com.

Carmichael, George. 1974-1975. "A Natural History of Lowest Bucks County." *Bucks County Audobon Society Newsletter.*

Carson, Linda Loeser. 1960. *Our Heritage: A History of the First Presbyterian Church of Strasburg, Pennsylvania as it relates to the growth of the Strasburg Community.* Strasburg, Pennsylvania: The Women's Association of the First Presbyterian Church of Strasburg, Pennsylvania.

2016. "Cary Family Genealogy."

Check, Gail. 1987. "Historians to produce 1798 map of Lower Makefield." *Yardley News,* April 2.

Chesner, Petra Ann. 1981. "Five Mile Woods formal opening is set for Monday." *Yardley News,* September 17.

Clark, Kathleen. 2006. *Images of America: Bucks County.* Charleston, South Carolina: Arcadia Publishing.

Cohn, Roger. 1978. "Woods with that lived-in look." *Philadelphia Inquirer,* May 5.

Colletti, Cathy. n.d. "The Great Frog Hunt." *Courier Times.*

Conservation News. 1976. "Five Mile Woods." June.

Conservation News. June 1977. "Five Mile Woods."

Conservation News. 1974. "Five Mile Woods." December.

Courier Times. 1979. "Five Miles Woods project to get $300,000 grant." June 10.

Courier Times. 2016. "George Carmichael." April 27.

Courier Times. 1998. "Voters to say if Preserve branches out." November 2.

Cupper, Dan. 2002. *Railroad Museum of Pennsylvania: Pennsylvania Trail of History Guide.*

Mechanicsburg, Pennsylvania: Stackpole Books.

Dale, Frank. 2003. *Bridges over the Delaware River: A History of Crossings.* New Brunswick,New Jersey: Rutgers University Press.

Dalton, Richard. 2006. "Physiographic Provinces of New Jersey." *New Jersey Geological Survey Information Circular.* Department of Environmental Protection.

David Amers and Linda McClelland. 2002. "Historic Residential Suburbs." *National Register Bulletin.*

Davis, Larry. December 23, 2004. "Aerial Infrared Deer Count Report."

Davis, W. W. H. Vol 2. "The Two Makefields." *Papers Published by the Bucks County Historical Society.*

Davis, W. W. Vol. 1. "The Poets and Poetry of Bucks County." *Papers Delivered Before the Bucks County Historical Society.*

Davis, W. W. H. 1876. *The History of Bucks County, Pennsylvania, From Discovery of the Delaware to the Present Time.* Doylestown, Pennsylvania: Democrat Book and Job Office Print.

1690. "Deed Book 1, Page 301." *Deeds, Bucks County.* Doylestown, Pennsylvania.

1988. "Deed Book 13, Page 926-928." *Deeds, Bucks County.* Doylestown, Pennsylvania.

1963. "Deed Book 1693, Page 187." *Deeds of Bucks County.* Doylestown, Pennsylvania.

1966. "Deed Book 1828, Page 145." *Deeds, Bucks County.* Doylestown, Pennsylvania.

1968. "Deed Book 1911, Page 102." *Deeds of Bucks County.* Doylestown, Pennsylvania.

1968. "Deed Book 1919, Page 643." *Deeds, Bucks County.* Doylestown, Pennsylvania.

1696. "Deed Book 2, Pages 94-95." *Deeds, Bucks County.* Doylestown, Pennsylvania.

1976. "Deed Book 2207, Page 0252." *Deeds, Bucks County.* Doylestown, Pennsylvania.

1978. "Deed Book 2325, Pages 1104-1106." *Deeds, Bucks County.* Doylestown, Pennsylvania.

1979. "Deed Book 2358, Page 840-845." *Deeds, Bucks County.* Doylestown, Pennsylvania.

1980. "Deed Book 2398, Page 0609-0614." *Deeds, Bucks County.* Doylestown, Pennsylvania.

1981. "Deed Book 2417, Page 1169-1171." *Deeds, Bucks County.* Doylestown, Pennsylvania.

1982. "Deed Book 2458, Page 0706-0711." *Deeds, Bucks County.* Doylestown, Pennsylvania.

1983. "Deed Book 2497, Page 1066-1066." *Deeds, Bucks County.* Doylestown, Pennsylvania.

1985. "Deed Book 2655, Page 0797-801." *Deeds, Bucks County.* Doylestown, Pennsylvania.

1986. "Deed Book 2662, Page 50-54." *Deeds, Bucks County.* Doylestown, Pennsylvania.

1911. "Deed Book 365, Page 5." *Deeds of Bucks Country.* Doylestown, Pennsylvania.

2006. "Deed Book 4002, Page 1591." *Deeds of Bucks County.* Doylestown, Pennsylvania.

1918. "Deed Book 401, Page 447." *Deeds, Bucks County.* Doylestown, Pennsylvania.

2004. "Deed Book 4010, Page 1941-1943." *Deeds, Bucks County.* Doylestown, Pennsylvania.

2007. "Deed Book 5324, Page 1848." *Deeds of Bucks County.* Doylestown, Pennsylvania.

1737. *Deed of Indians to William Biles.* Doylestown, Pennsylvania: Bucks County Historical Society.

2016. *Delaware Expressway: Historic Overview.* Accessed October 4 2016. http://www.phillyroads.com/roads/delaware/.

Delaware River Joint Toll Bridge Commission. 2007. *2006 Annual Report.* New Hope, Pennsylvania: Delaware River Joint Toll Bridge Commission.

c 1977. "Developer's Plan for the 5 Mile Woods (DFC)."

June 20, 1975. "Donald Formigli to Lower Makefield Board of Supervisors (DFC)."

July 17, 1974. "Donald Formigli to Michael Cutler."

October 23, 2016. "Donald Formigli to Peter Osborne."

December 15, 2016. "Donald Formigli to Peter Osborne."

December 1977. "Donald Formigli: The need to preserve natural resources." *Fairless First.*

1974-1975. "Draft of Letter from Lower Makefield Park and Recreation Board (DFC)."

Dubois, Carol, interview by Peter Osborne. 2017. (March 25).

Dyer, Charlotte. 1978. "To develop or not to develop." *Bucks County Courier Times*, January 30.

2016. "E. W. James on designating the Federal-aid system and developing the U.S. numbered highway plan." *Federal Highway Administration - Highway History.* Accessed August 4, 2016. http://www.fhwa.dot.gov/infrastructure/ewjames.cfm.

December 20, 1974. "Edgar Wherry to Donald Formigli (DFC)."

Edgar Wherry, John Fogg and Herbert Wahl. 1979. *Atlas of the Flora of Pennsylvania.* Philadelphia, Pennsylvania: Morris Arboretum of the University of Pennsylvania.

Edmond Cocks, A. Krout. Vol. 7. "Early History of the Public School System in Bucks County." *Papers Read Before the Bucks County Historical Society.*

Ely, Warren. Vol. 5. "Turnpike Roads in Bucks County." *Papers Read Before the Bucks County Historical Society.*

Emerson, Robert. 1989. *The Pennsylvania Railroad Historical Collection 1939-1989.* Strasburg, Pennsylvania: Friends of the Railroad Museum.

English, Chris. 2007. "Supervisors mull archery deer hunt." *Courier Times*, December 12.

Espenshade, Howry. 1925. *Pennsylvania Place Names.* Harrisburg, Pennsylvania: The Evangelical Press.

Fackenthal, B. F. 1932. Vol. 6, "Improving Navigation on the Delaware River." *Papers Read Before The Bucks County Historical Society.* .

Fairless First. 1977. "Seasons Greetings." December.

Falls Township Board of Supervisors. March 24, 2000. "Falls Township Receives $228,000 Grant for Coastal Plain Forest Nature Preserve."

Falon, Janet. April 19, 1979. "The Origins of the Earth Beneath You." *Bucks County Courier Times.*

—. 1981. "These ballads are tuned into Bucks County." *Bucks County Courier Times*, June 11.

Faris, John. 1917. *Old Roads out of Philadelphia.* Philadelphia: J. B. Lippincott.

Farkas, William, interviews by Peter Osborne. 2012-2015.

Fischer, David Hackett. 2004. *Washington's Crossing.* New York, New York: Oxford University Press.

Fisher, Elizabeth. 2000. "Township seeks funds to purchase farm site." *Courier Times*, March 14.

November 1976. "Five Mile Woods." *Conservation News* VIII (2).

August 28, 1978. "Five Mile Woods Management Plan."

June 7, 1979. "Five Mile Woods Preserve: Guide for Preservation."

1982. "Five Mile Woods: A Forest Preserve (Brochure)."

c. 1983. "Five Mile Woods: A Forest Preserve."

Fleishman, Jeffrey. 1991. "Fairless Steel Furnaces Mark A Last, Sad Date." *Philly.com*, August 9.

Formigli, Donald, interview by Peter Osborne. September 15, 2016.

Formigli, Donald, interview by Peter Osborne. July 29, 2016. ( ).

Formigli, Donald. 1975. "1976 Park and Recreation Board Budget Request (DFC)."

Formigli, Donald. 1981. "Dates to Remember (DFC)."

—. February 4, 1979. "Five Mile Woods Program and Nature Photography Show (DFC)."

Formigli, Donald. 1975. *Five Mile Woods: Lower Makefield and Falls Townships, Bucks County, Pennsylvania.* Doylestown, Pennsylvania: Bucks County Conservancy.

Formigli, Donald. 2016. "Land Parcels of Five Mile Woods (DFC)."

Formigli, Donald. c. 1974. "Notes for News Article (DFC)."

Formigli, Donald. c. 1975. "Notes from News Article (DFC)."

—. 1974. "Open Space Newsletter - Draft of Article (DFC)."

Formigli, Donald. 1978. "Planning for the Future of the Five Mile Woods."

Formigli, Donald. 1979. "Programs Presented (DFC)."

—. 1979. "Text for Five Mile Woods Slide-Tape Program (DFC)."

Formigli, Donald. 1975. "The Five Mile Woods (DFC)."

Forstall, Richard. 1990. *Population of States and Counties of the United States: 1790-1990.* Washington, D.C.: Department of Commerce, US Bureau of Census,.

2016. "Fossils of the Northeastern US: a brief review." *The Paleontological Research Institution.* Accessed June 16, 2016. http://geology.teacherfriendlyguide.org/index.php/fossils/a-brief-review.

Foulds, James, interview by Peter Osborne. 2016. (December 13).

Foulds, James, interview by Peter Osborne. 2016. (December 5).

Foulds, Laura, James, interview by Peter Osborne. 2016. (November 30).

October 11, 1979. "Fred Owen to Patricia Delmar (DFC)."

November 3, 1980. "Fred Owen to William Carlin (DFC)."

2017. *Friends of the Delaware Canal.* Accessed April 12, 2017. https://www.fodc.org/about-the-canal/.

1987. "Friends of the Five Mile Woods - Incorporation Files."

1987. "Friends of the Woods receive state commendations." December 10.

Gale, Dick. 1975. "A new idea whose time is coming."

2016. *Geology - Franklin College.* Accessed May 26, 2016. http://www.gly.uga.edu/railsback/1122EUSMISR.html.

April 3, 1975. "George Carmichael to Donald Formigli."

Gilbert, Jodi. 1997. "New Naturalist at 5 Mile Woods." October 2.

Gold, Russell. 1995. *Philly.com.* June 2. Accessed October 3, 2016. http://articles.philly.com/1995-06-02/news/25690179_1_tullytown-landfill-fish-story-waders.

1910. *Granites of the Southeastern Atlantic States, Bulletin 426.* Washington: United States Geological Survey, Government Printing Office.

2017. *Great Falls Park, Virginia.* Accessed January 6, 2017. https://www.nps.gov/htm.

Hardesty, Gail. March 22, 1981. "Friends of the Woods review of the Mellon Master Plan for the Five Mile Woods."

Heilferty, John, interview by Peter Osborne. 2016. (June 11).

Heilferty, John, interview by Peter Osborne. 2016. (October 9).

Heilferty, John, interview by Peter Osborne. 2017. (February 21).

Heilferty, John, interview by Peter Osborne. 2016. (December 16).

Heilferty, John. April 4, 2017. "Notes from Manuscript."

Heilferty, John. December 31, 2016. "Notes to Manuscript."

Heinz, Helen, interview by Peter Osborne. 2016. (July 26).

Heinz, Helen, interview by Peter Osborne. 2016. (October 6).

Heinz, Helen, interview by Peter Osborne. 2016. (December 1).

Heinz, Helen, interview by Peter Osborne. 2017. (February 23).

Heinz, Helen. December 11, 2016. "Notes to Manuscript."

Heinz, Helen. April 7, 2017. "Notes to Manuscript."

Heinz, Helen. July 30, 2016. "Notes to Manuscript."

Heinz, Helen. September 24, 2016. "Notes to Manuscript."

October 3, 2016. "Helen Heinz to Peter Osborne."

January 16, 2017. "Helen Heinz to Peter Osborne."

December 13. 2016. "Helen Heinz to Peter Osborne."

January 16, 2017. "Helen Heinz to Peter Osborne."

Hellyer, Joan. 2016. "$4M considered for open space." *Bucks County Courier Times*, December 7.

January 2, 2017. "Henry Miiller to Peter Osborne."

January 21, 2017. "Henry Miiller to Peter Osborne."

Hertkom, Tim, interview by Peter Osborne. 2016. (April 15).

Hill, David. 1981. "Five Mile Woods dedicated to the public." *Yardley News*, November 26.

2016. *Historic Bolton Mansion*. Accessed September 17, 2016. http://www.boltonmansion.org/history.html.

2016. "Historic Fallsington Walking Guide."

1947, 2008. *Historic Fallsington: The Story of an Early Bucks County Village*. Fallsington, Pennsylvania: Historic Fallsington, Inc.

Hobaugh, Maurice. 1978. *Woodland Management Plan for the Five Mile Woods*. Pottstown, Pennsylvania: Department of Environmental Resources.

Hondras, Tina. 1974. "Citizen's unit works for open space." *Bucks County Courier Times*, December 2.

—. 1974. "Citizen's unit works for open space." *Bucks County Courier Times*, December 2.

Hudson, John. 2002. *A Regional Geography of the United States and Canada*. Baltimore: Johns Hopkins University Press.

Huets, Jean. 2013. "The Fall Line's Fault." *New York Times*, January 16.

Hughes, Thomas. 1858. *Farm Map Lower Makefield Township Bucks County, Pennsylvania*. Philadelphia: Friend and Aub.

Hughes, Thomas. 1858. *Farm Map of Falls Township, Bucks County, Pennsylvania*. Philadelphia: Friend and Aub.

April 1978. "Insert in April 1978 Lower Makefield Township Newsletter: Five Mile Woods Question on May 16 Primary Ballot (DFC)."

2015. "Interpretive Panels, History Museum, Steamtown National Historic Site."

2016. *Interstate 95*. Accessed October 4, 2016. http://www.pahighways.com/interstates/I95.html.

J. H. Battle, Editor. 1887. *History of Bucks County*. Philadelphia: A. Warner & Co.

Jack and Lorraine Seabrook. 2000. *Images of America: Hopewell Valley*. Charleston, South Caroline: Arcadia Publishing.

2016. *Jacob Hibbs Genealogy*. December 1. Accessed December 1, 2016. http://person.ancestry.com/tree/20101244/person/18184542785/facts.

Jan McFarlan and Ron Montgomery. 1995. *Fact Sheet: Five Mile Woods*. Friends of Five Mile Woods.

Janet Brittingham, Mildred Williams. n.d. *1784 Return of Land, Bucks County, Pennsylvania: Transcripts of Dwellings and Outhouses, White and Black Inhabitants, Return of Land*. Will-Britt Books.

February 14, 1984. "Jeffrey Garton to James Dillon (DFC)."

May 30, 1997. "John Heilferty to Terry Fedorchak."

John Lawrence, Brian Albright. 2012. *Data Recovery Archaeological Investigation Report: River Road Site (36bu379) I-95 Scudder Falls Bridge Improvement Project, Lower Makefield Township, Bucks County, Pennsylvania*. New Hope, Pennsylvania: Delaware River Joint Toll Bridge Commission.

Johnston, Edward Harrington and Diane. 2005. *Solebury Township: From 500,000 BC to the Beginning of the Calamitous Twentieth Century*. Vol. I and II. Carversville, Pennsylvania: The Hillside Press.

Kenderine, Thaddeus. 1918. "Historical Reminiscences of the Cuttalossa Creek in Solebury Township." *Papers Read Before the Bucks County Historical Society, Vol. 5.*

Kennedy, Thomas. 1817. "A Map of the County of Bucks."

Kiscaden, Lester. 1973. "A History of the Strasburg Rail Road, 1832-1862." Lancaster, Pennsylvania: Lancaster Historical Society.

Lauren Poster, Ann Rhoads and Timothy Block. 2013. "Vascular Flora and community assemblages of Delhaas Woods, A Coastal Plain Forest in Bucks County, Pennsylvania." *Journal of the Torrey Botanical Society.*

LaVo, Carl. 2016. "Hard Lessons in The Ink Bottle." *Bucks County Courier Times*, September 26.

1991. *Lawmaking and Legislators in Pennsylvania: A Biographical Dictionary 1682-1709.* Philadelphia: University of Pennsylvania Press.

Lempert, Barbara. 1986. "Five Mile Woods: The last of its kind." *Courier Times*, November 7.

Leslie, Vernon. 1976. *The Battle of Minisink: A Revolutionary War Engagement in the Upper Delaware Valley.* Middletown, New York: T. Emmett Henderson.

2016. *Lincoln Highway Association.* Accessed October 20, 2016. https://www.lincolnhighwayassoc.org/info/pa/.

2016. *Lincoln Highway Heritage Corridor.* Accessed October 20, 2016. http://www.lhhc.org/.

2016. *Living Places - Fairless Hills.* Accessed December 23, 2016. http://livingplaces.com/PA/Bucks County/Falls_Township/Fairless_Hills.html.

April 22, 1975. "Lloyd Klatzkin to Patrick Noonan."

Lloyd, John, interview by Peter Osborne. 2016. (August 12).

Lloyd, John, interview by Peter Osborne. 2016. (December 12).

—. November 21, 2016. "Notes to Manuscript."

Long, David, interview by Peter Osborne. 2017. (February 21).

Long, David B. 2010-2013. "The Birds of Five Mile Woods." *Cassinia.*

1972. *Lower Bucks County Street and Road Map.* Alfred B. Patton, Inc.

Lower Makefield Historical Commission. 1992. *Tri-Centennial Commemorative History of Lower Makefield Township 1692-1992.* Lower Makefield Township, Pennsylvania.

Lower Makefield Historical Society, The Township Historical Commission, The Historical Architectural Review Board. 1998. *A Guide to Lower Makefield's Historic Landmarks.* Yardley, Pennsylvania: Lower Makefield Township, Pennsylvania.

June 30, 1975. "Lower Makefield Open Space Committee - Report on 1975 Survey (DFC)."

Lower Makefield Open Space Committee. 1973. *Facts About Open Space in Lower Makefield (DFC).*

April 1975. "Lower Makefield Questionnaire (DFC)." *Conservation News* VII (1).

Lower Makefield Township Historical Commission. 1998. *A Guide to Lower Makefield's Historic Landmarks.* Lower Makefield Township Historical Commission.

Lower Makefield Township Newsletter. Winter 1996-1997. "Nature at its best in LMT: A Visit to 5 Mile Woods."

April 1998. "Lower Makefield Township Open Space Plan."

January 4, 1982. "Lower Makefield Township Resolution No. 466, Bill No. 682 (DFC)."

Lower Makefield Township. June 1977. "Planning and Zoning Update." *Township Newsletter (PMC).*

MacReynolds, George. 1955. *Place Names in Bucks County, Pennsylvania: Alphabetically Arranged in an Historical Narrative.* Doylestown, Pennsylvania: The Bucks County Historical Society.

Manegold, C. S. 1981. "L. Makefield pool opens with fanfare." *Courier Times*, May.

1860. "Map of the Vicinity of Philadelphia: Lower Makefield Township section."

Mark Reinberger, Elizabeth McLean. July 2007. "Pennsbury Manor: Reconstruction and Reality." *Pennsylvania Magazine of History and Biography* Vol. CXXXI (3).

Marshall, Jeff, interview by Peter Osborne. 2017. (February 22).

Marshall, Jeff. April 7, 2017. "Notes to Manuscript."

—. June 8, 2016. "The Garden Party, Aldie Mansion, Doylestown, Pennsylvania."

Marshall, Jeffrey. 2009. *Bucks County Farmhouses*. Marshall Family Press.

Martellaro, John. 1980. "New zoning ruling to preserve nature." *Courier Times*, June 10.

Marthaler, Joseph. 2002. "Five Mile Woods Receives Plaque in Recognition of Service." *Times Publishing Newspapers*, June 14.

Mary Dunn, Richard Dunn, editors. 1982. *The Papers of William Penn*. University of Pennsylvania Press.

Mellon, Rick, interview by Peter Osborne. 2017. (February 28).

Mellon, Rick. 1981. *Master Plan for the Five Mile Woods Preserve*. Lower Makefield Township, Pennsylvania: Mellon Biological Services.

—. April 7, 2017. "Notes to Manuscript."

2015. *Mergers and Bankruptcies, Railroads: The 1960s and 1970s*. Accessed May 13, 2015. www.american-rails.com.

Messer, David. 1999. *Triumph II: Philadelphia to Harrisburg 1828-1998*. Baltimore, Maryland: Barnard, Roberts and Company.

Michael Williamson and Michael Wallace. 2007. *The Lincoln Highway: Coast to Coast from Times Square to the Golden Gate*. New York: W. W. Norton and Company.

August 10, 2001. "Michelle Batcheller to Terry Fedorchak."

Miiller, Hank. September 26, 1977. "Ecological Assets: A Winning Approach."

Miiller, Hank. April 7, 2017. "Notes to Manuscript."

Miiller, Pat, interview by Peter Osborne. 2016. (September 14).

Miiller, Pat, interview by Peter Osborne. 2016. (September 14).

—. November 11, 2016. "Notes to Manuscript."

Miiller, Pat. October 5, 2016. "Notes to Manuscript."

Miller, L. A. 1985. "Mall, park deal approved by L. Makefield." *Courier Times*, August 28.

—. 1985. "Mall, park deal approved by L. Makefield." *Courier Times*, August 28.

April 1, 1987. "Minutes, Five Mile Woods Business Meeting."

June 15, 1988. "Minutes, Friends of the Five Mile Woods."

January 9, 2004. "Minutes, Friends of the Five Mile Woods."

July 9, 1979. "Minutes, Lower Makefield Board of Supervisors Meetings."

March 1, 1979. "Minutes, Lower Makefield Park and Board Meeting."

June 7, 1979. "Minutes, Lower Makefield Park and Board Meeting."

April 28, 1977. "Minutes, Lower Makefield Park and Recreation Board (DFC)."

November 3, 1977. "Minutes, Lower Makefield Park and Recreation Board (DFC)."

December 1, 1977. "Minutes, Lower Makefield Park and Recreation Board (DFC)."

January 5, 1978. "Minutes, Lower Makefield Park and Recreation Board (DFC)."

November 2, 1978. "Minutes, Lower Makefield Park and Recreation Board (DFC)."

June 30, 1976. "Minutes, Lower Makefield Park and Recreation Board (DFC)."

January 6, 1977. "Minutes, Lower Makefield Park and Recreation Board (DFC)."

March 4, 1976. "Minutes, Lower Makefield Park and Recreation Board (DFC)."

August 5, 1976. "Minutes, Lower Makefield Park and Recreation Board (DFC)."

September 8, 1977. "Minutes, Lower Makefield Park and Recreation Board (DFC)."

February 2, 1978. "Minutes, Lower Makefield Park and Recreation Board (DFC)."

October 5, 1978. "Minutes, Lower Makefield Park and Recreation Board (DFC)."

November 2, 1978. "Minutes, Lower Makefield Park and Recreation Board (DFC)."

February 1, 1979. "Minutes, Lower Makefield Park and Recreation Board (DFC)."

August 2, 1979. "Minutes, Lower Makefield Park and Recreation Board (DFC)."

November 1, 1979. "Minutes, Lower Makefield Park and Recreation Board (DFC)."

September 4, 1980. "Minutes, Lower Makefield Park and Recreation Board (DFC)."

December 4, 1980. "Minutes, Lower Makefield Park and Recreation Board (DFC)."

March 10, 1981. "Minutes, Lower Makefield Park and Recreation Board (DFC)."

February 5, 1981. "Minutes, Lower Makefield Park and Recreation Board (DFC)."

December 7, 1978. "Minutes, Lower Makefield Park and Recreation Board (DFC)."

July 7, 1978. "Minutes, Lower Makefield Park and Recreation Board (DFC)."

January 6, 1977. "Minutes, Lower Makefield Park and Recreation Board (DFC)."

October 6, 1977. "Minutes, Lower Makefield Park and Recreation Board (DFC)."

February 3, 1977. "Minutes, Lower Makefield Park and Recreation Board Minutes (DFC)."

October 6, 1976. "Minutes, Lower Makefield Park and Recreation Board (DFC)."

June 1, 1978. "Minutes, Lower Makefield Park and Recreation Board (DFC)."

Mullaney, Thomas. 1951. "Giant Steel Mills Replace Farmers." *New York Times*, January 30.

2017. *National Interstate and Defense Highways Act.* Accessed April 12, 2017. https://www.our-documents.gov/doc.php?flash=true&doc=88.

National Park Service. 2016. *The Earliest Americans Theme Study.* Accessed July 21, 2016. https://www.nps.gov/archeology/pubs/nhleam/f-northeast.htm.

2016. "National Society, Sons of the American Revolution." *Sons of the American Revolution Membership Applications, 1889-1970* . Accessed April 10 , 2016. www.ancestry.com.

April 28, 2004. "Natural Areas Program: Grant Application Review."

1978. "Natural Areas Survey." *Conservation News.*

Nazzaro, William. 1979. "Unique Woods to be Saved." *The Bulletin*, June 17.

n.d. *Neeld Octagonal Schoolhouse Files.* Yardley, Pennsylvania: Lower Makefield Township Historical Society.

Newill, Bill. 1978. "Route 413 - bulldozer alley." *Bucks County Courier Times*, July 5.

Noll, E. P. 1891. *Atlas of Bucks County, Pennsylvania.* Philadelphia: E. P. Noll & Co., Map Publishers.

April 3 1995. "Notes, Lower Makefield Township Meeting."

Nyholm, Birgitta. 1978. "Conservancy is an unsung pioneer." *Sunday Times Advertiser*, October 8.

—. 1979. "Arbor Day: Conservancy searching for rare, old trees." *Trenton Times*, April 27.

—. 1978. "L. Makefield asks $900,000 to buy Woods." *Trenton Times*, September 20.

—. 1978. "Makefield signs deal to buy 5 Mile Woods." *Trenton Times*, November 14.

—. 1977. "Makefield to vote on Woods plan." *Trenton Times*, July 27.

—. 1978. "Rare orchid stands in way of development." *Trenton Times*, December 5.

—. 1978. "Woodlands rezoning approved." *Trenton Times*, March 28.

Nyholm, Birigtta. 1977. "Bucks group hopes to buy Five Mile Woods acreage." *Trenton Times*, April 15.

Nyholm, Brigetta. 1977. "Independence Square buys five acres for open space." *Courier Times*, September 7.

—. 1977. "Builder modifies Woods Offer." *Courier Times*, October 18.

—. 1977. "Makefield to vote on Woods plan." *Trenton Times*, July 21.

O'Brien, Ray. 1988. *Bucks County: A Journey Through Paradise: From the Peaceable Kingdom to the Suburban Dream.* Dubuque, Iowa: Kendall/Hunt Publishing Company.

April 25, 1974. "Oliver Stark to Donald Formigli (DFC)."

November 19, 1974. "Open Space Meeting (DFC)."

Osborne, Peter. 2014. *No Spot in This Far Land Is More Immortalized: A History of Pennsylvania's Washington Crossing Historic Park.* Yardley, Pennsylvania: Yardley Press.

—. 2007. *Perseverance & Vigilance: The History of the Old Decker Stone House.* Port Jervis, New York: Minisink Press.

Osborne, Peter. 2017. "Property Research Records."

—. 2012. *Where Washington Once Led: A History of New Jersey's Washington Crossing State Park.* Yardley, Pennsylvania: Yardley Press.

Oscar Sanodval, Thomas Carroll and Lewis Morgan. 2005. "Morrisville Yard: Improving NJ Transit Service on the Northeast Corridor."

January 5, 1978. "P&R Board Recommendation on the Five Mile Woods (DFC)."

P. Lea Thomas Holmes. 1687. "A mapp of ye improved part of Pensilvania in America, divided into countyes, townships, and lotts."

Papers Read Before the Bucks County Historical Society. n.d. "Early Botanists of Bucks County."

Pasko, Kathy. April 7, 2017. "Notes to Manuscript."

2016. *Penn Pilot: Historic Aerial Photographs of Pennsylvania.* Accessed October 16, 2016. www.pennpilot.psu.edu.

2016. *Penn Treaty Museum.* Accessed July 21, 2016. http://www.penntreatymuseum.org/wordpress/history-2/peace-treaty/.

2016. *Pennsbury Manor: Plan Your Visit.* Accessed July 18, 2016. http://www.pennsburymanor.org/plan-your-visit/.

2016. *Pennsbury Manor: People at Pennsbury.* June 4. Accessed June 4, 2016. http://www.pennsburymanor.org/the-manor/people-at-pennsbury/.

Pennsylvania Geological Survey. 1982. "Dr. Edgar Wherry." *Pennsylvania Geology.*

—. 1959. *Geology and Mineral Resources of Bucks County, Pennsylvania.* Harrisburg, Pennsylvania: Commonwealth of Pennsylvania.

—. October 1982. "Dr. Edgar Wherry." *Pennsylvania Geology.*

2017. *Pennsylvania Highways.* Accessed April 13, 2017. http://www.pahighways.com/interstates/I95.html.

November 28, 1979. "Pennsylvania Railroad Rolling Stock Thematic Resource Nomination to the National Register of Historic Places."

2017. *Pennsylvania Turnpike.* Accessed April 12, 2017. https://www.paturnpike.com/yourTurnpike/ptc_history.aspx.

2015. "Pennsylvania, Wills and Probate Records, 1683-1993." *Ancestry.com.* Accessed June 20, 2016.

July 20, 1977. "Peter Kostmayer to Martin Convisser (DFC)."

2017. *Philadelphia Botanical Club: Herbarium.* Accessed January 6, 2017. http://darwin.ansp.org/hosted/botany_club/herbarium.html.

Philadelphia Inquirer. 1982. "Mr. Edgar Wherry, 96 of Germantown." May 25.

2010. *PHMC Historic Resource Survey Form: Pennsylvania Railroad Morrisville Line; Trenton Cut-off.* Harrisburg, Pennsylvania: Pennsylvania Historical and Museum Commission.

Pickering, Corts & Summerson. April 28, 2004. "Banko Property - Natural Resources and Site Capacity."

October 1975. "Progress Report - Lower Makefield Open Space Committee (DFC)."

1974. "Property Owners (Five Mile Woods) (DFC)."

1976. "Proposed Park and Recreation Program for Lower Makefield (DFC)."

n.d. *Quaker Genealogy, Vol. II.*

2015. *Railroad History, An Overview of the Past.* Accessed May 13, 2015. www.american-rails.com.

No. 59, 1916. "Railway Review." Chicago, Illinois.

July 7, 1696. "Report - Road Leading from Newtown to Jenk's fulling mill." Doylestown, Pennsylvania: Bucks County Historical Society.

June 20, 2007. "Report of the Bucks County Open Space Task Force."

April 4, 1808. "Report on Roads and Canals, Communicated to the Senate ." Washington, D.C.

1997. "Resume of John Heilferty."

2016. *RG-34. Records of the Department of Community Affairs.* Accessed December 29, 2016. http://www.phmc.state.pa.us/bah/aaGuide/AA-RG-34.html.

Rhoads, Ann. April 7, 2017. "Notes to Manuscript."

Rhoads, Ann and Paul, interview by Peter Osborne. 2017. (February 23).

Rhoads, Paul, interview by Peter Osborne. 2017. (March 3).

Rhoads, Paul, interview by Peter Osborne. 2017. (March 31).

Rhoads, Paul. c. 1978. "Cutler Tract Deed Search."

Rhoads, Paul. 1998. "Pennsbury Manor to Fairless Works of U.S. Steel Corporation: A Chronology."

Richard and Amy Wagner. 2010. *Levittown.* Charleston, South Carolina: Arcadia Publishing.

Richards, Horace. 1956. *Geology of the Delaware Valley.* Philadelphia: Mineralogical Society of Pennsylvania.

Richman, Steven. 2005. *The Bridges of New Jersey: Portraits of Garden State Crossings.* New Brunswick, New Jersey: Rutgers University Press.

2017. *Rick Mellon.* Accessed January 15, 2017. https://www.linkedin.com/in/rick-mellon-7a1a498b/.

March 20, 2017. "Rick Mellon to Peter Osborne."

Rinehart, Norman. 1974. "Bucks transfer plan meets with criticism." *Trenton Times,* October 20.

Rivinus, Willis. 2004. *Guide to the Delaware Canal: Along the Delaware River Between Bristol and Easton, Pennsylvania.* Eighth Edition.

March 13, 1986. "Robert Gray to James Dillon."

February 17, 1977. "Robert Pierson to Bradford Northrup (DFC)."

December 7, 1976. "Robert Pierson to Bruce Howard (DFC)."

January 5, 1975. "Robert Pierson to Donald Formigli (DFC)."

June 8, 1976. "Robert Pierson to John Fullam (DFC)."

August 10, 1976. "Robert Pierson to Juliann Whelan (DFC)."

Roberts, David. 1996. *A Field Guide to Geology: Eastern North America.* New York: Houghton Mifflin Company.

Robertson, Marion. 1971-1972. "Walter MacKinnett Benner (1888-1970)." *Bartonia.*

Robinson, George. 1986. "Five Mile Woods offer guide training course." *Yardley News,* June 5.

November 6, 1978. "Ronald Chase to Don Formigli (DFC)."

2016. *Route 1, John H. Ware III Memorial Highway.* Accessed October 4, 2016. http://www.pa-highways.com/us/US1.html.

2016. *Route 13.* Accessed October 20, 2016. http://www.pahighways.com/us/US13.html.

2016. *Royal Family History.* Accessed May 30, 2016. http://www.britroyals.com/kings.asp?id=anne.

Satterthwaite, Elizabeth. 1945. "The Old Friends' Meeting of Falls." Speech, Falls Township, Pennsylvania.

Schaffhausen, Florence. 1978. "Save farmland a battle cry." *Bucks County Courier Times*, May 22.

Schlatter, D. E. 1986. "Supervisors pass farmland preservation ordinance." *Yardley News*, May 1.

Schuyler, Alfred. 1979. "Five Mile Woods (Bucks County, Pennsylvania) Revisited."

Scott, Hugh. 1951. "Our Industrial Boom." *Philadelphia Inquirer Magazine*, November 11.

Scott, J.D. 1876. *Combination Atlas Map of Bucks County, Pennsylvania*. Philadelphia: Friend & Aub.

Selda, LInda. 1987. "Lower Makefield warns hunters to avoid woods." *Courier Times*, January 27.

2017. *Sesame Place*. Accessed April 13, 2017. https://sesameplace.com/en/langhorne/park-info/about-sesame-place/history-of-sesame-place.

Shafer, Craig. April 15, 2003. "Comments on An Evaluation of Sites Representing the Fall Line Zone by Ann Rhoads (NNL nomination package)."

Shandle, Jack. 1985. "Five Mile Woods: Last remaining coastal plain forest." *Courier Times*, May 6.

Sheppard, Walter, ed. 1970. *Passenger and Ships prior to 1684*. Baltimore: Genealogical Publishing Co.

2017. *Shop Rite*. Accessed February 12, 2017. http://newsroom.shoprite.com/shoprite/news/new-shoprite-to-open-in-yardley-pennsylvania.htm.

Silkwood, Susan. 1977. "Residents like space over cash." *Bucks County Courier Times*, February 23.

Sill, Mary Ann. 1974. "Conservationists working to preserve prized area." *Bucks County Courier Times*, November 21.

Simms, Lynn, interview by Peter Osborne. 2017. (January 9).

c. 1975. "Slide Program - What's Worth Preserving in Lower Makefield as Open Space (DFC)."

Smyth, Gordon. Vol 4. "Bucks County Pioneers in the Valley of Virginia." *Papers Delivered Before the Bucks County Historical Society*.

Snipes, Samuel, interview by Peter Osborne. 2017. (February 16).

—. 2001. *The History of Falls Township 1692-1992*. Falls Township, Pennsylvania: Falls Township.

Spivey, Justin. 2001. *Philadelphia & Reading Railroad, Delaware River Bridge (HAER No. Pa 513)*. Washington D.C.: National Park Service.

Stanert, Shaun. 1987. "Township reviews plans for water storage tower." October 22.

Stanton, James. 1996. "Woods get new curator." *Courier Times*, January 21.

Steil, Karen. 2016. "Little Known Facts About Lower Makefield Township (LMTHS)."

July 24, 1985. "Stipulation for Agreed Order of Court - Independence Development Corp v. Lower Makefield Township."

Stockham, Ronald, interview by Peter Osborne. 2017. (February 16).

Stoffer, Harry. 1979. "Antique Trains Soon to Be Property of Pennsylvania." *Bucks County Courier Times*, December 10.

Strausbaugh, Joseph. 2006. "The Influence of the Pennsylvania Mainline of Public Works." *The Gettysburg Historical Journal*, 18-30.

Taber, Thomas. 1987. *Railroads of Pennsylvania: Encyclopedia and Atlas*. Muncy, Pennsylvania: .

Terry McNealy and Francis Waite. 1982. *Bucks County Tax Records 1693-1778*. Doylestown, Pennsylvania: Bucks County Genealogical Society.

2016. *The Founding of the Quaker Colony of West Jersey*. Accessed July 18, 2016. www.ushistory.org/penn/pennnj.htm.

The Froghorn. Summer 2016. "George R. Carmichael Jr. June 26, 1929 - April 27, 2016."

The Makefield Monograph. January 2014. "Lower Makefield Roads."

1997-2015. *The Most Perfectly Planned Community in America: Levittown, Pennsylvania*. Accessed

January 6, 2016. http://www.levittowners.com/.

1981. "The Nature Conservancy Recommendations to the Five Mile Woods Preserve."

2016. *The Philadelphia Chapter of the National Railway Historical Society.* Accessed August 8, 2016. www.trainweb.org/phillynrhs/rdg.html.

2016. *The Religious Society of Friends.* Accessed February 11, 2016. www.quaker.org.

2016. *The Township of Lower Makefield (Bucks County, Pennsylvania).* . Accessed May 9, 2016. http://www.lmt.org/township-information/statistical-information/.

2016. *The Township of Lower Makefield, Bucks County, Pennsylvania.* Accessed July 14, 2016. http://www.lmt.org/township-information/history-of-lower-makefield/.

May 1978. "Think! Then Vote No on the Five Mile Woods Question in the May 16 Primary (DFC)."

Thomas Holmes, Lloyd Smith. c. 1705. "Map of the Improved Part of the Province of Pennsylvania in America - 1681."

Thomas Tyler Moor Associates. 1981. "Report on the Hydrology of Five Mile Woods, Lower Makefield Township, Bucks County, Pennsylvania."

Thompson, Ralph. 1997. *Historic Sites in & adjacent to Five Mile Woods (Revised edition).* Lower Makefield Historical Society.

Thompson, Ralph. 1988. "Lower Makefield Township Bucks County, Pennsylvania Map of Original Grantees."

Thompson, Ralph. 1988. "Lower Makefield Township, Bucks County Pennsylvania: Historical Map 1798."

Thompson, Ralph. n.d. "Research Report on the Octagonal Schoolhouse."

Thompson, Ralph. 1991. *Slate Hill Cemetery National Register of Historic Places Registration Form.* Yardley, Pennsylvania: Lower Makefield Township Historical Committee.

May 8, 2016. "To the Editor from Donald Formigli, Pat Fair, Gail Hardesty (DFC)."

Fall 1976. "Township Newsletter, Lower Makefield ."

June 1979. "Township Newsletter, Lower Makefield ."

February 1978. "Township Newsletter, Lower Makefield."

February 1977. "Township Newsletter, Lower Makefield."

Fall 1976. "Township Newsletter, Lower Makefield."

June 1977. "Township Newsletter, Lower Makefield."

June 1978. "Township Newsletter, Lower Makefield."

February 1978. "Township Newsletter, Lower Makefield Township."

April 1978. "Township Newsletter, Lower Makefield Township."

March 1987. "Township Newsletter, Lower Makefield Township."

2016. *Township of Falls, Bucks County, Pennsylvania.* Accessed September 17, 2016. http://www.fallstwp.com/information-services/history-of-falls-township/three-arches.aspx.

Treese, Lorett. 2012. *Railroads of Pennsylvania.* 2nd Edition. Mechanicsburg, Pennsylvania: Stackpole Books.

Trenton Times. 1978. "$127,500 Lower Makefield park plan unveiled." June 13.

Trenton Times. 1981. "Formigli resigns post in L. Makefield Township." October 10.

Trenton Times. 1979. "Land Price reached in Makefield." May 30.

Trenton Times. 1975. "Open space plan urged by Cower." April 20.

2014. "U.S. Quaker Meeting Records 1681-1935." *Ancestry.com.* Accessed June 10, 2016. www.ancestry.com.

United States Geological Survey. 2016. *Earthquake Hazards Program: Pennsylvania Earthquake History.* Accessed July 28, 2016. http://earthquake.usgs.gov/earthquakes/states/pennsylvania/history.php.

2016. "Various Site Visits by Peter Osborne."

Viriginia and Lee McAlester. 1984. *A Field Guide to American Houses*. New York: Alfred Knopf.

2016. *Visit Bucks County*. Accessed August 25, 2016. www.visitbuckscounty.com/towns-main-streets/did you know Bucks County's early history/.

Wade, Jim. Summer 2008. "Summer's Journey: The Indian Shale Quarries of the Delaware River Valley and Beyond." *Nature's Grapevine*.

Walker, Tom. 1977. "Five Mile Woods: 375-acre sylvan battleground." *Bucks County Courier Times*, October 28.

Wandling, Patricia. 1977. "Fighting for the privilege of a woodland stroll." *Bucks County Courier Times - Accent Magazine*, November 13.

—. 1977. "L Makefield adopts bike path ordinance." *Bucks County Courier Times*, July 11.

—. 1977. "5-Mile Woods battle is seen at impasse." *Courier Times*, July 6.

—. 1978. "Woods rescue remains priority." *Courier Times*, April .

—. 1978. "Peering into the Past." March 20.

2004. "Watershed Restoration Action Strategy: State Water Plan Sub-basin 02E Pidcock Creek and Mill Creek and Tributaries to the Delaware River in Lower Bucks County, Pennsylvania."

Watson, Ed. 1996. "Naturalist has big plans for the Woods, preserve an oasis in the sea of development." *Yardley News*, February 29.

Werner, Jeff. Unknown. "National Designation sought for Five Mile Woods."

—. 1998. "At Five Mile Preserve, they're ready to roll: All-terrain wheelchair helps disabled hit the trail." *Yardley News*, April 30.

—. 2004. "Land Purchase adds acreage to preserve." *Yardley News*, March 25.

White, Florence. 1987. "Historian seek preservation of Octagonal Schoolhouse ." *Yardley News*, April 23.

—. 1992. "When the Lenape ruled the land." *Yardley News*, September 24.

Wilfred Jordan, editor. 1955. *Colonial and Revolutionary Families of Pennsylvania: Genealogical and Personal Memoirs*. New York: Lewis Historical Publishing Company.

1786. "Will of William Satterthwaite Jr." *Wills, Bucks County Records Department*. Doylestown, Pennsylvania.

Willard, Sam, interview by Peter Osborne. 2017. (April 19).

2016. *William Dark Genealogy*. Accessed June 15, 2016. http:/person.ancestry.com/tree/71676449/person/48246235742/story.

William Davis, Edited by Warren Ely and John Jordan. 1992-2002. *History of Bucks County (Revised)*. New York: Clearfield Company.

2016. *William Penn: Seed of a Nation Exhibit*. Accessed July 16, 2016. http://www.pennsbury-manor.org/the-manor/seed-of-a-nation-exhibit/.

2016. *William Penn's Country Estate Pennsbury Manor*. Accessed July 11, 2016. http://www.pennsburymanor.org/history/william-penn/.

2016. *William Penn's Country Estate Pennsbury Manor*. Accessed July 16, 2016. http://www.pennsburymanor.org.

2016. *William Satterthwaite Genealogy*. . Accessed June 14, 2016. http://person.ancestry.com/tree/46428928/person/6889711969/story.

December 1, 1976. "William Veitch to Robert Rodale (DFC)."

Williams, Francis. 1893. "Pennsylvania Poets of the Provincial Period." *The Pennsylvania Magazine of History and Biography* Vol 17 (No. 1).

Williams, Mildred Coursen. 1983. *Genealogical Miscellanea: Pennsylvania Families.*

Williams, Richard and Mildred. 1973. *Transcript of Tax: Bucks County 1779.* Dauphin, Pennsylvania.

Winchester, Simon. 2013. *The Men Who United The States.* New York: HarperCollins Publishers.

Wise, Dan. 1979. "Three vie for two open seats with L. Makefield supervisors." October 24.

Woestendiek, John. 1981. "They'll be strolling woods, not a development." *Philadelphia Inquirer,* November 21.

—. 1981. "They'll be strolling woods, not a development." *Philadelphia Inquirer,* November 21.

2016. *Yardley Historic District.* August 11. http://www.livingplacescom/PA/Bucks_County/Yardley_Borough_Historic_District.

Yardley News. 1987. "Ann Rhoads honored by Nature Conservancy." June 18.

Yardley News. 1997. "LMT historians showcase township's forest preserve." October 9.

Zimmerman, Albright. 2002. *Pennsylvania's Delaware Division Canal: Sixty Miles of Euphoria and Frustration.* Easton, Pennsylvania: Canal History and Technology Press.

COMMON BEECH

COMMON BEECH

INDEX

N

National Interstate and Defense Highways Act –118
National Lands Trust –16
National Natural Landmark –229, 246
National Wildlife Foundation –159
Native Americans –40, 47, 53, 58, 61, 62, 63, 70, 90, 101, 238, 242, 250
Natural National Landmark –246
Nelson, Thomas –199
Neshaminy Creek –47, 98, 136
New Hope, Pennsylvania –59, 102, 103, 128
New House –74, 75, 78, 79, 85, 86
Newtown, Pennsylvania –59, 69, 91, 94, 95, 97, 149, 209, 219, 232
New York City, New York –39, 41, 46, 47, 63, 90, 92, 93, 96, 98, 103, 105, 107, 113, 118, 124, 128, 130, 145, 146, 147, 264
New York, New York –39, 41, 46, 47, 63, 90, 92, 93, 96, 98, 103, 105, 107, 113, 118, 124, 128, 130, 145, 146, 147, 264
Nield Schoolhouse –83
Noise from Route 1 –192, 205, 247, 253
Northampton County –59
North Pennsylvania Railroad –107, 118
Northrup, Bradford –162, 195
Nuttall, Thomas –30

O

Oakview Drive –98
Open space –16, 136, 137, 138, 139, 142, 151, 152, 153, 154, 155, 159, 162, 163, 171, 177, 179, 180, 186, 190, 193, 203, 209, 216, 221, 226, 227, 231, 246, 247, 254, 255, 267, 268, 270, 279
Oreo Cookie analogy –177
Otter Creek –43, 44
Otter, John –46
Oxford Creek –99
Oxford Glen –148, 150, 253
Oxford, Pennsylvania –91, 98, 100
Oxford Valley Assn. –143
Oxford Valley Park –43, 44
Oxford Valley, Pennsylvania –98, 99, 128
Oxford Valley Road –42, 62, 79, 83, 97, 98, 99, 100, 109, 110, 141, 149, 150, 218, 219, 221, 223, 231

P

Paleo-Indian Period –60
Palmer House –201
Palmer, John –79, 98
Palustrian (wooded) wetlands –49
Park and Recreation Board Citizen Survey Forms –168

COMMON BEECH

COMMON BEECH

ACKNOWLEDGEMENTS

HOW CAN ONE EXPRESS THE NECESSARY gratitude to Don Formigli for all that he did and continues to do for the Five Mile Woods Preserve? He was the visionary who began the effort four decades ago to save what was then the largest remaining forested area in lower Bucks County and a place of such geological significance. Don saw the effort through the various stages including creating a vision, finding support, raising awareness, helping to bring together an equally determined group of interested people, and seeking support from a diverse group of organizations, legislators, Township officials, botanists and volunteers. He gathered together the remarkable stars of the world of botany at the time to come and help create a groundswell of support.

In reading the minutes of the Township's Park and Recreation Board, one can only marvel at Don, and the dedication of his fellow board members, in attending meeting after meeting, dealing with a multitude of challenges simultaneously and bringing them to a successful conclusion. This was a critical moment in the Township's history, a one-time opportunity to guide the development process in a way that addressed quality-of-life issues. If they had not been willing to make great sacrifices at that moment the opportunity would have been lost forever. There were certainly frustrating moments along the way and early into the effort Don was quoted as saying:

It's a daily battle; you win some, you lose some. But we give it a good try.[1]

On December 11, 1978, the first tract of land was purchased and the most significant acreage within the Five Mile Woods was set aside for future generations to enjoy. Then, three years later, the Preserve was officially dedicated. That would be an amazing accomplishment for most people but Don maintained a remarkable archive of photographs and manuscripts that tell the story of how the Preserve came to be created, and that document its fascinating plant life and geological wonders. He photographed events, recorded the various stages of the project, and supported its programs by giving of himself and inspiring others.

Spring Beauties

Finally, he commissioned this book. He shared all of his files with me and generously gave of his time as I asked him countless questions while we walked in the Preserve, had lunch, and traipsed into the areas of the Preserve where most do not go. Don drove me all around the region as I tried to place the history of the Preserve into a larger context of residential and commercial development in lower Bucks County.

He gave me access to the remarkable collection of photographs he has taken over the last four decades. Don never told me what to write, how to go about my job or how to interpret the materials he gave me. He encouraged me with leads on where to do research and was fascinated by what I found. My persistent questioning often found him trying to remember things that had happened almost forty years ago.

Aside from the creation of the Preserve, this book is perhaps his greatest gift because those efforts of long ago and all the information that was found and compiled will be saved for future generations. Staff, volunteers and visitors will be able to better understand the history, the geology, the flora and the beauty of the place that so many have worked hard to save. Having written several institutional and park histories, I know that this book will live on long after both Don and I are gone and will continue to provide insights into this special place.

And that is only part of the story as Don also created the Township's *Bikeway Master Plan* and was instrumental in creating the *Fee-In-Lieu-Of Program* that allowed for the funding of Lower Makefield's recreational resources. In a resolution passed by the Board of Supervisors on January 4, 1982, officials expressed the sentiments of many when they said:

On behalf of all present and future residents the Supervisors offer its thanks and appreciation.[2]

That is exactly what has happened since the late 1970s and continues to happen. His colleagues at the Bucks County Audubon Society and the Bucks County Conservancy (now the Heritage Conservancy) also recognized him with special awards. We offer too our collective thanks to Don.

Pat Miiller, the current President of the Lower Makefield Historical Society, was a major contributor to the project. Not only is she the leader of the historical organization but she was intimately involved with the creation of the Preserve, its early operation, and the development of the Township's recreational resources that so many now use. Pat sat on the Park and Recreation Board at the same time as Don and attended meeting after meeting looking to the Township's future. As with Don, if she had not been in the thick of the fight for quality-of-life issues at that time, the Township would be a different place than it is today. She succeeded him as the chairman and brought many of the visions that they had worked on to a successful conclusion. While she now lives in Yardley, the impact of her time in Lower Makefield is immeasurable.

She provided access to the Society's collection and gave me many insights into the Township's past, along with the Preserve's history, most found their way into this manuscript. In addition, she vouched for me on occasion, graciously introduced me to colleagues and other local resources, read the manuscript a number of times and offered corrections and insights. She was not bashful in suggesting ideas to me. The cover of the book is one that she suggested after I had picked another.

Helen Heinz is my kind of historian. She looks beyond the obvious or the easy and delves more deeply into why things happen. Her family has been drawn into this history business as well including her son who owns the former Mark Palmer boarding house, called Greenlawn, which is in the former railroad community of Lizette. This whistle-stop on the former Reading Line figures into the Five Mile Woods story. Other children, some of whom I met, also had the history bug.

Helen was incredibly generous with her time, expertise and many, many of the threads of our conversations found their way into this book. She is particularly expert at the arcane and the kinds of sources of material that are often overlooked or difficult to research. We are grateful for her insights and assistance. The acknowledgements in the well-written *Guide to Lower Makefield Historic Landmarks* said it perfectly:

Her breadth of knowledge about local and national history, architecture, sociology, combined with detective-like deed research skills enabled us to assemble this unprecedented collection of landmark synopses. . . We are all in her debt for the countless hours, patient guidance and cheerful diligence she offered . . .[3]

From the moment I met John Heilferty I realized we were of like mind and both have had a long interest in parks, preserves and forests. How can one not like a fellow who climbs up into tall trees checking on bald eagle chicks? In our many conversations, I learned much from him because my professional interest is in history while his professional interest is in the natural world but from those long talks came a book that reflected both of our interests. I am grateful for his help in making this book possible.

John Lloyd has served as the chairman of the Friends of the Five Mile Woods for more than two decades. That is a long time for anyone to serve in that kind of leadership position successfully. It takes great dedication and a generosity of spirit. In my various meetings with John, I gained many insights into the history of the Preserve and its environment. He willingly shared with me all his files, both inherited and collected over the years, and gave me tours of the Preserve which allowed me to gain an even greater perspective. He is a great tour guide and answered many, many questions and helped find information for me right up until the last minute.

Jan McFarlan, a volunteer with the Friends since 1987, met with me to discuss the challenges that faced the Preserve and offered her valuable insights into what the future might hold.

Ann and Paul Rhoads sat with us for a delightful interview discussing the history of the efforts to save the Preserve, the National Natural Landmarks nomination, her work, and Paul's efforts to document the Preserve's history and the Brelsford House in particular, and also the story of the Fairless Works. They also provided some of the arcane information that we had been trying to track down. A memorable moment came when Paul remembered that someone had told him that the Woods should not be the Five Mile Woods, but the Seven Mile Woods. Fortunately for me he could not remember who it was or the context in which it was said as that might have required a lot of changes in the book and at the Preserve! Ann assisted in the creation of the listing of plant species at the Preserve. My initial effort had many omissions and mistakes and she corrected them all.

John Heilferty refined it even further. Thank you, Ann and John.

Carol Dubois and I had a fascinating conversation over her involvement in the efforts to save the Woods. She had been involved in the local historical commission and had a love of American history, politics and government. She confirmed what so many said to me during the course of the project and that was that Don's efforts had been central to the saving of the Woods. She likened his leadership to having been the hub of a wheel with the spokes leading out representing the people and organizations that were involved.

When I think of Jeff Marshall, I think of him as a Bucks County institution. He would probably reply, as Mae West did, although in a different context to:

Marriage is a great institution, but I'm not ready for an institution.

Jeff has done so much for Bucks County's history and heritage, never mind preserving its open space and educating the public about those resources. He has written about the county's architecture, is an expert on the Commonwealth's barns, and inventoried the county's historic sites for its various townships. His long career and the work he has accomplished at the Heritage Conservancy will live on long after he is gone. Plus, he is a delightful guy to talk history with. We are grateful for his help with this project, his insights into the architectural heritage at the Preserve, and also for the Heritage Conservancy's acceptance of the book as a gift from Donald Formigli and agreeing to publish and distribute it. This will allow for the book to live on long into the future.

As with Don, speaking with Rick Mellon was a great pleasure. So much of what the Preserve is today has its origins in the precedents and programs that he set in motion while working there. His knowledge of things natural was amazing and his ability to recall so much of the Preserve's early years was so important to this project. Seeing him and Don together again at Rick's home, after all these years, was a delight. As I listened to them both reflect on the Woods there was this sense, just like I had at the Heritage Conservancy's Garden Party, that I was honored to be in the presence of these two pivotal figures in the Preserve's history. We are grateful for Rick's help.

Hank Miiller provided me with a number of insights into the time he was active in helping to save the Woods and the actions of the Township's Board of Supervisors. Those insights made the book a better one and we are appreciative for his sharing them and facts about local history.

We are grateful to Lynn Sims Lang, the Bucks County Balladeer, for allowing us to reproduce her two ballads written for and performed as part of the successful effort to raise awareness and to save the Woods. Her *Bucks County Ballads* were all recorded and are still available. When she sent them along to me, she felt I would not want to listen to the body of her work, but just the songs about the

Woods. I disregarded her admonition and listened to her beautiful voice and all her haunting music which is just amazing. In discussing the Woods efforts with her we both agreed that it had been a remarkable effort led by remarkable people. I am grateful for her insights.

Laura and Jim Foulds provided a great deal of contemporary information and insights about how the Preserve property had been used since 1945 when Jim's father bought the piece of land that neighbors the Preserve along Big Oak Road. They gave the author many pieces of valuable information that found their way into the book. Jim was kind enough to take us on walks through the Woods on two occasions pointing out features that I had seen but was not quite sure of what they were. He also had an excellent memory of the people who were neighbors and how they had used their respective properties. My favorite fact that Jim revealed was that the Preserve's parking lot was once fertile ground for growing potatoes.

Sam Willard gave us important insights into the operation of the evergreen nursery, and most importantly, the location of the Satterthwaite *New House*. He was also able to give us additional information about the name of the Woods and other details that proved to be very valuable. We were grateful for his taking time out to meet us.

To the venerable Sam Snipes, Falls Township historian, author, lawyer and colleague we offer our sincere appreciation. He answered many of our obscure questions about local history that only he could address given his long interest in the Township's history, the county's history and American Quakerism. The first time I met Sam was during the writing of my Pennsylvania Crossing park book and I was just amazed at his memory. For this project, I taxed his memory clear back to the 1600s and he provided insights and important information that clarified many issues for me. He also relayed how he had gone to the dedication of the Fairless Works and gained entry with a wedding invitation and not with an official invitation. The guard never looked closely as Sam went by.

I am also grateful to his legal colleague, Ronald Stockham, who made the arrangements for our meeting with Sam, and provided valuable insights into the region's recent history and technical assistance with a deed we were having problems with.

David B. Long was kind enough to share his insights into the Preserve, the bird listing he created for the Delaware Valley Ornithological Club and the knowledge that he had of the Sadowski farm purchase by Falls Township that included part of the Five Mile Woods. His ties to the Preserve go back to his youth when his mother voted for the purchase of the first parcels that made up the Preserve. We are grateful for his willingness to meet with us.

Tim Hertkorn, the tenant at the Preserve, and I met early on during my research and he was fascinated by what we were finding. It was his introduction of me to Helen Heinz that proved to be one of the most important connections in the life of this project. He also pointed out the foundation of the old barn that stands just beyond the parking area which also proved to be an important part of the story. This book will provide him with lots of new material that I am sure he will pass on to visitors.

The following institutions, organizations and people provided research assistance including Donna Humphrey, the library assistant at the Bucks County Historical Society's Spruance Library in Doylestown, the Bucks County Historical Society, the Bucks County Library staff at the Yardley-Lower Makefield facility, the staff at the Land Records section of the Bucks County Recorder of Deeds Office (and in particular one staff member who refused to give me her name to be attributed but has been so generous with her time every time I visited), Arden Williams, an Administrative Assistant at the Silver Lake Nature Center, Jim Puzo, Collin Stuart, Hart Rufe, Larry Miller, Steve Myers all were good enough to talk about the Preserve with me along with Connor and Jaclyn Gray and Dominick and Jarry Fantano. Also, Chris Myers, Chloe Myers, Ayden Boccamfuso and Tyler Rugarber. Lower Makefield Township's Barbara Ellison, Lynn Todd and Terry Fedorchak provided assistance by allowing access to several of the deeds related to the Preserve.

The Pennsylvania Historical and Museum Commission through its good offices provided valuable assistance to this project. The staff at Pennsbury Manor was generous with their time and expertise including Todd Galle, Museum Curator; Mary Ellyn Kunz, Museum Educator, and Sarah Taylor, a summer intern. They provided access to their archives, library and offered me many helpful insights. Kurt Bell, the Railroad Collections Archivist at the Pennsylvania State Archives in Harrisburg, and I have worked on several other projects together, most notably a comprehensive history of the Washington Crossing Historic Park and an institutional history of the Railroad Museum of Pennsylvania. He generously assisted by providing information about the Trenton Cutoff, and the Pennsylvania and Reading railroads. Janet R. Johnson, the Curator in the State Museum's Archaeological Section reviewed records to see if any archaeological work might have been done in the immediate Five Mile Woods area.

I am grateful to the following individuals, institutions and publications from which photographs and graphic materials were obtained including: Donald Formigli, the Five Mile Woods Preserve, Pat Miiller, John Heilferty, Penn Pilot: Historic Aerial Photographs of Pennsylvania, the Pennsylvania Geological Survey, Pennsylvania's Department of Conservation and Natural Resources, the United States Geological Survey, the National Park Service, the Library of Congress, the Lower Makefield Historical Society, the Heritage Conservancy, United States Direct Tax Lists, Bucks County Land Records, the late Ralph Thompson, Rachel Stenftennagel, Sharon Guzikowski Stewart, Sandy Guzikowski, John Lloyd,

Helen Heinz, and Gary Street. Graphics were also taken from the *Master Plan for the Five Mile Woods Preserve: Lower Makefield Township Pennsylvania, Report on the Hydrology of the Five Mile Woods,* and the *Genealogy of the Satterthwaite Family* and various Bucks County atlases.

I also want to recognize all of those who provided essays including Donald Formigli, Pat Miiller, John Lloyd, John Heilferty and Jeff Marshall. Their essays are insightful and reveal their deep passions about the Preserve and open space in general. I am grateful to the readers of the manuscript although I take complete responsibility for any typos, mistakes or errors which remain as I am sure there are still some. They include: Sue Gotta, Don Formigli, Pat Miiller, John Heilferty, Kathy Pasko, Jan McFarlan, Helen Heinz, John Lloyd, Hank Miiller, Ann and Paul Rhoads, Jeff Marshall, Rick Mellon, Rachel Stenftennagel and Kurt Bell. They were all kind enough to read the manuscript for mistakes and context and made many good suggestions. They did a remarkable job given that it was such a hefty project to read on a tight deadline.

Then there are those who fall under the category of technical assistance but without whose help the project could not proceed: Michael McCann, Esq., O'Keefe and McCann; and Eileen Lindsey, Esq., who provided important software assistance allowing the project to move along smoothly. Bill Farkas, for whom I have written three other books, deserves special credit because during those projects he took me all over Lower Bucks County showing me various historic sites whose histories found their way into the narrative of this book. My sister, Elizabeth, and her husband Gary Stenftennagel, provided lodging, good cheer and encouragement (along with their two dogs, Dakota and the late Ginger and cat, Eleanor).

I am sure that the Preserve's staff, professional and volunteer, and visitors all felt like I was a new version of Columbo, the 1970s-television detective played by Peter Falk. He would wear his suspects down with an unending number of questions. As I met with all of them I found myself often saying, near closing time or in the middle of an event, project or just a lovely walk:

Just one more question . . .

They were forever patient and gracious, probably wanting to hide when they saw me coming. To all of those listed, unlisted and those who have passed on, we offer our sincere thanks for making this book possible.

Red Cloud, Nebraska
April 30, 2017

COMMON BEECH

COMMON BEECH

ABOUT THE AUTHOR

PETER OSBORNE IS AN INDEPENDENT HISTORIAN, writer and lecturer who has worked in the public history field for more than thirty-five years. Born in Paterson, New Jersey, he holds a Bachelor of Arts degree from Rutgers, the State University of New Jersey. Osborne's professional interests include Theodore Roosevelt, Franklin and Eleanor Roosevelt, the state and national park systems, the Civilian Conservation Corps, and the famed Corps of Discovery Expedition led by Captains Meriwether Lewis and William Clark.

Osborne has been published widely over the last two decades. He has written four books on the Depression era and state parks including *We Can Take It! The Roosevelt Tree Army at High Point State Park 1933-1941, Images of America Series: High Point State Park and the Civilian Conservation Corps, Images of America: Hacklebarney and Voorhees State Parks (New Jersey)* and *Images of America: Promised Land State Park (Pennsylvania)*.

Between 2012 and 2014 he wrote a comprehensive two-volume, twelve-hundred-page history about the state parks at the site of Washington's famed Crossing of the Delaware River. They were commissioned by William Farkas, president of Yardley Press of Yardley, Pennsylvania and entitled *Where Washington Once Led: A History of New Jersey's Washington Crossing State Park* and *No Spot In This Far Land Is More Immortalized: A History of Pennsylvania's Washington Crossing Historic Park*. They will be an important resource for park historians and students of the famed Christmas Crossing of 1776 for many years to come.

Over the years, Osborne has written about a variety of topics. In 2011, he co-authored *So Many Brave Men: A History of the Battle at Minisink Ford* with Mark Hendrickson and Jon Inners which was considered for the George Washington Book Prize. In early 2016 he finished writing the first institutional history of the Commonwealth of Pennsylvania's official railroad museum. The book is entitled *The Trains of Our Memory: A History of the Railroad Museum of Pennsylvania 1965-2015*.

Osborne was the Executive Director of the Minisink Valley Historical Society in Port Jervis, New York, from 1981-2009, and the Port Jervis City Historian from 1989-2003. During his directorship he was responsible for the Society's

Fort Decker Museum of History. He then served as the Curator of Education and Special Events at the Red Mill Museum Village in Clinton, New Jersey from 2010-11. Since then he has been working as an independent historian and writer.

During his long career, he has served on the board of directors of the Depot Preservation Society, the Port Jervis Centennial Committee, the Orange County Historical Society, the Grey Towers Heritage Association (Treasurer), the Delaware and Hudson Transportation Heritage Council (Treasurer), the Upper Delaware Scenic Byway (Original incorporator and Treasurer) and the Unitarian-Universalist Fellowship of Sussex County, New Jersey (Webmaster).

He owns the Wild Horse Creek Company and splits his time between Red Cloud, Nebraska and North Haledon, New Jersey. The mission of his company is to provide exciting journeys of discovery into our nation's history through presentations, lectures, demonstrations, motor coach tours and publications. The Wild Horse Creek Company (and its predecessor, the Pienpack Company) has been providing programs for civic, historical, fraternal, church groups, seminars, meetings, Elder hostel and Road Scholar programs for more than thirty-five years.

Web Page: *www.wildhorsecreekcompany.com*
E-mail: *peter@wildhorsecreekcompany.com or peterosbornehistorian@gmail.com*
Phone: *845-551-0417*

Along the Missouri River on the trail of Lewis and Clark

COMMON BEECH

COMMON BEECH

COLOPHON

THE MANUSCRIPT WAS PREPARED IN MICROSOFT WORD and transferred into Adobe InDesign CS4 for production. The book block was typeset in Adobe Garamond Pro. The cover was set in Trajan Pro and Adobe Garamond Pro. The paper is White 50lb. The paperback cover is four-color with a gloss film lamination, and perfect-bound. The hardcover version also uses a White 50lb. paper with a four-color cover. The cover and the book's interior design were created by Peter Osborne and the Wild Horse Creek Company. The book was then converted into a PDF and printed in the United States by Lightning Source, Inc. located in La Vergne, Tennessee. It was originally published by the Wild Horse Creek Company in Red Cloud, Nebraska. The book is available for purchase from the Heritage Conservancy, local and regional book stores, major online retailers including Barnes and Noble and Amazon, and directly from the Five Mile Woods Preserve.

The picture used for the front cover of the book was taken by Donald Formigli in 2016 and showcases one of the numerous boardwalks that pass over the wet areas in the Preserve. The recommendation to use this photograph for the cover came from Pat Miiller who believed that it symbolized how the trails of the Preserve will lead one to many discoveries.

The photographs used for the back cover were also taken by Donald Formigli. The picture of the yellow trout lily in bloom was taken in the spring of 2016 and used by the Heritage Conservancy for their 2017 calendar. The picture of the author was taken at the foundation of the Dark and Satterthwaite homestead near the Queen Anne Creek in the Preserve.

The handsome beech line drawing that begins each chapter was described in the nineteenth century line art books as a *common beech*. There is no American species that is called by that name but there is an American beech (*Fagus grandifolia*) which is commonly found at the Five Mile Woods Preserve.

Courtesy Peter Osborne

Earth Day 2016
Five Mile Woods Preserve

If the reader has additional historical materials or items of interest related to the natural environment at the Preserve, please feel free to contact the staff at:

Five Mile Woods Preserve
1305 Big Oak Road, Yardley, Pennsylvania 19067
Phone:
215-493-6652
E-mail:
Fivemilewoods@yahoo.com
Web Page:
www.lmt.org/departments/park-recreation/five-mile-woods-nature-preserve

WHAT OTHERS HAVE WRITTEN ABOUT PETER OSBORNE'S BOOKS

THE TRAINS OF OUR MEMORY:
A HISTORY OF THE RAILROAD MUSEUM OF PENNSYLVANIA 1965-2015

An institutional history might seem like dull reading, but Peter Osborne has written an easy-to-digest account of the first 50 years of the Railroad Museum of Pennsylvania . . . Perhaps the best way to convey the scope of the book is to put it in terms of page counts: 16 pages of front matter, nearly 400 pages of history, 82 pages of essays by principals in the story, 39 pages of endnotes, 18 pages of index listings, and 16 pages of bibliography . . . This book is a magnum opus. All museums, especially railroad museums, should be so fortunate to have such an encyclopedic and exhaustive record of their mission and work.

Dan Cupper
Deputy Editor, Railroad History magazine

WHERE WASHINGTON ONCE LED:
A HISTORY OF NEW JERSEY'S WASHINGTON CROSSING STATE PARK

The Committee was certainly impressed with the scholarship and exhaustive effort that went into *Where Washington Once Led*. One of our Committee members commented that this was indeed the 'Bible of Washington Crossing Park' and we all agreed. The topographical nature of the history was outstanding and the detail was immense, which will be a huge boon for future researchers. The maps and illustrations are wonderful and many Committee members commented that other state parks cry out for such professional and similar coverage.

New Jersey Studies Academic Alliance - Author Awards Committee

Sometimes people get the impression of history being stagnant and dull. Washington Crossing State Park, however, is a dynamic place, with a dynamic history reflecting changes in how we relate to our past that can be just as instructive and entertaining as the events it memorializes. It was especially interesting to read the personal accounts of some of the superintendents as well as Osborne's own observations in a chapter called *A Year in the Life of the Park*. Osborne has done a wonderful job bringing that long story to life with this comprehensive history.

GSL Reviews, GardenStateLegacy.com, Issue 21, September 2013 (New Jersey)

I think most people would readily agree that setting aside areas of natural beauty such as the National Parks so that we as well as future generations may enjoy them is a national priority. Far fewer, unfortunately, would agree that historical areas and buildings should be preserved and honored. These places are our *landmarks* where we tell our American story to our own generation and preserve it for generations to come. This book is about the Washington Crossing Park in New Jersey which honors one of the pivotal points in the American Revolution - Washington's surprise attack on the Hessians at Trenton on December 26, 1776. This book is not about the attack itself. You can read about that in one of my all-time favorite history books - *Washington's Crossing* by David Hackett Fischer.

This book is about how the park came to be. The story is full of quirks, characters and odd turns-of-events. It has been superbly researched and written by Peter Osborne who has a number of other historical publications to his credit. It is a lesson for all of us about how to guard the places and buildings which earlier generations have made historic by their actions. For this reason alone, the book is worth the time to read.

Perhaps, more importantly, it is also the story about how the park evolved and was shaped by succeeding generations. A historical park is nothing if it does not tell its story afresh and invite people to share its story while enjoying the site which has been set aside. Peter captures the ongoing history of this park which continues to tell its story and involve people from far and near. *Where Washington Once Led*, we must now lead. This book will help us do it.

Dogearred Bookmarker
Review on Amazon.com

CHRISTMAS 1776

No Spot in this Far Land is More Immortalized
A History of Pennsylvania's Washington Crossing Historic Park

On Christmas night in 1776, George Washington and 2,400 men crossed the icy Delaware River into Trenton and then later Princeton, where they went on to win decisive victories that changed the course of the Revolutionary War. But it wasn't until 1895 that efforts to memorialize the event and place began. Twenty-two years later, in 1917, a park commission was created, and in 1921 the group formally dedicated Washington Crossing Park to pay tribute to the famed crossing.

Yet in the nearly one hundred years that (the) Washington Crossing (parks), both in New Jersey and in Pennsylvania, existed, perhaps no in-depth research has been done on the scale of what writer and historian Peter Osborne has accomplished. Osborne, who has a degree in American history, this past July published *No Spot In This Far Land Is More Immortalized: A History of Washington Crossing Historic Park,* which focuses on Pennsylvania's park, after publishing *Where Washington Once Led: A History of New Jersey's Washington Crossing State Park*, which focuses on New Jersey, in December 2012. Both books were sponsored by Yardley Press.

Combined, the books total more than twelve hundred pages and reveal how park administrators overcame many challenges to organize ideas, raise funds and develop the public areas.

Times of Trenton (New Jersey)

I bought this book for my son-in-law's birthday . . . he and my daughter just love the Washington Crossing area . . . so much so they were married there and every year they go to dinner at the Washington Crossing Inn . . . and delight in every minute of it . . . So, I held my breath . . . but Chuck's smile says it all!

TS
Review on Amazon.com

CPSIA information can be obtained
at www.ICGtesting.com
Printed in the USA
BVOW08s2314220517
484883BV00002B/3/P

9 780692 842348